# Jesus and the Gospels

## An Introduction to Gospel Literature and Jesus Studies

**JARL FOSSUM**
UNIVERSITY OF MICHIGAN

**PHILLIP MUNOA**
HOPE COLLEGE

**WADSWORTH**
━━━✶━━━ ™
**THOMSON LEARNING**

Australia • Canada • Mexico • Singapore • Spain
United Kingdom • United States

**Publisher:** Holly J. Allen
**Religion Editor:** Steve Wainwright
**Assistant Editors:** Lee McCracken,
Anna Lustig
**Editorial Assistant:** Melanie Cheng
**Marketing Manager:** Worth Hawes
**Marketing Assistant:** Kristi Bostock
**Advertising Project Manager:** Bryan Vann

**Print/Media Buyer:** Karen Hunt
**Permissions Editor:** Kiely Sexton
**Production Service:** Ruth Cottrell
**Copy Editor:** Ruth Cottrell
**Cover Designer:** Yvo Riezebos
**Compositor:** Argosy Publishing
**Text and Cover Printer:** Webcom Limited

Printed in Canada
1 2 3 4 5 6 7 07 06 05 04 03

For more information about our products, contact us at:
Thomson Learning Academic
Resource Center
1-800-423-0563

For permission to use material from this text, contact us by:
**Phone:** 1-800-730-2214
**Fax:** 1-800-730-2215
**Web:** http://www.thomsonrights.com

**Library of Congress Control Number:**
2003105185
ISBN 0-534-63504-0

**Wadsworth/Thomson Learning**
10 Davis Drive
Belmont, CA 94002-3098
USA

**Asia**
Thomson Learning
5 Shenton Way #01-01
UIC Building
Singapore 068808

**Australia/New Zealand**
Thomson Learning
102 Dodds Street
Southbank, Victoria 3006
Australia

**Canada**
Nelson
1120 Birchmount Road
Toronto, Ontario M1K 5G4
Canada

**Europe/Middle East/Africa**
Thomson Learning
High Holborn House
50/51 Bedford Row
London WC1R 4LR
United Kingdom

**Latin America**
Thomson Learning
Seneca, 53
Colonia Polanco
11560 Mexico D.F.
Mexico

**Spain/Portugal**
Paraninfo
Calle/Magallanes, 25
28015 Madrid, Spain

*For Ellen and Kathy*

*"Many women have done excellently,*
*but you surpass them all."*

*Proverbs 31:29*

# Contents

# Preface

We spent several years writing this book. Its gestation took place in a major public research university, where it appeared in lecture form for a course on Jesus and the Gospels. After that it found its way to another Jesus and the Gospels course at a private liberal arts college. In both instances, students new to the field of gospel literature used the materials that make up this text. Although there are some useful books that introduce students to gospel literature, we believed that another text was warranted. Our book goes beyond other texts by introducing beginning students to the field of gospel studies while at the same time orienting students to the accompanying field of historical Jesus studies. Several books have tried to do both, and those usually compressed their material and thus left out important topics that are essential to the study of gospel literature and the historical Jesus.

In addition to blending of gospel studies with historical Jesus studies, we intentionally addressed issues of scholarly methodology when studying the Gospels, the broader literary context of early gospel literature, and pedagogical concerns that beginning students face when they attempt to master material that is foreign to them. Our text introduces students to five major methodologies (textual, source, redaction, form, and tradition) so students can develop their own scholarly perspectives and skill in reading gospel literature and thinking about the historical Jesus. We intend to be nonsectarian in approach and employ a scholarly, critical perspective that is in common use among biblical scholars teaching in universities and colleges.

This text also introduces and describes noncanonical gospel literature. Too often canonical gospel literature is presented to the exclusion of noncanonical gospel texts that are important for both gospel studies and Jesus studies. To overcome this common deficiency, we have included chapters on the *Gospel according to Thomas* and the Jewish-Christian Gospels. Lastly, students wondering what they should know about chapter topics or where they can look for more in-depth coverage will find help at the end of every chapter. Each chapter concludes with a brief summary, a list of key terms, study questions, and a short bibliography for further study. Essential terms are also printed in bold type the first time they appear in the text, and their definitions can be located in the glossary at the end of the book. The order of our chapters is such that it can serve as an outline for a semester course on Jesus and the Gospels—as it has already done successfully for several years.

Like most textbooks, this one would never have been completed had it not been for the careful work of editors and readers. As authors, we are thankful for the reviewers who carefully examined and commented on this text. At times, it seemed as if the rounds of readers would never end—and this is not to say that our work is done. Textbook improvements are like death and taxes! Nevertheless, the corrections, suggestions, and comments of the reviewers always improved this text and were an indispensable element in making it more useful to students. We thank Daniel Breslauer, University of Kansas; Greg Carey, Winthrop University; Russell Fuller, University of San Diego; Edwin C. Hostetter, George Washington University; Cheryl Kirk-Duggan, Graduate Theological Union; Christopher Scott Langton, Principia College; Tony S. L. Michael, University of Toronto; Stacy L. Patty, Lubbock Christian University; William L. Petersen, Pennsylvania State University; Jeffery Warren Scott, Radford University; Mahlon H. Smith, Rutgers University; Jeff Staley, Seattle University; and, J. Lyle Story, Regent University. Our editors at Wadsworth, Peter Adams and Steve Wainwright, gave direction and encouragement whenever needed. Lee McCracken was very helpful at important junctures. Ruth Cottrell was exceptional in taming our prose. Thanks must also be given to Pam Valkema, our administrative assistant, who helped in the typing and editing of our manuscript. Finally, we thank our patient and supportive wives, Ellen and Kathy. You never tired of listening, encouraging, and loving.

Spring 2003
Jarl Fossum and Phillip Munoa

# PART I

# Introduction to Jesus and the Gospels

# 1

※

# The Gospel
# and the Gospels

## THE TERM *GOSPEL*

The term **gospel**[1] derives from an Old English word, godspell, meaning good news (god = good, spell = news). It is a direct translation of the Greek noun *euangelion,* which is used in the titles of the books of the **New Testament** ascribed to Matthew, Mark, Luke, and John.

Although the mother tongue of Jesus and his **disciples** was Aramaic, the New Testament was written in Greek. In the wake of the conquests of Alexander the Great (356–323 BCE), Greek was substituted for Aramaic as the diplomatic language throughout the Near East. By means of the Greek language, people from the different countries of the empire of Alexander and his successors could communicate with each other. When the Romans became masters of the Eastern Mediterranean world (during the first century BCE), Greek continued in use as the diplomatic language.

In the period when the New Testament was written, *euangelion* had acquired a religious meaning. **Oracles** by the gods were referred to as *euangelia* (plural of *euangelion*). Some shrines were popular sites where **cultic functionaries** conveyed oracles, counsels, and prophecies from the divine world to people of high and low station.

The immediate background of the New Testament usage of the noun *euangelion* can be found in the **imperial cult.**[2] The Roman emperor was seen as a sav-

---

[1] All **boldfaced** words are defined in the glossary.

[2] The verb *euangelizesthai* (proclaim good news) is used in some passages of the Greek translation of the prophet Isaiah, where it denotes the proclamation of the imminence of the new age that will be characterized by God's sovereign lordship (40:9; 52:7; 61:1; cf. Ps. 95:2 and Isa. 60:6), where it is also used with reference to salvation. The noun *euangelion* occurs only three times in the Greek Old Testament (2 Sam. 4:10; 18:22, 25), where it means simply "(good) news" without any religious meaning.

ior who protected the state and its people. He was believed to be able to work miracles such as healing people. The emperor was even thought to have power over the forces of nature; winds and waves were supposed to be subject to his command.

When an emperor died he was usually deified. However, some emperors were acknowledged as divine during their lifetimes, either by themselves or by their supporters. In the eastern part of Rome's empire, where the cult of the ruler originated, this divination was self-evident. An inscription from a city on the west coast of Asia Minor hails Augustus, during whose reign Jesus was born, as "Son of God," and even "God." In a resolution passed by the provincial assembly in Asia Minor, Augustus was hailed as a "savior" who brought peace to humankind. It is also said that "the birthday" of the god (Augustus) was for the world the beginning of the "good news."

Jesus was born five years after this inscription was put up in the marketplace in Priene, a town near Ephesus. The Gospel according to Luke says that when Jesus was born an angel appeared to some shepherds in the fields and proclaimed, "Do not be afraid; for see, I am bringing you good news of great joy for all the people: to you is born this day in the city of David a Savior. . . ." (2:10–11). After this announcement, an entire chorus of angels appeared, singing, "Glory to God in the highest heaven, and on earth peace among those whom he favors!" (v.14).

Similarities in terminology and thought between the inscription from Priene and Luke's account are easily observable; the terms *good news, savior,* and *peace* were all used with reference to the birth of the person in question. Christians seem to have adopted terms and ideas used in the imperial cult. One of those terms and ideas was that of *euangelion* (good news).

In the imperial cult the term *euangelion* referred to the appearance of the emperor in the world, and his accession to the throne and his decrees were referred to as *euangelia*. All the emperor's decrees were believed to entail salvation and peace for the subjects of the empire. To the first Christians, however, salvation was not rescue from catastrophes in nature, war, and the enemies of the state. In the New Testament salvation is deliverance from sin, the devil, and death. This kind of salvation was effected in a different way from that of salvation in the imperial cult. To Christians, salvation was effected through the death and resurrection of Jesus. In the beginning, the Christians used *euangelion* with reference to those events.

Some twenty-five years before Luke produced his gospel, the Christian missionary Paul wrote to the Church that he had established in Corinth several years before, saying:

> Now I would remind you, brothers and sisters, of the good news that I proclaimed to you, which you in turn received, in which also you stand. . . . For I handed on to you as of first importance what I in turn had received: that Christ died for our sins in accordance with the scriptures, and that he was buried, and that he was raised on the third day in accordance with the scriptures, and that he appeared to Cephas, then to the twelve (1 Cor. 15:1, 3–5).

This appears to be an early summary of the Christian faith—that is, a mini-gospel. Paul described it as something he himself had received and had preached to the people at Corinth.

Another summary of the faith is found at the very beginning of Paul's letter to the Christian community in Rome. Paul opened his letter by stating that he had been

> called to be an apostle, set apart for the gospel of God, which he promised before-hand through his prophets in the holy scriptures, the gospel concerning his Son, who was descended from David according to the flesh and was declared to be Son of God with power according to the spirit of holiness by resurrection from the dead, Jesus Christ our Lord. . . . (Rom. 1:1-4).

The Christian gospel, then, was originally an oral message about the significance of Jesus. How did it come to be used as a literary term, as a designation of a certain kind of writing?

The Gospel according to Mark, which was written about the year 70 CE, begins in the following manner: "The beginning of the good news of Jesus Christ, the Son of God" (1:1). Mark tells about Jesus' death and resurrection, and he also gives information about Jesus' teaching and miracles. The "gospel" of Paul does not include the latter. It is probably not the case that Mark 1:1 simply denotes the author's writing. Mark uses the term *gospel* several times, and it is always used with reference to the message proclaimed by Jesus (1:14–15; 8:35; 10:29) or the message proclaimed about him (13:10; 14:9). Mark obviously conceived of the work of John the Baptist—his preaching and **baptism** of repentance (1:2–9)—as the beginning of the gospel. However, although Mark did not refer to his literary creation by the term *gospel*, it is clear that the term is no longer used in the same way as it was expressed in Paul's letters. What brought about this new usage?

The need to know more about the savior—what kind of person he was, why he was executed, and so on—must always have been present. In the beginning, this need was satisfied by an **oral tradition** based on the accounts of eyewitnesses. When those eyewitnesses died, committing their accounts to writing was a natural option. This option was favored by the circumstances created by the rapid expansion of Christianity out into the Roman empire. Oral tradition was not an adequate means of preserving information about Jesus in communities far removed from the country and socio-political milieu in which he had lived.

Mark was apparently not the first writer to use the term *gospel* in a broader sense. In the Acts of the Apostles, a missionary speech delivered by Peter—one of Jesus' disciples—to certain Gentiles defines the "good news of peace by Jesus Christ" in the following way:

> . . . the message he sent to the people of Israel, preaching peace by Jesus Christ—he is Lord of all. That message spread through Judea, beginning in Galilee after the baptism that John announced: how God anointed Jesus of Nazareth with the Holy Spirit and with power; how he went about doing good and healing all who were oppressed by the devil, for God was with him. We are witnesses to all that he did both in Judea and Jerusalem. They put him to death by hanging him on a tree; but God raised him on the third day and allowed him to appear (10:36–40).

The speech goes on to say that Jesus was made manifest only to those whom God had chosen, and that God commanded them to proclaim Jesus as the one whom God had ordained to be the judge of all humankind (10:42).

This speech is some sort of a mini-gospel, as in 1 Cor. 15:3–5. It is an account prefacing the significance of Jesus, his death, and his resurrection by the story of his ministry that led up to the events surrounding his death.

Mark's work, as well as the mini-gospel in Acts 10, presupposes the view that there is only one gospel. It took some time before the word *euangelion* was used in the plural, *euangelia*, to denote the books written under the names of Matthew, Mark, Luke, and John. The idea that there is only one gospel is still maintained in the titles of these writings, "the [one] Gospel according to [the version of] Mark," and so on. Justin Martyr, a Christian philosopher who suffered martyrdom in Rome about 165 CE, was the first one to use the plural *euangelia* to designate the writings that set forth the words and deeds of Jesus as well as his passion, death, and resurrection.

However, even after the time of Justin, the idea that there was only one gospel prevailed. About 175 CE, Tatian, who had studied under Justin, produced a book called the *Diatessaron,* "Out of Four, One," a harmonization of the gospel writings. This approach apparently presupposed the view that the essential gospel is one.

In the beginning of the third century the term *evangelist* was used to mean "author of a gospel." In the New Testament, however, this term is always used of the wandering preacher of the gospel who announced the saving event, the death and resurrection of Jesus (Acts 21:8; Eph. 4:11; 2 Tim. 4:5). In the beginning of the third century, the expression "in the Gospels" was used of a word handed down in only one of the Gospels.

## CANONICAL AND APOCRYPHAL GOSPELS

At the beginning of the third century, many books known as Gospels were in circulation. Why did only four of them come to be regarded as canonical—that is, authoritative, infallible, or even divine? The answer to this question is bound up with that of the origination of the New Testament **canon** as a whole.

The Greek word *kanon* (reed, rod, measuring-stick; hence standard, norm, criterion)[3] was not used with reference to the books of the Bible until the middle of the fourth century CE. In 380 CE, the Council of Laodicea in Phrygia declared that noncanonical writings should not be read in the Church. The Council even drew up a list of the canonical writing comprising the Christian Bible. In the second and third centuries CE, the correct beliefs and practices could be denoted by terms such as *canon of truth, canon of faith,* and *canon of the Church,* but the writings containing these beliefs and doctrines were never referred to as canonical.

As a designation of books recognized by the Church the term *kanon* is outdated by another Greek word, *diatheke,* a juridical term; it was used of a testament, the declaration of a person's will with regard to the disposal of his or her personal property after death. In the Greek translation of the **Hebrew Bible,** however,

---

[3] *Kanon* could be used of both the carpenter's stick and the moral law, "the basic rules for the right use of the free will" (Epictetus). Compare this with the usage of *kanon* in Gal. 6:16, where it is translated as "rule."

*diatheke* was used to render the term *berith*, which denoted the covenant between God and the People of Israel (for example, Gen. 17:2,4,7; Exod. 19:5; 24:8). Believing that, through Jesus, God had established a second covenant, the first Christians spoke of the new as well as the old covenant (Luke 22:20; Heb. 8:7–13). The use of the words *old covenant* (or testament) as a literary reference is already found in one of Paul's letters (2 Cor. 3:14, "when they hear the reading of the old covenant"). At the end of the second century, Melito, bishop of Sardis in Asia Minor, gave a list of "the books of the Old Covenant." Subsequently, the Christian theologian Clement of Alexandria divided the books of the Church into the New Testament and the Old Testament.

Because Christianity grew out of Judaism, it is only logical that the "testament" of the first Christians as well as that of Jesus was the **Jewish Bible** (consisting of the "Law," the "Prophets," and a loosely circumscribed category referred to as the "other books" or "Writings"). How did the idea of a new "testament" originate, as witnessed to by Clement?

In Paul's writings, a couple of Jesus' words had already been cited as being authoritative (1 Thess. 4:15; 1 Cor. 9:14). Citations of Jesus' words are also found in other writings that came to be included in the New Testament (Acts 20:35; 2 Pet. 3:2). In the beginning, these words circulated orally; however, their oral form did not diminish their authority. Around 130 CE, Papias, bishop of Hierapolis in Asia Minor, said that he regarded a living oral tradition as more valuable than written works. As a matter of fact, Jesus' sayings that were not derivable from written Gospels were quoted as being just as authoritative as words from written Gospels until the middle of the second century CE.

Paul appears to have believed that what he spoke was the "word of God" (1 Thess. 2:13), or at least that he was "one who by the Lord's mercy is trustworthy" (1 Cor. 7:25), but he did not seem to have regarded his letters as being on the same level as **Scripture.** In the first part of the second century, however, the author of the Second Epistle of Peter mentions an unspecified collection of Paul's writings as being among the "Scripture" (3:16).

In the same century as the Second Epistle of Peter, the *Second Letter of Clement,* written under the name of a bishop of Rome, quoted Matthew 9:13 as "Scripture" (2:4). Around 150 CE, Justin Martyr testified to the **liturgical** use of the Gospels according to Matthew, Mark, and Luke (which he identified as "the memoirs of the apostles") as well as the Old Testament.

One figure was particularly significant in the development of the canon. Around 140 CE, a Christ teacher in Rome named Marcion asserted that Christians should dispense with the entire Old Testament. Moreover, according to Marcion, the only gospel that had merit was the Gospel according to Luke. In addition to Luke, Marcion would include in the canon ten letters ascribed to Paul (excluding 1 and 2 Timothy and Titus). Arguing that the Old Testament's conception of God was wholly incompatible with the image of God in the teachings of Jesus, Marcion purged Jewish elements from the Gospel according to Luke and his ten Pauline letters. In effect, Marcion was the first person to create a New Testament canon, although he did not use the term as such.

Marcion was expelled from the greater Church and formed a church of his own that existed for quite some time. The greater Church had to meet the challenge of

Marcion's canon. It has been said that Marcion was the creator of Christian holy Scripture, but that statement is not accurate. As we pointed out, moves toward the authorization of parts of Christian literature had been taken before Marcion's time. However, the development of formal authorization did not take place everywhere in the same way and at the same time. Thus, whereas Papias in Asia Minor honored oral traditions about Jesus more than the written Gospels, around 150 CE the Church in Rome seems to have regarded the Gospels as Scripture—that is, equal in value to the Old Testament. Marcion seems to have had a catalyzing and synthesizing effect on the development of the canon: A need was felt to produce a catalog of writings that contained the correct delineation of Scripture.

The need for this catalog encouraged a process of not only embracing books that Marcion had thrown out but also rejecting some writings that were held in esteem in certain quarters of Christianity. Rejected writings were called **"apocryphal"** writings. The Greek word *apocrypha* means "things that are hidden." Originally, *apokryphos* was used of a book that was withdrawn from common use because of its esoteric, secret contents. Clement of Alexandria testified to the existence of a *Secret* (apocryphal) *Gospel according to Mark*. Works of other types were also called apocryphal. From the first part of the second century, there is the *Apocryphon of John,* which claims to contain secret teachings conveyed by Jesus to his disciple John after Jesus' resurrection.

The greater Church adopted the term *apocryphal*, which was used by some groups to describe secret teachings, taking this term instead to designate books that ought to be hidden away because of their fraudulent nature. Writing against all the "heresies" within the Church, Irenaeus, bishop of Lyons in southern France around 180 CE, spoke of the **heretics**' "apocryphal and falsified writings" (*Against the Heresies,* 1:20:1).[4]

When arguing for the recognition of the Gospels according to Matthew, Mark, Luke, and John as Scripture, Irenaeus said,

> It is not possible that the Gospels can be either more or fewer in number than they are. For since there are four zones of the world in which we live, and four principle winds, and while the Church is scattered throughout all the world, and the "pillar and ground" (1 Tim. 3:15) of the Church is the Gospel and the Spirit of Life, it is fitting that She should have four pillars breathing out immortality on every side and vivifying people anew (3:11:8).

A few decades after Irenaeus wrote against the heresies, a list of canonical books was drawn up somewhere in the Western hemisphere of Christianity, probably in Rome around 200 CE.[5] Named the *Muratorian Canon* after the Italian

---

[4]The term *apocryphal* also came to be used for a body of Jewish writings dating from about 200 BCE to 100 CE. These books were included in the Greek translation of the Hebrew Bible but were denied canonical status by the Synagogue. The Church, however, found these writings edifying and even authoritative. In the late fourth century, Jerome included these writings in his Latin translation of the Old and the New Testaments, the so-called *Vulgate* (common) edition that is still the official Bible of the Roman Catholic Church.

[5]Weighty arguments for a fourth-century date and an eastern provenance of this canon have been advanced. However, it seems prudent to maintain the accepted view that it originated in the West around 200 CE.

librarian L. A. Muratori who published it in 1740, the catalog contains the four Gospels found in the New Testament (whereas other New Testament books—such as Hebrews, 2 Peter, and 3 John—are missing, and the Old Testament apocrypha—the *Wisdom of Solomon*—is included). We cannot know whether the *Muratorian Canon* was an official document or drawn up for a private person, but later official lists all contain the four New Testament Gospels.

Even so, the question about the identity and number of authoritative Gospels was by no means settled by the end of the second century. In some quarters there was an objection against the acceptance of the Gospel according to John. John was a favorite work in the second-century **gnostic** school of Valentinus; the earliest commentaries on the Fourth Gospel come from two of Valentinus's pupils, Ptolemaeus and Heracleon. Moreover, Montanus, the founder of a church based on "new prophecy" granted to him in the middle of the second century, taught that he himself was the advocate promised in the Gospel according to John (14:16–17, 26). Consequently, a few authors belonging to the greater Church turned against the common opinion that the gospel had been written by a disciple of Jesus.

Late in the second century, Serapion, bishop of Antioch in Syria, gave permission for the *Gospel according to Peter* to be read in the congregation. Although Serapion later changed his mind, the third-century Syrian writing known as the *Teaching of the Apostles* makes free use of this gospel.

Some years after Serapion permitted the use of the *Gospel according to Peter* in Syria, Clement of Alexandria asserted that the *Secret Gospel according to Mark* derived from the hand of the same author who wrote the Gospel according to Mark. He wrote that the Gospel according to Mark set forth what was most suitable for beginners in the faith, whereas the *Secret Gospel according to Mark* was to be used by those who were perfected in the faith.

Early in the fourth century, Eusebius, bishop of Caesarea in Palestine, drew up a list of "acknowledged," "disputed," and "spurious" New Testament writings, which appears to have had great influence in the Church. Eusebius reckoned that only the Gospels according to Matthew, Mark, Luke, and John were "acknowledged," but he is well aware of the fact that a gospel known as the *Gospel according to the Hebrews* was held by many to enjoy the same status.

The writings from Eusebius' first two categories were used to make up the first list containing the twenty-seven books of New Testament as it is now known. This list is found in the famous *Paschal Letter* that Athanasius, bishop of Alexandria, circulated in 367 CE. Although Athanasius's list influenced the Western Church, it had little influence upon Syrian Christianity when it was introduced. In the Syrian churches, Tatian's *Diatessaron* was preferred over the four Gospels until well into the fifth century.[6]

---

[6]In spite of its name, Tatian's gospel harmony should not be taken as a witness to an early acceptance of the fourfold gospel. Some scholars argue that Tatian actually used a fifth source.

# THE QUESTION OF GENRE

It is important to determine a book's **genre**—that is, the type of writing it is. For instance, people reading novels have certain expectations of novels. A reader may know nothing about a novel's actual content, but familiarity with the genre of the novel prepares a reader for a specific kind of writing. If the novel turns out to have a form totally unlike that of other novels, the reader is likely to be confused. It is extremely important to understand what genre the Gospels represent. If the Gospels are misidentified, readers may not understand their contents. Different types of writing must be interpreted in their own terms. This principle applies to the Gospels as well as to other types of writing; a document's genre qualifies its interpretation.

What is a gospel? What kind of writing is it? What were the expectations of the first "readers" of the Gospels? They were not readers in the modern sense because printing had not yet been invented; not many people could write, and not many copies of the Gospels were available for the few who could read. The Gospels were read by one person to an assembly of listeners. What did the assembly of listeners compare them with? Were the Gospels comparable to other New Testament writings?

There are several types of writings in the New Testament. The book of Acts can be categorized as an historical monograph composed of loosely sequenced events and speeches (Greek *praxeis*) of famous men. Acts includes religious interests, but even Herodotus's great history portrayed God as the shaper of history.

Paul's epistles (letters) fit into the genre of letters. This form of writing was well established in the first century as attested to by the letters of Cicero (50 BCE). Despite Paul's modification of the typical letter format, his letters are best placed alongside other ancient letters. The book of Revelation (Revelation = **Apocalypse**) can be set alongside Jewish apocalypses like Daniel. This type of writing usually discloses a revelation or unveiling of the history of the world, especially of the end of the age. While Revelation is not **pseudepigraphical** like other apocalypses, it does present a series of revelations about the future. It is obvious that the Gospels represent a type of book that is different from other New Testament writings.

Many readers of the Gospels think of them as biographies. This interpretation was popularized in the nineteenth century when scholars generally understood the Gospels to be records of the life of Jesus. This tradition goes back to the second-century apologist, Justin. He said that the *euangelia* (Gospels) are "memoirs of the apostles." Thus he thought of the Gospels as biographies, a genre that was popular in Justin's day.

However, some people in the ancient Church had a different, more perceptive view than Justin's notion about the genre of the Gospels. Approximately fifty years after Justin, Clement of Alexandria described the Gospel according to John as a "spiritual gospel." According to Clement, only Matthew, Mark, and Luke were historically reliable. He believed that John should not be compared with them because John set forth the spiritual truth underlying the historical facts. Today all four Gospels are interpreted by scholars as setting forth what their authors think is spiritual truth. Overall, however, Clement's distinction between the first three Gospels on the one hand and John on the other is still useful to scholars. That is why scholars identify Matthew, Mark, and Luke as **synoptic** Gospels.[7]

Justin's view, which portrayed the Gospels as biographies, prevailed up to the twentieth century. In the nineteenth century, many writers tried to stitch together pieces from all four Gospels in order to write a modern biography of the life of Jesus. Tatian, Justin's pupil, was the first to write a "biography" with his work, the *Diatessaron*. Tatian agreed with Justin that the Gospels really say the same thing and serve as biographies of Jesus.

However, there is a difference between Tatian's biography and the nineteenth-century's biographies. Scholars in the nineteenth century tried to fill in the gaps in the life of Jesus, which are found, in varying degrees, in the four Gospels. Questions having to do with the time between Jesus' birth and baptism needed to be answered. Consequently, nineteenth-century writers, by drawing on their own imaginations and the apocryphal Gospels, produced biographies of Jesus that smoothed out the shortcomings of the Gospels. The idea that the Gospels were biographies clearly affected their research.

Besides being concerned about the gaps found in the Gospels, nineteenth-century scholars also wanted to understand Jesus' motivation. Why did Jesus do this or that? These scholars recognized that the Gospels needed to include psychological explanations if they were to serve as biographies. In Mark 8, Peter confessed that Jesus was the **Messiah,** and this confession was a crucial turning point in the life of Jesus with his disciples. Before this confession very little was said about the messiahship of Jesus. However, after Peter's confession, Jesus taught his disciples that he was the Messiah and that he had to suffer. Scholars felt a need to explain the change in Jesus' behavior after the confession. The biographers of the previous century said that Jesus perceived that the crowds did not grasp his intention and therefore—encouraged by Peter's confession—he gave his attention instead to the disciples. This is a psychological construction of Jesus' motives and behavior. The explanation is weakened, however, when we realize that the Gospel according to Mark is not a primitive biography of Jesus with an accurate chronology.

Why do scholars doubt that Mark's gospel is a biography? Scholars understand that Mark's gospel does not have the characteristics of ancient biographical literature. There are biographies from Jesus' time, such as the *Life of Apollonius*, a famous miracle worker. Mark's work is different from this one in two ways. First, we know something about Philostratus, the author of Apollonius's biography, whereas Mark, as well as the other gospel authors, is anonymous. The familiar headings of the Gospels (the Gospel according to Mark, and so on) were not part of the original manuscripts but were added in the second century. Second, unlike ancient biographies, the Gospel according to Mark is not very descriptive of the main character, Jesus. Considered the earliest gospel, Mark begins by saying that

---

[7] *Synopsis* is a Greek word that can be translated as "common perspective." The perspective shared by the first three evangelists made it possible for editors to produce a "synopsis" by placing their materials in parallel columns. John, however, does not fit in so easily. Simply browsing through any modern synopsis illustrates how seldom John's column is filled out in accordance with the other Gospels.

Jesus went to John for baptism. The writer said that Jesus came from Nazareth but said nothing about his parents, his occupation, his larger family, what he looked like, and so on. Did he have a beard? Probably, because all male Jews had beards. Was he married? The overwhelming majority of grown-ups were. Nothing was said about a wife of Jesus, but nothing is said about Peter's wife either, although he certainly was married (Mark 1:30; 1 Cor. 9:5). Historical interests, essential to ancient biographies, are not treated in the Gospels.

Jesus is introduced as a figure more or less known to the readers. The Gospel according to Mark is kerygmatic literature. *Kerygma* is the Greek word for "preaching," and it is used in the New Testament to describe the proclamation of the gospel or its content. Mark's gospel represents the narrative form of the Church's gospel. The Gospels are therefore meant primarily to strengthen faith. They are also missionary literature: They address people who have heard something about Jesus and want to hear more.

The original gospel as detected in the mini-gospel of Paul (1 Cor. 15:3–5) was the oral proclamation of the death and resurrection of Jesus. His death and resurrection effected salvation. This belief is fundamental to the Gospels. Mark has been characterized as a **passion** story with a very long introduction. Everything in Mark is oriented toward the death and resurrection of Jesus. Nothing similar to this exists in ancient biographical literature. The Gospels reveal no interest in the external or internal history of Jesus.[8]

There is in fact no genre that bears a close similarity to the gospel genre. The Gospels describe the work of the savior. In a wider sense, that work included Jesus' teaching and miracles, but those were not recorded in a chronologically accurate way, as even the earliest witness to the Gospels, Papias (about 130 CE), observed. The usual biographical interest is simply not to be found in them. We can see this from the way in which Matthew and Luke handle the traditional material, altering the form of the material they are working with in their Gospels.

The Gospels do have what may be called a biographical framework. All the Gospels describe Jesus' life from his baptism by John to his execution by Pilate, but their overall coverage is markedly different from that of any biography, ancient as well as modern. However, it is inappropriate to take a part of the Gospels and define it as the whole. The primary focus of the Gospels has to do with Jesus' death at Jerusalem.

Furthermore, biographies, then and now, contain anecdotes that serve as entertaining stories. There is very little anecdotal material in the Gospels. The story of the death of John the Baptist in Mark 6 is a true anecdotal piece. It describes the dancing stepdaughter of Herod Antipas, who dances so well that Herod promises her anything. She then asks, after being coaxed by her mother, for the head of John the Baptist on a platter. This story qualifies as an anecdote, but this literary form is rare in the Gospels. The genre of the gospel is not a biography in the Greco-Roman tradition.

---

[8]Mark served as the model for the Gospels according to Matthew and Luke. These Gospels expand on the material of Mark, but even so they do not parallel the biographical works of the ancient world. Matthew may depict the birth of Jesus, and Luke may describe an incident at the temple when Jesus was twelve years old, but huge spans of Jesus' life are still overlooked.

What can be called Jewish memoir literature—such as Old Testament evidence about prophets and later Jewish evidence about charismatic individuals, miracle workers, and **sect**-leaders—highlights the distinctive character of the Gospels. We can locate reports on the teaching and actions of these people and reports on their relationship with different groups of opponents; but they lack an emphasis on the death of the hero and its significance. The death of the main character, in contrast, is the essence of the Gospels, and death is never the chief feature of a biography.

A comparison can be made between the Gospels and ancient Greek tragedies. In the tragedies we find an emphasis on the death of the main character, but this character is not sent from the divine world to reveal God's will before going to his death. Moreover, the tragic figure's death has no stated purpose.

Whereas many scholars identify the Gospels as *sui generis* (Latin: one of a kind), some scholars detect enough significant parallels with a Greco-Roman biographical genre known as a life (Greek: *bios*; Latin: *vitae*) to argue that such a category is fitting for the Gospels. Ancient forms of biography do have some characteristics that are shared with the Gospels. For instance, they are similar in length to the Gospels (10,000–20,000 words). Like the gospel authors, some ancient biographers devoted a similar amount of space to their subject's final days (15–20 percent). However, a *bios/vitae* was not defined as a genre by the ancients and stands as a category delineated only by contemporary scholars. By virtue of the fact that a single figure is their subject, the Gospels parallel ancient biographical texts in some ways, yet as their distinctive features demonstrate, the Gospels exceed the boundaries of biographical literature.

## SUMMARY

The term *gospel* underwent a transformation over time. Beginning among Jews and Gentiles as a common term that denoted an announcement, among the **apostles** it came to mean the proclamation of Jesus' death, burial, and resurrection. To this core message were added further details about Jesus' life as Mark's gospel illustrates. Ultimately, the texts preserving the gospel came to be known as Gospels, and the memory of oral Gospels was lost.

The development of the canon was thus a slow process, proceeding at different speeds in different quarters; the determination of the canon also reflects power struggles and political issues. Bishops, the leaders of Christian communities, disagreed among themselves about the delineation of Scripture and competing parties were formed. Bishops who agreed met, drew up canonical lists, distributed them to their congregations, and thereby discarded other interpretations of Jesus and Christianity. The New Testament is the canon of the party that proved to be the strongest one in the end. Marcion's canon was refused; it was rejected as too small and bearing the mark of a **heterodox** editor. The Gospel according to John was finally accepted. However, Gospels that lacked **catholicity,** like the *Gospel according to Peter,* were refused, whereas Gospels reckoned as **unorthodox,** like the *Secret Gospel according to Mark,* were branded as heretical.

As to form, the Gospels do not intend to be simple biographies or to serve as careful historical reports. Is it still possible that they contain historical truth or even intend to do so? That is, do the Gospels convey historical truth while being something other than biographies? Two things should be noted: (1) The Gospels do not conform to the biography genre, and (2) the Gospels actually do not fit into any literary category and represent a genre of their own.

## KEY TERMS FOR REVIEW

| | | | |
|---|---|---|---|
| Gospel | *Diatessaron* | Scripture | *Muratorian Canon* |
| Greek | Evangelist | Apocryphal | *Paschal Letter* |
| Salvation | Canon | Genre | |
| Oral tradition | Testament | Biography | |

## QUESTIONS FOR REVIEW

**1.** How did the meaning of the term *gospel* change from Paul to Mark to Justin Martyr?

**2.** Why is Marcion important in the development of the canon?

**3.** Why is the question of the Gospels' genre a complex one to answer?

## SUGGESTIONS FOR FURTHER READING

Aune, D. *The New Testament in Its Literary Environment.* Philadelphia: Westminster, 1987.

Baukham, R. ed. *The Gospels for All Christians: Rethinking the Gospels Audiences.* Grand Rapids: Eerdmans, 1998.

Burridge, R. *What Are the Gospels?: A Comparison with Greco-Roman Biography.* Cambridge: Cambridge University Press, 1992.

Talbert, C. *What Is a Gospel: The Genre of the Canonical Gospels.* Philadelphia: Fortress, 1977.

# 2

※

# Evidence for Jesus

## DID JESUS EVEN EXIST?

Although the vast majority of historians accept that Jesus existed, from time to time a few people pose the question of Jesus' historicity. Some argue that early Christians turned a mythical savior into a historical figure, and parallels between the Gospels and pagan **myth** are often used in support of this contention. Birth from a divinely impregnated woman was claimed for several gods in the ancient world. Plutarch, a Greek biographer who was a contemporary of the New Testament authors, said that intercourse between a male god and a mortal women was conceded by all. The "divine" Augustus was rumored to be the son of Apollo. Furthermore, the idea that a god was put to death and then resurrected was not uncommon in the old myths. Dionysus, the Greek deity who was restored to life by his father Zeus, is just one example of this well-known tradition. Other such figures would include Adonis, Osiris, and Tammuz.

However, mythical parallels do not disprove the existence of Jesus. They merely illustrate that the significance of Jesus was presented in a form familiar to a first-century audience. Religious missionaries know that they have little chance of success if they cannot establish contact with other people through their already existing religious world. In some cases, upon close inspection the mythical parallels are found to be superficial and offer only a few points of correspondence.

Those who deny that Jesus existed also point to the fact that the earliest Christian **creeds,** such as the summary of the faith found in 1 Cor. 15:3–5 and even in Paul's letters at large, do not mention the crucifixion under Pilate or events in the life of Jesus. This is the so-called argument from silence: What is unmentioned did not happen (that is, if no wife of Jesus is referred to, then Jesus was not married). It is much more likely that these topics were not pertinent to the interests of the New Testament writings. They were not part of the gospel, and therefore not important enough to be mentioned in creedal formulations. In Paul's writings, 1 Thess. 2:14–15 is the most specific reference to those responsible for Jesus' death, and in this instance Paul refers only to the "Jews." This identification is, of course, a very general one, but it is nonetheless historically accurate that Jesus was rejected by a segment of first-century Jews living in the Roman province of Judea. The earliest creedal statements do not include any references to those associated with Jesus' death, like the Roman governor Pilate or the high priest Caiaphas. Paul was so absorbed by his faith in Jesus as the savior risen from the dead that he had little need or occasion to speak of Jesus' ministry. In addition, Paul admits that he was not an eyewitness of the passion events and had no first-hand knowledge of Jesus' life.

The greatest weakness for the hypothesis that Jesus never existed is the fact that the Christians really had no compelling reason to transform a mythical savior into a historical figure. In the first century many religions had mythical savior figures, and these figures were *acceptable* to their religious adherents. At the time these religions were not criticized because their saviors were not historical figures.

Many historically detailed traditions are described in the Gospels, and it would border on incredulity to label them as mere inventions. The Gospels do not show telltale signs of being produced when Christianity moved out into the Greco-Roman world. All the discussions between Jesus and the Jewish authorities meant nothing to non-Jews, yet they are significant portions of every gospel. Similarly, the geographical details were meaningless to non-Palestinian readers. The first Christians could not have fabricated these traditions in Palestine as a justification for their own preaching. Their Palestinian contemporaries would have simply identified Jesus as a product of fantasy. Non-Christian sources, both Roman and Jewish, never question the existence of Jesus. Jewish sources, as quoted by the anti-Christian writer Celsus (Origen, *Against Celsus* 1:32), assert that Jesus was the bastard son of a Roman soldier. It is therefore too implausible to argue that within thirty years there had evolved a fairly coherent and consistent complex of traditions about a nonexistent figure.

## NON-CHRISTIAN LITERARY EVIDENCE

Non-Christian literary evidence comes in two forms: Greco-Roman and Jewish. Historians seek early, independent accounts of Jesus and accept the reality that ancient literary sources are biased in varying degrees. Greco-Roman literary evidence does not surface until the second century and, even then, references to Jesus are indirect and imprecise. This scarcity comes as no surprise because Christianity was then viewed by many Romans as a Jewish sect of no consequence to the empire. Jewish literary evidence, with the exception of Jospehus, comes later and is at times rather cryptic in nature. Scholars believe that other literary references to Jesus were probably lost when Christians persecuted the Jews following the empire's embrace of Christianity. Many Jewish writings were burned by Christians, and Jews appear to have either destroyed or blacked out references to

Jesus in their writings. Despite the scarcity and quality of literary evidence, scholars are struck by the fact that these texts always assume Jesus' existence.

## Greco-Roman

In general, none of the Greco-Roman writers said much about Jesus. Pliny, a governor of Asia Minor, provided the earliest non-Christian gentile testimony to early Christianity. Writing to the emperor Trajan about 111 CE, Pliny was puzzled about the followers of Jesus and asked if Christians were to be considered criminals. He described early Christian devotion to Jesus with the following words: "They were in the habit of meeting on a fixed day before sunrise and reciting an antiphonal hymn to Christ as god" (*Epistles* 10:96). Pliny depicted Christians as decent people, who neither stole nor committed adultery.

Many Christians already worshipped Jesus as a god by the beginning of the second century. Perhaps Pliny meant to say that Jesus (Christ) was in reality no god and that Christians only treated Christ as a god. Pliny did not make any references to the life and teaching of Jesus, and he provided only traditions that he may have drawn from Christian sources at his disposal. In addition, the ethical standards of the Christians may or may not go back to the teachings of Jesus. Even if the Christians claimed that the standards go back to his teaching, it does not have to be true; the moral code is too general for us to tell.

Tacitus, a Roman historian writing shortly after Pliny (116 CE), identified Christians as the ones who were blamed by the emperor Nero for the fire which partially destroyed Rome in 64 CE. He stated that these people, being most despicable, "got their name from **Christ,** who was executed by sentence of the procurator Pontius Pilate in the reign of Tiberius" (*Annals* 15:44). Tacitus regarded *Christ* as a proper name, even though it is a Greek translation of the Hebrew word *messiah*. Originally, *messiah* was used as a royal title in the Jewish Bible; it later became a designation for the divinely appointed savior expected by many Jews. Furthermore, Tacitus dated Christ's death to the time when Pilate was governor of Palestine (26–37 CE). Can this dating serve as independent evidence? Unfortunately, Tacitus did not provide independent historical evidence. In all likelihood, the name *Christ* and the date for Pilate came from Christian sources. Interestingly, Tertullian, the early third-century Latin theologian, claimed that Roman records could provide verification for the execution of Jesus by Roman authorities (*Apology* 21).

Suetonius, a near contemporary of Tacitus (12 CE), wrote that on a certain occasion the emperor Claudius "expelled the Jews from Rome, on account of the riots in which they were constantly indulging, at the instigation of Chrestus" (*Claudius* 25:4). Because Claudius was emperor from 41 to 54 CE, something seems to be wrong with the statement for Suetonius to think that Chrestus was a living person at that time and that he showed up in Rome (although one later Christian writer did say that Jesus was crucified during the reign of Claudius). Suetonius may have been referring to a Jewish riot that was brought about by a quarrel over whether or not Jesus was the Messiah (Christ [Christos] being misspelled as Chrestus). Perhaps Suetonius should not even be understood to mean that Christ (Chrestus) was in the city. He may have spoken about a later time. Many Jews were living in Rome, and most of the first Christians in the city were

Jews. Early Christian missionaries, as described in the book of Acts, always sought to convert Jews (13:13–14). Possibly two parties were present among the Jews in Rome: one believing that Jesus was the Messiah (Chrestus), and the other believing that the messiah was yet to come.

What about the name *Chrestus?* It may not be a misspelling on the part of Suetonius. In Greek, *Chrestus* means the "Good One" and may have been used as a title for Jesus. *Christos,* the Greek translation of *messiah,* means the "Anointed One." Anointing was part of the royal installation ritual in the Near East; oil was poured over the head of the king and he was called the Anointed One. Greeks and Romans, however, did not anoint their rulers, and the term was used as a name because it meant nothing to them as a title. Paul's letters reflect both Jewish and non-Jewish usage. Sometimes Paul put the article before Christ (the Christ) and thus correctly treated it as a title. In other passages, Paul used Christ without the article, treating it as a proper noun: Jesus Christ, Christ Jesus, and even Christ. In this light, Chrestus, the Good One, may be a deliberate alteration of Christos, or Anointed One, which was meaningless to Greek and Roman ears. In any event, Suetonius does not say anything about the historical Jesus.

A letter written in Syriac that can be dated sometime after 73 CE, but probably no later than the third century, is another Greco-Roman Jesus text. Its author, Mara bar Serapion, was writing to his son to encourage him in the pursuit of wisdom. He presented Jesus, along with Socrates and Pythagoras, as examples of unjustly murdered wise men, whose teachings continue as a legacy. Jesus was identified as a king rejected by his people. Concerning Jesus the letter reads, "What advantage did the Jews gain from executing their wise king? It was just after that their kingdom was abolished. . . . Nor did the wise king die for good; he lived on in the teachings which he had given" (*British Museum Syriac MS* Additional 14,658).

Mara bar Serapion does not appear to be a Christian, or else he would have referred to the resurrection of Jesus. The reference to the Jews as Jesus' executioners, and not the Romans (as Tacitus did), suggests his dependence on Christian traditions. Yet, although comments on the resurrection are missing, he took the existence of Jesus for granted.

## Jewish

Non-Christian Jewish documents provide more information than Greco-Roman sources. Stories about Jesus appear in rabbinic sources, such as the legendary material in the **Talmud.** In one famous passage, found in *Sanhedrin* 107b, Jesus is called a magician. The text reads, "Jesus the Nazorean[1] practiced magic and led astray and deceived Israel." This accusation must be placed within the sphere of competitive religious claims. In the context of rival religions, what is miraculous for one group is simply interpreted as magical by another group. Therefore, the **rabbis** interpreted Jesus' works as magical deeds whereas Christians interpreted them as miracles. This rabbinic tradition does not amount to a corroboration of

---

[1] The Babylonian Talmud, in which *Sanhedrin* is found, dates to the fifth century. It contains mainly legal material and a discussion of the law, but it also has legends about Jewish teachers.

the gospel stories about Jesus as a miracle worker because it may be based on Christian tradition.

Another Talmudic text says that Jesus was the fruit of a union between Mary and a Roman soldier named Pantera. Clearly, the claim is antagonistic, presupposing the Christian story of the virgin birth. Other Talmudic Jesus traditions are more difficult to account for. Another story, in *Sanhedrin* 107b, states that Jesus was a pupil of a teacher who lived one hundred years before the date normally accepted for Jesus' birth (8–6 BCE). This story adds that Jesus, after his teacher rebuked him, lapsed into heresy by setting up a brick and worshipping it.

Some Jewish Jesus traditions are not antagonistic; they provide a more positive view of Jesus. One refers to Jesus' followers as great healers "in the name of Jesus." Another states that a "word" of Jesus (Greek: *agraphon*) was found pleasing to one of the Jewish authorities on the law.

One rabbinic tradition dealing with Jesus' execution is particularly significant. *Sanhedrin* 43a states that

> On the eve of the Passover they hung Yeshu the Nazarene. And the crier went out before him for forty days saying, "Yeshu the Nazarene is going to be stoned, because he has practiced magic and deceived and led astray Israel. Any one who knows anything in his favor, let him come and tell about him." And they found nothing in his favor. And they hung him on the eve of the Passover.

This tradition can be linked to the Gospel according to John. Whereas the synoptics related that Jesus was apprehended, interrogated, and sentenced to death all in one night, John implied that formal moves against Jesus were made some time before his apprehension and crucifixion. Even more interesting is the statement that Jesus was executed on the **Passover** eve. This statement is also in agreement with John's gospel (18:28; 19:14). In contrast to John, the synoptics said that Jesus shared a Passover meal with his disciples and was crucified the following day. The talmudic account corroborates John's version.

Josephus, a first-century Jewish historian, is the most important Jewish source for Jesus. His writings supply references to John the Baptist, Jesus, and James, the brother of Jesus who became the leader of the first Christian community in Jerusalem. According to Josephus's *Antiquities,* written around 92 CE, the high priest of Jerusalem had James stoned in 62 CE. He also confirmed Acts and later Christian sources that presented James as an important figure in Jerusalem. Moreover, Josephus referred to James as "the brother of Jesus, the so-called Christ." This wording demonstrates that he knew that Christ was a messianic title. Despite Josephus's brevity and indirectness, this writing is helpful evidence for the existence of Jesus because Jesus is identified as the "*so-called* Christ," not simply as "the Christ," which would suggest that a Christian had tampered with the text.

In an earlier passage, Josephus dealt directly and extensively with Jesus, but Christians probably altered the text, or perhaps they even wrote it altogether.

> About this time arose Jesus, a wise man, if indeed it be lawful to call him a man. For he was a doer of wonderful deeds, and a teacher of men who gladly receive the truth. He drew to himself many both of the Jews and of the Gentiles. He was the Christ; and when Pilate, on the indictment of the principal men among us, had condemned him to the cross, those who had loved him at the first did not cease to

do so, for he appeared to them again alive on the third day, the divine prophets having foretold these and ten thousand other wonderful things about him. And even to
this day the race of Christians, who are named for him has not died out.
(*Antiquities* 18:63)

Josephus called Jesus a wise man ("if it is right to call him a man"). Historians
doubt that a non-Christian Jew would write the latter, but would such a Jew write
that Jesus was a "wise man"? Josephus also called Jesus a miracle worker and
teacher of truth-loving people. Some scholars argue that no Christian would present such a low **Christology,** and that this terminology must go back to a Jewish
source. But could such an assessment be possible in first-century Jewish circles? No
such depiction of Jesus as a wise man can be found in early Judaism—much less
the judgment that he was a miracle worker! Some scholars consider the whole
passage a clever fabrication. Josephus's description of Jesus may have been written
by a Christian who wanted to make Christianity less offensive to the Romans, for
whom the *Antiquities* were written. Jesus was portrayed as a member of the Jewish
nation, and Judaism was tolerated by the Romans as a legal religion.

The text then states that Jesus was the Messiah (Christ). This statement is
clearly not traceable to Josephus. Afterward, Josephus stated that Jesus was executed by Pilate at the instigation of the leaders of the Jews. Several scholars maintain that a Christian interpolator would have been more anti-Jewish because the
Gospels blame the Jews for the execution of Jesus. However, the question
remains: What if the interpolator was a Jewish Christian who felt an allegiance to
his Jewish traditions? Josephus also noted that Jesus rose after three days and
appeared to his disciples, all in accordance with Jewish prophecy. This last statement cannot derive from Josephus. Scholars have reconstructed this text to sal-
vage it as historical evidence, but would a revision be justifiable?

An original Josephus text that touched on Jesus directly may never have
existed. The Church father Origen of Alexandria, who lived in the third century,
read the entire *Antiquities* and often made references to the passage on James, but
his extant writings make no mention of the longer account of Jesus. In any case,
Josephus probably referred indirectly to Jesus but did not add to what is known
about Jesus of Nazareth.

## ARCHAEOLOGICAL EVIDENCE

**Archaeology** cannot prove Jesus' existence, but archaeological finds may throw
light on the Gospels and create a greater appreciation for the integrity of the
social and cultural milieu that they associate with Jesus. Major excavations exist
in Jerusalem and Galilee—including the cities of Nazareth, where Jesus lived, and
Capernaum, which seems to have been a center for his activities. Some of the
archaeological evidence confirms the veracity of historical descriptions found in
the Gospels and their Jewish environment. As evidence, the Gospels reflect Jewish
life in Israel as opposed to gentile interests in the greater Roman empire.

Excavations in Capernaum unearthed a church from the fourth century. The
graffiti scratched by Christians on the plaster walls and partitions of this church
identify it as having originally been the house of Peter. If true, this house is where

Jesus cured Peter's mother-in-law of fever (Mark 1:29–31). Archaeologists have also discovered that this church was built on the site of a first-century house that was rebuilt in the fourth century. Was it really the house of Peter? Christian tradition says so, whereas archaeology can only confirm the existence of such sites.

In November 1990, a dump truck accidentally smashed through the roof of an ancient burial tomb during some work at the Jerusalem Peace Forest. Inside the tomb were found a number of ossuaries, small stone boxes for retaining bones of the deceased. This practice thrived for less than a century and was generally limited to Jerusalem. One ornate ossuary was inscribed with the name "Yehosef bar Qafa" (Joseph, son of Caiaphas). Bronze coins minted in 42–43 CE during the reign of Herod Agrippa I were also found in the cave. According to the Gospels, a high priest named Caiaphas presided over the trial of Jesus in Jerusalem shortly before his crucifixion under Pontius Pilate in 30 CE. Outside of the Gospels, Jospehus was the only ancient writer to speak of a Caiaphas.

In the fall of 2002, an even more intriguing ossuary surfaced. Oded Golan, a Tel Aviv engineer who describes himself as a collector of biblical artifacts, brought forward an ossuary that he said he had purchased thirty-five years earlier from an antiquities dealer whose name he could not recall. On the ossuary are inscribed the Aramaic words, "James, son of Joseph, brother of Jesus." Scholars have since debated the authenticity of the inscription. Some argue for its authenticity and the likely possibility that it confirms New Testament references to Jesus, his brother James, and Joseph. The odds against names like James, Joseph, and Jesus being related the way they are in the inscription is used as evidence to support a connection to Jesus of Nazareth. Other scholars have argued that the inscription is suspect; apparent differences in the handwriting have raised the possibility that an ancient or modern forger added the inscription, either whole or in part. Unfortunately, the mystery that remains surrounding the ossuary's discovery (it appears to be a looted artifact that was clandestinely sold on the antiquities market) and the ambiguity of its inscription (no one doubts the antiquity of the ossuary itself) stand in the way of a scholarly consensus over the ossuary's historical value.

Mark 14 relates a story about a woman anointing Jesus with a bottle of perfume. According to the evangelist (14:3), she had to break the bottle to open it. This story had puzzled scholars until archaeologists unearthed small glass bottles with extremely long necks. This type of bottle would have been ideal for keeping perfume. Opening such a bottle involves breaking or smashing the neck before pouring the perfume.

All the Gospels relate that Jesus was nailed to the cross. This tale has been embarrassing for Christians because there was no evidence that the hands and feet of those who were crucified were nailed to the cross. Normally people were bound to the cross with ropes and hung there until they died of thirst and exhaustion. Such was the case for those who were crucified after the great insurrection of 6 CE. But now, due to recently discovered remains of people who were crucified, we have evidence supporting the nailing of victims to the cross. Moreover, archaeologists now know that instead of nailing the hands to the cross, the crucifiers put nails through the wrists—apparently because the wrists could better support the weight of the body. With regard to the nailing of feet, one particularly grisly artifact still has the nail in the petrified heel bone of the unfortunate victim.

Most representations of the crucified Jesus are anachronistic and show Jesus' hands nailed to the cross, but one allegedly old representation of Jesus shows holes in the wrists: the Shroud of Turin that pious Catholics have long regarded as the cloth in which the dead body of Jesus was buried. This shroud shows the contours of a body that seems to have undergone extensive torture. The first time a photograph was taken of the shroud, the photographer received something of a shock; a very realistic picture of a crucified man appeared on the negative!

During the seventies and eighties an international team of scholars worked intensively on the shroud. Their examination concluded that the body whose imprint is formed on the shroud seems to have undergone a type of torture similar to that predicated of Jesus in the Gospels. One of the more striking details involves a great number of peculiarly formed blood marks over the entire body. They appear to be the result of a beating with a Roman *flagrum,* a whip with several leather tails tipped with metal hooks. By using a sophisticated astronomical camera, two researchers from the United States Air Force found that the face on the shroud had true three-dimensional qualities. As for the shroud itself, grains from plants that grew in and around Palestine in the first century were found in it.

However, only a radiocarbon analysis of cloth fragments could demonstrate the age of the shroud. According to this test, which was carried out in 1988, the shroud proved to be only 700 years old. As a whole, the Shroud of Turin is medieval.[2] The *Gospel according to the Hebrews,* one of several noncanonical **Jewish-Christian** Gospels, may have contributed to the tradition of Jesus' burial cloth that lies behind the Shroud of Turin. According to Jerome's quotation of this gospel in the fourth century, Jesus, after his resurrection, gave his burial cloth to the servant of the priest.

## SUMMARY

Although some people may insist that Jesus never existed, the literary and archaeological evidence strongly suggests that Jesus is an historical figure. The arguments against Jesus' existence are offset by ancient writers, both Christian and non-Christian. The archaeological materials do not prove Jesus' historicity, but they do testify to the plausibility of the New Testament Gospels as reflecting first-century Jewish life under the Romans. The important issue that remains is the reliability of the New Testament Gospels. Their accurate descriptions of life in Jesus' day do not necessarily ensure that their presentations of Jesus are free of distortions. Whereas Jesus was a historical figure, was he later presented with the features of mythical figures?

---

[2]In 2000, Dr. Shimon Gibson, the director of the Jerusalem Archaeological Field Unit, was giving a tour of first-century tombs in the Hinnom Valley south of Jerusalem and chanced upon a 2,000-year-old corpse that was wrapped in a burial shroud. Carbon dating places this shroud in the first fifty years of the first century CE. News services speculated that it could be that of a witness to Jesus' crucifixion— a very remote but real possibility.

# KEY TERMS FOR REVIEW

| | | |
|---|---|---|
| Myth | Suetonius | Josephus |
| Mythical saviors | Mara bar Serapion | Archaeology |
| Pliny | Talmud | Shroud of Turin |
| Tacitus | Rabbis | |

# QUESTIONS FOR REVIEW

1. Why do some people doubt Jesus' existence?
2. What do Greco-Roman writers say about Jesus?
3. Why is Josephus an ambivalent factor in deciding Jesus' existence?
4. How do archaeological finds relate to the setting given to Jesus' life in the Gospels?

# SUGGESTIONS FOR FURTHER READING

Helms, R. *Gospel Fictions.* New York: Prometheus, 1988.

Meyers, E. and Strange, J., *Archaeology, The Rabbis and Early Christianity.* London: SPCK, 1984.

Van Voorst, R., *Jesus Outside the New Testament: An Introduction to the Ancient Evidence.* Grand Rapids: Eerdmans, 2000.

Wells, G., *The Historical Evidence for Jesus.* New York: Prometheus, 1972.

Wenham, D., ed. *The Jesus Tradition Outside the Gospels.* Sheffield: JSOT Press, 1985.

# 3

# Jesus and Modern Scholarship

## THE HISTORICAL JESUS ENTERPRISE

In 1967, Hugh Anderson counted more than 60,000 published biographies of Jesus and asked, "Who of sufficient range of intellect and breath of vision is to survey and measure an enterprise so massive, to bring order into the chaos of the lives of Jesus?" Many more biographies of Jesus have been published since Anderson asked that question, and the task is no less challenging today. Any introduction to Jesus and the Gospels needs to take into account these efforts.

The vast array of Jesus studies involves mutually exclusive models of understanding Jesus that elicit strong, sometimes-heated rebuttals. Some people are acquainted with the **"Jesus Seminar"**—a group of Jesus scholars who have been meeting since 1985 with the agenda of dispelling ignorance about Jesus by acquainting interested readers with modern gospel scholarship. Their high profile has resulted in a fair amount of media coverage, and their effort produced the book, *The Five Gospels: The Search for the Authentic Words of Jesus* (1993), which color codes Jesus' words according to their degree of authenticity. One member unofficially suggested this interpretation of the colors: red, That's Jesus; pink, Sure sounds like Jesus; gray, Well, maybe; and black, There's been some mistake. Luke Johnson is one scholar who has pointedly responded to the Jesus Seminar's efforts in his book, *The Real Jesus: The Misguided Quest for the Historical Jesus and the Truth of the Traditional Gospels* (1996), and he expresses serious reservations about the seminar's scholarship and conclusions regarding Jesus.

It is important to define what Jesus scholars mean by the phrase, ***historical Jesus.*** Historical Jesus refers to Jesus as he lived in first-century Palestine according to historical research. On the other hand, scholars also use the phrase ***Christ of Faith,*** to describe Jesus as he is worshipped by the Church and defined by its **creeds** and **confessions.** Historical Jesus scholars commonly distinguish the historical Jesus from the Christ of Faith. The former is the result of historical investigation whereas the latter is the substance of Christian faith and reflection. The relationship between these two perspectives is complex and sometimes extremely contentious.

## THE OLD QUEST FOR THE HISTORICAL JESUS

The first period of historical Jesus research is called the "Old Quest." It began in the eighteenth century and was typified by a growing skepticism about the historical reliability of the Gospels. At the end of the nineteenth century scholars eventually portrayed Jesus as a moral teacher who was misrepresented by his disciples as a Jewish Messiah, announcing the promised Kingdom of God. Convinced that the Gospels were biographies, scholars of the Old Quest wanted to produce a biographical re-reading of the Gospels that would be free of their supernatural, nonhistorical elements. In *The Aims of Jesus and His Disciples* (1778) Hermann Reimarus began this approach. Seeking to interpret Jesus within the context of first-century Jewish life, Reimarus wrote that Jesus was a failed Jewish revolutionary whose dead body was stolen by disciples who proclaimed him as the redeemer. David Strauss, with his book *The Life of Jesus* (1835), objected to treating the miracle accounts as simple historical texts. Instead, he identified the Gospels as religious literature and treated their miracle stories as myths— Christian stories symbolizing the truth that Jesus is the Messiah.

Together, Reimarus and Strauss were like lightning rods, igniting scholarly responses and new accounts of Jesus' life. Earnest Renan's *Life of Jesus* (1863) embodied the spirit of the Old Quest by presenting Jesus as a teacher of ethical ideals, not as a founder of theological dogmas. Renan echoed a theme common to several predecessors and argued that Jesus would not recognize the Church's ideology: A rabbi had been transformed into a god.

Old Quest methodology represented a clear departure from the past. Prior to the eighteenth century, canonicity was the only test for determining the authenticity of the sayings and deeds of Jesus. All texts included in the New Testament were considered authentic and noncanonical texts were historically suspect. Reading the Gospels was *the* means of finding out about Jesus. Underlying this practice was the assumption that the Gospels are inspired memoirs of Jesus' eyewitnesses. The Old Quest, which was a child of the **Enlightenment** and accepted its emphasis on reason and scientific ways of knowing, rejected these assumptions. No longer could a text be accepted as historically accurate simply because it was in the New Testament. Investigation and reason became the basis for historical knowledge.

The Enlightenment's new paradigm also questioned the claims of supernatural causation. Everything had to be understood within a natural system of cause and effect. It was Benedict Spinoza's work, *Tractatus Theologico-Politicus* (1670), that encouraged a thoroughly historical form of biblical interpretation. Consequently, the task of Jesus historians was no longer a simple chronicling of events reported in the Gospels. The new historical consciousness moved historians to evaluate the history reported in the Gospels. Discriminating judgments about their accounts had to be made in the effort to find out, "what really happened." As a result, each scholar's rationalism became his tool for discovering the historical Jesus.

Albert Schweitzer evaluated the efforts of Reimarus and other questors. His book, *The Quest of the Historical Jesus* (1906), was dedicated to his teacher, Heinrich Holtzmann, by his "grateful pupil" Albert. In it, Schweitzer surveyed historical Jesus studies over the previous 100 years, applauded a handful of scholarly advances, and concluded that except for a few scholars, the whole enterprise was a failure. Holtzmann, famous for his view that Jesus was a teacher of ethical ideals, found his position criticized as biased, subjective, ethnocentric, and ultimately non-Jewish. On the basis of a **critical** yet straightforward reading of the Gospels, Schweitzer presented Jesus as a determined messianic prophet who died in his attempt to bring in the kingdom (reminiscent of Reimarus's view). For Schweitzer, previous attempts to grasp the historical Jesus missed the mark because they ventured into historical speculation and did not interpret the Gospels consistently. Too many views of Jesus mirrored the idealistic interests of his biographers. The views were as much a flawed reconstruction as the ancient creeds of Nicea and Chalcedon, which many in the Old Quest wanted to replace.

Schweitzer's own spin on the historical Jesus as a resolute visionary focused on a future kingdom, which itself owed much to J. Weiss's *Jesus' Proclamation of the Kingdom of God* (1892), was a significant counterpunch to the prevailing view and gained new adherents. However, his book's critique of the historical Jesus search created a kind of nuclear winter by undermining what had come to be a thriving industry. Confidence was lost in the ability to determine who Jesus was. For many readers the choice was between Schweitzer's martyred Messiah, an interpretation that rested on a comparatively careful and historical reading of the Gospels but whose fruitless death was unnerving for some, and Holtzmann and company's teacher of ethical ideals, the reigning paradigm.

Ironically, Old Quest scholarship was evolving in ways that would undermine scholarly confidence in historical Jesus reconstructions. Nineteenth-century gospel scholarship had invented the science of **source criticism** and argued that Mark's gospel was a source for Matthew and Luke (John was deemed to be theologically speculative and of little historical value). Mark was therefore used as the primary document for constructing Jesus' biography. As the earliest text it was considered "purer," meaning it was more simple and unadorned in describing Jesus than other Gospels, which were viewed as Markan supplements. William Wrede's *The Messianic Secret of Mark* (1901) countered the assumption of Markan historical reliability. Wrede argued that Mark was a contrived text that had no historical advantage over the other Gospels and that all of them should be viewed with suspicion. Mark's presentation of Jesus as the Messiah was an early Christian construct that rendered Mark nonhistorical and thus unreliable. Wrede's treatment of Mark was a foreshadowing of **redaction criticism,** which sees each gospel as an editor's interpretation of Jesus. The Old Quest was familiar with historical difficulties in the Gospels but was certain that **literary criticism** and

Markan priority, in the hands of able scholars, would produce an accurate picture of the historical Jesus. Wrede's interpretation of Mark eroded this belief and provided a basis for historical skepticism regarding the historical Jesus.

## NO QUEST FOR THE HISTORICAL JESUS

Ultimately, the question, "Who was Jesus?," was asked less and less because its relevance, indeed the very possibility of answering it, was being debated more and more. Some scholars were asking, "Does it matter who Jesus was?" At the beginning of the twentieth century a growing number of scholars, led by Rudolf Bultmann, said that questions about the historical Jesus could not be answered. Building upon the claims of Martin Kähler's book, *The So-Called Historical Jesus and the Historic Biblical Christ* (1892), Bultmann said that the Gospels cannot be used biographically, were never intended to serve as biographies, and that the historical Jesus does not matter. In Bultmann's thinking, the Gospels are artificial constructions, mixing historical facts and pious fictions that cannot be disentangled, and more importantly, this state of affairs does not matter. It is best to treat the Gospels as unique texts of early Christian preaching and thus aim to discern Jesus' message through them, not his life. Bultmann began a phase that Marcus Borg has amusingly called, "No Quest of the Historical Jesus."

It became clear to many that Schweitzer's legacy for historical Jesus studies was an extreme skepticism that discouraged scholars interested in Jesus' biography. That was not Schweitzer's expressed intention. Yet, although he believed that scholars had ignored the historical evidence of the Gospels, he did think that the historical Jesus remained something of a mystery for modern readers, "One unknown," because of his strangeness as a Jewish apocalypticist who expected the end of this age. Schweitzer, who appears to have fashioned Jesus along the lines of Friedrich Nietzsche's "superman" (who blends power, virtue, and courage), followed Jesus by heroically serving others. All in all, the combined weight of Schweitzer, Wrede, and Kähler crushed the Old Quest's dream of biography.

Bultmann sensed that a critical mass had been reached in historical Jesus studies and ignored Jesus' life. He based his view of Jesus on the few sayings he found to be authentic through his use of **form criticism**—a literary program that identifies the Gospels as a collection of different types of sayings and deeds, all in varying degrees of authenticity. Bultmann's method for recovering the historical Jesus was quite different from the Old Quest. He settled for the recovery of Jesus' message by identifying the authentic Jesus sayings in the Gospels. His plan, explained in his *History of the Synoptic Tradition* (1921), for singling out Jesus' words, was to identify the authentic Jesus traditions from secondary additions. He identified them by applying what scholars now call the **criteria of authenticity**—principles for identifying which sayings are probably authentic—to each Jesus saying of the Gospels. He was left with meager results, which led him to conclude that Jesus' message was an existential call to a decision that leads to self-understanding.

Using existential philosophy as an interpretive grid, Bultmann said that Jesus called human beings to face the future with the freedom that God can give. He argued that this was Jesus' idea of the Kingdom of God. Bultmann's agenda was an **apologetic** effort to render Jesus relevant to modern people. His task, called the "demythologizing" of the New Testament, involved the reinterpretation of items that he understood as myths—like heaven, hell, and resurrection—to make Christianity meaningful for twentieth-century readers.

## THE NEW QUEST FOR THE HISTORICAL JESUS

Bultmann's own disciples challenged their teacher's disregard for the historical Jesus. In a paper read in 1953 entitled "The Problem of the Historical Jesus," Ernst Käsemann treated his teacher more kindly than Schweitzer did his, but he still contradicted Bultmann and said that the historical Jesus must matter for the Church, or else Jesus will become a meaningless buzz word. Käsemann began what James Robinson later named in 1960, "The New Quest of the Historical Jesus."

The goals of this second quest were more modest than those of the first. This quest did not seek to give as long, or as certain, an answer to the question, "Who was Jesus?," but its constituents were certain that some answer was necessary. Whereas the Gospels remained faith documents and not historical records that could serve as biographical fodder, they still needed to be investigated for the history that is in them. If they were not investigated, a complete break between the Jesus of history and the Christ of Faith might result. This New Quest was not a return to a traditional, pre-Enlightenment reading of the Gospels. Although it rejected Bultmann's extreme historical skepticism, it did not reject Bultmann's rational methodology, form criticism (which became confining because of its demanding criteria for authenticity), or his insistence on existential interpretation.

The movement's apex was reached in 1960 with the publication of Gunther Bornkamm's *Jesus of Nazareth*. He studied the synoptic gospel stories individually, thinking that any attempt to present them in a sequential fashion is historically impossible. In doing so, he found historical materials intertwined with materials that he considered legendary embellishments, like Jesus' miracles and resurrection. The recoverable historical items allowed Bornkamm to propose a sketch of Jesus' life, but Jesus' message continued to be understood existentially as the "No Quest" counseled: Jesus brings us a new history that is no longer ours, but his too.

## THE THIRD QUEST FOR THE HISTORICAL JESUS

Thomas Wright, in his book *The Interpretation of the New Testament 1861–1986* (1988), dubbed the most recent quest for the historical Jesus, the Third Quest. This quest has some very real differences with the Old and New Quests. Unlike the Old Quest, it is not rooted in an effort to present Jesus as some type of idealistic moral instructor detached from his Palestinian environment. With regard to the New Quest, the Third Quest rejects existentialism as the key for understanding Jesus' message. The Third Quest does have methodological characteristics that were inherited from its predecessors, like source, form, and redaction criticisms. However, one distinct interest distinguishes the Third Quest: to present Jesus as a figure within first-century Palestinian life with the help of new advancements in the historical, literary, and social sciences.

Interestingly, Jewish non–Christian scholars are primarily responsible for initiating the Third Quest. David Flusser's book, *Jesus* (1969), and Geza Vermes' book, *Jesus the Jew* (1973) (which for its day was provocatively entitled), ignored the scholarly consensus that both underplayed Jesus' ethnicity and the possibility of confidently describing not only his teachings but also his life. Flusser and Vermes did not write long, exhaustive treatments, but their accounts positioned Jesus forcefully within his age in a way that made him more than a talking head offering moral platitudes, asserting apocalyptic demands, and promoting existential well-being. They injected Jesus studies with a renewed confidence in describing their subject with greater balance. As a consequence, the 1980s and 1990s saw some of the most provocative accounts of the historical Jesus. It is a good time to be interested in the historical Jesus.

Today E. P. Sanders is the best-known historical Jesus scholar. His 1985 work, *Jesus and Judaism,* sets out his interpretive fix on Jesus, and his more recent work, *The Historical Figure of Jesus* (1993), is a serious yet popular offering of his views. Sanders has much in common with Schweitzer; both understand Jesus as an eschatological prophet convinced that Israel's promises of a new kingdom would soon be fulfilled. He departs from Schweitzer by focusing on one of Jesus' acts, the disturbance in the temple, as his defining moment. This shift is a methodological break from form criticism's preference for Jesus' sayings over his actions. Sanders' preference for Jesus' actions is based on A. E. Harvey's argument in his book, *Jesus and the Constraints of History* (1982). Harvey and Sanders agree that Jesus' crucifixion makes sense only against a dramatic act like that of Jesus' disturbance in the temple.

For Sanders, Jesus' temple disturbance symbolized the temple's ultimate destruction because of its corruption and foreshadowed a new temple and messianic age. Jesus fit within what Sanders calls "Jewish restoration **theology**." Because Sanders does make use of form criticism and discounts so many of Jesus' words as inauthentic, few Jesus statements place Jesus at odds with Judaism. Therefore, Sanders says that Jesus was not at great conflict with his Jewish environment. Rather, Jesus' temple behavior led to his arrest, trial, and execution at the hands of a priestly aristocracy and Roman governor. Sanders is silent on just what encouraged Jesus' followers to establish a church after his death, but whatever it was, Sanders says it must have been dramatic.

Marcus Borg takes issue with Sanders' eschatological interpretation of the historical Jesus. He first presented his view in his dissertation, *Conflict, Holiness, and Politics in the Teachings of Jesus* (1984), and later sharpened it in his 1987 study, *Jesus: A New Vision.* As in Sanders' view, Jesus remains a Jewish holy man, sage, and prophet, but Borg adds the setting of Jesus' sociological conflict with Judaism at large over the issue of holiness.

Borg argues that Jesus took issue with the **Zealots** who wanted to establish purity by ridding the land of foreigners, with the **Essenes** who wanted to purify themselves by separating from society, and with the **Pharisees** and **Sadducees,** who wanted to attain purity by separating within society. According to Borg, Jesus rejected these views and substituted a radical alternative—internalizing holiness as compassion. Borg connects this "holiness as compassion theme" with a noneschatological interpretation of the Kingdom of God. The phrase *Kingdom of God* is symbolic of the presence and power of God in the lives of Jesus' followers. It is thus something of a mystical experience that enables them to act and live in compassion.

To support a noneschatological Jesus, Borg argues that Jesus used traditional eschatological language in a novel fashion—to describe God's mystical encounter with human beings—and that the familiar "Son of man" sayings—attributed to Jesus and often used to describe a future kingdom age—are secondary additions to the Gospels. Although Borg has connected Jesus to an important element of first-century Jewish life, holiness, he has also severed Jesus from the eschatological ideas of that period.

Burton Mack shares Borg's fondness for a noneschatological Jesus. In his earlier study of Mark's gospel, *The Myth of Innocence: Mark and Christian Origins* (1988), and in his more recent study, *The Lost Gospel: The Book of Q and Christian Origins* (1993), Mack presents his theory of Christian origins and suggests a distinctive view of Jesus and the Gospels. For Mack, the Gospels consist of multiple layers of Jesus traditions, with each tradition representing a different period of the Jesus movement. He comes to this conclusion through his use of source criticism and its identification of multiple traditions behind the Gospels. Mark's gospel is of no historical value to Mack because he accepts Wrede's position that it is a contrived and unreliable guide to the historical Jesus. What Mack does cherish is **Q,** a hypothetical Jesus sayings tradition isolated by Old Quest scholars and thought to have been a source for Matthew and Luke. Mack designates Q as the earliest and most authentic Jesus tradition. The scholars of the Old Quest liked Q too, but they always used it in conjunction with Mark in their search for the historical Jesus.

According to Mack, Q has gone through several stages, and its earliest stage provides a glimpse of the historical Jesus. Q1, as Mack calls it, preserves several sayings that fit the form criticism category called sapiential or wisdom sayings. These sayings comprise some **proverbs** and **parables** and include several anecdotes about Jesus. As a group, these authentic sayings portray Jesus as critical of social pretensions. With this profile, Mack insists that first-century Palestine was Hellenized to a great degree, and he concludes that Jesus was a wandering **Cynic** sage who never waxed apocalyptic, looked forward toward the kingdom, judged his opponents, or even spoke critically toward others.

For Mack, Jesus was a confident, clever mocker of social convention. In fact, not only was Jesus not apocalyptic, he was not concerned with many traditional Jewish interests and was thus more Hellenistic than Jewish. Mack believes that most gospel materials were created by succeeding groups of Jesus' followers, who created all manner of sayings, deeds, and apocalyptic judgments as a response to the hostilities they faced. Mack is not the first to connect Jesus to the Cynic movement; Johannes Weiss suggested this possibility back at the turn of the century. Mack's contribution is basing his Cynic interpretation of Jesus on what he thinks are the authentic Jesus sayings preserved in Q. The most controversial issue for Mack, besides his reductionist approach to the gospel materials, is his claim for the presence of the Cynic movement among the Jews of first-century Palestine.

Another scholar, John Dominic Crossan, modifies Borg's noneschatological Jesus and Mack's Cynic Jesus. He recently weighed in with an impressive statement on the historical Jesus that has garnered praise from fellow Jesus scholars. Borg calls Crossan the "premier Jesus scholar in North America." His scholarly contribution is a 500-page opus entitled *The Historical Jesus: The Life of a Mediterranean Jewish Peasant* (1991). Shortly after its publication, this big Jesus book gave birth to what has affectionately been dubbed, Crossan's "baby Jesus" book, *Jesus: A Revolutionary* (1993). In essence, this smaller Jesus book has repackaged Crossan's fix on Jesus, but without the methodological procedure for unearthing the historical Jesus, which is his earlier book's most significant part. His big book has even produced a "grandchild," *The Essential Jesus* (1994), which contains the few Jesus sayings Crossan thinks are authentic.

Crossan's importance lies in his development of a more refined methodological procedure. When describing his motivation in researching Jesus, Crossan says he was troubled by the methodological sloppiness characteristic of Jesus scholars, which he calls "something of a scholarly bad joke." His recourse is to adopt a twofold methodological regiment.

First, Crossan assesses what traditions may be attributed to Jesus. Jesus accounts are categorized in one of four time frames: 30–60, 60–80, 80–120, and 120–150 CE. In the earliest layer he places Q, the *Gospel according to Thomas* (a sayings gospel whose date is disputed), the *Gospel according to Peter* (a passion narrative dated by a majority of scholars to the second century), and a few accounts from the New Testament Gospels. Crossan then counts the number of independent attestations for each unit (saying or deed) of the Jesus traditions he has just layered chronologically. Every unit of tradition has two numbers. Because Q is placed in the earliest time frame, a saying from it would be given a 1. If the same saying were to appear in another text besides Q, it would be given a 2. A rating of 1-2 would designate this Q saying as both belonging to the earliest (and best) layer of the Jesus traditions, and as having two independent occurrences. The earlier the layer, and the greater the number of independent occurrences, the greater the probability of the tradition's authenticity. All the Jesus materials are scored in this way. This first step is Crossan's modification of form criticism's multiple attestation criterion: Multiple independent attestations of a Jesus saying or deed increases the likelihood of its authenticity.

Second, after assessing Jesus traditions, Crossan interprets the earliest, most likely authentic Jesus traditions. Here Crossan sets those traditions traceable to Jesus within a multidisciplinary and cross–cultural context, employing insights from different branches and models of anthropology, sociology, religion, psychology, philosophy, medicine, and economics. All these resources give Crossan's historical Jesus study the appearance of comprehensiveness, objectivity, and precision. It is a grand effort at tightening up what scholars, beginning with

Schweitzer, had complained about—the arbitrary nature of scholarly research on the historical Jesus.

Because Crossan shares Mack's interest in Q, he produces a Cynic-like Jesus whom he identifies as nonapocalyptic. However, his use of sociological and economic models of the ancient world pushes him beyond Mack. Crossan adds that Jesus was a poor, illiterate, peasant leader who had a social vision marked by egalitarianism. Because he favors studies of ancient magic and medicine, Crossan makes Jesus out to be a healer-magician who used his healings to challenge and subvert established religious power, like the priestly class of his day that held sway over medicine and healing. Crossan's Achilles' heel is the same as Mack's—a reductionist's approach to the traditional sources used by Jesus studies that downplays the significance of canonical texts like Mark and a scarcity of evidence for Jewish Cynicism in Palestine.

## THE THIRD QUEST DISSIDENTS

The Third Quest also includes a number of scholars whose research has not divorced the historical Jesus from the Christ of Faith. Every quest, from Old to Third, has had its share of scholars who questioned the prevailing tendency to drastically re-evaluate Jesus historically. Sometimes their actions were reactionary, responding to what were seen as extreme scholarly revisions of the Gospels. Others were motivated by apologetic interests, attacking critical views in defense of the Christ of Faith, rather than employing their scholarly skills in an attempt to describe Jesus of Nazareth positively. However, several scholars are using important methodologies, not merely to defend a more traditional reading of the Gospels, but to assert views of Jesus that have scholarly integrity and are "user friendly" for traditional believers.

This company of scholars includes John Meier, who is writing a multivolume study, *Jesus: A Marginal Jew* (1991; 94; 01); Thomas Wright, who is also in the midst of a multivolume study entitled *Christians Origins and the Question of God* (1992; 96; 03); and Ben Witherington, who matches Meier's and Wright's prolific writing with his own works, *The Christology of Jesus* (1990) and *Jesus the Sage: The Pilgrimage of Wisdom* (1994). These scholars are not in complete agreement, but they are like concentric circles, sharing a common center: The historical Jesus can support the Christ of Faith.

A common interest in their works is the view that the canonical Gospels preserve a reliable account of Jesus that needs to be taken seriously as an expression of sound historical judgment. Other noncanonical gospel texts are to be rejected by the Church because they are secondary fabrications. These scholars argue that the Church's traditional preference for the canonical Gospels is based on their historical value, not just their theological contents. In them the Church senses both the voice of an exalted Jesus and the testimony of dependable witnesses. In light of these recent studies, and many others that are too numerous to decide, at the start of the twenty-first century Jesus studies appear to be in full bloom, with no letup in sight.

# SUMMARY

The efforts of Jesus scholars to describe the historical Jesus followed the Enlightenment and resulted in several identifiable stages. In the eighteenth and nineteenth centuries, scholars of the Old Quest set aside traditional assumptions about the Gospels' reliability and discerned a moral teacher who had been transformed into an apocalyptic messiah by his followers. At the beginning of the twentieth century, Albert Schweitzer's critique of the Old Quest as subjective and non-Jewish stifled scholarly search for the historical Jesus. Later in the twentieth century, the historical skepticism of scholars like Rudolf Bultmann, which resulted in No Quest, was overcome by the New Quest as scholars renewed their interest in describing Jesus' life to avoid detaching Jesus and Christian faith from history.

The last quarter of the twentieth century has witnessed the rise, vigor, and variety of the Third Quest, with its commitment to describe Jesus in first-century terms. Established methods, as well as new scholarly advances, were used by E. P. Sanders, Marcus Borg, Burton Mack, and John Dominic Crossan to describe Jesus in ways ranging from eschatological reformer to peasant Cynic leader. This Third Quest also includes the work of scholars who seek to maintain a connection between the historical Jesus and the Christ of Faith by arguing for the reliability of the canonical Gospels.

## KEY TERMS FOR REVIEW

| | | |
|---|---|---|
| Historical Jesus | Albert Schweitzer | Gunther Bornkamm |
| Christ of Faith | William Wrede | Third Quest |
| Old Quest | Rudolf Bultmann | Geza Vermes |
| Herman Reimarus | Demythologizing | E. P. Sanders |
| Enlightenment | New Quest | Third Quest Dissidents |

## QUESTIONS FOR REVIEW

1. How do the terms *historical Jesus* and *Christ of Faith* differ?
2. How did scholars of the Old Quest change the way the Gospels were traditionally read?
3. Why did Albert Schweitzer dismiss the Old Quest as a failure?
4. Why did Rudolf Bultmann prefer Jesus' words over his actions?
5. What interests gave rise to the Third Quest?

# SUGGESTIONS FOR FURTHER READING

Bennett, C. *In Search of Jesus: Insider and Outsider Images.* Herndon: Continuum, 2001.

Borg, M. *Jesus in Contemporary Scholarship.* Valley Forge: Trinity, 1994.

Meier, J. "The Present State of the 'Third Quest' for the Historical Jesus: Loss and Gain," *Biblica* 80 (1999) 459–487.

Powell, M. *Jesus as a Figure in History.* Louisville: Westminster John Knox, 1998.

Schweitzer, A. *The Quest of the Historical Jesus.* New York: Macmillan, 1966; German original, 1906.

# PART II

## Studying the Gospels

# 4

# Textual Criticism

## WHAT WAS IN THE ORIGINAL GOSPEL TEXT?

The original **manuscripts** of the New Testament no longer exist. In their stead are a huge number of more or less complete copies, more than 6,000 in total, scattered throughout the libraries of the world. These copies are copies of copies. In the process of copying the original writings, what scholars call **autographs,** alterations were made, some unintentional but some no doubt intentional. Sometimes the **scribe**'s eyes may have skipped a line that ended in the same way as the one he just had copied. Perhaps some letters were not clear. Capital G in Greek is very similar to capital T; capital O can be confused with Θ, a letter corresponding to the English th- sound. The original manuscripts were written in capital letters without any space between the words and without punctuation marks, so it is easy to see how mistakes could have been made.

Mark 1:1 exists in two different versions. The longer version reads, "The beginning of the good news of Jesus Christ, the Son of God." But some copies leave out the title "Son of God." Did the hurried hand of a scribe inadvertently skip the title, or did a later copyist intentionally add "Son of God"?

The first task of the student of the Gospels is to determine the form of the original text.[1] This is what is meant by **textual criticism.** If the author of Mark's gospel called Jesus the "Son of God" in the opening of his book, we can assume

[1]Every discipline that depends on written documents, especially ancient documents that came into existence before the invention of the printing press, begins with determining the original forms of the texts being used.

that he assigned great significance to this Christological title. Therefore, determining the correct version of Mark 1:1 is an important task.

Determining the correct reading of a disputed textual reading often depends on the age of the copies being examined. The earlier the copy, the greater the possibility that it preserves a reading closer to the original. How can the ages of the different manuscripts be determined? This is the task of **palaeography** (from the Greek words, *palaios,* "old," and *graphe,* "writing"), the science of describing ancient writings. The approximate age of a manuscript can be determined on the basis of the style of forming letters, abbreviations, the type of writing materials used, and in some cases, carbon dating.

However, textual criticism is not simply a matter of finding the oldest manuscripts. A later manuscript may go back to an earlier early copy that is now lost. In addition to searching for the oldest manuscripts, we must ask certain questions that can help us decide whether a particular reading, regardless of the age of the manuscript, is reliable or not. We need methods to do so.

## MATERIALS OF TEXTUAL CRITICISM

Before dealing with the methods of textual criticism, we must look at the manuscripts and their nature. The first printed editions of the New Testament, produced in the sixteenth century, were based on manuscripts copied after the ninth century. These were written in cursive using capital and lowercase letters **(minuscules)**, a form of writing that did not develop until the ninth century. Before that time, books were written in capital letters **(majuscules** or **uncials).**[2] Thus it is understandable that the minuscule manuscripts contain a large number of errors that had accumulated over the centuries of copying the texts of the New Testament.

The Greek manuscripts fall into two categories: (1) **papyri** and (2) **parchments.** Some eighty-eight papyri manuscripts exist, all of them more or less fragmentary. They are made from the spongy center of the stalk of the papyrus plant that grows in the Nile delta region. Accordingly, the papyri were discovered in the sands of Egypt.

The oldest known papyrus fragment of a New Testament writing is P52 of the John Rylands Library in Manchester, England (the number refers to the listing sequence; P52 was thus catalogued rather late); it stems from the beginning of the second century CE and contains parts of John 18:31–33 and 37–38. Somewhat younger than P52 is the Egerton Papyrus 2 (the name refers to the original owner). Egerton 2, which is now located in the British Museum, London, joins the story of the healing of the leper in Mark 1:40–42 to an account

---

[2]All New Testament manuscripts are in book (codex) form. The codex was made by folding leaves of paper, stacking them in layers, binding them by waxed tablets, and fastening them together by a thong hinge. The **codex** was much easier to use than a scroll, which was a roll of sheets glued together up to 35 feet in length and wound up on a stick. Some of the first New Testament writings may have been written on scrolls, but they no longer exist.

of an attempt to stone Jesus (compare with John 8:59). A reference to an otherwise unknown healing by Jesus also appears there. This papyrus is thus the earliest evidence for a noncanonical gospel text. Moreover, it is the earliest evidence for an otherwise unknown gospel.

M. Martin Bodmer, a Swiss book collector and humanist, acquired an important collection of papyri in 1955–56. One of the oldest papyri (P66) dates from around 200 CE and contains two large portions of the Gospel according to John. P75, from about the same time, preserves the earliest known copy of the Gospel according to Luke and one of the earliest copies of the Gospel according to John.

In the early 1930s, American millionaire Chester Beatty, then living in Ireland, obtained a substantial papyri collection. These papyri, most of which are located in the Chester Beatty Library in Dublin, include one-seventh of the Gospels and Acts (P45), a large portion of Paul's letters plus Hebrews (P46), and about one-third of the Revelation to John (P47). They all date from the third century.

The last acquisition of gospel papyri to be mentioned is the discovery made by two British scholars, B. Grenfell and A. Hunt, who turned up a considerable amount of papyri by digging in the rubbish heaps in Egypt around the turn of this century. The gospel texts they found were shown to date from around 200 CE. The texts, which were later established to derive from the *Gospel according to Thomas,* created quite a stir because they could be made out to be more than one hundred years older than the oldest New Testament manuscripts known at that time.

Besides papyri fragments, some New Testament writings are preserved on parchment, animal skin prepared for writing by being soaked, scraped, dried, and rubbed to a smooth surface. This process produced an excellent writing material, and by the fourth century parchment had replaced papyrus.

A very important parchment manuscript is *Codex* [book] *Sinaiticus* (ℵ), the Sinai Book, now in the British Museum. Written in the fourth century, it was acquired in 1859 by the German scholar Konstantin von Tischendorf who, after fifteen years of endeavor, was successful in obtaining it from the monastery of St. Catherine in the Sinai desert. It includes the entire New Testament and a couple of other early Christian writings as well as most of the Old Testament.

The sister **codex** of *Sinaiticus* is *Codex Vaticanus* (B), the Vatican Book, which also dates from the fourth century. Both codices, as well as most of the early papyri, belong to the Alexandrian "family," a group of texts that can be shown to have common Egyptian ancestors. Errors, corrections, and additions made in Alexandria were perpetuated elsewhere in Egypt and more or less adjacent countries. Thus, the influence of *Sinaiticus* and *Vaticanus* can be seen in the Coptic (Egyptian) translations of the Biblical books.[3] Readings in Latin translations and the writings of the early teachers of the Roman Church are evidence of a Western text.

A chief representative of the Western text is *Codex Bezae* (D), a late fifth- or early sixth-century manuscript of the Gospels and Acts that was presented to the

---

[3]What is known as *Codex Alexandrinus* (A), preserved in the British Museum, is a fifth-century manuscript that represents a mixed text type. The Gospels are actually of a later text type known as Byzantine, whereas the rest of the New Testament resembles the Alexandrian type.

University of Cambridge, England, by the Swiss scholar Theodore de Beza in 1581. D contains a very significant *agraphon* (a noncanonical Jesus saying) between Luke 6:4 and 5: "At the same day, he [Jesus] saw a man working on the Sabbath. And he said to him 'Man, if you know what you did, you are blessed; but if you do not know, you are cursed and a transgressor of the Law!'"

In addition to the different papyri and parchment codices, the textual critic has to take into consideration the early translations of the New Testament writings, called **versions,** and the quotations of the New Testament writings from the **church fathers.** Two incomplete manuscripts represent the Old Syriac version. They preserve a text that dates from the close of the second or beginning of the third century. From about the same time we have evidence of many Old Latin versions, none of which is entirely extant. The Church Father Jerome produced the best-known Latin translation, the Vulgate or the authorized version of the Roman Catholic Church, in 384. The Coptic translations were made early in the third century.

New Testament quotations by Christian writers can also be used in the effort to identify the best form of a biblical text. The most useful quotations are found from around 100 CE (*The First Epistle of Clement*) to the eighth century. Such evidence must be used with caution because the author may be quoting from memory or conflating (combining) different texts. Moreover, copyists also transmitted the writings of the Fathers, so it is not always easy to identify what the text that is quoted originally was.


## METHODS OF TEXTUAL CRITICISM

The first **critical** editions of the New Testament began to appear in the eighteenth century. These editions are called *critical* because, in addition to the text, they include the **variant** readings of a given passage. But how is it possible to obtain a preferred text given all the sources for the writings of the New Testament? What criteria should be used for detecting the best possible reading?

First of all, the external evidence supporting the different readings—such as the papyri, manuscripts, versions, and quotations—must be weighed. Textual scholars evaluate the age, quality, and geographical distribution of their readings. This demands a very careful study of all the pertinent materials because no one reading is inherently superior and beyond criticism. Textual scholars have divided the manuscripts into three types (or families, because each type stands for manuscripts that share the same family characteristics): Alexandrian, Western, and Byzantine. Scholars generally believe that Alexandrian manuscripts are the best, whereas Byzantine are the poorest (and most numerous). However, scholars are reluctant to simply assume the superiority of one text type over another and always consider internal evidence.

Internal evidence takes into consideration the roles of both the original authors and the scribes who subsequently copied their texts. Two kinds of internal evidence are: (1) **transcriptional probability,** which refers to the kind of change or error the scribe probably made, and (2) **intrinsic probability,** which bears upon the question of what the author was most likely to have written.

The three rules of transcriptional probability are: (1) The more difficult reading is probably the original because scribes tended to make the text easier to understand. No fewer than seven readings of John 7:39 exist. The best reading is undoubtedly, "Now he said this about the Spirit, which believers in him were about to receive, for as yet there was no Spirit, because Jesus was not yet glorified." This reading (found in P75 and S) is difficult to interpret, hence some versions read, "for the Holy Spirit was not yet upon them" (D), "for the Holy Spirit was not yet given" (B), and so on. If either of these readings were original, it would be incomprehensible for a scribe to change it to "for as yet there was no Spirit." (2) The shorter reading is probably the original because the scribes tended to elaborate on the text. For instance, after Matthew 6:13, some manuscripts (all of them late) add as a doxology, "For the Kingdom, and the power, and the glory are yours forever. Amen." This elaboration is based upon 1 Chronicles 29:11–13 and is obviously secondary. (3) A reading that differs from a parallel reading in another text is probably original. The tendency of scribes to harmonize the texts makes this last rule necessary. Matthew's version of the Lord's Prayer begins, "Our Father in heaven" (6:9), whereas Luke reads simply, "Father" (11:2). Some manuscripts (for example, A and D) conformed Luke's text to that of Matthew, but it is probable that the shorter reading of Luke (as found in P75, S, and B) is original.

Intrinsic probability bears upon the author's style, vocabulary and ideology. To decide whether or not "the Son of God" was part of the original text of Mark 1:1, we need to know the theology of the Gospel according to Mark. Textual criticism scholars ask, "Is the title significant for Mark's Christology?"

The conclusions reached on the basis of internal evidence may conflict with the conclusions regarding the external evidence. Moreover, the different operations of internal evidence may conflict with one another. The basic rule of Textual criticism is that the reading that can explain the origin of the other readings, but which cannot be explained by them, is probably the original.

## AN EXERCISE IN TEXTUAL CRITICISM: MARK 1:1

### External Evidence

The reading "(the) Son of God" is included by (א), B, and D but omitted by S, a fifth-century uncial. Thus some preference exists for the inclusion of the title.

### Internal Evidence

*Transcriptional Probability:* (1) Whether "(the) Son of God" is read does not make the text either easier or more difficult. (2) The title may be seen as an amplification of the original text. (3) No parallel material exists. Therefore, on the basis of transcriptional probability, there is a slight preference for the exclusion of the title.

*Intrinsic Probability:* Mark cites the title "Son of God" in important places— that is, in the story of Jesus' baptism (1:11), in the transfiguration story (9:7), and when the Roman centurion witnesses the crucifixion of Jesus (15:39). On intrinsic probability, the title thus seems to have been part of the original text.

## Conclusion

Considering the external and internal evidence together, the vote goes to the inclusion of the title "(the) Son of God." Whereas one of the rules of transcriptional probability argues for exclusion, both the external evidence and the intrinsic probability suggest that Mark 1:1 included the title.

The application of the basic rule, however, reverses what seems obvious. There is no reason for a scribe to have left out the title if he found it in his exemplar. On the other hand, we can easily explain why a scribe would have added an important Christological title in the very first verse of the gospel.

## SUMMARY

Despite the loss of the original New Testament writings, many handwritten copies of the originals remain. These copies date from the second century and vary from paper copies called *papyri* to animal skin copies called *parchment*. Intentional and unintentional errors were introduced by copyists and complicated the process of identifying the original readings. The science of identifying the original readings, textual criticism, has provided a credible reading of these writings, through the application of a methodical approach. Scholars rely on external and internal evidence when they examine a variant. When textual evidences conflict, the scholar is guided by the principle that the reading that can explain the origin of the other readings, but which cannot be explained by them, is probably the original.

## KEY TERMS FOR REVIEW

| | | |
|---|---|---|
| Autographs | Uncials | *Codex Siniaticus* |
| Scribes | Papyri | Versions |
| Textual criticism | Parchment | Variant |
| Palaeography | P52 | External evidence |
| Minuscules | Codex | Internal evidence |

## QUESTIONS FOR REVIEW

1. Why is textual criticism a necessary first step for students of the Gospels?
2. What types of materials were used for the writing of the New Testament documents?
3. How does external evidence differ from internal evidence?

# SUGGESTIONS FOR FURTHER READING

Greenlee, J. *Scribes, Scrolls, and Scripture: A Student's Guide to New Testament Textual Criticism.* Grand Rapids: Eerdmans, 1985.

Epp, E. and Fee, G. *Studies in the Theory and Method of New Testament Textual Criticism.* Grand Rapids: Eerdmans, 1993.

Metzger, B. *The Text of the New Testament: Its Transmission, Corruption, and Restoration,* 3rd ed. New York: Oxford University Press, 1992.

# 5

✳

# Source Criticism

## HOW ARE THE GOSPELS RELATED?

The first three Gospels in the New Testament are called the synoptic Gospels because they are so closely related that they must be viewed together (*synopsis* is a Greek word that means "seeing the whole together," "common perspective"). Matthew, Mark, and Luke see the whole of Jesus' works and words in a similar way; they share a perspective. How is this common perspective to be explained? It is the aim of **source criticism** to find out how the synoptic Gospels are literarily related to one another.

Although the synoptic Gospels are similar they are not identical. They often recount the same incident or teaching in different ways. This problem that the source criticism student has to solve is known as the **synoptic problem.** How can we explain the similarities and differences among the synoptic Gospels?

Source criticism does not deal with the question of whether a certain saying of Jesus was really uttered by him or was put into his mouth by the early Christians. However, source criticism does hold certain implications for the history of Jesus because it deals with the question of which text is the oldest one and thus presumably the most reliable (although an older source is not necessarily more reliable than a younger text).

## THE QUESTION OF PRIORITY

Several answers are available for the problem of priority among Matthew, Mark, and Luke. The older attempts are three in number.

(1) Working independently of one another, the three synoptic authors drew on a common oral tradition, which is illustrated in Figure 5.1.

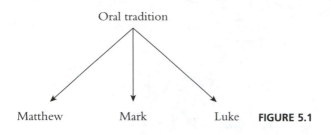

Oral tradition

Matthew          Mark          Luke        **FIGURE 5.1**

One weakness of this construction is that it cannot explain the verbal agreements that appear among the Gospels in particular cases. This criticism can be met by modifying the theory in question and arguing that the Gospels are made up of a large number of initially independent oral collections of Jesus traditions. The construction would look like Figure 5.2.

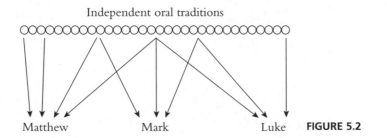

Independent oral traditions

Matthew          Mark          Luke        **FIGURE 5.2**

Thus, one segment of the tradition about Jesus may turn up not only in one but also in two, or even in all three, of the synoptic Gospels. This theory can explain verbal agreements among the authors, but it cannot explain the agreement in the order of the different units that is also found. The frequent agreement in the sequence of the different segments, as well as the verbal agreement, cannot be pure coincidence.

(2) One author copied another, or even both of the two other synoptics. But who copied whose gospel? Traditionally, Matthew's gospel is held to be the oldest one (that is why Matthew is placed first in the New Testament). Papias, a second-century Christian, was quoted as saying that Matthew wrote down the "sayings" (Greek: *Logia*) and that others translated them—a tantalizing comment whose exact meaning remains unclear. Yet Papias is also quoted as saying that Mark's gospel used Peter as its source for Jesus' sayings and deeds. In the fifth century Augustine argued that Mark used Matthew and said that Luke then used them both. J. Griesbach argued for a different form of Matthean priority in 1789 by reversing the order of Mark and Luke (see Figure 5.3).

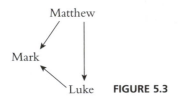

Matthew

Mark

Luke        **FIGURE 5.3**

However, Matthean priority will not work because it cannot account for the differences among the Gospels. Mark's gospel is substantially shorter than Matthew's. Why would Mark abbreviate Matthew, even leaving out the Sermon on the Mount, obviously an important **pericope**? Why would Luke break up the sermon and scatter Jesus' sayings throughout his gospel, even dropping some of them altogether?

(3) All three synoptic authors used a **primitive** gospel that is now lost (see Figure 5.4).

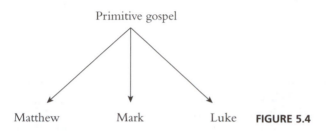

Primitive gospel

Matthew          Mark                Luke          **FIGURE 5.4**

This theory seems at first glance to explain the differences; each author adapted the primitive gospel in his own way. Any agreements existing among the three also seem to be explained by the fact that they had the same text in front of them.

On closer inspection, however, the construction fails. It can explain only the agreements among all the synoptics. Matthew and Luke can be observed to contain common material not found in Mark. In fact, the reconstruction turns out to be unable to explain the differences.

To improve the theory of a lost primitive gospel as the basis of the three synoptic Gospels, scholars have suggested that Mark had only an abridged version of the primitive gospel to work from. Between the primitive gospel and Mark, we need to insert a gospel that is an abridgment of the former. The assumption of an unknown $y$ as well as an unknown $x$ makes this modification of the primitive gospel theory hypothetical. Moreover, the modified theory cannot really explain why the primitive gospel was abbreviated in the first place.

Having discarded these three approaches to the synoptic problem, we can examine the theory that is now widely accepted among gospel scholars today. Many have observed that the Gospels are not the same length. Mark is much shorter than Matthew and Luke. Moreover, as already noted, these three Gospels have both verbal parallels and a frequent common order of events. This similarity suggests **Markan priority.** Leaving aside the question about non-Markan material in Matthew and Luke for the time being, we can consider the model in Figure 5.5.

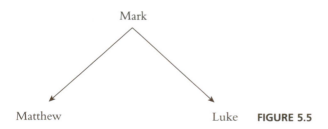

Mark

Matthew                              Luke          **FIGURE 5.5**

It is in fact not so difficult to support the priority of Mark. The order in which Matthew and Luke wrote their Gospels is never the same unless Mark is in agreement with them, and where Matthew and Luke disagree on the sequence of events, Mark is in agreement with one of them. This order can be diagrammed as shown in Figure 5.6.

| Matthew | Mark | Luke | |
|---------|------|------|---|
| A | A | A | |
| D |   | B | |
| C | C | E | |
| B | D | D | **FIGURE 5.6** |

Furthermore, we can make a similar observation about the wording of the text as about the sequence of events. Verbal agreement sometimes exists among the three synoptics, and where Matthew and Luke are different, Mark is in agreement with one of them. We can easily see that Matthew and Luke try to make stylistic or theological improvements of the Markan material. Some examples illustrate this.[1]

Mark 10:17–18: 17 As he was setting out on a journey, a man ran up and knelt before him, and asked him, "Good Teacher, what must I do to inherit eternal life?" 18 Jesus said to him, *"Why do you call me good? No one is good but God alone."*

Matt. 19:16–17: 16 Then someone came to him and said, "Teacher, what good deed must I do to have eternal life?" 17 And he said to him, *"Why do you ask me about what is good? There is only one who is good.* If you wish to enter into life, keep the commandments."

Working on the assumption that Mark is original, why did Matthew abridge his source? Matthew did not write that the questioner knelt before Jesus. We can also note that the question is different. According to Mark, the man says, "Good teacher, what must I do . . . ?' In Matthew's gospel, he asks, "Teacher, what good deed must I do . . . ?" The adjective *good* does not refer to the same noun. Should we connect this change with Matthew's deletion of the notice that the man knelt? Kneeling is an act of reverence, and in Matthew's form of the question, the status of Jesus is not the concern. The explanation of Matthew's changes is given at the end of the story. Mark states that Jesus denied that he was good and said, "There is only one who is good." Matthew obviously had difficulty with this ending and so made the adjective refer to the deed and not to Jesus. His ending is essentially the same as Mark's, but it does not make good sense, for he has to contrast a deed to a person, whereas Mark's version contrasts two persons to each other. In the interest of avoiding the impression that Jesus is not good, Matthew abbreviated and changed Mark.

---

[1]The examples are taken from R. M. Grant, *A Historical Introduction to the New Testament* (New York: Harper and Row, 1963).

In another incident Matthew avoided the impression that two disciples are selfish.

Mark 10:35–38: 35 *James and John, the sons of Zebedee, came forward to him* and said to him, "Teacher, we want you to do for us whatever we ask of you." 36 And he said to them, "What is it you want me to do for you?" 37 And they said to him, "Grant us to sit, one at your right hand and one at your left, in your glory." 38 But Jesus said to them, "You do not know what you are asking. Are you able to drink the cup that I drink, or be baptized with the baptism that I am baptized with?"

Matt. 20:20–22: 20 Then *the mother of the sons of Zebedee came to him* with her sons, and kneeling before him, she asked a favor of him. 21 And he said to her, "What do you want?" She said to him, "Declare that these two sons of mine will sit, one at your right hand and one at your left, in your kingdom." 22 But Jesus answered, "You do not know what you are asking. Are you able to drink the cup that I am about to drink?" They said to him, "We are able."

Although Mark's version reads that James and John put a selfish question to Jesus, Matthew apparently wants to exonerate them and says that it was the mother of the two disciples who wanted her sons to sit next to Jesus in the hereafter. That Matthew is secondary is shown quite indisputably by his preservation of Jesus' answer, for the Greek pronoun in verse 22 is in the plural form referring to James and John.

Sometimes Matthew and Luke improve on the writing style and the theological interests of Mark.

Mark 1:32–34: 32 *That evening, at sunset,* they brought to him all who were sick or possessed with demons. 33 And the whole city was gathered around the door. 34 And he cured many who were sick with various diseases, and cast out many demons; and he would not permit the demons to speak, because they knew him.

Matt. 8:16–17: 16 *That evening* they brought to him many who were possessed with demons; and he cast out the spirits with a word, and cured all who were sick. 17 This was to fulfill what had been spoken through the prophet Isaiah, "He took our infirmities and bore our diseases."

Luke 4:40–41: 40 *As the sun was setting,* all those who had any who were sick with various kinds of diseases brought them to him; and he laid his hands on each of them and cured them. 41 Demons also came out of many, shouting, "You are the Son of God!" But he rebuked them and would not allow them to speak, because they knew that he was the Messiah.

Mark begins with a redundancy, "That evening at sunset." Both Matthew and Luke made a stylistic improvement by removing the Markan redundancy.

Mark also says that "all who were sick or possessed by demons" were brought to Jesus. Matthew says that "many" possessed people were brought, whereas Luke follows Mark and says "all" were brought (however, he reads only "sick with various kinds of diseases," a phrase found later in Mark's text). After giving the picturesque detail that "the whole city was gathered around the door," Mark says that Jesus "cured many" and "cast out many demons." Both Matthew and Luke leave out this picturesque detail, focusing on the healings and exorcisms themselves. According to Matthew, Jesus "cured all who were sick." Here he changed Mark who says that Jesus duly healed "many." Luke agrees with Matthew that Jesus healed all the sick, but in Luke's version Jesus is an even greater healer than in Matthew's gospel, for Matthew says that "many" were brought to Jesus, whereas Luke follows Mark and says that "all" the sick were brought to Jesus.

In a final example, Matthew and Luke remove another Markan redundancy.

| Mark 1:40–42: 40 A leper came to him begging him, and kneeling he said to him, "If you choose, you can make me clean." 41 Moved with pity, Jesus stretched out his hand and touched him, and said to him, "I do choose. Be made clean." 42 *Immediately the leprosy left him, and he was made clean.* | Matt. 8:2–3: 2 and there was a leper who came to him and knelt before him, saying, "Lord, if you choose, you can make me clean." 3 He stretched out his hand and touched him, saying, "I do choose; be made clean!" *Immediately his leprosy was cleansed.* | Luke 5:12–13: 12 Once, when he was in one of the cities, there was a man covered with leprosy. When he saw Jesus, he bowed with his face to the ground and begged him, "Lord, if you choose, you can make me clean." 13 Then Jesus stretched out his hand, touched him, and said, "I do choose. Be made clean." *Immediately the leprosy left him.* |

Again Matthew and Luke can be seen to have made stylistic improvements in Mark's story, which they obviously found **pleonastic;** what Mark says in 1:42 was changed, but in different ways, by Matthew and Luke.

In the first two examples, Matthew can be seen to have changed Mark for theological reasons. In the third example, both Matthew and Luke can be observed to have changed Mark for stylistic as well as theological reasons. In the fourth and final example, Mark's text at 1:42 was not stylistically acceptable to Matthew and Luke.

Summing up the discussion of this section, we can draw two conclusions: (1) The Gospel according to Mark should be given priority; it can be shown to have been used by Matthew and Luke. (2) Matthew and Luke worked independently of one another; neither agrees against Mark in the sequence of the different paragraphs or in their wording.

## THE MINOR AGREEMENTS

The claim that Matthew and Luke do not agree against Mark needs to be qualified. Scholars talk about **"minor agreements"** between Matthew and Luke. The two occasionally agree over against Mark in wording. Their agreements are minor but they do exist and must be examined. In the third example in the preceding section, both Matthew and Luke left out Mark's picturesque detail about the whole city being gathered at the door (Mark 1:33). The final example shows an even more striking agreement between Matthew and Luke. Whereas Mark's text reads, "Moved with pity, Jesus stretched out his hand and touched him, and said to him. 'I do choose. Be made clean'" (Mark 1:41), Matthew and Luke agree in reading, "He stretched out his hand and touched him saying, 'I do choose. Be made clean'" (Matt. 8:3; Luke 5:13). Both changed Mark in the same way, leaving out that Jesus was "moved with pity" (Mark 1:41).

This omission does not have to be explained by resorting to the assumption that either Matthew or Luke knew the other's text. Rather, the two evangelists independently thought that it did not befit Jesus to feel pity, because that made him too human. Thus, they omitted a psychological reference to Jesus.

This explanation of the minor agreement between Matthew and Luke against Mark 1:41 is even more convincing if we realize that Mark's gospel actually read "anger" instead of "pity." Although weakly attested to by external evidence (supported mainly by D, *Codex Bezae,* and some of the old Latin versions), "moved with anger" makes a rather difficult reading that would be easy to explain as having given rise to the variant, "moved with pity." If the original text contained the latter reading, it would be hard to explain the change. The difficulty of the reading as well as the psychological reference would be a reason for Matthew and Luke to drop it.

The so-called minor agreements can be explained without abandoning the theory of Markan priority. The agreements between Matthew and Luke are few, and they can be explained by assuming that Matthew and Luke responded similarly to Mark's text. Moreover, the agreements consist mainly in omissions. Where agreements that do not consist simply in omissions are found between Matthew and Luke, they never share entire sentences beyond Mark's text. Given the problem of the minor agreements, the best conclusion is that Matthew and Luke changed Mark on grammatical, stylistic, or ideological accounts.

Another problem should be dealt with at this point. Mark contains a couple of sections that are not found in Matthew and Luke: the parable of the seed growing secretly, 4:26–29, and the healing of a blind man in Bethsaida, 8:22–26. Why do Matthew and Luke omit these stories? A simple solution is that they read a more primitive version of Mark, a version that did not have these passages.

This theory can also be used to explain some of the minor agreements between Matthew and Luke. They reproduced the primitive text of Mark, a text that was changed later.

Two conclusions come to the forefront: (1) Mark is the oldest gospel and was used by Matthew and Luke. Actually, both may have used a primitive version of Mark that was finalized later. (2) No literary connection exists between Matthew and Luke.

## MATTHEW'S AND LUKE'S ADDITIONAL SOURCE

As we have shown, Matthew and Luke usually agree in sequence where they reproduce Mark. But Matthew and Luke also had common material—approximately 230 verses deriving from a source other than Mark—and this material was inserted in different places in the sequence taken from Mark. For instance, the

Sermon on the Mount is found in both Matthew and Luke, but not in Mark. In Luke, the sermon is given on a plain instead of on a mount, but that placement is not important. However, the sermon was inserted in different places in the structure that Matthew and Luke inherited from Mark. That is, Matthew inserted the main part of the Sermon on the Mount after Mark 1:39—that is, after the election of the twelve disciples—and he also scattered words from the sermon throughout his gospel.

What does this difference demonstrate? Apart from providing an additional argument for the view that Matthew and Luke worked independently, it also shows that Matthew and Luke used a second source in addition to Mark, a proposal commonly known as the **two source hypothesis.** This second source is known as Q, the first letter of the German word *Quelle,* meaning "source." Two German scholars, C. G. Wilke and C. H. Weisse, were the first to propose this theory and apply it to the synoptic Gospels in 1838. This synoptic "butterfly" in Figure 5.7 is the result.

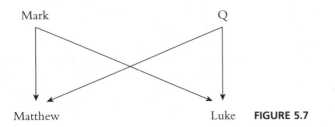

Mark                                    Q

Matthew                        Luke     **FIGURE 5.7**

Keep in mind that the "Mark" identified here may have been a primitive form of the Gospel according to Mark.

This scheme suggests that Matthew used Mark and Q, and Luke used Mark and Q. Furthermore, no connection exists between Matthew and Luke, and no connection exists between Mark and Q.

More can be said about Q. The story of John the Baptist is presented differently by Matthew and Luke when compared with Mark. Both Matthew and Luke build on Mark 1. For instance, Matt. 3:1–6 and Luke 3:1–6 incorporate much of Mark 1:2–6. Although their parallels are not identical, they do illustrate their dependence on Mark. However, Matthew and Luke go further than Mark; Mark does not render the teaching of John, and both Matthew and Luke do. Moreover, the penitential speech of the Baptist in Matthew and Luke is almost identical in wording, Matthew 3:7–10 corresponding to Luke 3:7–9. This material is thought to come from Q.

> Matt. 3:7–10: 7 But when he saw many Pharisees and Sadducees coming for baptism, he said to them, "You brood of vipers! Who warned you to flee from the wrath to come? 8 Bear fruit worthy of repentance. 9 Do not presume to say to yourselves, 'We have Abraham as our ancestor'; for I tell you, God is able from these stones to raise up children to Abraham. 10 Even now the ax is lying at the root of the trees; every tree therefore that does not bear good fruit is cut down and thrown into the fire."

Luke 3:7–9: 7 John said to the crowds that came out to be baptized by him, "You brood of vipers! Who warned you to flee from the wrath to come? 8 Bear fruits worthy of repentance. Do not begin to say to yourselves, 'We have Abraham as our ancestor'; for I tell you, God is able from these stones to raise up children to Abraham. 9 Even now the ax is lying at the root of the trees; every tree therefore that does not bear good fruit is cut down and thrown into the fire."

But Luke goes further than Matthew when describing John's instructions to the penitent. The message in Luke 3:10–14 has no parallel in Matthew, which indicates that Luke had access to additional material beyond that of Mark and Q. The same holds true for Matthew; some parts of Matthew are found in neither Mark nor Luke, like Matt. 13:36–52. This fact demands a modification of the synoptic butterfly. Material peculiar to Matthew and material peculiar to Luke, abbreviated as **p–Matthew** and **p–Luke,** respectively, should be added. This modification results in what B. F. Streeter called the **four source hypothesis** in 1924 (see Figure 5.8).

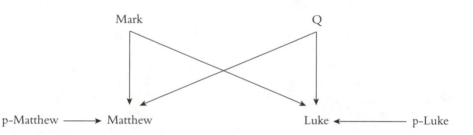

**FIGURE 5.8**

To explain more fully the role of Mark in Matthew and Luke and their minor agreements, **primitive Mark** needs to be inserted under the title **Ur-Mark** (a German expression that means early Mark). Ur-Mark and material peculiar to Mark make up Mark (see Figure 5.9).

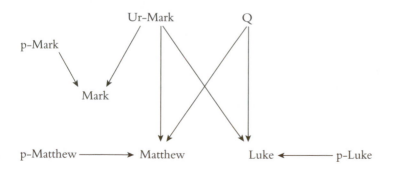

**FIGURE 5.9**

## THE Q SOURCE

The only source that we have not discussed is Q. What kind of source is Q? Judging from the similar materials in Matthew and Luke, Q consisted almost entirely of Jesus sayings, making it analogous to the *Gospel according to Thomas,* a collection of Jesus sayings that dates to the second century or perhaps earlier. It is a hypothetical source, reconstructed from the common materials of Matthew and Luke. We cannot know its full contents or even if it had a **passion narrative.**[2] Whereas Q has traditionally been dated to the second half of the first century, more and more scholars are arguing for a date as early as 50 CE.

The identical wording in John the Baptist's penitential speech seems to indicate that the source was a written one. An examination of the Sermon on the Mount in Matthew and the corresponding sermon in Luke shows that they are similarly composed. The two sermons have the same format. Matthew's version seems at first to be an expansion of Luke's version. However, a large part of the material in Matthew's sermon, which is not found in Luke's sermon, occurs elsewhere in Luke's gospel. This appearance does not appear to be coincidence. It indicates that Q was a written source. The simplest explanation is that Matthew and Luke worked independently of one another without adhering to the sequence of Q.

Consider also that Jesus spoke Aramaic, a language closely related to Hebrew, in which the Jewish Bible was written. By Jesus' day Aramaic had displaced Hebrew as the language of Palestine. Some parts of the Jewish Bible, the Old Testament, are even written in Aramaic. Thus, Jesus' words were translated when they were written because the Gospels are in Greek. Even Q seems to have existed in written form in Greek because Matthew and Luke possess the same Greek word order. If Q were an oral tradition, it does not seem likely that the words of Jesus would have been transmitted orally in exactly the same form, or that Matthew and Luke would have arrived at exactly the same translation. The Baptist's penitential preaching is a good case in point.

Furthermore, there is the important evidence of **doublets**—that is, the same saying of Jesus occurring in two different places in the same gospel. Why would Matthew and Luke use the same saying twice? This repetition suggests that Q was written, and that Matthew and Luke reproduced it mechanically. Luke 8:16 bears this out: "No one after lighting a lamp hides it under a jar, or puts it under a bed, but puts it on a lampstand, so that those who enter may see the light." This saying in Luke occurs in a sequence that corresponds with Mark's ordering of material.

Now consider Mark 4:21: "Is a lamp brought in to be put under the bushel basket, or under the bed, and not on the lampstand?" What is different from Luke's version? Mark presents Jesus' words in the form of a question. Luke is obviously dependent on Mark, yet he changed Mark's word order. Luke repeats the saying found in 8:16 in 11:33: "No one after lighting a lamp puts it in a cellar, but on the lampstand so that those who enter may see the light." Here it is

---

[2]Most scholars believe that Q lacked a passion narrative, but it is entirely possible that Matthew and Luke chose Mark's passion narrative over Q's. Perhaps some of Matthew's or Luke's distinctive passion elements are borrowed from Q.

not in interrogative form as it is in Mark. This form is the clue to the question of why Luke changed Mark's word order in 8:16. The Q form of the saying, which he also reproduces in 11:33, influenced him. That the saying was found in Q is proved by the fact that it also occurs in Matthew 5:15: "No one after lighting a lamp puts it under the bushel basket, but on the lampstand, and it gives light to all in the house." Matthew's form matches Luke's. Moreover Matthew, like Luke, includes the idea of "seeing light." The context of the saying in Matthew is different from that in Mark 4 and Luke 8. Both Matthew and Luke bear witness to the Q form of the saying. When Luke reproduced Mark in 8:16, he altered Mark's form of the words on the basis of Q.

All this evidence suggests that at least part of Q existed in written form. If it were simply an oral tradition, why would Luke pick up these words at all after he already had reproduced it based on Mark? A written source with a certain structure is more authoritative than words from an oral tradition. In addition, it is more plausible that Luke changed Mark on the basis of a written text he had before him than on the basis of words from an oral tradition. If Q were only an oral tradition, Luke would probably have changed the Q version, found in 11:33, and made it conform to Mark's written version, which he reproduced in 8:16.

But there are difficulties with the view that Q existed as a written source. It can be shown that both Matthew and Luke faithfully reproduced Jesus' sayings in Mark. As for the narrative material, both made changes, but the changes made in the sayings in Mark consist of only stylistic and grammatical alterations. The hypothetical Q is primarily a sayings source. The important question, then is this: Do Matthew and Luke treat this source, Q, in the same way they treat the sayings of Jesus in Mark? That is, can they be shown to be in close agreement? In Matthew 5:25–26 and Luke 12:58–59 we find a saying that is not reproduced in the same way.

> Matt. 5:25–26: 25 Come to terms quickly with your accuser while you are on the way to court with him, or your accuser may hand you over to the judge, and the judge to the guard, and you will be thrown into prison. 26 Truly I tell you, you will never get out until you have paid the last penny.

> Luke 12:58–59: 58 Thus, when you go with your accuser before a magistrate, on the way make an effort to settle the case, or you may be dragged before the judge, and the judge hand you over to the officer, and the officer throw you in prison. 59 I tell you, you will never get out until you have paid the very last penny.

Another example is found in Matthew 5:44. "But I say to you, 'Love your enemies and pray for those who persecute you.'" Luke 6:27–28 reads, "But I say to you that listen, 'Love your enemies, do good to those who hate you, bless those who curse you, pray for those who *abuse* you.'" Here Luke has two clauses that Matthew lacks: "do good . . . , bless . . ." Moreover, Matthew includes "pray for those who persecute you."

How can differences such as these be accounted for if Q was a written source? Were there different editions of Q? That is not impossible, and it may be the case that Matthew and Luke used different editions of Q. Perhaps Q was a conglomeration of sources, partly written and partly oral. Whereas Q therefore appears to be a written source for non-Markan material, scholars cannot rule out the possibility that it consisted of both written and oral materials. The full picture, then, is shown in Figure 5.10.

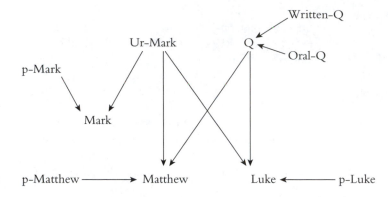

**FIGURE 5.10**

## SUMMARY

Source criticism aims to discover the sources behind the synoptic Gospels and thus explain the similarities and differences among the synoptic Gospels. Several explanations have been suggested, but most scholars have argued that the Gospel according to Mark was written first and was in turn used independently by Matthew and Luke. The material in Mark not found in Matthew and Luke can be best explained by Matthew and Luke using primitive versions of Mark. In addition to Mark, the authors of Matthew and Luke both used a sayings source that scholars have named Q, along with sources that were peculiar to each author.

## KEY TERMS FOR REVIEW

| | | |
|---|---|---|
| Synoptics | Markan priority | Synoptic butterfly |
| Source criticism | Minor agreements | p-Matthew |
| Synoptic problem | Ur-Mark | p-Luke |
| Oral tradition | Q | Doublets |
| Primitive gospel | Two source hypothesis | Four source hypothesis |

## QUESTIONS FOR REVIEW

1. What is the task of source criticism?
2. Why is Markan priority preferred as an explanation for the synoptic problem?

3. What is meant by the phrase *minor agreements*?
4. Why do scholars feel the need to postulate a hypothetical source named Q?
5. How do Matthew's sources compare with Luke's?

## SUGGESTIONS FOR FURTHER READING

Black, D. and Beck, D. eds. *Rethinking the Synoptic Problem*. Grand Rapids: Baker Academic, 2001.

Farmer, W. *The Synoptic Problem: A Critical Analysis*. New York: Macmillan, 1964.

Kloppenborg, J. *The Formation of Q: Trajectories in Ancient Wisdom Collections*. Philadelphia: Fortress, 1987.

Stein, R. *The Synoptic Problem: An Introduction*. Grand Rapids: Baker, 1987.

# 6

✳

# Redaction Criticism

## MATTHEW, MARK, AND LUKE AS EDITORS

Textual criticism scholars ask: What was the original reading of this particular text? Often the manuscripts contain variant readings, and it is necessary to choose one. Scholars cannot be arbitrary in their choices, however. They must be critical and employ a method so others can evaluate their work. In source criticism the different stories and traditions of Matthew, Mark, and Luke are studied in relationship to one another. Here the source criticism scholar asks: What sources were used and in what order or priority?

Once the questions of text, source, and priority have been examined, one question remains, "Can the differences among the evangelists tell us anything of significance about the evangelists themselves?" This type of question led to the development of an additional method of gospel scholarship, redaction criticism. The word *redaction* derives from the German word, *Redakteur,* which means "editor." An editor (or redactor) is one who edits manuscripts for publication. Editors may correct accounts within a manuscript, supplement its material, rearrange details, delete unnecessary items, or simply polish its prose. Newspapers have editors; major newspapers have several editors who are responsible for their own news fields—a sports editor, an editor of foreign politics, and so forth. Among the many editors a newspaper may employ is an editor-in-chief who is responsible for the paper at large. When the Gospels are examined source critically, as they were in the preceding chapter, there is a tendency to regard Matthew, Mark, and Luke as compilers of sources and traditions. But those responsible for the synoptic Gospels not only collected the material; they also adapted it and edited it to their own interests. Although the gospel writers were not journalists, they can be likened to newspaper editors because they acted like editors for their audiences as they prepared their Gospels.

Yet newspapers differ among themselves; they have editorial policies that reflect their particular interests. They often do not report the same event in exactly the same way. A politically conservative newspaper, like the *Washington Times,* and a politically liberal newspaper, like the *Washington Post,* may run the same story, but an examination of that story may reveal something about the newspaper from which it came, especially if the story is political in nature. By looking at the way in which the story is presented a reader can draw some con- clusions: This has to be a conservative paper, that a liberal one, this a Republican paper, that a Democrat one. A careful reader can make these assumptions because he will be aware of the editorial policy of those responsible for the paper.

The Gospels are similar to newspapers. The Gospels, like newspapers, have editorial procedures and policies. Readers can ask, "How did the author employ his source(s)?" This general question leads to more precise questions: What did he include? What did he omit? What did he change? How did he arrange the material? Readers can also ask if the author drew on his own imagination. This type of redaction criticism is called **emendation analysis** because the focus is on how an evangelist used, emended, his sources.

Once these questions have been answered, the reader can search for the author's particular emphases and distinctive purpose. Questions such as "why did he do what he did?" and "what were the criteria by which he worked?" will help. These questions allow the reader to understand the **ideological** or theological concerns of the author. Here we need to address the author's own situation and the needs of his specific audience. These sociological and **ecclesiastical** aspects are important because it has become obvious to scholars that like most writings in general, the Gospels were targeted toward specific audiences. This type of redaction criticism is known as **composition analysis** because the focus is on the overall interests of the evangelist's composition.

The redaction-critical approach is evident when source criticism scholars deal with Markan priority. The interests of Matthew and Luke are clearer when their use of Mark is examined: (1) Matthew did not approve of Mark's account that Jesus denied that he was good and altered it (Matt. 19:16–17, compare with Mark 10:17–18); (2) Matthew did not approve of Mark's account that the disciples asked for special privileges and altered it (Matt. 20:20–22, compare with Mark 10:35–38); (3) Matthew and Luke did not approve of Mark's stylistic redundancy and altered it (Matt. 8:16–17 and Luke 4:40–41, compare with Mark 1:32–34).

## EXAMPLES

Several examples of redaction-critical analysis help to illustrate the method of redaction criticism.

### (1) Jesus' Healing of a Boy Possessed by a Demon

(Mark 9:14–29; Matt. 17:14–20; Luke 9:37–43)

Matt. 17:14–20: 14 When they came to the crowd, a man came to him, knelt before him, 15 and said, "Lord, have mercy on my son, for he is an epileptic and he suffers terribly; he often falls into the fire and often into the water. 16 And I brought him to your disciples, but they could not cure him." 17 Jesus answered, "You faithless and perverse generation, how much longer must I be with you? How much longer must I put up with you? Bring him here to me." 18 And Jesus rebuked the demon, and it came out of him, and the boy was cured instantly. 19 Then the disciples came to Jesus privately and said, "Why could we not cast it out?" 20 He said to them, "Because of your little faith. For truly I tell you, if you have faith the size of a mustard seed, you will say to this mountain, 'Move from here to there; and it will move; and nothing will be impossible for you.'"

Mark 9:14–29: 14 When they came to the disciples, they saw a great crowd around them, and some scribes arguing with them. 15 When the whole crowd saw him, they were immediately overcome with awe, and they ran forward to greet him. 16 He asked them, "What are you arguing about with them?" 17 Someone from the crowd answered him, "Teacher, I brought you my son, he has a spirit that makes him unable to speak; 18 and whenever it seizes him, it dashes him down; and he foams and grinds his teeth and becomes rigid; and I asked your disciples to cast it out, and they could not do so." 19 He answered them, "You faithless generation, how much longer must I be among you? How much longer must I put up with you? Bring him to me." 20 And they brought the boy to him. When the spirit saw him, immediately it convulsed the boy, and he fell on the ground and rolled about, foaming at the mouth. 21 Jesus asked the father, "How long has this been happening to him?" And he said, "From childhood. 22 It has often cast him into the fire and into the water, to destroy him; but if you are able to do anything, have pity on us and help us." 23 Jesus said to him, "If you are able!—All things can be done for the one who believes." 24 Immediately the father of the child cried out, "I believe; help my unbelief!" 25 When Jesus saw that a crowd came running together, he rebuked the unclean spirit, saying to it, "You spirit that keeps this boy from speaking and hearing, I command you, come out of him, and never enter him again!" 26 After crying out and convulsing him terribly, it came out, and the boy was like a corpse; so that most of them said, "He is dead." 27 But Jesus took him by the hand and lifted him up, and he was able to stand. 28 When he had entered the house, his disciples asked him privately, "Why could we not cast it out?" 29 He said to them, "This kind can come out only through prayer."

Luke 9:37–43: 37 On the next day, when they had come down from the mountain, a great crowd met him. 38 Just then a man from the crowd shouted, "Teacher, I beg you to look at my son; he is my only child. 39 Suddenly a spirit seizes him, and all at once he shrieks. It convulses him until he foams at the mouth; it mauls him and will scarcely leave him. 40 I begged your disciples to cast it out, but they could not." 41 Jesus answered, "You faithless and perverse generation, how much longer must I be with you and bear with you? Bring your son here." 42 While he was coming, the demon dashed him to the ground in convulsions. But Jesus rebuked the unclean spirit, healed the boy, and gave him back to his father. 43 And all were astounded at the greatness of God.

Scholars agree that Matthew and Luke used Mark's gospel. Their accounts of Jesus' healing of a boy possessed by a demon are much shorter than Mark's. Was this story also in Q, and is that the reason why Matthew and Luke are shorter than Mark—that is, their accounts are based on Q? This explanation is not likely because their divergences from Mark are not identical. Matthew and Luke appear to have edited Mark's text in different ways.

How did they edit Mark? Matthew and Luke shared the same approach. Mark carefully recounted the symptoms of the boy as verses 18, 20, 22, and 26 illustrate.

Mark 9:18: and whenever it seizes him, it dashes him down; and he foams and grinds his teeth and becomes rigid; and I asked your disciples to cast it out, but they could not do so."

Mark 9:20, 22 and 26: 20 And they brought the boy to him. When the spirit saw him, immediately it convulsed the boy, and he fell on the ground and rolled about, foaming at the mouth . . . 22 It has often cast him into the fire and into the water, to destroy him; but if you are able to do anything, have pity on us and help us . . ." 26 After crying out and convulsing him terribly, it came out, and the boy was like a corpse, so that most of them said, "He is dead."

What about Matthew and Luke?" Luke has two verses, 39 and 42. Matthew had only one verse, 15.

Luke 9:39 and 42: 39 Suddenly a spirit seizes him, and all at once he shrieks. It convulses him until he foams at the mouth; it mauls him and will scarcely leave him. . . . 42 While he was coming, the demon dashed him to the ground in convulsions. But Jesus rebuked the unclean spirit, healed the boy, and gave him back to his father.

Matt. 17:15: ". . . Lord, have mercy on my son, for he is an epileptic and he suffers terribly; he often falls into the fire and often into the water.

Evidently, Matthew and Luke found that Mark dwelt too much on the outer event and did not focus on what they thought to be the deeper meaning of the healing miracle. Luke ascribed the ultimate reason for the miracle to the power of God (9:43 "And all were astounded at the greatness of God"), whereas Matthew appended a lesson about faith (17:20: if great faith is present, everything is possible). Mark, in contrast, contains an ending that deals with healing methods and says nothing about theology. Matthew and Luke interpreted Mark's text and edited the story accordingly.

## (2) Jesus' Healing of a Deaf Mute

### (Matt. 15:29–31; Mark 7:31–37)

Matt. 15:29–31: 29 After Jesus had left that place, he passed along the Sea of Galilee, and he went up the mountain, where he sat down. 30 Great crowds came to him, bringing with them the lame, the maimed, the blind, the mute, and many others.

They put them at his feet, and he cured them, 31 so that the crowd was amazed when they saw the mute speaking, the maimed whole, the lame walking, and the blind seeing. And they praised the God of Israel.

Mark 7:31–37: 31 Then he returned from the region of Tyre, and went by way of Sidon towards the Sea of Galilee, in the region of the Decapolis. 32 They brought to him a deaf man who had an impediment in his speech; and they begged him to lay his hand on him. 33 He took him aside in private, away from the crowd, and put his fingers into his ears, and he spat and touched his tongue. 34 Then looking up to heaven, he sighed and said to him, "Ephphatha," that is, "Be opened." 35 And immediately his ears were opened, his tongue was released, and he spoke plainly. 36 Then Jesus ordered them to tell no one; but the more he ordered them, the more zealously they proclaimed it. 37 They were astounded beyond measure, saying, "He has done everything well; he even makes the deaf to hear and the mute to speak."

Are Matthew and Mark telling the same story? It appears in the same place in the two Gospels, after the healing of the daughter of the Syro-Phoenician woman and before the feeding of the four thousand. The wider context is also identical; thus Matthew follows Mark's order. But the two stories are rather different. Whereas Mark narrates the healing of a deaf-mute, Matthew's version contains a summarizing healing report. Luke is of no help, for it lacks a corresponding story. Is it possible that Ur-Mark, which was used by Matthew and Luke, did not have the story? Are these two stories then from sources peculiar to Mark and Matthew (p-Mark and p-Matthew)? If this was the case then it was by coincidence that different writers inserted both stories at exactly the same place in the arrangement of the different sections. Such a coincidence is certainly possible, but it doesn't appear to be probable.

Mark says that Jesus went from Tyre through, or by way of, Sidon to the Sea of Galilee in the region of the Decapolis (verse 31). Actually, a better translation would read "in the midst of the region of the Decapolis" rather than "in the region of the Decapolis." However, the correct translation of the Greek preposition *ana meson* does not matter much in this instance. Either way Mark was misinformed. One doesn't travel by way of Sidon, or go through the Decapolis, if traveling from Tyre to the Sea of Galilee. Mark cannot have been to Palestine. The correct translation of *ana meson* as "in the midst of" serves only to strengthen this point.

Matthew was better informed about the topography of Palestine; he skipped any mention of Decapolis, saying that Jesus went from the general district of Tyre and Sidon (compare Matt. 15:29 with 15:21) directly to the Sea of Galilee.

Thus it is clear that Matthew presupposed Mark's text and emended it. This emendation was not done accidentally because Matthew completely rewrote the story. The decision was editorial, and Matthew's rewriting appears to be theologically motivated. Matthew apparently felt that Mark's story was too magical. Jesus used certain ritual actions—put his fingers into the man's ears, spit, touched the man's tongue. Saliva was widely employed in ancient magic and medicine. Jesus also looked up to heaven. Why? Probably to draw down power from heaven from whence the Holy Spirit descended (Mark 1:10). He also used a magical formula, the Aramaic word, *Ephphatha,* which means, "Be opened!" In the first century

words in foreign languages were thought to be powerful and were used by miracle workers. Here, in a Greek text, written for Greek-speaking people, we find
an Aramaic word. Many scholars believe that the whole story serves as an instruction to the Christian miracle worker-healer.

The story is similar to miracle stories found in both Jewish and gentile liter-
ature. Others also employed the means and acts employed by Jesus. But to
Matthew, the other miracle workers were magicians. This calls to mind the adage,
"My miracle is your magic." Matthew would not have Jesus appear as a magician.

The same avoidance of the magical can be observed in the fact that neither
Matthew nor Luke included the Markan story about the healing of the blind man
in Bethsaida (Mark 8:22–26). Matthew followed Mark's sequence of events but
did not include this story. This story was cited as an example of p-Mark material,
but it may have been found in Ur-Mark. If so, it was left out by both Matthew
and Luke. In this episode Jesus took the man aside, spit on his eyes, and laid his
hands on him (Mark 8:23). It is also probable that it was Jesus who looked
intently, not the man, as 8:25 might suggest.

In view of this redaction-critical analysis, we can conclude that Mark 8:22–26
was omitted in Matthew's gospel out of a theological concern. Thus, the story of
the healing of the blind man in Mark, Chapter 8, may have been there all the
time. Perhaps the only story not found in the primitive version of Mark was the
parable about the seed growing secretly (4:26–29).

## (3) John the Baptist

### (Mark 1:2–6; Luke 3:1–6)

Mark 1:2–6: 2 As it is written in the prophet Isaiah, "See, I am sending my messenger ahead of you, who will prepare your way; 3 the voice of one crying in the wilderness: 'Prepare the way of the Lord, make his paths straight'" 4 John the baptizer appeared in the wilderness, pro-claiming a baptism of repentance for the forgiveness of sins. 5 And people from the whole Judean countryside and all the people of Jerusalem were going out to him, and were baptized by him in the river Jordan, confessing their sins. 6 Now John was clothed with camel's hair, with a leather belt around his waist, and he ate locusts and wild honey.

Luke 3:1–6: 1 In the fifteenth year of the reign of Emperor Tiberius, when Pontius Pilate was governor of Judea, and Herod was ruler of Galilee, and his brother Philip ruler of the region of Ituraea and Trachonitis, and Lysanias ruler of Abilene, 2 during the high-priesthood of Annas and Caiaphas, the word of God came to John son of Zechariah in the wilderness. 3 He went into all the region around the Jordan, proclaiming a baptism of repen-tance for the forgiveness of sins, 4 as it is written in the book of the words of the prophet Isaiah, "The voice of one crying in the wilderness: 'Prepare the way of the Lord, make his paths straight. 5 Every val-ley shall be filled, and every mountain and hill shall be made low, and the crooked shall be made straight, and the rough ways made smooth; 6 and all flesh shall see the salvation of God.'"

It is easy to determine what Luke retained of Mark 1:1–3, but what did he add? *Add* refers to the addition to the core (the basic story given in Mark) from blocks of material not dealing with John the Baptist. Luke did not begin his gospel at the same place as Mark did and added source material not found in Mark: two chapters of nativity and infancy narratives in Luke 1 and 2 and 3:1–2a, is an historical preface. What do these differences reveal about Luke's concerns? He was concerned about giving his gospel some biographical and historical characteristics. In the beginning of Chapters 2 and 3, Luke placed his story in the context of Roman secular history. He linked his account of the gospel to contemporary historical events in a way that Mark did not (see also the book of Acts, which appears to have the same author as Luke).

What did Luke omit? He omitted Mark's quotation of Malachi found in Mark 1:2b: "I am sending my messenger ahead of you who will prepare your way." How can we explain this omission? (1) Mark identified a quote as coming from Isaiah that is really from Isaiah and Malachi. Thus, Luke wanted to correct Mark and left out the Malachi quotation altogether. However, this may not be the full story because Matthew does the same thing (Matt. 3:1–6). Did Matthew arrive at the same conclusion? Or were Matthew and Luke following Q? The latter is probable because they both quoted the Malachi passage elsewhere (Matt. 11:10; Luke 7:27); thus both knew that Mark was wrong about the Isaiah reference and that the Malachi quotation belonged in a different setting. They had Q, where the Malachi reference was placed in a later context. Luke's omission does not really say anything about his theological concerns, only that he knew the scriptures better than Mark did.

Did Luke expand his source? Yes, he quoted more extensively from Isaiah 40 than Mark. He cited Isaiah in 3:6, "and all flesh shall see the salvation of God." Why did he do that? Luke emphasized throughout his work, both the gospel and the book of Acts, that the salvation Jesus brings is for all humankind.

Whereas the universal appeal of the gospel is one of Luke's theological concerns, the character of Luke's community is ambiguous. Would this concern indicate that his community was a gentile Christian community? Or a community concerned about the validity of the gospel for Gentiles and not only for Jews? To answer the question of Luke's community we need a more in-depth study of Luke's gospel and the Books of Acts. A tension between Jesus' movement and Judaism exists in Luke, but it is a tension between a form of Judaism wanting to include the Gentiles and a conventional form of Judaism.

Did Luke rearrange Mark's material? Luke took the presentation of John the Baptist (Mark 1:4) and put it before the prophetic passage quoted in Mark 1:3. Thus, John the Baptist is more clearly identified as the person about whom Isaiah speaks. This rearrangement was done in the interest of presenting John as a prophesied figure.

This discussion leads to one last point: Luke used material from Q and from p–Luke to present John as the forerunner of Jesus, which is demonstrated by Luke's additional source material. After John the Baptist's penitential speech, which came from Q (Matt. 3:7–10; Luke 3:7–9), Luke went beyond Matthew in adding special material from p–Luke (Luke 3:10–14).

## (4) Jesus' Stilling of the Storm

(Matt. 8:23–27; Mark 4:35–41)

Matt. 8:23–27: 23 And when he got into the boat, his disciples followed him. 24 A windstorm arose on the sea, so great that the boat was being swamped by the waves; but he was asleep. 25 And they went and woke him up, saying, "Lord save us! We are perishing!" 26 And he said to them, "Why are you afraid, you of little faith?" Then he got up and rebuked the winds and the sea; and there was a dead calm. 27 They were amazed, saying, "What sort of man is this, that even the winds and the sea obey him?"

Mark 4:35–41: 35 On that day, when evening had come, he said to them, "Let us go across to the other side." 36 And leaving the crowd behind, they took him with them in the boat, just as he was. Other boats were with him. 37 A great windstorm arose, and the waves beat into the boat, so that the boat was already being swamped. 38 But he was in the stern, asleep on the cushion; and they woke him up and said to him, "Teacher, do you not care if we are perishing?" 39 He woke up and rebuked the wind, and said to the sea, "Peace! Be still!" Then the wind ceased, and there was a dead calm. 40 He said to them, "Why are you afraid? Have you still no faith?" 41 And they were filled with great awe and said to one another, "Who then is this, that even the wind and the sea obey him?"

Matthew's version is shorter and reveals an abridgment of Mark's version. Several words and phrases of the Markan narrative have been omitted: verse 36, "Other boats were with him"; verse 37, "so that the boat was already being swamped"; verse 38, Jesus was asleep "in the stern . . . on the cushion"; verse 39, "the wind ceased"; verse 41, the disciples spoke "to one another."

All this abridgment by Matthew is not simply a space saver, as if Matthew was trying to make a long story short; it is a method of interpretation. Matthew concentrated on essentials, and he wanted to reach these essential points more rapidly. What is his interest?

Matthew's concern was christological. He concentrated on Jesus Christ, the worker of the miracle, not on the details that served to fill out the setting and highlight the wonder. In Matthew no rhetorical question raises the issue of Jesus' compassion as it does in Mark (4:38). Of course Jesus cares according to Matthew. In Matthew 8:25 he responded to the disciples' plea, "Lord, save us! We are perishing!" which indirectly serves as a kind of proclamation acknowledging Jesus' importance. This statement is no question as in Mark, but a prayerlike confession of Jesus' significance.

Matthew knew what sort of man Jesus was because in verse 25 the disciples addressed him "Lord." In Mark he was called "Teacher." "Lord" is a loftier epithet. "Lord" (Greek: *kyrios*) is the name of God in the **Septuagint,** the Greek translation of the Old Testament.

In the light of Matthew's designation of Jesus as "Lord," Matthew 8:23 is important. Here the redaction focuses solely on Jesus and the disciples. No mention was made of the crowds or other boats in the vicinity, as it was in Mark 4:36. In Matthew, Jesus led his disciples into the boat, and he was alone with them.

The verb in Matthew 8:23 is also important. The disciples *followed* Jesus. This verb is also used in the New Testament to define a disciple of Jesus. For instance, the same verb is used in Matthew 9:9 in the calling of the tax collector, "Come, follow me."

Matthew also placed the miracle of the stilling of the storm in a context different from Mark's. Mark narrated the story immediately after a collection of parables, whereas Matthew's account of Jesus stilling the storm is located before a similar collection of parables that is given in Matthew 13. Instead of having parables precede this miracle, Matthew placed two stories, which served to enhance the meaning of Jesus' miracle, before the stilling of the storm.

> Matt. 8:18–22: 18 Now when Jesus saw great crowds around him, he gave orders to go over to the other side. 19 A scribe then approached and said, "Teacher, I will follow you wherever you go." 20 And Jesus said to him, "Foxes have holes, and birds of the air have nests; but the Son of Man has nowhere to lay his head." 21 Another of his disciples said to him, "Lord, first let me go and bury my father." 22 But Jesus said to him, "Follow me, and let the dead bury their own dead."

The verb *follow* is central to both stories (verse 19 and verse 22), and both uses refer to discipleship. The story about the stilling of the storm begins with the same verb in verse 23. Thus, Matthew intended that his readers think of discipleship as they continued reading. The hand of Matthew the redactor (editor) is evident.

In verse 22 the disciple who asked to "first let me go and bury my father" is challenged to follow Jesus. Then Matthew wrote that the disciples followed him into the boat. The story about the stilling of the storm illustrates the nature of discipleship. The presence of other boats, as found in Mark's version, adds nothing to this motif and has been dropped by the editor Matthew.

In Matthew 8:25, the disciples pray to be saved by Jesus, their Lord. This is a significant change of Mark. The verb *went (proserchomai)* does not occur in Mark's version. The verb denotes the solemn approach to a deity and accords with the disciples' prayer: "Lord save us! We are perishing!" In Matthew Jesus appears as a redeemer god.

Jesus' response in Matt. 8:26 seems strange. Mark contains Jesus' word about faith after the miracle, which seems more natural (Mark 4:40). Matthew included the word about faith before the demonstration of divine power because his version is a lesson in discipleship. People should remain disciples, have full faith, even when the situation seems very dangerous. The expression "you of little faith" characterizes the faith of the disciples as weak and immature. They are faithful, but not faithful enough.

In Mark, the disciples are filled with awe and fear in response to the miracle. In Matthew's version they marvel. This difference is necessary because Matthew had already dealt with the fear of the disciples in 8:26 where he connected this motif to that of their faith. When Jesus did speak in Matthew's version, he did not use the word "disciples" (8:23), but "you of little faith" (8:26). Who is the "you"?

Matthew widened the perspective of Jesus' reply. The response is made to those to whom the story was addressed, not to the twelve disciples. The "you" is representative of Matthew's community. The people were, or should have been, impressed by Jesus' presence as Lord in the midst of the difficulties that faced the Church. The central line in the story is Jesus' words in verse 26. The words are addressed to the Church as a challenge to fidelity. There is no need to fear, the Lord is near.

## SUMMARY

Redaction criticism sees the gospel writers as editors who prepared their Jesus traditions for their audiences. As editors they arranged and modified their sources in an effort to present their own accounts of Jesus. Their editorial work can best be seen in the modifications that Matthew and Luke introduced when they used Mark. These modifications touch upon theological, ecclesiastical, and stylistic interests. In this light, the Gospels take on an individuality that highlights their peculiar interpretations of Jesus.

## KEY TERMS FOR REVIEW

| | | |
|---|---|---|
| Redaction criticism | Emendation analysis | Theological interests |
| Editor | Composition analysis | Ecclesiological interests |
| Audience | Ideological interests | Stylistic interests |

## QUESTIONS FOR REVIEW

1.  How did the practice of source criticism encourage the practice of redaction criticism?
2.  How are the evangelists similar to newspaper editors?
3.  How does emendation analysis differ from composition analysis?
4.  What kinds of questions will a redactor ask when examining a gospel story?

## SUGGESTIONS FOR FURTHER READING

Perrin, N. *What Is Redaction Criticism?* Philadelphia: Fortress, 1969.

Marxsen, W. *Mark the Evangelist.* Nashville: Abingdon, 1969.

Rohde, J. *Rediscovering the Teachings of the Evangelists.* Philadelphia: Westminster, 1969.

Stein, R. *Gospels and Tradition: Studies on Redaction Criticism of the Synoptic Gospels.* Grand Rapids: Baker, 1991.

# 7

# Form Criticism

## BEFORE THE GOSPELS

Jesus died around 30 CE. Mark, the oldest gospel, was written around 70 CE; Matthew and Luke were written in the seventies or eighties. Some blocks of Jesus traditions, consisting of Q material, were probably put into writing before 70, as were parts of p-Matthew and p-Luke. However, the fixation of the Gospels in written forms is a late phenomenon.

Thus, there are three layers (or phases) behind the writing of the Gospels: (1) the layer of Jesus, (2) the layer between Jesus and the evangelists, and (3) the layer of the evangelists (see Figure 7.1).

| | Some Q, p-Matthew, and p-Luke materials | |
|---|---|---|
| Jesus ———— | were probably written | ———— Mark, Matthew, Luke |
| 30 CE | | 70–95 CE |

**FIGURE 7.1**

Thus far, the third layer, belonging to the evangelists, has been the focal point of scholarly explanation: textual criticism, source criticism, and redaction criticism. The second layer, the oral stage preceding the written Gospels, sometimes known as the tunnel layer, needs explanation.

During the tunnel layer, a period of some 40 years, the Jesus tradition (sayings and deeds) was used and preserved by Jesus' followers prior to being finalized in the Gospels. Scholars ask, *How* was the Jesus tradition preserved during this interval? Q did not have a narrative structure, was essentially a sayings source, and did not establish a historical, chronological sequence. This same lack of sequence is also suggested for p–Matthew and p–Luke. Mark, on the other hand, contains a story, a narrative. Could the entire contents of Mark have been memorized and preserved orally? Or can it be shown that Mark is made up of originally disparate units (forms)? Jews in Jesus' day prized oral traditions, and scholars are convinced that Jesus' earliest followers passed on their knowledge of Jesus orally (Luke 1:1–4; 1 Cor. 15:3). The task of **form criticism** is, in essence, to isolate and ana-lyze the individual units making up the Gospels. Form criticism is thus named after its aim of examining the units, or forms, of the Gospels.

Only after a form critical analysis of a Jesus tradition has been made can scholars ask about the historical Jesus. Then the central question is, "What are the criteria for determining the authenticity of a Jesus saying or deed?"

## FORM CRITICISM

A form-critical analysis involves three stages: (1) Isolate the individual units of narratives and sayings, that is, separate Jesus **tradition** and the evangelist's **redac-tion;** (2) determine the **form** of these isolated units of narratives and sayings for the purpose of understanding them as self-contained individual texts; and (3) identify the function of these forms.

The first stage of form criticism involves the analysis of the literary framework to separate tradition—the Jesus traditions of the early Church that do not come from the hands of the gospel writers—and redaction—the editorial additions of the authors of the Gospels. Many scholars have noticed how individual scenes in Mark are tied together in time and space.

In the introduction of Mark, three scenes are linked. First is the appearance and preaching of John (1:2–8). Then follows the story of the baptism of Jesus (1:9–11). After the baptism, Mark narrates the story of the temptation (1:12–13). How were these three segments made into a sequence? How are they tied together?

The beginning of the story of the baptism says that Jesus came to John and was baptized in "those days"—that is, the time during which John was active—but what about the beginning of the story of the temptation? After his baptism Jesus was "immediately" led into the wilderness to be tempted according to Mark (1:12). At this point the synoptic parallels differ. After Jesus' baptism Matthew says, "Then Jesus was led up by the Spirit" (4:1). After Jesus' baptism, Luke inserts the genealogy of Jesus (3:23–38). Afterward, Luke says, "Jesus, full of the Holy Spirit, returned from the Jordan and was led . . ." (4:1). Matthew and Luke modify Mark's abrupt introduction of the temptation. Mark frequently employs the word *immediately* as a redactional link between his stories (see 1:18, 20) much more often than Matthew and Luke do. As for the use of *immediately* in Mark 1:12, it suggests that the story of the temptation originally circulated independently of the story of the baptism and was later appended to it.

Another unit of redaction and tradition follows the final scene of Mark 1:2–13. Verse 14 links a summary formulation of the teaching of Jesus in 1:15 with the temptation story (1:13). This linkage says, "Now after John was arrested, Jesus came to Galilee, proclaiming . . ." This verse appears to underscore the appear-ance and work of Jesus after the appearance and work of John; Jesus is presented as the successor of John. The rest of Mark, Chapter 1, continues in this manner, and Chapters 2 and 3 are quite similar, representing scenes from Jesus' life (tradition) that are linked together by the gospel writer (redaction).

From the material that has been examined, we can see that Mark is comprised of a number of originally self-contained narratives that the author more or less skillfully linked together. This linkage was done with reference to time and place: "And the Spirit immediately drove him out into the wilderness" (1:12); "Now after John was arrested, Jesus came to Galilee, proclaiming the good news of God" (1:14).

After analyzing and isolating tradition from redaction, scholars can perform the second task of form criticism: to determine the form of the individual units. The form-critical scholar searches for the smallest self-contained unit because the addition of material is more probable than the deletion of material in the process of transmission. Thus one has to start with the smallest identifiable section to identify the specific form of the tradition.

To determine the forms of the tradition, scholars need to distinguish between narrative material and sayings material.[1] Then they can subdivide these two basic groups into subgroups. Miracle stories constitute an important subgroup under narrative material. The miracle stories, in turn, can be divided into **healing miracles** and **nature miracles.** The other important subgroup under narrative material is a complicated one because two theoretically distinguishable categories, history and **legend,** are mixed. The nativity accounts of Jesus are usually considered legends by form-critical scholars, whereas the baptism accounts of Jesus are historical even though they have some elements that many consider legends, such as the descending bird and the voice from heaven (Mark 1:10–11). The passion story certainly has a historical foundation, but it has also been embellished with legendary motifs, such as an earthquake and many resurrections when Jesus died (Matt. 27:51–53).

In the second major group, sayings material, we find three subgroups: (1) **dominical sayings,** or sayings by the *dominus* (Latin: "Lord"); (2) parables; and (3) **apophthegms,** or sayings. The dominical sayings are sayings by Jesus as the lord of the Church—an **eschatological** prophet, a creator-regulator of church life and order, and a teacher of wisdom who shares proverbs. Thus the Sermon on the Mount is comprised of dominical sayings; so is the eschatological discourse in Mark 13, commonly known as the "little apocalypse." Whereas parables may function as dominical sayings, form-critical scholars put them in a separate category. The term *apophthegms* is from the Greek word, *apophthegma,* and denotes a short, instructive saying that often appears at the climax of a speech or dialogue, as in Mark 2:27–28. There Jesus words, "The sabbath was made for humankind, and not humankind for the sabbath, so the Son of Man is Lord even of the sabbath," conclude a dispute over plucking grain on the Sabbath (Mark 2:23–28). There are two different kinds of dialogues: controversy dialogues in which Jesus argues with his opponents and gets the final word (Mark 2:23–28) and scholastic dialogues in which Jesus appears as a scholar responding to a certain question (Matt. 22:34–40).

---

[1]Form criticism scholars have used different terms to describe the various forms of narrative and sayings material. R. Bultmann's terminology has been used here, in part because he is the most important form criticism scholar of the twentieth century.

But an apophthegm is not always the punch line of a dialogue. We also find biographical apophthegms—so-called because they convey some information about Jesus and his way of life (Mark 1:16–20).

Why is it necessary to categorize the different Jesus stories according to form? Can a formal categorization reveal anything important or essential? The determination of form is important because the form of stories helps to shape their content. Personal letters, for instance, are expected to contain certain features. When a close relative is addressed, certain items are standard: (1) an indication of place and date; (2) a personal address, such as "Dear Aunt"; (3) a statement about one's own health and the wish that the recipient is in good health; and (4) perhaps even an apology for not having written sooner! The letterform shapes the letter's contents to a certain extent. So it was in antiquity. The very form evoked certain expectations. The recipient had a certain knowledge of formal contents, which triggered certain expectations when she started reading.

A brief examination of the healing miracles will help illustrate this point. In the ancient world, healing miracles were related in a certain way and followed a more or less fixed pattern. This form is brought out clearly in the story of the healing of Peter's mother-in-law in Mark 1:29–31.

> Mark 1:29–31: 29 As soon as they left the synagogue, they entered the house of Simon and Andrew, with James and John. 30 Now Simon's mother-in-law was in bed with a fever, and they told him about her at once. 31 He came and took her by the hand and lifted her up. Then the fever left her, and she began to serve them.

Verse 29 is clearly a redactional link ("As soon as" . . . "house of Simon and Andrew"). The miracle story proper consists of two verses involving three elements: (1) a description of the illness (verse 30); (2) the cure (verse 31); and (3) the illustration of the cure's effects (verse 31).

It is a fact that the three elements of Mark 1:30–31 are common in miracle stories in the ancient world. In some miracle accounts, a fourth element appeared: the impression the miracle made on those present (Mark 2:1–12, especially verse 8).

The last task of form criticism is to identify the way in which a form functions in its community. To do so the form-critical scholar must consider the sociological (and/or ecclesiastical) situation of the different forms. Every tradition, especially one that was handed down orally, stands in an immediate relationship with a community that both hands down the tradition and also helps shape it. Therefore, form and community shape the tradition. The same story is not related in exactly the same way to all people. In telling a story, people reflect the social, political, religious, and philosophical ideas of their context. The question about context includes a question about the setting in life. Form-critical scholars use the German phrase **Sitz im Leben,** "setting in life," to describe this sociological interest in the way that a form functions in its community situation. Form criticism argues that units of Jesus traditions were used in different ways for different purposes (instruction, worship, evangelism, church order, and defense) by early Christian communities and asks, "Under what conditions were the forms used and passed on?"

Jesus' healing of the leper in Mark will help illustrate this aspect of form critical analysis. Mark 1:40–45 contains the story about cleansing a leper. The three formal characteristics of the miracle story are evident (a description of the illness [1:40]; the cure [1:41]; and the illustration of the cure's effects [1:42]). At the end of the story it is said that Jesus commanded the leper to present himself to the priest and sacrifice what was commanded in the Law; the Law required that a healed leper should be inspected by a priest and offer sacrifice (Leviticus 14).

What does the end of the story reveal about its *Sitz im Leben*? It says that people who have been healed should go to the temple. How far back into the tunnel does the story go? Apparently it dates to a Jewish-Christian community before 70 CE. The story couldn't have been fabricated in a gentile milieu, nor could it have been fabricated after the temple was destroyed in 70 CE. Does the story take us all the way back to Jesus and his time? Form critics are not certain because Jesus' earliest followers, Jews living in Palestine before 70 CE, could have created this story. What is clear is that it dates from the earliest period of the Jesus movement and was probably used to teach believers about proper conduct after being healed.

## CRITERIA OF AUTHENTICITY

The Gospels set forth the significance of Jesus many years after his death; the earliest gospel, Mark, was written about 40 years after the execution of Jesus. The Gospels also draw on oral traditions. Mark put together many disparate stories that existed first in oral form, then later in written form. Given this situation, form criticism scholars (and now Jesus scholars in general) ask, "How can a reader decide whether or not a particular Jesus tradition goes back to Jesus himself?"

In some cases it is possible to get far back in the tunnel. For example, the story of the cleansing of the leper in Mark 1:40–45 witnesses the existence of a community of Jewish Christians in Palestine before 70 CE. It is not known if the story reports something that actually happened. The reason that readers cannot trust all the stories is that the stories lack the characteristics of eyewitness reports, and one gospel explicitly identifies itself as secondary (Luke 1:1–4). The stories rarely include memorable details or exact biographical or topographical precision. Where did the cleansing of the leper in Mark 1 take place? The verse prior to the healing miracle simply says, "And he went throughout Galilee, proclaiming the message in their synagogues and casting out demons" (1:39). Then it reads, "A leper came to him . . ." The story itself conforms to the common pattern found in healing miracle stories throughout the Hellenistic world, but readers are not left with the impression of having an eyewitness report.

The story about the blessing of the children given in Mark 10:13–16 appears to take place in a house because the preceding story takes place in a house; Mark says, "Then in the house the disciples asked. . . ." (10:10). But whose house is it? The meal with the tax collectors and sinners takes place in a house (Mark 2:15–17). Again, whose house is it? It actually seems to be the house of Jesus, but Mark joined the story to the call of Levi, and Luke, who put the two stories together, said that it was the house of Levi (Luke 5:29). An eyewitness would have been able to provide more information.

Is it possible to get out of the tunnel and recover the original words and works of Jesus? Form criticism pioneered this effort and used specific criteria to help identify **authentic** words and works of Jesus. Whereas some of the other interests of form criticism are at times underused by scholars, these criteria continue to be important in describing the historical Jesus.

## (1) Criterion of Dissimilarity (Discontinuity)

The first criterion is based on the idea that a Jesus tradition may be found authentic if it can be distinguished from what is characteristic of the **early Church** and/or first-century Judaism. Some scholars depict this criterion as a criterion of awkwardness or discomfort or embarrassment, applying it only to the assessment of Jesus' words and actions in relation to early Christianity. If a Jesus tradition is dissimilar to the general teaching and practice of the early Church, then the early Church can hardly have created it. This approach is limited in that it authenticates only those Jesus traditions that are unique, overlooking traditions that Jesus may have shared with other Jews and his followers.

In Mark's story about the young man asking Jesus what he had to do in order to enter the Kingdom of God, the young man addressed Jesus as "Good Teacher," whereupon Jesus said, "Why do you call me good? No one is good except God alone" (10:17). The first Christians held that Jesus was good, and Matthew accordingly changed the question and answer, "Why do you ask me about what is good? There is only one who is good" (Matt. 19:17). On the basis of the criterion of dissimilarity, Mark has preserved Jesus' words, or at the least his basic opinion.

Another example of this criterion can be found in Mark 3:21. There it says that the family of Jesus thought he was crazy and "went out to restrain him, for people were saying, 'He has gone out of his mind.'" This example probably reflects historical reality because the family of Jesus believed in him after the resurrection and was held in high esteem in the early Church. It must be noted that the Greek text does not say that Jesus' family came to get him because of what people were saying; it says "they were saying." The Greek text has *elegon,* "they were saying," which refers to people in general, and modern translations reflect this interpretation, but the subject, Jesus' family, is naturally suggested by the context. In addition, the verb *restrain* is a very strong expression; it denotes "to take hold in order to control." The family of Jesus wanted to get him under its control. Matthew and Luke left out this story, and perhaps they did not do so simply because people said Jesus was crazy, because they did report it (Matt. 12:24; Luke 11:15). When it was reported to Jesus that his family had come to get him, he did not go out to them. Instead, he pointed to those sitting around him, saying, "Who are my mother and my brothers?" (Mark 3:33). Thus, there was a conflict between Jesus and his family; they thought he was crazy.

Another example can be found in the story of Jesus' baptism as described in Mark 1:4–11. Jesus was baptized by John, and according to Mark, his baptism was for repentance of sins. Mark's account is historical because the early Christians would never have fabricated the tradition that Jesus was baptized by John. Matthew provided a theological explanation for Jesus' baptism by John and Luke diverted attention from the fact of his baptism by John by not describing Jesus' baptism by John (Matt. 3:15 and Luke 3:21). Together, the synoptic accounts of Jesus' baptism appear to illustrate how some of the evangelists were uneasy, and perhaps even embarrassed, because Jesus was baptized by his perceived inferior, John.

In some cases Jesus deviated from Judaism as well as from the early Church. Mark 2:18 says that John's disciples and the Pharisees fasted, and that fasting was a cause of offense because Jesus and his disciples did not practice fasting. Moreover, from Matthew's gospel (6:16–18) we see that the early Christians fasted and even ascribed this practice to Jesus. Matthew is corroborated by an early Christian writing (*Didache* 8:1) not found in the New Testament. Thus, it seems certain that Mark is right that Jesus did not fast and did not enjoin his disciples to fast. Here Jesus deviated from Judaism as well as from Christianity.

Thus, it is possible to say something about the historical Jesus. We must be careful, however, when applying the criterion of dissimilarity, especially when we compare Jesus with Judaism. We need to keep two things in mind. First, not much is known about Judaism in the first century CE. In 1947 the discovery of scrolls at **Qumran** brought to light the writings of a particular Jewish sect. These writings show a view of divorce that is quite similar to Jesus' teaching, but before 1947 we knew nothing about such a view in Judaism apart from Jesus' teaching. Did the Qumran discovery force scholars to say that Jesus' view of divorce as unlawful is something that has been ascribed to him? No, because the early Church did allow for the possibility of divorce. The fact that in the Gospels Jesus is seen to agree with the view of a certain Jewish sect does not have to mean that he did not hold that view.

Second, Jesus was a Jew, and if he is said to be in agreement with Judaism, this agreement does not automatically mean that readers are dealing with an inauthentic Jesus tradition. The same holds true for Jesus traditions that are in agreement with the teachings of the early Church. However, authenticity is more likely if there is a dissimilarity between Jesus and the early Church because it is unlikely that the early Church would create a Jesus tradition that ran counter to its own teaching. And authenticity is most likely if there is a dissimilarity between Jesus and Judaism as well as early Christianity. Because Jesus was a Jew and had followers in the early Church, it is obvious that many materials in the Gospels will be ruled out by the criterion of dissimilarity.[2] This criterion's advantage is that the traditions that do meet its requirements will have a high probability of authenticity.

## (2) Criterion of Coherence

After having determined that some traditions can be regarded as genuine Jesus traditions, readers may find passages that are not dissimilar from passages established as authentic. Such passages, which cohere with those already established by the criterion of dissimilarity, are often identified as historical by scholars. The criterion of

---

[2]Some scholars seemingly reverse the interests of the criterion of dissimilarity and argue that Jesus traditions in agreement with first-century realities (historical, social, and theological) are more likely to be authentic. According to this view, known as the criterion of suitability, Jesus sayings, deeds, and experiences that can be situated in the context of the first century are more likely to be reliable (S. Case, *Jesus: A New Biography* (Chicago: University of Chicago Press, 1927).

coherence is often used to enlarge the meager number of Jesus traditions that have passed the stringent requirements of the dissimilarity criterion. This criterion, however, appears to be inadequate because decisions regarding coherence are frequently subjective; it is difficult to define coherence with precision.

## (3) Criterion of Multiple Attestation

If something attributed to Jesus—like an action, saying, idea, or tradition—can be found in different sources, especially sources that are early and independent (Mark, Q, p-Matthew, p-Luke, Paul[3]), it is probably historical. Jesus' fellowship with "tax-collectors and sinners" can serve as an example of this criterion. According to the criterion of dissimilarity, this practice of fellowship may be regarded as historical because both Judaism (***Mishnah Tohoroth*** 7:6) and early Christianity (Matt. 18:17) affirmed that the righteous should turn their backs on sinners. But both Mark 2:13–17 and Q (Matt. 11:19; Luke 7:34) testify to Jesus' association with tax collectors and sinners. Moreover, another early and independent source, p-Luke, also testifies to this practice (Luke 15:1).

This criterion of multiple attestation also authenticates Jesus' friendship with women. In some Jewish circles, rabbis who associated with women came under severe criticism, and this was also the case for teachers in early Christianity. However, Jesus' concern for women is a striking trait in all the Gospels and all the sources.

## (4) Criterion of Palestinian Coloring

This criterion of Palestinian coloring is defined as the possibility of translating a Jesus saying smoothly back into Aramaic. This translation is usually possible, but such translations do not really count for much because the earliest Christian community was Aramaic speaking and could have composed such sayings. This approach has force only when a clumsy or obscure Greek text can be made more intelligible by being translated back into Aramaic. This undertaking can, of course, be very subjective. What constitutes clumsy or obscure Greek?

In John 3:3, Jesus told Nicodemus that he must be "born from above." Nicodemus replied by asking Jesus, "How can anyone be born after having grown old?" (3:4). Nicodemus's assumption that he must literally be born again is based on the Greek word attributed to Jesus in 3:3, *anothen,* which means both "from above" and "again." In Aramaic, the language of Jesus,[4] no such confusion arises because the word for "from above" is different from the word for "again." Therefore, the type of misunderstanding that John 3:4 describes is possible only in Greek. According to the criterion of Palestinian coloring, the wording of this passage in Aramaic undermines its historical value. Many scholars believe that John 3:3 illustrates how Jesus' teachings were elaborated on and reworked by the author of John.

---

[3]Paul is the earliest Christian writer, and his reflections on Jesus, though few in number, are valuable as an early, independent source.
[4]Because of the Aramaic words that surface on the lips of Jesus in Mark and the other Gospels (i.e., Mark 14:36) scholars have assumed that Jesus' everyday language was Aramaic.

Scholars consider references made to religious, social, and domestic customs of Palestine because a Jesus tradition that was anachronistic and/or did not conform to its era could not be considered authentic. In Matthew 18:17, Jesus told his disciples that they were to report a stubborn, unrepentant brother "to the church." The term *church* came to be used as a technical phrase for the Christian community in the early Church only after Jesus died. Therefore, in Matt. 18:17 Matthew introduced an anachronism that represents an inauthentic element.

Many accurate references to Palestinian customs before 70 CE occur in the Gospels. However, these references do not necessarily mean that their Jesus traditions go back to Jesus himself any more than an impeccably researched novel means that its story is true. Some scholars modify this criterion of Palestinian coloring by including a criterion of orality and/or form. This modification is based on the premise that Jesus directed his teaching to rural and largely illiterate people in Galilee. Therefore his words would had to be vivid and striking if they were to be remembered and transmitted orally before being written down. Thus, Jesus' sayings would include aphorisms—brief, pithy sayings—that would make people sit up and take notice, as in Mark 7:15 where Jesus says, "there is nothing outside a person that by going in can defile, but the things that come out are what defile." Here, form and content are not easily distinguishable. Yet why would the first Christians not come up with aphorisms too? Each aphorism has to be assessed on the basis of dissimilarity because form alone is not a sufficient test of authenticity.[5]

The criteria of authenticity, although important in evaluating the Jesus traditions, are not foolproof in categorically identifying what the historical Jesus actually said or did. The criterion of dissimilarity, a primary tool for many scholars, can be draconian in its effects, and thus coherence, multiple attestation, and Palestinian coloring are also needed to test for Jesus sayings and deeds that are not peculiar to their period of time. However, the application of these tools always depends on the individual scholar, and that element introduces a subjectivity. For this reason, scholars demand that method, and not whim, play a central role in gospel scholarship.

## FORM CRITICAL ANALYSIS OF SOME PASSAGES

Mark 10:13–16: Jesus' blessing of the children:

> Mark 10:13–16: 13 People were bringing little children to him in order that he might touch them; and the disciples spoke sternly to them. 14 But when Jesus saw this, he was indignant and said to them, "Let the little children come to me; do not stop them; for it is to such as these that the kingdom of God belongs. 15 Truly I tell you,

---

[5]The one exception may be Jesus' parables. Few parables exist outside the Gospels, and some form critics have argued that many, if not most, of Jesus' parables in the Gospels are authentic. This does not mean that every element of a Jesus parable is authentic (many scholars question the applications and interpretations that accompany the parables), but it does mean that parables appear to be a distinctive Jesus form that the early Church did not mimic or borrow from the larger Jewish community (where parables were used to elucidate Scripture).

whoever does not receive the kingdom of God as a little child will never enter it."
16 And he took them up in his arms, laid his hands on them, and blessed them.

First the scholar has to separate tradition from redaction. A careful reading reveals that Mark 10:13–16 is unrelated to what precedes it and what follows it in the text. The scholar then asks, "What kind of material is this, narrative or sayings material?" The important part of the story is what Jesus said, not what happened; thus this passage from Mark consists of sayings material. But what kind of sayings material? Because 10:13–16 is an anecdote, climaxing in an emphatic utterance, it should be classified as an apophthegm. Moreover, because it is not a controversy dialogue or a scholastic dialogue, but an anecdote providing some information about Jesus, it should be classified as a biographical apophthegm.

Note that Jesus gave two different explanations that do not harmonize in verses 14 and 15. Verse 14 says that children enter the Kingdom of God, whereas verse 15 says that one enters the kingdom by being like a child. Whereas verse 14 speaks about children, verse 15 speaks about adults. This difference may indicate that only one answer was original and that a second answer was added.

To test this possibility, read Mark 10:13–16 twice, and leave each of the disputed answers out of one of the readings. Here Mark 10:13–16 appears without the answer of verse 15.

Mark 10:13–16: 13 People were bringing little children to him in order that he might touch them; and the disciples spoke sternly to them. 14 But when Jesus saw this, he was indignant and said to them, "Let the little children come to me; do not stop them; for it is to such as these that the kingdom of God belongs. 16 And he took them up in his arms, laid his hands upon them, and blessed them.

Now Mark 10:13-16 appears without the answer of verse 14.

Mark 10:13–16: 13 People were bringing little children to him in order that he might touch them; and the disciples spoke sternly to them. 15 Truly I tell you, whoever does not receive the kingdom of God as like a little child will never enter it." 16 And he took them up in his arms, laid his hands on them and blessed them.

The answer of verse 14 fits as an organic apophthegm, whereas verse 15 is an inorganic apophthegm and does not fit the setting. A scholar has to distinguish between organic and inorganic apophthegms. In the former, the organic apophthegm, the scene and the words belong together; the disciples restricted the children and Jesus spoke up for the children. In the latter, the inorganic apophthegm, the words originally existed independently of the scene; the disciples restricted the children and Jesus said one must be childlike to enter the kingdom—the scene and the sayings do not follow and were apparently joined together. Evangelists often created a scene to provide a suitable framework for an isolated apophthegm. However, such is not the case in Mark 10:13–16, for verses 13–14 and 16 clearly make up an apophthegm, the point of which is Jesus' words in verse 14.

Matthew does not have Mark 10:15 in the same scene as Mark does; he reproduced this verse in another context.

Matt. 18:1–3: 1 At that time the disciples came to Jesus and asked "Who is the greatest in the kingdom of heaven?" 2 He called a child, whom he put him among them, 3 and said, "Truly, I tell you, unless you change and become like children, you will never enter the kingdom of heaven. . . ."

Matthew also provided another application in the verse. He probably knew the verse as a self-contained unit. At least he saw that it did not fit with the setting given in Mark 10:13–16. Thus an originally inorganic apophthegm, Mark 10:15, was made into an organic one through the addition of a scene that suits it. As in some other biographical apophthegms, the words of Jesus are not the end of the story.

What does this formal analysis reveal about the *Sitz im Leben*—the life setting, the sociological situation—of the apophthegm in 10:13–16? The original apophthegm (10:13–14,16) addresses church order and says that children are to be admitted into the Church, the members of which constitute the people who will live in the future Kingdom of God. Verse 16 no doubt reflects a practice in Mark's community. This saying's importance for Mark is demonstrated by its placement at the beginning of the gospel and by Mark's addition that Jesus prayed. This practice—that of praying over children—was practiced in his community. The form-critical analysis has certain consequences for theological interpretation. Mark 10:13–14 and 16 teach that the kingdom is a gift that is received without personal efforts.

It is difficult to demonstrate the authenticity of the apophthegm in verse 14. Some rabbis also taught that children have a share in the kingdom so it does not pass the criterion of dissimilarity, nor are there multiple independent attestations for it. Interestingly, scholars are hard pressed to find an early Christian text apart from the Gospels that exhibits sympathy toward young children. This lack has led some to argue that this saying's perspective coheres with a theme that can be authenticated as a Jesus tradition—Jesus' sympathy for the marginal members of society.

Scholars can now interpret verse 15, which formulated the condition for entrance into the kingdom. People must accept the kingdom "as a little child"; no one is entitled to it. This explanation shows why verse 15 was inserted into this apophthegm. The two themes were combined on the basis of the words "child" and "kingdom," which are common to verses 14 and 15. With regard to authenticity, the apophthegm in Mark 10:15 fares better than that of Mark 10:14. The saying in Mark 10:15 is independently attested to by a version in the *Gospel according to Thomas* (logion 22), a collection of Jesus sayings that scholars date anywhere from the first to the second century. There is also a note of dissimilarity, because using children as religious models for adults would have insulted both gentile and Jewish adults in ancient Mediterranean societies.

## SUMMARY

Form criticism takes gospel students back to the oral period, prior to the writing of the Gospels, when early Christian communities were using and preserving the Jesus traditions. The Gospels are thought to consist of Jesus traditions that were preserved by these communities in various forms of sayings and deeds that later served as the substance of the written accounts called Gospels. Form criticism's aims are to isolate Jesus traditions within the Gospels from the evangelists' redaction, determine the specific forms of the Jesus traditions, identify how these forms functioned in the life setting of early Christian communities, and comment on their authenticity by means of the criteria of authenticity.

## KEY TERMS FOR REVIEW

| | | |
|---|---|---|
| Tunnel layer | Forms | Narratives |
| Form criticism | Sayings | *Sitz im Leben* |
| Tradition | Dominical | Criteria for authenticity |
| Redaction | Apophthegm | |

## QUESTIONS FOR REVIEW

1. How does the tunnel layer differ from the other two layers behind the writing of the Gospels?
2. Why is form criticism so named?
3. What are the three stages of form–critical analysis?
4. What was the function of early Christian communities in the preservation of Jesus traditions?
5. What are some of the sub-groups of the forms known as sayings and narratives?
6. How does the criterion of dissimilarity function in authenticating a Jesus tradition?

## SUGGESTIONS FOR FURTHER READING

Bultmann, R. *History of the Synoptic Tradition.* New York: Harper & Row, 1963.

McKnight, E. *What Is Form Criticism?* Philadelphia: Fortress, 1969.

Travis, S. "Form Criticism," in I. Howard Marshall (ed.), *New Testament Interpretation: Essays on Principles and Methods.* Grand Rapids: Eerdmans, 1977, pp. 153–164.

# 8

# Tradition Criticism

## WHICH ACCOUNT IS ORIGINAL?

Source criticism established that Matthew and Luke made use of earlier sources. In many instances they duplicate one another in their accounts of Jesus' life. These duplications can be traced to their shared sources, Mark and Q. When material from Mark was used, it is usually clear that Mark's account is the more original. However, when Matthew and Luke make use of Q, it is not immediately obvious whose account of Q is closer to the original. Can the originality of one version of Q over the other even be demonstrated?

The task of **tradition criticism** is to identify the more original version of those accounts duplicated in the Gospels. By studying Matthew and Luke's duplications of Q, scholars can speculate on which version is more authentic and thus closer to the historical Jesus—although the process is formidable and may produce less than firm results. While reflecting on these duplications, tradition criticism also encourages scholars to comment on the development and use of the Jesus traditions *(Sitz im Leben)* shared by the Gospels, an activity that associates tradition criticism with form criticism and redaction criticism (both of which are special applications of tradition criticism).

Tradition criticism is not an exact science. The cumulative evidence is important and must be weighed. Scholars give careful attention to each version's context, setting, and peculiarities (the differences between duplications) and consider whether these items argue for originality. As long as a scholar can accumulate evidence for one view without coming up with counterarguments, she is building a case for one version as opposed to another.

# TRADITION CRITICISM
# OF THE LORD'S PRAYER

Papias (second century) and Augustine (fifth century) testified that Matthew was regarded as the earliest gospel. Consequently, Matthew's version of the Lord's Prayer soon became popular in teaching and preaching. Scribes who made copies of the New Testament even changed Luke's version, aligning it with Matthew's version. However, in the earliest manuscripts, the Lord's Prayer is not identical in Matthew and Luke and, fortunately, modern translations have preserved their differences. Which is the more original version of the Lord's Prayer?

The Q passages, from which the Lord's Prayer was drawn, do not follow an arrangement similar to that of the adaptation of Mark by Matthew and Luke. Matthew placed the Lord's Prayer within the Sermon on the Mount (6:9–13); Luke placed it in another setting, prompted by the request, "Lord, teach us to pray. . . ." (11:1–4). In Matthew, the Lord's Prayer is part of a continuous sermon; in Luke, it is an answer to a disciple's request. Which setting is the least original one?

The wider context may be helpful in discerning originality. In Matthew, the Lord's Prayer is given in 6:9–13. What follows it and what precedes it? In Matthew, the Lord's Prayer is inserted in the middle of three different instructions—instructions regarding alms giving, prayer, and fasting. Alms giving and prayer are dealt with first, then fasting. They serve as particular examples of practicing piety before others (6:1). In all three cases, readers are told not to follow the example of the hypocrites, but to give alms, to pray, and to fast in a different way. The structure is this: "Whenever you . . . , do not act like the hypocrites who . . . , but when you . . . , do it this way." The passage on prayer is very long and out of proportion to the material dealing with alms giving and fasting. The practical and general instructions on how to pray differently from the "hypocrites" and Gentiles have been expanded by an exact prayer formula. What follows immediately after the Lord's Prayer? A section on the forgiveness of sins taken from Mark 11:25. This placement was probably occasioned by the fact that forgiveness of sins is spoken of toward the end of the prayer. Thus the long Lord's Prayer and the added section on the forgiveness of sins spoil the balanced parallel structure of the sayings on alms giving, prayer, and fasting, which may indicate that the Lord's Prayer does not occur in its correct place and that the Gospel according to Matthew has inserted it in a literary structure in which it does not naturally belong.

Is Luke's context better? In Luke 11:1, Jesus is said to have prayed in a lonely place. When Jesus returned, his disciples said, "Lord, teach us to pray, as John taught his disciples." After the prayer, Luke continues with p-Luke material. Luke often has Jesus praying alone before significant events, whereas both Mark and Matthew are silent about Jesus praying before the same events: before the Spirit descends on him after his baptism (3:21), before the appointment of the twelve apostles (6:12), before Peter's confession that Jesus is the Messiah (9:18), and before Jesus' transfiguration on the mountain (9:28). Luke's references to Jesus praying before significant events appear to be a redactional link that is analogous to Mark's use of *immediately* as a redactional link (for example, 1:12, 18, 20). Thus, his information about Jesus praying at these times is open to question because it may be a secondary editorial interest rather than a primary Jesus tradition.

But what about the disciples' request, "Lord, teach us to pray."? Different Jewish groups had different ways of praying. John's followers apparently had a prayer of their own, as Luke 11:1 makes clear. John the Baptist was a religious leader in his own right and had his own disciples, who apparently prayed according to John's instructions. The Christians, on the other hand, made John into a forerunner of Jesus and would have no compelling reason to invent a community of disciples devoted to John. Thus, the immediate context of Luke seems more plausible than that of Matthew. Jesus taught the Lord's Prayer when his followers asked him how to pray. Luke did not put the Lord's Prayer into the middle of a long sermon as Matthew did, one which could not have been memorized by anyone anyway. Luke's *Sitz im Leben* is more suitable, and therefore Luke 11:1 may be closer to the actual setting.

In addition to the context and setting of the Lord's Prayer, we need to examine both versions of the prayer itself. Matthew included two petitions not found in Luke: (1) "Your will be done, on earth as it is in heaven" (6:10b and 10c) and (2) "But rescue us from the evil one" (6:13b). If Matthew and Luke had one source with the same wording, it would be difficult to explain why Luke would have left these petitions out. In any case, at some point in the transmission of the Lord's Prayer, before Luke or with Luke, there appears both a long version and a short one. Which one is closer to the original?

It is possible to explain why the longer version arose. Matthew 6:10a, which matches Luke 11:2c (at the end), says: "Your Kingdom come." People may have asked, "How?" "How is the Kingdom to come?" Matthew may have provided an answer: When God's will is done by people on earth as it is by the angels in heaven. If Matthew's explanation was original, it would be difficult to think of a reason for Luke to drop it.

Furthermore, Matthew knew a similar saying from Q in 7:21. There he reported that Jesus said: "Not everyone who says to me, 'Lord, Lord,' will enter the kingdom of heaven, but only the one who does the will of my Father in heaven." This is from Q, for Luke 6:46 also uses it. Thus, Matthew 6:10b appears to be an adaptation of a Q saying in answer to the question, "How is the Kingdom to come?"

As for Matthew's ending of the Lord's Prayer, "But rescue us from the evil one," we can find a similar explanation. It is a filling out of the preceding words, "And do not bring us to the time of trial." The conjunction *but* is a strong adversative in Greek; it implies an opposition to what has gone before. Thus, the two petitions are intimately connected. Again, there seems to be no reason to drop the last petition. It is easier to regard it as an addition.

Two other important differences occur between the versions of the Lord's Prayer in Matthew and Luke. These differences are not additions or omissions but simply variations of the text. The first one is extremely important because it goes beyond the question of the more accurate version to the question of the words of Jesus himself. How does the Lord's Prayer begin? Matthew begins with the words, "Our Father in heaven." Luke begins differently, "Father." Here we can be certain which was the original version. "Our . . . in heaven" is an expression also found in Jewish prayers. So is Matthew's version original? Why would Luke have abridged such an expression? The prayer has clear signs of being translated from a Semitic original, and the Greek word for Father *(pater),* which itself is not a diminutive, may be a translation of a diminutive form, *abba* (Aramaic).

A diminutive is a word formed from another to express diminished size, or familiarity. Johnny is a diminutive meaning John. *Abba* was not used in Jewish prayers; Jews did not address God as *Abba* because it was considered too informal for addressing God. It is a diminutive meaning Dear Father, Dad, or even Daddy (*Abba* corresponds to the Aramaic word *Imma,* which means Dear Mother, Mom, or Mommy). If Father is traceable to *Abba,* then Luke 11:2 can be translated, "When you pray, say, 'Dad, hallowed be Your Name.'" *Abba* is a word used by children; it expresses familiarity and intimacy. It was not used in first-century Jewish prayers, as illustrated by the **eighteen benedictions,** where we find formal references to God as Lord. There would have been no way for the Christians to hit upon such an original expression if their savior had conformed to Jewish standards; the Christians would have spoken of "the heavenly Father" or of "our Father in heaven."

We can corroborate this inference. Paul used the word *Abba* twice, once in Gal. 4:6 and again in Rom. 8:15. In both cases, the possession of the Spirit was said to confirm to the believers that they are children of God who can exclaim, *"Abba"! Abba* is an Aramaic word. The congregations in Galatia and Rome spoke Greek, and Paul wrote to them in Greek, which suggests that *Abba* was a particularly important word and not Paul's invention. Paul's coining of such a prayer would be incomprehensible. *Abba* must have derived from a tradition, even a very sacred tradition.

After comparing the versions of the Lord's Prayer carefully and noting the context, setting, and differences between Matthew and Luke, we must give Luke's version priority. When we examine the context and setting for the Lord's Prayer in Luke, the immediate context and setting are plausible: the plea of the disciples, "Teach us to pray!" This occasion is more plausible for the origination of the Lord's Prayer than that of Matthew's sermon, in which the Lord's Prayer is immersed in other material. Matthew inserted the Lord's Prayer into a section of the Sermon on the Mount that had a carefully balanced structure, and this insertion spoiled the structure. It seems more likely that the Sermon on the Mount consists of material drawn together from different quarters. Various collections of traditions about Jesus, both oral and written, were probably put together at some point in time and utilized by the evangelists.

Some scholars suggest that Jesus gave the Lord's Prayer on two different occasions, which would explain the different forms in Matthew and Luke. Each gospel may have preserved a different version of the two versions given by Jesus. In this case the Q source would not have been used as a source of the Lord's Prayer that was modified by Matthew and Luke. Despite the attractiveness of this solution, a close look at the placement of the Lord's Prayer in the two Gospels reveals how tenuous it is. In Matthew, the Lord's Prayer is given at the outset of Jesus' activity; in Luke, it appears somewhat later. In Luke, the disciples said, "Teach us to pray!" If we accept the Gospels at face value, a problem arises. The disciples should have known how to pray because they had heard the Sermon on the Mount! There would be no reason for their request. Thus both Matthew and Luke used Q as a source for the Lord's Prayer and edited it accordingly.[1]

When we consider the further differences between the Lord's Prayer in Matthew and Luke, it is clear that the two versions cannot have been independent of one another, as well as its being clear that Luke must be given priority. There would have been no reason for Luke to abridge the Lord's Prayer.

Matthew included two petitions not found in Luke. The passages, "Your will be done, on earth as it is in heaven" and "But rescue us from the evil one," are intimately connected with the material preceding these two petitions. It is best to explain these passages as additions that elaborate on the preceding petitions. There is no ready explanation to be found for Luke's shorter version if Matthean priority is maintained. Nor can we find an explanation for Luke's shorter version if we assume his independence. Why would Jesus on one occasion leave out what he had previously included in the prayer? Jesus' simple identification of God as Father (in all likelihood *Abba*) in Luke's version is highly original, whereas Matthew's "Our Father in heaven" is conventional and fits first-century Jewish prayers. Again, we must give Luke priority. If we assume independence, why would Jesus on one occasion teach people to address God as "Father" and on another occasion use the more common phrase "Our Father in heaven"? In Matthew, the Sermon on the Mount is not addressed solely to the disciples, although they are included among the recipients. No evidence exists to the effect that Jesus gave the disciples a secret teaching. Any theory of independence has to answer such questions.

One variation between the two versions does seem to argue for Matthean priority. Matthew reads, "Give us this day our daily bread" (6:11). The word for daily is *epiousios,* which does not occur anywhere else. It probably derives from *epiousa,* which means "following." Thus the text says literally, "Give us today bread for the following"—that is, the following, coming, day. According to Jerome, the second-century *Gospel according to the Nazoreans* reads, "Give us our bread of tomorrow" (Aramaic: *mahar*), which may be an interpretation of *epiousios.* The twenty-four hour day of the Jews began at sundown, so reciting this petition of the Lord's Prayer in the evening or even in the morning makes good sense. The prayer implies an ever-present urgency that reveals something about the needy socio-economic status of the followers of Jesus.

Luke's version lacks Matthew's sense of urgency. Instead of the verb form "give," he has a word meaning "keep on giving." Instead of "this day," he has "each day." Thus he literally says, "Keep on giving us each day our bread for the following day." Urgency is not the focus in Luke's version. The perspective is longer; it includes the future, "Keep on giving us" "each day." The prayer is not desperate. Here the concern of surviving from day to day is not present. The text

---

[1] Whereas in principle Jesus may have repeated his teachings, this approach to duplicate traditions is often motivated by a concern to harmonize the Gospels and remove what may be perceived as contradictions or discrepancies. Such an approach may lead to strained and unreasonable explanations, such as Jesus "cleansed" the temple twice, once at the beginning of his ministry (John 2: 13–17) and a second time at the end of his ministry (Mark 11:12–14).

seems to give evidence that the followers of Jesus have settled down in the world somewhat and are able to look ahead. They are not concerned about surviving until the next day.

We have examined both versions of the Lord's Prayer, including their different contexts, settings, and peculiarities (the two additional petitions in Matthew's version [6:10b and 13b] and Luke's petition for bread [11:3]). Except in the case of the petition for bread, Luke seems to have priority and to have preserved the version closer to the original. A sound conclusion is that Luke preserved the more original version but changed it at one point. Luke may not have been the one to change it though; Luke may simply have transmitted the text that he found in Q. In any event, on the whole Luke is more reliable.

## TRADITION CRITICISM OF THE SERMON(S) ON THE MOUNT (PLAIN)

Matthew and Luke each preserved sermons of Jesus which are quite alike in content but which have different characteristics in both Gospels (Matt. 5:1–7:27; Luke 6:17–49). In Matthew Jesus gave the sermon on a mountain. In Luke Jesus gave the sermon on a level plain. In Matthew the sermon precedes the call of the disciples. In Luke the sermon follows the call of the disciples. In Matthew the sermon is lengthy and is the first of a series of discourses. In Luke the sermon is shorter, and the contents of Matthew's sermon that are not found in it are distributed throughout Luke's gospel. However, the same order is generally preserved.

The beginning of the sermon is identical in both Gospels. It is found only in Matthew and Luke; Mark has no counterpart. Scholars therefore identify it as Q material. As a Q text the Jesus saying was preserved without a narrative context. The narrative context given to the sayings is secondary. The form of the beginning of the sermon is a series of Jesus sayings known as beatitudes. A beatitude is a declaration of blessing that states, "Blessed are . . . ." This type of saying is common in Jewish literature. Thus the sermons begin with a series of dominical sayings.

The first beatitude in Matthew reads, "Blessed are the poor in spirit" (Matt. 5:3). Luke begins with "Blessed are you who are poor" (Luke 6:20). What does Matthew mean by "poor in spirit"? Is it certain that Matthew's version means the same thing as Luke's? If both versions mean the same thing, the question of which is more original still remains. What was the wording in the Q source?

The form of the saying may be helpful in deciding originality. Jewish beatitudes were usually formulated in the third person. On this formal basis Luke may seem to be secondary because he used the second person: "Blessed are you who are poor." But then Luke appears more primitive and simple than Matthew does. Luke has, "Blessed are you who are poor, . . . you who are hungry now" (6:21). Luke also preserves a sense of urgency in 6:21 with the adverb *now.* Matthew notes the "poor in spirit" and "hunger and thirst for righteousness" (5:3 and 6). Matthew seems to elaborate on the "poor" and those that "hunger" in much the same way he elaborated parts of the Lord's Prayer.

But Luke may have a redactional interest in the poor and the rich. Elsewhere in his gospel Luke has a manifest interest in the poor; he also has a bias against the rich. After the beatitudes he has two "woes" (judgments) against the rich (verses 24–26). Luke uses the word "poor" ten times (twice as often as Matthew). Luke speaks about the "rich" eleven times (Matthew only three). Only Luke has the verb to "be" rich. In the material peculiar to Luke (p-Luke) we find traditions that focus on the motif of wealth: the parable of the rich fool (12:13–21), the parable of the rich man and Lazarus (16:19–31), and the story of the rich tax collector (19:1–10).

We must ask whether Luke edited the beatitudes according to his own interests. Perhaps Luke as well as Matthew did redactional work on this Q material. That Matthew did editorial work is suggested by the phrase "hunger and thirst *for righteousness*" in 5:6. The word *righteousness* is a favorite of Matthew's. It does not occur in Mark and occurs only once in Luke (1:75), whereas Matthew has it five times in the Sermon on the Mount. It is reasonable to argue that Matthew inserted it into his Q material. Luke 12:31 says, "strive for his kingdom, and these things will be given to you as well." These words concern cares about earthly things. Matthew's parallel, in 6:33, adds the word *righteousness* and reads, "But strive first for the kingdom of God and his righteousness, and all these things will be given to you as well."

It is not easy to decide the content of Q in this instance. Is it "Blessed are you who are hungry now," as Luke has it (6:21)? Or is it "Blessed are those who hunger and thirst for righteousness," as Matthew has it (5:6)? Both writers promoted theological interests. Perhaps the Q saying was "Blessed are those who hunger," which eliminates the poverty interest of Luke and the righteousness interest of Matthew.

In Matthew 5:9, Jesus said, "Blessed are the peacemakers, for they will be called children of God." In the full context of Matthew's gospel this is a little strange because later Jesus declares that he has not come to bring peace:

> Matt. 10:34–36: 34 "Do not think that I have come to bring peace to the earth; I have not come to bring peace, but a sword. 35 For I have come to set a man against his father, and a daughter against her mother, and a daughter-in-law against her mother-in-law; 36 and one's foes will be members of one's own household."

Luke's gospel contains another version of this Q saying:

> Luke 12:51–53: 51 "Do you think that I have come to bring peace to the earth? No, I tell you, but rather division! 52 From now on five in one household will be divided, three against two and two against three; 53 they will be divided: father against son and son against father, mother against daughter and daughter against her mother, mother-in-law against her daughter-in-law and daughter-in-law against her mother-in-law."

Here we have at least an apparent contradiction between Matthew 5:9 and 10:34–36.

*Peace* is a special theme in Luke, and this word occurs thirteen times in his gospel. In Matthew *peace* occurs only four times. Interestingly, Matthew 5:9 has no parallel in Luke. Why would Luke, with his special interest in peace, leave out this passage if it were in Q? This omission may suggest that it was not in Q. That Matthew, as a redactor, is responsible for the saying is suggested by the fact that the word "peacemakers" occurs only in Matthew 5:9 and nowhere else in the New Testament. This word seems to designate those who settle quarrels.

We need to consider the Q passage about division in households. Is this a genuine Jesus passage? *Peace* and *sword* are used here with reference to family quarrels. Did Jesus realize that he would not bring peace because the decision about whether or not to follow him would break up families? We can easily imagine that Zebedee, the father of James and John, was angry when his sons suddenly left the family business to follow Jesus (Mark 1:19–20). The peace in Zebedee's household was surely disrupted. It is possible though that the saying referred not to the families of the disciples, but to the disquieting experience of the early church.

The two versions about divisiveness are not identical. In Matthew the hostility is that of the younger generation against the older, which is based on Micah 7:6 and quoted by Matthew in 10:35–36. In Luke the hostility between generations is mutual. Luke's version does not quote Micah. A staunch form critic would be apt to say that the Matthean form of the saying was shaped in the early church on the basis of Micah 7:6. Micah took the corrupt social life of his time as a sign that the end was near; now God would have to act and change things. Matthew's community saw its own experience of trial and division as the fulfillment of Micah's prophecy and thus integrated it into one of Jesus' sayings.

## TRADITION CRITICISM OF THE PARABLE OF THE WEDDING FEAST/GREAT BANQUET

Matthew and Luke both preserve a Q text having to do with a parable about a wedding feast (Matthew) or a great banquet (Luke).

> Matt. 22:1–14: 1 Once more Jesus spoke to them in parables, saying: 2 "The kingdom of heaven may be compared to a king who gave a wedding banquet for his son. 3 He sent his slaves to call those who had been invited to the wedding banquet; but they would not come. 4 Again he sent other slaves, saying, 'Tell those who have been invited: Look, I have prepared my dinner, my oxen and my fat calves have been slaughtered, and everything is ready; come to the wedding banquet.' 5 But they made light of it and went away, one to his farm, another to his business, 6 while the rest seized his slaves, mistreated them, and killed them. 7 The king was enraged. He sent his troops, destroyed those murderers, and burned their city. 8 Then he said to his slaves, 'the wedding is ready, but those invited were not worthy. 9 Go therefore into the main streets, and invite everyone you find to the wedding banquet.' 10 Those slaves went out into the streets and gathered all whom they found, both good and bad; so the wedding hall was filled with guests. 11 "But when the king came in to see the guests, he noticed a man who was not wearing a wedding robe, 12 and he said to him, 'Friend, how did you get in here without a wedding robe?' And he was speechless. 13 Then the king said to the attendants, 'Bind him hand and foot, and throw him into the outer darkness, where there will be weeping and gnashing of teeth.' 14 For many are called, but few are chosen."

Luke 14:16–24: 16 Then Jesus said to him, "Someone gave a great dinner, and invited many. 17 At the time for the dinner he sent his slave to say to those who had been invited, 'Come; everyone is ready now.' 18 But they all alike began to make excuses. The first said to him, 'I have bought a piece of land, and I must go out and see it; please accept my regrets.' 19 Another said, 'I have bought five yoke of oxen, and I am going to try them out; please accept my regrets.' 20 Another said, 'I have just been married and therefore I cannot come.' 21 So the servant returned and reported this to his master. Then the owner of the house became angry and said to his slave, 'Go out at once into the streets and lanes of the town, and bring in the poor, the crippled, the blind, and the lame.' 22 And the slave said, 'Sir, what you ordered has been done, and there is still room.' 23 Then the master said to the slave, 'Go out to the roads and lanes, and compel people to come in so that my house may be filled. 24 For I tell you, none of those who were invited will taste my dinner.'"

Matthew's account is much longer than Luke's. It includes the additional passage about the servants being killed (v. 6) and the additional passage about the guest who does not have the proper garment (v. 11–14). It also makes reference to the host sending his armies to destroy those who refused the first invitation by burning their city (v. 7) and to cast out a man without a wedding garment (v. 11).

Luke's account, on the other hand, has a more elaborate version of the second instruction to the servant about the guests who would replace those who had been invited initially (v. 21). He tells us a little about the kind of person who was summoned to the feast: the poor, the crippled, the blind, and the lame (v. 21).

Thus, both evangelists seem to have read a deeper significance into the story than it may have contained in the first place. Luke's addition about the character of those invited is consistent with his overall concern about the outcasts and follows Jesus' command to invite the "poor, the crippled, the lame, and the blind" (14:13–14), which immediately precedes the parable. In Luke's account these types of people show the most enthusiasm for Jesus and his gospel.

Matthew's concerns were different. The servants of the king were killed (v. 6). He probably had the prophets of Israel in mind here. One guest was without a proper garment, and he was punished (v. 13). This punishment may reflect Matthew's insistence that there be no slackening of the understanding of righteousness. According to Matthew, the righteousness of the Christians had to exceed that of the scribes and Pharisees (5:20). The tree had to bear good fruit or else it would be cut down (7:19). Thus, disciples of Jesus must demonstrate discipleship. This explanation may be the clue to the symbolism of the wedding garment that the king expected of his guests (v. 12).

The revenge taken by the king on his ungrateful guests is clearly allegorical and shows that the parable went through a transition involving a change of material. The host was a king, evidently God himself. Those who were first invited were the members of the covenant. The servants of the king were prophets. The destruction of the city of the ungrateful people was the destruction of Jerusalem. The guests who filled the wedding hall were the Gentiles.

Luke seems to have substantially preserved the original form of the parable. It is not necessary to give a special meaning to each and every element in the story. Form critically, we can argue that the parable was used in the church's preaching *(Sitz im Leben)* as a way of speaking about the crisis facing the people listening to the gospel. As with the guests who were initially invited to the wedding feast, there would be no second chance. Now was the time for a decision. A refusal meant that the opportunity would be gone for good. This message may also reflect the teaching of Jesus.

## SUMMARY

Tradition criticism seeks to identify the more original version of duplicate accounts in the Gospels. This task is important because duplicate accounts are not uncommon; both Matthew and Luke used Q as a source. By examining the context, setting, and peculiarities of each version of a duplicated tradition, students of the Gospels can comment on the originality of the shared tradition. Tradition criticism also reflects form criticism and redaction criticism in its interest in a passage's *Sitz im Leben* and the way it has been modified in accordance with a gospel's theology.

## KEY TERMS FOR REVIEW

| | | |
|---|---|---|
| Tradition criticism | Cumulative evidence | Peculiarities |
| Original version | Context | Q |
| Duplicate accounts | Setting | |

## QUESTIONS FOR REVIEW

1. Why is tradition criticism required?
2. What does tradition criticism have in common with form criticism and redaction criticism?
3. What kinds of reasons might a student give for favoring a Matthean version of a shared tradition over a Lukan version?

## SUGGESTIONS FOR FURTHER READING

Barbour, R. *Traditio-Historical Criticism of the Gospels.* London: SPCK, 1972.

Catchpole, D. "Tradition History," in *New Testament Interpretation,* ed. I. Marshall. Grand Rapids: Eerdmans, 1977, pp. 165–80.

Stanton, G. *Jesus Christ in New Testament Preaching.* Cambridge: Cambridge University Press, 1974.

# PART III

# The Canonical Gospels

# 9

✳

# The Gospel according to Mark

## INTRODUCTORY QUESTIONS

### Authorship

Eusebius, a historian of the Christian Church who wrote in the fourth century, reported that a certain Papias of Hierapolis in Asia Minor, who lived sometime in the first part of the second century, maintained that Mark's gospel was written by Mark, the secretary of the disciple Peter. Papias is reported to have said that although Peter provided quite accurate information, the Gospel according to Mark does not give a correct chronological order of the events.

In another place, Eusebius quoted Clement of Alexandria to the effect that Mark accompanied Peter to Rome. In 1 Peter 5:13, the author of the letter, writing from Rome, mentioned his associate Mark whom he called "my son." In both the Acts of the Apostles and the letters ascribed to Paul, Paul had an associate called Mark (Acts 12:25; Col. 4:10). Acts 12:12 identifies John Mark as a member of the primitive community in Jerusalem.

When we piece all this information together, we end up with the following picture: The Gospel according to Mark was written by John Mark, who belonged to the first Christian community in Jerusalem and for a while accompanied Paul on his travels. Later John Mark associated himself with Peter and even went to Rome with Peter, Jesus' leading disciple. This picture of the gospel's author is the traditional one.

Are there methods we can use to find out whether a writing was actually written by the author to whom it has been ascribed? Extreme caution is necessary. The burden of proof rests on the person contesting authenticity. If we doubt the traditions regarding the origin of Mark, we must provide good reasons for doing so. Now, do we have reasons for doubt? The first question to be asked is, "Did the author state his identity?" The next question is, "If the author's name was passed on only by tradition, what is the age of that tradition and who were the authorities behind it?" We need to examine the tradition by critical methods.

We can analyze the tradition behind Mark's gospel. Who was this John Mark of Jerusalem mentioned in Acts? Who was this Mark mentioned in Paul's letters? John Mark was not connected to Peter or to the Gospel according to Mark in Acts or in Paul's letters. Furthermore, we can detect no trace of Paul's theology in Mark. Peter is no help because first we need to settle the question of whether 1 Peter was written by Jesus' disciple called Peter. According to many scholars, Jesus' disciple Peter did not write 1 Peter. Even if 1 Peter was written by Peter the disciple, who is the Mark referred to in 5:13? Nothing is said in 1 Peter about Mark being the author's secretary or his having written a gospel.

What about Papias? The text of the gospel does not bear out the information that Mark was Peter's secretary/interpreter. In Chapter 7, the itinerary of Jesus from the Sea of Galilee, as related in verse 31, could not have been written by anyone familiar with the geography of Palestine. Peter would never have given Mark this itinerary. Other similar problems exist.

Mark 7.3 is another example that the person who put together the Gospel according to Mark could not have been well acquainted with or informed about first-century Palestine: "For the Pharisees, and all the Jews, do not eat unless they thoroughly wash their hands. . . ." This writer did not know the Pharisees. Did they differ from the rest of the Jews? They did. Here the author of Mark tried to have it both ways. The Pharisees are distinctive, and yet they are not. Peter would have been better acquainted with the Jews of Palestine.[1]

Thus, we can learn something about the anonymous author of Mark's gospel. His description of Jesus in Mark 7 shows that he was probably not Peter's secretary, or even a disciple of Paul (who, like Peter, was familiar with Palestine and the Pharisees). This deduction is negative knowledge, but it is a corrective against past misunderstandings about the authorship of Mark.

## Date

This discussion revolves around Mark's relation to the first Jewish revolt. Romans entered Palestine in 63 BCE and ruled the Jews throughout the life of Jesus. The Roman presence eventually resulted in a great revolt that was crushed by the Romans (66–70 CE). One catastrophic result for the Jewish people was the destruction of

---

[1]Some scholars have argued that these passages from Mark 7, which support a non-Palestinian source or origin, may be **interpolations** and are thus additions to a preexisting text that could have originated in Palestine. In addition, Mark includes some Aramaic words and constructions, both of which may be evidence of a Palestinian starting point. Mark, like the other Gospels, was probably edited from other sources so interpolations are a possibility. Unfortunately, no textual support exists for these passages in Mark 7 as interpolations. As for the Aramaic words and constructions, they are not proof of a Palestinian origin. Mark does translate the Aramaic words, something that would not be necessary for Palestinian readers (are the translations interpolations?). Several of Paul's letters include Aramaic words and constructions but were written outside of Palestine.

their temple in Jerusalem. Mark 13:1–2 states that Jesus foretold that great catastrophe.

> Mark 13:1–2: 1 As he came out of the temple, one of his disciples said to him, "Look, Teacher, what large stones and what large buildings!" 2 Then Jesus asked him, "Do you see these great buildings? Not one stone will be left here upon another; all will be thrown down."

How could Jesus have prophesied the temple's destruction? Because he was Jesus, the Son of God, according to Christian tradition. That argument is not a good one in this context; historians must treat Mark's gospel as an historical document, not as a divine revelation. Documents from the same time frame as Mark's gospel, like Suetonius's account of the caesars, represent the emperor as a god who could foretell the future and work miracles. Such documents are not accepted uncritically by historians as factual.

Mark 13:1–2 seems to be a prophecy that was put into the mouth of Jesus after 70 CE. Note, however, that the prophecy goes on to say that people ought to flee up into the hills when the destroying forces draw near, "But when you see the desolating sacrilege set up where it ought not to be (let the reader understand), then those in Judea must flee to the mountains" (13:14). People could not have followed Jesus' advice. When closing in on the city, Roman troops controlled the entire terrain surrounding Jerusalem. Christian tradition, as reported by Eusebius, also says that shortly before 70 CE the Christians fled across the river Jordan, not into the hill country around Jerusalem.

In any event, Mark's gospel must have been written around 70 CE, either just after the fall of the temple, or just before, by a person who saw the events. This person was not well acquainted with the geography of Palestine or the customs of the Jews.

## Language

The language of Mark's gospel is very simple. The Greek is primitive and colloquial. Matthew and Luke improved on Mark's language in a number of cases. Interestingly, Mark's Greek cannot be proven to rest upon Aramaic, the spoken language of Palestinian Jews in Jesus' day (which would have been the case if Peter and John Mark of the Jerusalem community were the authors).

## The Audience (Recipients of the Gospels)

Mark wrote for a Greek-speaking audience because he wrote in Greek. The quotations from the Jewish Bible were taken from the Greek version. The author also paused to interpret certain Hebrew and Aramaic words such as *Ephphatha* (be opened) in 7:34 and *Golgotha* (place of the skull) in 15:22. He also tried to explain the customs of Jewish groups like the Pharisees, as in 7:3, or the Sadducees, who did not believe in the resurrection of the dead (12:18), for an audience unfamiliar with Jewish traditions and beliefs.

Thus, Mark probably wrote for Greek-speaking Christians who lived outside of Palestine. There must have been a large number of Gentiles among his audience because Mark felt it necessary to explain certain things that pertained only to Jews, even to Jews in Palestine; only Palestinian inhabitants would have been familiar with the Sadducees. However, because he did not accurately depict Palestinian life, he himself was probably not a Palestinian Jew. Despite the lack of certainty over the audience, many scholars have suggested that it was Rome, whereas others have argued for a territory near Palestine, like Syria.

## Sources

The author of Mark, the earliest gospel, seems to have used several sources. Source criticism has argued for Ur-Mark and p-Mark. Stages of development and the addition of source materials best explain why the parable of the seed growing secretly in 4:26–29 is not found in Matthew and Luke. These two authors had no reason to drop it. Originally that parable was not in Ur-Mark, the form of Mark used by Matthew and Luke. In Mark 4:10–12 we find a passage about the parables, the subject of the entire context, that does not show up in the other synoptics. It is probable that written sources existed before Ur-Mark. The collection of parables in Chapter 4 and the passion story in Chapters 11 through 16 may have been drawn from previously existing documents.

## Structure

Did Mark put together his material with a certain plan in mind? The basic structure is this: (1) Chapters 1–9 deal with Jesus' ministry in Galilee. The key theme throughout these chapters is the proclamation of the Kingdom of God and its subsequent rejection; (2) Chapters 11–15 deal with Jesus' passion in Jerusalem. Chapter 10 is a link between the two sections. It deals with Jesus' journey from Galilee to Jerusalem. The gospel does not end with Chapter 15. Chapter 16 is an epilogue dealing with the empty tomb. The gospel originally ended with 16:8.

The second part of Mark's gospel, Chapters 11 through 15, is very long. More than one-third relates to the passion narrative (Jesus repeatedly predicted his passion in 8:31, 9:31, and 10:33–34), although the passion events occurred within a few days. According to Mark, Jesus' entire ministry spanned one year. It has been said that the Gospels are "passion stories with an extended introduction," which is correct insofar as the passion, death, and resurrection of Jesus constituted the gospel at the beginning of Christianity. But when dealing with the Gospels proper—that is, literary works including the ministry of Jesus—the question of structure cannot be so easily solved. What comes before the passion is not simply introduction.

The messiahship of Jesus is an obvious theme in Mark. However, Mark formulated this interest in a distinctive manner. In the first part, he emphasized over and over that Jesus' true identity had to be kept hidden. Demons and disciples are repeatedly told not to announce Jesus' identity as "the Holy One of God" (1:24) or "the Messiah" (8:29). In the second part of the gospel, the messiahship of Jesus is pronounced openly to the disciples, to the high priest, and finally to the bystanders by the centurion beneath Jesus' cross. Thus, the first part of the gospel is no introduction in the sense that it introduces all of that which is to come later. Mark implicitly emended the gospel proper by adding Chapters 1 through 9.

An ancient literary study may shed some light on Mark's gospel.[2] In the fourth century BCE, Aristotle (*Poetics*) said that all tragedies should have a middle portion that would serve an essential function. This portion might be a scene in which the hero was recognized for what he was. This recognition would bring about the friendship of some and the enmity of others. Also, there should be a reversal in the hero's destiny; from now on he should go to his passion and death. Aristotle's model fits reasonably well with the Gospel according to Mark. In Chapter 8 Peter acknowledged Jesus as the Messiah. In Chapter 9, this acknowledgment was confirmed by a voice from heaven. Then, in Chapter 10, Jesus began his journey to Jerusalem, where he was rejected.

Admittedly, there is no exact parallel between Aristotle's theory and Mark. For Aristotle, people who were not close friends of the hero suddenly realized his true nature and then became his friends, whereas in Mark it was Jesus' good friend who realized his true nature. Although Mark probably did not read Aristotle, Aristotle appears to have exercised a powerful influence on storytellers and, in one way or another, Mark apparently came under his influence.

Thus, the structure of Mark can be accounted for by the prefacing of the primitive Christian gospel with a section that turned the whole story into some sort of a classical tragedy.

## THE THEOLOGY OF MARK

Why was the Gospel according to Mark written? Luke's gospel has an explicit statement in 1:1–4 that answers the question of why he wrote his gospel. He wanted to set the record straight and clear up any misunderstandings about Jesus. John's gospel also has a purpose statement in 20:30–31, which probably served as the ending of the original gospel. John's gospel was written so people would believe that Jesus was the Messiah, the Son of God.

Mark's gospel contains no such statement, yet we can discover his aim by comparing his gospel with the other Gospels and by asking how and why he differs from them. What are Mark's specific themes? What did he want to say? As redaction criticism has emphasized, each of the four Gospels has a particular point of view about Jesus.

### (1) The Passion

The passion of Jesus has a significant place in Mark. It constitutes one-third of the entire gospel. Mark also has many allusions to the passion before the passion narrative begins, which is especially apparent in the passion pronouncements of Chapters 8, 9, and 10, where we find the turning point of the story: The messi-

---

[2]Scholars have increasingly turned to traditional aspects of literary criticism (that is, narrative structure, plot, and character development) when interpreting the Bible and the field of narrative criticism, studying the formal literary characteristics of biblical literature. For further explanation, see M. Powell, *What Is Narrative Criticism?* (Minneapolis: Fortress, 1990).

ahship of Jesus was made known. Thus, passion and messiahship belong together in Mark. Jesus was the Messiah, of course, but what kind of Messiah? A suffering one who was put to death!—that is, a Messiah who was not at all the type expected by Palestinian Jews. Although Dead Sea Scroll scholars have come across several fragments that may associate messiahship with suffering within the Qumran community, the only explicit reference to a dying messiah in first-century Judaism is found in *2 Esdras* 7:28–29. Here we find no hint of suffering or rejection, but of a messiah who died after ruling for 400 years. Evidently, it was important to Mark to drive home this point of a suffering Messiah.

There can be no doubt that Mark knew about the appearances of the resurrected Jesus. He referred to them twice. In 14:28, in one of Jesus' prophecies about his resurrection, he said that he would go before the disciples to Galilee. Thus, the resurrected Jesus was expected to appear to the disciples in Galilee. This prophecy was repeated by the angel whom the women found at the empty tomb (16:7), but Mark did not narrate these appearances. The original gospel ends with the next verse, which says that the women fled in fear and "said nothing to anyone" (16:8). The "longer ending" (verses 9–20), which describes the appearances of the resurrected Jesus, was not found in the earliest manuscripts.

The ending of Mark's gospel presents a problem. Why would a copyist have dropped the ending? There would have been no reason for him to do so. Had a leaf been lost? Yet Matthew and Luke were acquainted with Mark up to only 16:8, and no trace whatsoever of a continuation of Mark exists. Verses 16:7 and 14:28 may help. In 16:7 the angel's words, "just as he told you," refer to the prediction of Jesus in 14:28, that he would meet the disciples in Galilee. A reading of 14:28 in its context is revealing.

> Mark 14:26–31: 26 When they had sung the hymn, they went out to the Mount of Olives. 27 And Jesus said to them, "You will all become deserters; for it is written, 'I will strike the shepherd, and the sheep will be scattered.' 28 But after I am raised up, I will go before you to Galilee." 29 Peter said to him, "Even though they all become deserters, I will not." 30 Jesus said to him, "Truly, I tell you, this day, this very night, before the cock crows twice, you will deny me three times." 31 But he said vehemently, "Even though I must die with you, I will not deny you." And all of them said the same.

Verse 28 is clearly a redactional addition; it does not have anything to do with the theme of the passage, which is that of falling away. Note that Peter and the disciples did not react at all to the prophecy of Jesus' post-resurrection appearance, responding only to Jesus' words about falling away. Possibly, then, the original gospel did not even contain the prophecy of the post-resurrection appearances of Jesus.

This theory, however, does not solve the problem. Why would the author of Mark add these prophecies but leave out any word of their fulfillment? Perhaps he added the prophecies because he knew of Jesus' appearances. Then why did he not highlight their fulfillment? Some postulate that the original ending of Mark was lost. In light of Mark's overall thrust, others believe that 16:8 may serve as a dramatic punch line. As the text now stands, the gospel ends with the empty tomb and the fear of the women, which results in a very strong emphasis on the passion and death of Jesus. Mark wanted to tell his readers that Jesus was the suffering Messiah. This theme fits in with the other Markan themes.

## (2) The Misunderstood Messiah

Mark's gospel ends by describing the fear and silence of the women. They misunderstood the young man they met at the tomb. We find the motif that Jesus was misunderstood throughout the gospel. He was misunderstood by his opponents and by the people at large. Even his family misunderstood him (3:20ff). When Jesus once stopped in his hometown, his family tried to seize him because it was rumored that he was mad. His family did not understand that he was the Son of God. This theme of misunderstanding extended to his disciples. They did not understand his parables (4:13; 7:18) or his miracles (6:52; 8:17, 21), which was strange, because Mark said that the disciples received special instruction. After Jesus spoke to the people, he customarily taught his disciples.

By these passages, Mark admitted that the gospel is a mystery; it cannot be immediately understood. Mark even taught that the disciples did not understand Jesus and that they lacked faith. Thus the disciples were unable to perform miracles (9:19). They did not even understand Jesus' words about his death and resurrection, so the disciples fell away. During Jesus' passion, the disciples denied Jesus and fled.

## (3) The Teaching of Jesus

Mark often stated that Jesus was a teacher. However, in comparison with the other Gospels, Mark contains very little information about what Jesus taught. As a whole, this gospel gives the impression that Jesus was a miracle worker, not a teacher. Yet, Mark said that Jesus taught. Jesus was addressed as "teacher." Mark's version of the stilling of the storm says that Jesus' disciples addressed him as "teacher," whereas in Matthew's version Jesus was called "Lord."

When Jesus did teach, he taught by parables. According to Mark, these parables confounded people. Verses 4.10–12 illustrate Mark's handling of Jesus' parables:

> Mark 4:10–12: 10 When he was alone, those who were around him along with the twelve asked him about the parables. 11 And he said to them, "To you has been given the secret of the kingdom of God, but for those outside, everything comes in parables; 12 in order that 'they may indeed look but not perceive, and may indeed listen but not understand; so that they may not turn again and be forgiven.'"

In this parable Mark shows that it takes something special to believe: "to you has been given the secret of the kingdom . . . those outside, everything comes in parables. . . ." Yet even the disciples did not understand. What is Mark's point?

## (4) The Messianic Secret

Ever since William Wrede argued that the author of Mark's gospel added Jesus' call for secrecy regarding his special status (to explain why Jesus never announced himself as the Messiah even though his followers did), Mark's "messianic secret" has been an important concern of scholars. The messianic secret theme pervades

Mark and determines its structure. In the first part of Mark's gospel, Jesus emphatically commanded that his true identity must not be made known. This prohibition is often connected with the miracle stories. The demons, because of their supernatural power, knew who Jesus was, but Jesus silenced them. He also stated that the miracles themselves must not be made known; however, his secrecy charges were disobeyed. People did not pay heed to Jesus' prohibition, and Mark himself wrote about this. Mark began his gospel with the statement: "The beginning of the good news of Jesus Christ" (1:1). This statement shows that Mark did not write in order to announce that Jesus was the Messiah; his readers already knew it.

Where Mark did report the miracles, it is clear that Jesus' prohibition was limited to specific incidents and was not a permanent secrecy charge. This point is clearly demonstrated in 9:9, when Jesus and his most intimate disciples (Peter, James, and John) were coming down from the mountain where Jesus had been transfigured and declared to be the Son of God by a voice from heaven. Jesus charged his disciples not to tell anyone about this. This specific charge is the motif of the messianic secret. However, there is an addition: ". . . he ordered them to tell no one about what they had seen, until after the Son of Man had risen from the dead." Thus, a clear distinction exists between the times before and after the resurrection. The turning point of the gospel follows this event. Jesus began his fateful journey to Jerusalem. He started to tell his disciples about his identity and always included a prediction about his passion.

Actually, Jesus' first prediction is found right before the transfiguration story in Chapter 8, when Peter acknowledged Jesus as the Messiah.

> Mark 8:29–31: 29 He asked them, "But who do you say that I am?" Peter answered him, "You are the Messiah." 30 And he sternly ordered them not to tell anyone about him. 31 Then he began to teach them that the Son of Man must undergo great suffering, and be rejected by the elders, and the chief priests, and the scribes, and be killed, and after three days rise again. 32 And he said all this quite openly. And Peter took him aside, and began to rebuke him. 33 But turning and looking at his disciples, he rebuked Peter and said, "Get behind me, Satan! For you are setting your mind not on divine things but on human things."

Here Jesus charged his disciples not to tell anyone, and then he proceeded to speak of his suffering, death, and resurrection. Peter rebuked him for speaking of a crucified Messiah, whereupon Jesus rebuked Peter. Jesus' messiahship led to the cross. Moreover, upon Jesus' death, Mark presented the last affirmation of Jesus' divine status with the words of the centurion, "Truly this man was God's Son!" (15:39).

This affirmation shows that it is impossible to speak of the glory of Jesus without including his passion. It is the suffering and rejected Jesus who is the Son of God. The passion story is the key to the work of Jesus as a whole. This passion is the criterion by which Jesus has to be understood, and this interest best explains the secrecy motif of Mark.

Mark wanted to prevent a misunderstanding about Jesus. Mark knew about the miracle workers of his time, and he portrayed Jesus in their colors. Redaction criticism has shown that the Gospels according to Matthew and Luke are not parallel in this respect. These two Gospels did not paint a similar picture. They changed Mark; they did not want Jesus to appear to be another miracle worker. Nor did Mark, but he did adopt the form identified by form criticism as a miracle story.

Mark had another method of distinguishing Jesus from contemporary miracle workers. He underscored that Jesus told people not to tell about his miracles. How could people not tell? People do tell about miracles. Mark's admonition not to tell is clearly an editorial device. He did not want his readers to believe that it was the miracle worker who was the Son of God. In the Hellenistic world, the great miracle workers were called "divine" men. Mark did not intend to convey the impression that Jesus was regarded as divine because of his miracles. It was the suffering, rejected, and betrayed Jesus who was the miracle worker. The miracles must be understood in the light of the passion, which is the point of the messianic secret motif.

The messianic secret motif also solved the problem of why the resurrection and the post-resurrection appearances of Jesus were not related and why Mark placed all the emphasis on the passion and death of Jesus. The resurrection could be misunderstood as the central miracle of Jesus' life. If so, then Jesus' passion and death would simply be stages through which he had to pass in order to perform the greatest miracle of all. However, it is in the suffering and death of Jesus that Mark saw God's revelation in Jesus. Here Mark saw divine love fully manifested.

## (5) Suffering and Discipleship

The predictions of the passions are probably not genuine words of Jesus because they do not pass the criterion of dissimilarity. Instead they appear to be confessional statements of the Christian community that were credited to Jesus. Mark underscored the actual significance of these confessions by adding sayings about discipleship.

> Mark 8:34–37: 34 He called the crowd with his disciples, and said to them, "If any want to become my followers, let them deny themselves and take up their cross and follow me. 35 For those who want to save their life will lose it, and those who lose their life for my sake, and for the sake of gospel, will save it. 36 For what will it profit them to gain the whole world and forfeit their life? 37 Indeed, what can they give in return for their life?

> Mark 9:33–35: 33 Then came to Capernaum; and when he was in the house he asked them, "What were you arguing about on the way?" 34 But they were silent, for on the way they had argued with one another who was the greatest. 35 He sat down, called the twelve and said to them, "Whoever wants to be first must be last of all and servant of all."

> Mark 10:35–40: 35 James and John, the sons of Zebedee, came forward to him and said to him, "Teacher, we want you to do for us whatever we ask of you." 36 And he said to them, "What is it you want me to do for you?" 37 And they said to him, "Grant us to sit, one at your right hand and one at your left, in your glory." 38 But Jesus said to them, "You do not know what you are asking. Are you able to drink the cup that I drink, or be baptized with the baptism that I am baptized with?" 39 They replied, "We are able." Then Jesus said to them, "The cup that I drink you

will drink; and with the baptism with which I am baptized, you will be baptized; 40 but to sit at my right hand or at my left is not mine to grant, but it is for those for whom it has been prepared."

Thus, suffering is characteristic of the Christian community of Mark. Of course there were also healing miracles in the community of Mark, but Mark did not see decisive events for his community in the miracles of Jesus. The passion and death of Jesus, however, had great significance for Mark's community. When Mark wanted to tell his readers about what was divine, he did not cite the miracles, but discipleship. As disciples, people were informed of God's revelation; correspondingly, discipleship involved suffering.

Mark's interest in suffering and discipleship helped to explain the purpose of Chapter 13, often called the "little apocalypse," because of its eschatological contents. Mark may not have included this speech because it gave information about the last events. The scene was Jerusalem, and Mark's readers were a Greek-speaking community outside Palestine. There would be no point in telling this outside community what would happen in Judea at the end of time, but there are some general statements that apparently were of significance to Mark.

Mark 13:7–9: 7 When you hear of wars and rumors of wars, do not be alarmed; this must take place, but the end is still to come. 8 For nation will rise against nation, and kingdom against kingdom; there will be earthquakes in various places; there will be famines. This is but the beginning of the birth pangs. 9 "As for yourselves, beware: for they will hand you over to councils; and you will be beaten in synagogues; and you will stand before governors and kings because of me, as a testimony to them.

Mark 13:11–13 11 When they bring you to trial and hand you over, do not worry beforehand about what you are to say; but say whatever is given you at that time, for it is not you who speak, but the Holy Spirit. 12 Brother will betray brother to death, and a father his child, and children will rise against parents and have them put to death; 13 and you will be hated by all because of my name. But the one who endures to the end will be saved.

This description of the end of the age apparently said something to Mark's readers, who experienced exactly what is described here. It is linked to the words about discipleship. The persecution of Jesus' followers allowed believers to demonstrate their discipleship (v. 9 and 11).

It is often said that Peter's confession that Jesus was the Messiah (8:29) was a turning point in Mark's gospel; from this point on the disciples knew who Jesus was. That belief is not quite accurate although Mark has more or less unconsciously adapted Aristotle's theory of tragedy, according to which the tragedy has a middle section where the true nature of the hero is revealed and some people become his friends. Peter did not have greater insight than the demons; they too realized that Jesus was the Son of God. Peter misunderstood the nature of the divine sonship of Jesus and received Jesus' rebuke. Moreover, Mark's gospel continued to present the disciples as ignorant. What does this presentation reveal? The disciples knew, and yet they didn't. They didn't know what the divine sonship of Jesus really implied.

By this representation of the disciples, Mark was able to tell his community something very important. The disciples misunderstood Jesus' divine sonship; thus when Jesus was apprehended, they denied him and fled. The gospel ends by relating that the women did not tell anyone about the empty tomb. Then how did the Christian community come about? It did not owe its existence to faithless disciples. It originated in spite of the disciples. The Christian community, the Church, was founded on God's work.

By revealing the divine origin of the Church, Mark was also able to warn his readers: Do not be like the disciples! Follow Jesus! Accept suffering! Only by doing so will you be true disciples! It is only through suffering that it is possible to understand Jesus and thus God. Do not misunderstand what Jesus is all about.

This emphasis on suffering explains why Mark did not say much about what Jesus taught. His readers were probably informed about Jesus; there was no reason to believe that Mark told us all he knew about Jesus. He manifestly knew about the appearances of the resurrected Jesus, yet he did not narrate them for a good reason. His congregation, too, was probably familiar with them. They would also have known of Jesus' teaching. Mark said that Jesus sent out his disciples to teach (3:14; 6:7ff.). His congregation would have had some idea of what they taught, and therefore Mark did not elaborate on it. He stressed that discipleship is an imitation of Jesus' life; a teaching that is not followed up by such a discipleship is not worthy of anything, which was actually proven by Jesus' own disciples. Mark 10:44–45 epitomizes the entire gospel: "Whoever wishes to be the first among you must be slave of all. For the Son of Man came not to be served but to serve, and to give his life as a ransom for many."

## THE *SECRET GOSPEL* ## *ACCORDING TO MARK*

Some Jesus scholars, like John Dominic Crossan, have argued that the *Secret Gospel according to Mark* surpasses canonical Mark in historical significance. Evidence for a secret version of Mark's gospel was discovered by the American scholar Morton Smith in 1958. In the library of a Greek Orthodox monastery in the Judean desert southeast of Jerusalem, Smith found a copy of a letter written by Clement of Alexandria to a certain Theodore; the copy was made on the last blank pages of a book printed in 1646. Although the external evidence occurred at a very late date, experts seem to agree that this letter is a genuine copy. In this letter, Clement answered Theodore's questions about a certain Christian sect, the Carpocratians (named after their founder), who claimed to possess a *Secret Gospel according to Mark.*

Clement said that there was indeed such a gospel; it was to be used by those Christians who were perfected in the faith; the later "canonized" Gospel according to Mark was written for beginners in the faith. Clement even quoted two passages that were peculiar to the *Secret Gospel according to Mark.*

The first pericope is sandwiched between 10:34 and 35. Jesus and his disciples were on their way to Jerusalem, as told in Mark 10:32. After Jesus made a prophecy of his death and resurrection (verses 33–34), the *Secret Gospel according to Mark* continued by relating that they came to a certain town, where Jesus raised a young man from the dead. This story is similar to that of the raising of Lazarus from the dead in John 11. But the *Secret Gospel according to Mark,* according to Clement, went on to say that the youth loved Jesus and expressed a wish to remain with him. This incident does not appear in John's gospel. Jesus stayed in the young man's home for six days, after which period the *Secret Gospel according to Mark* states:

> "Jesus told him what to do, and in the evening the youth comes to him, wearing a linen cloth over his naked body. And he remained with Jesus that night, for Jesus taught him the mystery of the Kingdom of God."

This passage is intriguing. Next it is related that Jesus crossed the river of Jordan. The *Secret Gospel according to Mark* then continued with the request of John and James, as found in Mark 10:35 and the following verses.

The second fragment given by Clement is very short and was found in the middle of 10:46. After Jesus and his disciples reached Jericho on their way to Jerusalem, relatives of the young man who was raised from the dead wanted to meet Jesus, but he did not receive them.

The text of the *Secret Gospel according to Mark* used by the Carpocratians, however, contained additional material. Clement denied that this was part of the original secret gospel. He quoted one phrase, "naked man with naked man." Apparently the Carpocratians had rites of a homosexual nature and used this gospel to justify those rituals.

Morton Smith argued on the basis of the Greek text of the two fragments that the *Secret Gospel according to Mark* went back to an Aramaic source. The Carpocratian version also preserved elements from the Aramaic source. According to Smith, both canonical Mark and John used this source, canonical Mark actually being an abridgment of the *Secret Gospel according to Mark*. Smith argued that Mark 14:51–52 is one of the vestiges of the secret gospel in canonical Mark. After Jesus' arrest in the garden, it reads, "A certain young man was following him, wearing nothing but a linen cloth. They caught hold of him, but he left the linen cloth and ran off naked."

The initiation spoken about in the *Secret Gospel according to Mark* may have been some kind of baptismal ritual in which the one initiated ascended to heaven. The linen cloth may have been a symbol of the body that had to be put off, or left behind, when the soul ascended. The initiated was thus naked during the ritual. Later in Church history recipients of Christian baptism had to be naked. Smith combined this knowledge with the phrase "naked man with naked man" and suggested that the original ritual indeed had a homosexual nature. Furthermore, he argued that this ritual reflected Jesus' original teaching.

However, we cannot prove that there was an Aramaic source for the two fragments. It would seem that the *Secret Gospel according to Mark* abridged John 11 and supplemented it with many different synoptic texts. For instance, Luke 18:23 was quoted ("for he was very rich") when describing the young man. Smith maintained that this description must be ascribed to a later hand, but this statement appears arbitrary. Papyrus Egerton 2, three fragments that date to the second century CE, is also made up of different synoptic texts like the *Secret Gospel according to Mark.* In conclusion, it appears that the *Secret Gospel according to Mark* is a second-century text of secondary importance.

## SUMMARY

The Gospel according to Mark was written by an unknown follower of Jesus around 70 CE. It was read by Greek-speaking readers who were probably Gentiles not familiar with Palestine and Judaism. In all likelihood, its author used various sources to compose his account of Jesus, although none can be identified with certainty. The theme of the hiddenness and eventual revelation of Jesus' messiahship makes up the structural framework of the gospel. Whereas Mark did not explicitly identify his theological purpose, Jesus' distinctive messiahship appears to be its dominant interest. Jesus is described as a suffering, misunderstood Messiah who asked his disciples to follow his example if they truly wished to be his followers.

## KEY TERMS FOR REVIEW

| | | |
|---|---|---|
| Papias | Tragedy | Suffering |
| John Mark | Passion | Discipleship |
| Peter | Misunderstood Messiah | *Secret Gospel according to Mark* |
| 70 CE | Messianic secret | |

## QUESTIONS FOR REVIEW

1.  Why should we reconsider Papias' opinion about the identity of Mark's author?
2.  What light does Aristotle's view of tragedy shed on Mark's structure?
3.  How does Mark's abrupt ending in 16:8 bear out the gospel's message about Jesus?

## SUGGESTIONS FOR FURTHER READING

Hooker, M. *The Message of Mark.* London: Epworth, 1983.

Kingsbury, J. *The Christology of Mark's Gospel.* Philadelphia: Fortress, 1983.

Matera, F. *What Are They Saying about Mark?* New York: Paulist, 1987.

Rhoads, D. and Michie, D. *Mark as Story: An Introduction to the Narrative of a Gospel.* Philadelphia: Fortress, 1982.

Telford, W. *The Theology of the Gospel of Mark.* New York: Cambridge University Press, 1999.

# 10

✳

# The Gospel according to Matthew

## INTRODUCTORY QUESTIONS

### Authorship and Sources

Who wrote the Gospel according to Matthew? Papias of Hierapolis, who wrote during the early second century CE, said that "Matthew compiled the words (Greek: *logia*) of Jesus in the Hebrew language, and each interpreted them as he was able." Papias must have meant the Matthew found in all the lists of the Twelve Apostles of Jesus. In Matthew 10.3, Matthew is called a "tax-collector." In Mark 2:14, Jesus called a tax collector by the name of Levi, but in Matthew's parallel (9:9), the name appears as Matthew. Matthew's next chapter lists Matthew as one of the apostles (10:3). According to the tradition of the Church, Matthew was the author of the gospel, but such a statement was not made in the gospel itself.

It is unlikely that the author of Matthew was one of the apostles. Why would an apostle of Jesus base his story on that of a person who was not an apostle, namely Mark? Even after it had been established that both Matthew and Luke used Mark as a source, some conservative scholars tried to use Papias's information and argued for a Hebrew Matthew, or rather an Aramaic Matthew, as an Ur-gospel (see Figure 10.1).

But why would Mark abridge primitive Matthew? Why would he leave out the Sermon on the Mount? And why would Luke abridge the same sermon and break it up, scattering material from the Sermon on the Mount throughout his gospel? Further, if Mark were secondary, why was his structure of Jesus' life the one followed by Matthew and Luke?

The theory of an Ur-Matthew can be improved on by arguing that it was p-Matthew that really constituted a literary source. Perhaps Papias was referring

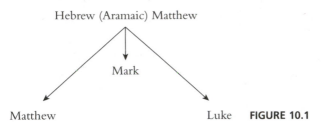

Hebrew (Aramaic) Matthew

Mark

Matthew                                         Luke     **FIGURE 10.1**

to p-Matthew? Even so, the material unique to Matthew (p-Matthew) is not found in any other gospel and shows no evidence of being shared as Papias suggested. Another difficulty with this interpretation is that the theory of a literary source requires us to isolate material making up a continuous thread. We cannot do so in this instance. Is it certain that Papias is right? He may have been misinformed, as he was in the case of Mark. Or did conservative scholars misunderstand Papias? Is it certain that *logia* refers to words spoken by Jesus, or even a gospel? The term *logia* is best translated as "oracles" (prophetic), whereas *logoi* is best translated as "words" or "sayings."

Matthew's gospel has a clear, systematic arrangement of material. His gospel is not biographical, as we might expect if it were an eyewitness report or if it were based on an eyewitness account. Even if the addition of Mark to this report confused the picture, we should be able to recover something of a biographical sketch concerning Jesus if Matthew's gospel was based on an eyewitness account, but we cannot. Would an apostle of Jesus, when putting together his gospel, rely on the structure of a gospel written by a person who was not an eyewitness (Mark)? That is doubtful. In addition, source criticism has identified Q as Matthew's second source.

It is not certain that Papias understood *logia* as denoting the "words" of Jesus. The word *logia* was most frequently used to identify passages from the Old Testament. Perhaps Papias meant that Matthew, an apostle, compiled a collection of Old Testament passages dealing with the Messiah and that various Christians used this collection to prove to the Jews that Jesus was the Messiah. Such collections of so-called messianic proof-texts, called "testimonia," exist from a later time, and scholars can make a case for the incorporation of such a source in Matthew.

## Date

Because Mark preceded Matthew, it follows that the Gospel according to Matthew was written later than 70 CE. Matthew's parable of the wedding feast climaxed with the burning of the city inhabited by those who refused the king's invitation (22:7). Many scholars have understood the conflagration as an allusion to the destruction of Jerusalem by the Romans in 70 CE. Because Ignatius of Antioch cited Matthew, it could have been written no later than 110 CE. Thus, this gospel is datable to the last decades of the first century. Matthew also appears to have written at a time when Christians were cast out of the **synagogues.** This expulsion may have taken place at different times in different places.

## Language

Matthew's style is more elegant than Mark's and includes more Jewish terminology. Instead of the phrase, "the Kingdom of God," Matthew substituted the phrase "the Kingdom of Heaven." The use of "Heaven" as a substitute for "God" is called a circumlocution. Many Jews used circumlocutions (that is, Power, Glory) for the divine name in an effort to avoid violating the commandment to "not make wrongful use of the name of the LORD your God" (Exod. 20:7). In English, such forms are called minced oaths (that is, "my goodness!" for "my God!").

## Audience

For whom was the Gospel according to Matthew written? Matthew seems to be at home in a Greek-speaking environment, even more so than Mark, whose language Matthew has improved upon. Matthew even has word plays that show a certain sophistication. Yet, it seems that his audience was comprised of Jews, thus it must have been the Jews of the dispersion who lived outside of Palestine and spoke Greek. For centuries Jews had lived outside of Palestine, either voluntarily (economic migration) or involuntarily (forcible exile). This phenomenon is named the **Diaspora,** after the Greek word for dispersion used in the Greek version of the Hebrew Bible known as the Septuagint. The theological characteristics of Matthew's gospel further bear out Matthew's Jewish orientation.

## Structure

The structure of Matthew is often said to be determined by major discourses: (1) Sermon on the Mount (5–7); (2) the apostolic commission (10); (3) parables (13); (4) church or community order (18); (5) criticism of the Pharisees (23); and (6) the end of the age (24–25). Except for the speech about the criticism of the Pharisees, all these speeches end with a similar phrase: "Now when Jesus had finished saying these things" (7:28). Because such an expression is found five times, some scholars have argued that Matthew arranged his gospel into five parts, each part beginning with narrative material and ending with a discourse by Jesus. In this manner, Matthew wanted to intimate symbolically that his gospel was to take the place of the five books of the **Torah,** the law. Thus, Jesus was presented as the new Moses who surpassed the original Moses with his assertions, "But I say to you . . ." (Sermon on the Mount, 5:22ff.).

However, this approach overlooks Jesus' criticism of the Pharisees in Chapter 23; there are six major discourses, not five. But if Jesus' criticism of the Pharisees and his discourse on the end of the age are grouped under the subject of judgment, then Matthew's gospel can be said to have five parts. There cannot be much doubt that Matthew tried to present Jesus as a new Moses, and a fivefold, torahlike collection of speeches with accompanying narratives supports this view.

Beyond these major discourses, it is difficult to detect an overall structure in Matthew. Mark is much better in that respect. We can divide Matthew into seven sections, which in turn can be divided into three parts: introduction, body, and epilogue.

Matthew's introduction consists of: (1) nativity legends (1–2) that are based on p-Matthew; (2) Baptist material drawn from Mark, Q, and p-Matthew (3); and (3) temptation material drawn from Q (4:1–11). Jesus' identity is laid down in the nativity legends. Jesus was not only the Son of God by adoption at baptism as in Mark but also God's divine son from birth. Matthew also gives his human lineage. Jesus was descended from David and from the patriarchs. The baptism of Jesus by John informs readers that Jesus was recognized as God's son—both by God and by men (John). John was presented as Jesus' forerunner who proclaimed the same message as Jesus (3:2 and 4:17). The temptation story confirms that Jesus was what the two preceding sections said: the Son of God.

Matthew's last four sections make up parts 2 and 3. Section 4, Jesus in Galilee (4:12–13:58); section 5, Jesus' travels in Galilee and Judea (14–20); and section 6, Jesus in Jerusalem (21–27), make up the body of his gospel. Section 7, Jesus' resurrection and appearance in Galilee (28) (which does not appear in Mark), serves as Matthew's epilogue. This last section describes how Jesus' resurrection overcame the efforts of the chief priests and Pharisees to guard his body (27:66; compare with 28:2–4), even though the priests and elders still spread the rumor of a stolen body (28:12–15). When Jesus did appear to his disciples, it was as the all-powerful Son of God (28:18)

## THE THEOLOGY OF MATTHEW

### (1) Discourses

The words of Jesus are gathered in major discourses, and several smaller discourse units also exist, which shows that Matthew endeavored to present Jesus as a teacher.

The way in which Matthew told the miracle stories created the same impression—that Jesus was a teacher—which we can easily see when we compare Matthew with Mark. The story about the healing of the epileptic boy highlights this theme (17:14–21). Matthew minimized the details and did not relate the symptoms of the child. Instead he added a saying on faith. According to Mark, Jesus said, "This kind can come out only through prayer" (Mark 9:29). (Jesus himself, though, did not use prayer but simply commanded the demon to leave the boy.) In Matthew, however, Jesus answered the disciples by saying that they did not have enough faith: "For truly I tell you, if you have faith the size of a mustard seed, you will say to this mountain, 'Move from here to there,' and it will move, and nothing will be impossible for you" (Matt. 17:20). Redaction critics ask why Jesus' saying, and not Jesus' miracle, is the important element in Matthew's version. The answer is that Matthew wanted to present Jesus as a teacher.

We can also see that Matthew put a higher priority on the *words* of Jesus than on the *works* of Jesus from the fact that Matthew, in the order of presentation of his material, placed the miracles of Jesus after Jesus' teachings. In Chapters 5 through 7, he collected the teachings of Jesus in the Sermon on the Mount. He followed the teachings with a collection of Jesus' miracles in Chapters 8 and 9. How is Mark ordered? The miracles appear immediately in Chapters 1 and 2. Some teaching appears in the latter part of Chapter 2, but miracles once again appear in Chapter 3. Only in Mark's Chapters 4 and 13 do we find extensive collections of Jesus' teachings.

Matthew was not the first to gather the teachings of Jesus in discourses. Mark revealed a similar tendency. However, Matthew advanced beyond both Mark and Luke. He must have had a definite reason for doing so. The reason may be illustrated by comparing the Sermon on the Mount in Matthew 5–7 with the Sermon on the Plain in Luke 6. Matthew's version is much longer than Luke's. Matthew lengthened his sermon by gathering Q material in these three chapters, which we can see by noting that many of the words found in Matthew 5–7 are also found in different places in Luke's gospel. In Matthew, Jesus was a teacher, even a scribe of the Torah.

## (2) Formula Quotations

Matthew has many formula quotations—citations of Scripture in the light of which we can interpret Jesus life and ministry. Matthew phrased such citations characteristically as, "All this took place to fulfill what had been spoken by the Lord through the prophet . . ." (1:22).

Quotations and allusions to the Jewish Bible are present in all the Gospels. These allusions are only natural because the Jewish Bible was also the Bible of the first Christians, renamed the Old Testament by later Christians. The religious language of the first Christians was based on the Bible. Often the use of the Bible was not conscious, and the biblical basis may have been forgotten, which we can see in Matthew's passion narrative. Here we find many biblical quotations and allusions to the text of the Jewish Bible—for example, Psalms 22 and 69. This use of the Jewish Bible informs readers about what went on before the passion narratives appeared in the New Testament. The first Christians had no fixed passion narrative. They knew Jesus had suffered and died, but how could they tell the story? They found the passion of Jesus alluded to in the Jewish Bible. Jewish Scriptures were used to describe Jesus' passion as a fulfillment of prophecy.

The Christian community reflected on Jesus' passion and wove the biblical material into the narrative of Jesus' life, so that what were originally seen as elucidations of Jesus' destiny were now regarded as historical events and fulfillments of prophecy. Psalm 69 has a description of a man who suffered at the hands of his enemies. The first Christians saw this as an allusion to the sufferings of Jesus. Verse 21 says that the sufferer was given poison for food and vinegar to drink. In the Gospels this story is regarded as an historical event in the passion of Jesus, but here we no longer see a conscious use of Psalm 69:21. The Scripture has been forgotten. Jesus uttered some words that were taken by the bystanders to be a cry to Elijah for help. (Elijah the prophet had been taken up to heaven alive.) Mark's gospel says: "And someone ran, filled a sponge with sour wine, put it on a stick, and gave it to him to drink, saying, "Wait, let us see whether Elijah will come to take him down" (Mark 15:36). No reminiscence of Psalm 69:21 appears here. In the psalm, the purpose of offering vinegar was totally different; it was an act of cruelty. In the Gospels, it was an act meant to prolong the life of the sufferer so that he might be saved by Elijah.

It is noteworthy that Matthew's gospel does not say that this happened to fulfill Scripture. If it was possible for Matthew to cite a scriptural "proof," he did not pass up a chance to do so. Jesus did not have to say or do much without Matthew stating that it was a fulfillment of Scripture.

These prophecies of the formula quotations may in fact be the *logia* of Hebrew Matthew about which Papias spoke. This view may be argued from the fact that the wording seems to be based on the Hebrew text, not on the Greek translation of the Old Testament. In addition, Papias' term, *logia,* was not normally used with reference to the sayings of Jesus (for which *logoi* was used) but instead used of passages from the Bible. Perhaps Papias meant that Matthew (or some other person) compiled a collection of Old Testament texts purporting to prove that Jesus was the Messiah.

In any event, Matthew's gospel thus shows a conscious, deliberate use of the Bible. Jesus fulfills Scripture.

### (3) The Law (Torah)

Matthew was very concerned with the law. As opposed to Mark, Matthew returned time and again to questions concerning the law. How often he referred to the law is not as important as the contexts in which he did so. Matthew 5:17–20 from the Sermon on the Mount is a very important passage:

> Matt. 5:17–20: 17 "Do not think that I have come to abolish the law or the prophets; I have come not to abolish but to fulfill. 18 For truly I tell you, until heaven and earth pass away, not one letter, not one stroke of a letter, will pass from the law until all is accomplished. 19 Therefore, whoever breaks one of the least of these commandments, and teaches others to do the same, will be called least in the kingdom of heaven; but whoever does them and teaches them will be called great in the kingdom of heaven. 20 For I tell you, unless your righteousness exceeds that of the scribes and Pharisees, you will never enter the kingdom of heaven."

Jesus is presented as one who had come to fulfill the law, God's will. In fact, the new and greater righteousness that he expounded was seen as fulfillment of the law. Matthew was the only one of the evangelists who talked about "righteousness"—a term denoting God's will and the Christian way of life—"unless your righteousness exceeds that of the scribes and Pharisees, you will never enter the kingdom of heaven" (5:20). All Jesus' teachings in 5:21–48, the core of the Sermon on the Mount, express the righteousness that God wants practiced in the lives of his people. In essence, Jesus told his followers how to "fulfill" the law and acquire the righteousness needed for God's kingdom.

Matthew even provided two summaries. Matthew 7:12 contains a summary known as the Golden Rule: "In everything do to others as you would have them do to you; for this is the law and the prophets." In 22:34–40, Jesus formulated the essence of the law in the commandment to love God and one's neighbor. The commandment to love is a summary of God's righteousness.

### (4) Polemic

Matthew's gospel contains polemic with a clear audience. All the Gospels have discussions between Jesus and the Jewish religious authorities. The discussions are not necessarily found in a polemical situation; they are sometimes used by the evangelists as warnings and admonitions to the Christians. Perhaps the evangelists adapted the discussions between Jesus and the Jewish religious authorities and turned polemics into warnings and admonitions to the Christian community. However, Matthew seems to have preserved a specific polemic against the Jewish religious authorities and even to have enhanced it.

In the Sermon on the Mount, this kind of polemic can be identified in the so-called antitheses, "You have heard that it was said, . . . but I say to you . . ." (5:21–48). These words are polemical because Jesus set up his authority against that of the scribes of the Pharisees. Only in Matthew did Jesus condemn the Pharisees with a series of prophetic "woes" (23:13–36). Luke, in his version of the sermon, also contains some of these woes, but in his gospel they are not polemical; they are not antitheses; they do not even specifically address the Jews. Matthew says, "You have heard that it was said, 'An eye for an eye and a tooth for a tooth.' But I say to you . . ." (5:38–39). Now consider Luke's version: "But I say to you that listen, Love your enemies, do good to those who hate you, bless those who curse you, pray for those who abuse you. If anyone strikes you on the cheek, offer the other also . . ." (6:27–29). No polemic exists against the Jewish authorities here. The words are not introduced by a thesis "You have heard that it was said," to which the evangelist conjoins an antithesis "But I say to you. . . ."

The resurrection narrative at the end of Matthew, which also functions in an apologetic fashion to discredit a false rumor about Jesus' body being stolen, contains a very important polemic against the chief priests and elders. In the first place, Matthew related that they devised a lie about the body of Jesus being stolen and removed from the tomb, a story that was current among Jews when Matthew's gospel was written (28:11–15). The Jews might very well have heard this explanation, but the fact that Matthew used this anti-gospel in his work tells us something about him. He did not have to, but he chose to include an account that was critical of Jewish religious authorities.

Matthew even prepared his readers for its inclusion. At the end of Chapter 27, he related that the chief priests and the Pharisees asked Pilate to place a guard at the tomb so the disciples could not steal Jesus' body, because Jesus had said that he would rise from the dead. Of course this story is probably not historical. None of the other evangelists related anything like this, nor were any of Jesus' followers among the chief priests and Pharisees. Matthew appears to have fabricated a story, or used a fabricated story, to introduce the Jewish anti-gospel.[1] Why did he do that?

---

[1]Arguments defending the historicity of Matthew's Jewish anti-gospel cannot be correct. (1) The chief priests and the Pharisees worked together on the Sabbath; they went to Pilate; they went to the tomb and placed the guard there. These actions are totally out of keeping with Jewish Sabbath practices. (2) The chief priests and the Pharisees remembered that Jesus had said that he would rise. This remembrance is utterly strange because Jesus' disciples did not remember this. They fled. They did not gather around the tomb. (3) The Roman guard at the tomb went back to Jerusalem and told the Jewish authorities what had taken place: an earthquake, an angel descending, the rolling away of the stone, and the resurrection. Why did the guard not go to his commander, Pilate? Matthew says that the soldiers were bribed by the Jews. Matthew even says that they kept their mouths shut. How could Matthew know what was said among the soldiers and the high priests? (4) Finally, the soldiers said that Jesus' disciples stole Jesus' body while they were asleep. Well, how would they know what went on while they were sleeping?

We can also find a polemic against the Jewish religious authorities in the passion narrative in Matthew. In the story about the Last Supper, Jesus called the cup of wine "my blood of the covenant" (26:28). His blood is to be poured out for the forgiveness of sins. The blood of Jesus stands for his death. In the story about the trial before Pilate, the chief priests and elders hand Jesus over to the governor because they are jealous of him (27:18). Later, before the crowd demanded Jesus' death and said, "His blood be on us and on our children" (27:25), Matthew noted that the chief priest and elders manipulated the crowd into demanding Jesus' death (27:20). Thus, according to Matthew, the Jewish religious authorities were culpable in orchestrating the death of Jesus. Matthew thus portrayed Jesus in conflict with Israel's religious authorities, namely the Pharisees, and the chief priests and elders, who were sometimes blended together (27:62).

In Matthew 8:12 we find a warning, if not a word of judgment, against Israel. In Chapter 8, Jesus said that Gentiles from the east and west would come and sit together at the table with the patriarchs in the coming kingdom, whereas the "heirs of the Kingdom will be thrown into the outer darkness" (8:12). The "heirs of the Kingdom" were of course the Jews. Neither Mark nor Luke said anything like this. Why did Matthew say it?

## (5) The Messiah and the People of God (the Church)

Matthew made negative comments about Israel's religious authorities, yet Jesus' ministry was directed only to Israel (10:5–6). The disciples were sent out with the command not to address Samaritans or Gentiles. Jesus was sent only to the "lost sheep of the house of Israel" (15:24).

How should we understand this seeming ambivalence? The clue appears in the ending of Matthew. Chapter 28:16–20 holds the conclusion to the story that Matthew told. The result of Jesus' life, passion, death, and resurrection was, first of all, that God had installed Jesus as the ruler of the world: "And Jesus came and said to them, 'All authority in heaven and on earth has been given to me'" (v. 18). The Messiah and Son of God about whom Matthew wrote was the king of the universe.

Furthermore, the result of Jesus' ministry, death, and resurrection was that the disciples proclaimed Jesus. The saying continues: "Go therefore and make disciples of all nations, baptizing them in the name of the Father and of the Son and of the Holy Spirit" (verse 19). Here are Matthew's Christology, his teaching about the person of Jesus, and **Ecclesiology,** his teaching about the Church (Greek: *ecclesia*).

The phrase "all nations" is important. The term was well-known in Jewish and early Christian literature. It designated the gentile world as distinct from Israel. The world was made up of Israel and the gentile nations. The result of the story and the significance of Jesus was that a Church came into existence—and this Church was drawn from *all* the gentile nations. The final commandment to the disciples was not to proclaim Jesus to all the nations and Israel. Israel, which played an important role throughout the gospel, is no longer exclusive. Matthew foresaw a Church in which Israel had no place. An all-powerful Jesus was now building a Church from all the nations.

What about Jesus' message to the disciples that they should address only Jews (10:6)? Something happened between the time those words were spoken and the commission described at the end of the gospel. Only the latter commission had continuing validity for Matthew's situation. What was that situation? Matthew's polemic against the Jewish religious authorities is integral in understanding Matthew's setting. This polemic is not just an echo of what once happened, of what went on when Jesus was on earth. This polemic appears in 28:15, which describes the conspiracy to disrupt the resurrection: "So they took the money and did as they were directed. And this story is still told among the Jews to this day." The phrase "to this day" relates to Matthew's day, to the time of Matthew and his community. Matthew and his community were in strife with the synagogue and non-Christian Judaism. The question was not primarily whether or not Jesus rose. The questions were: Where were the people of God? Who were the people of God? Was it the synagogue, Israel, or this assembly of people consisting "of all nations"? Matthew obviously opted for "all nations." What about Israel then? Were Israelites still God's people?

If the Church asserted that it was comprised of God's people, this assertion has to be demonstrated on the basis of Scripture. Now the purpose of the formula quotations becomes clear. Matthew did not want to show that the "Bible was or is right." That was self-evident to him. Matthew wanted to show that the Church that grew out of all the nations was comprised of the people of God spoken about in the Bible. And that meant the people that *God* spoke about. God spoke about the Christian Church in the Bible.

This view is demonstrated through the fulfillment of Scripture. Matthew asserted that what Scripture said about the people of God was now being fulfilled. It had to be shown that Jesus was the Messiah, the Messiah about whom Scripture had spoken. This point was absolutely crucial for Matthew. If Jesus was not the Messiah spoken about in the Bible, the Church was not comprised of the people of God. Jesus' birth, works, words, miracles, passion, death, and resurrection all proved that the end of the times about which the Scripture spoke had come about.

This view also meant that we can now fully understand Scripture for the first time. Now the promises and prophecies are fulfilled. The origin of a Church of all the nations was a fulfillment of Scripture, of God's will.

As a result, the synagogue, the nonbelieving Jewish community headed by its religious authorities, was not in accord with Scripture. This fact is quite clear when we understand the concept of the law in Matthew. The people of God and the law of God belong together. Where the law is observed, there God's people are found, which we can see at the end of the Sermon on the Mount. It is of no use to have the right belief and confess Jesus as Lord. It is of no use to drive out evil spirits. It is of no use to prophesy. The law has to be fulfilled (7:21). The people of God have to bear fruit. Matthew's gospel presents Jesus as the interpreter and fulfillment of the law. Furthermore, in Matthew Jesus opposed another interpretation of the law, "You have heard said . . . ," because Jesus continued, "But I say unto you," it is clear that the former interpretation is wrong. Thus, the representatives of the Jews do not know how to expound the law, and as a result, the Jews do not fulfill God's will. Now it is clear why the concept of the law is so important in Matthew.

Matthew's version of the parable of the wicked husbandmen concludes with a Jesus saying that is not found in Mark or Luke: "Therefore I tell you, the kingdom of God will be taken away from you and given to a people that produce the fruits of the kingdom" (21:43). According to Matthew, the Israelites, as led by their religious authorities—the chief priests and the Pharisees (21:45)—were taught and knew what God required of them but came up short. This view was made clear in the Sermon on the Mount and in the summary of the law (7:12; 22:34–40). God's people properly observed God's law, and those who did not were not God's people. Consequently Matthew emphasized that Jesus was a teacher. Matthew identified two kinds of teachers: the Pharisees and Jesus. The Pharisees were "blind guides" whose instruction led people only to hell (23:15, 24). To Matthew it was important to show what Jesus taught, in contrast to Mark who was not interested in sectarian Jewish interests. What Jesus taught was the final word about God's will. Therefore, it was important that his disciples were bidden to go out in the world to teach all nations to do what Jesus commanded.

We can also see the importance of Jesus' teaching in the way that Matthew represented the miracles. They were in fulfillment of Scripture (8:16–17; 12:17ff.). They were acts of mercy and mercy expressed God's demands according to Hosea the prophet: "I desire mercy, not sacrifice." This Scripture is quoted in Matthew 9:13 as the conclusion of the story about Jesus' association with tax collectors and sinners. Thus, when Jesus healed people, when he associated with tax collectors and sinners, he fulfilled God's will. When the Pharisees criticized him, they opposed God's will.

Throughout Matthew, the Church is presented as taking the place of Israel (16:17–20). Israel's history has come to an end. In the story about the healing of the servant of the Roman officer, it was said that "many will come from east and west and will eat with Abraham and Isaac and Jacob in the kingdom of heaven, while the heirs of the kingdom will be thrown into the outer darkness . . ." (8:11–12). In the parable of the vineyard, the same idea is present: "Therefore I tell you, the kingdom of God will be taken away from you and given to a people that produces the fruits of the kingdom" (21:43). The last expression of this teaching appears at the end of the gospel where "all nations" take the place of Israel (28:19). The last thing said about Israel appears in 28:15—that Israel subsisted on a lie, on the anti-gospel spread by the priests and elders: "His disciples came by night and stole him away while we were asleep (28:13)." The words "to this day" (28:15) give notice that in Matthew's day Israel still believed this report.

The message that the people of God were manipulated by their leaders into demanding the killing of God's Son is tragic. Barabbas went free; Jesus was executed. Thereby Israel rejected Scripture, even God himself. Thus, the Israelites could no longer be God's people. A new people out of all nations appeared in their stead.

If the people who were once the people of God were rejected, what about the new people of God? Were they guaranteed to remain the people of God? When Matthew described how the previous people failed, he also warned the Church that history can repeat itself. Warnings and admonitions were joined to Jesus' teachings and his discussions with the Jewish religious authorities. Of course, Matthew did not warn and admonish those to whom he did not write or those about whom he wrote—that is, the rejected people of God. His audience was clearly the Church. Matthew used the parable about the weeds in the field (13:24–30) to explain what was going to happen to the Church at the end of time (verses 36–43). At the end of the age the Church, the righteous would be rewarded, whereas the evildoers, the unrighteous, would be punished. The story about Peter's denial showed what could happen to people confessing Jesus. Matthew's admonitions were determined by his main concern—how the new people of God were created and how they lived and must live in order not to be rejected.

## SUMMARY

The Gospel according to Matthew was written by an unknown follower of Jesus sometime after the Gospel according to Mark (70 CE). Its language suggests a Greek-speaking Jewish readership living outside of Palestine. Matthew's structure is more complicated than Mark's. He presented Jesus' words in the format of major speeches, and he gave more descriptions of Jesus' life. In this way, Matthew's sources greatly lengthened his gospel in comparison with Mark's. Theologically, Matthew presented Jesus as a teacher of the law who established the Church, which consisted of Jesus' followers who were drawn from among the nations, as a successor to Israel. Jesus was righteous in doing so because he fulfilled God's law and thus carried out God's will.

## KEY TERMS FOR REVIEW

| | |
|---|---|
| *logia/logoi* | Torah |
| Kingdom of Heaven | Formula quotations |
| Diaspora | Polemic |
| Discourses | Ecclesiology |

## QUESTIONS FOR REVIEW

1. Why have Papias' comments about Matthew confused scholars about Matthew's authorship?
2. How does Matthew's structure differ from Mark's?
3. How does Matthew's polemic help explain his Ecclesiology?

## SUGGESTIONS FOR FURTHER READING

Edwards, R. *Matthew's Story of Jesus.* Philadelphia: Fortress, 1985.

Luz, U. *The Theology of the Gospel of Matthew.* New York: Cambridge University Press, 1995.

Overman, J. *Matthew's Gospel and Formative Judaism: The Social World of the Matthean Community.* Minneapolis: Fortress, 1991.

Senior, D. *What Are They Saying About Matthew?* New York: Paulist, 1983.

# 11

✳

# The Gospel
# according to Luke

## INTRODUCTORY QUESTIONS

### Authorship

According to tradition, the author of the Gospel according to Luke was a physician who was one of Paul's associates. Around 180 CE, Irenaeus, the bishop of Lyon in southern France, said that the author of Luke's gospel was a companion of Paul who followed the latter on his missionary travels. Irenaeus pointed to New Testament evidence. He identified the "we" passages in the Acts of the Apostles as ones written by the same person who wrote the Gospel according to Luke. The writer abruptly changed from the third person, "he," to the first person, "we," in describing certain episodes. At the beginning of Chapter 20, the author, "Luke," related that Paul came to Macedonia and then went to Greece, staying there for three months. Verse 20:6 relates that Paul decided to return to Macedonia, and the text says, "*we* sailed from Philippi [a city in Greece]."

Irenaeus also appealed to Paul's letters. At the end of the letter to Philemon, Paul mentioned a certain Luke among his fellow workers. At the end of the letter to the Colossians, the author spoke of "Luke, the beloved physician" (4:14; see also 2 Tim. 4:11). However, it is difficult to believe that this person was the author of the Gospel according to Luke. The author of the Acts of the Apostles did not explicitly associate himself with Paul. Moreover, we find no significant Pauline influence on Luke's theology, which is what we would expect if Luke accompanied Paul. Finally, the author did not refer to or quote Paul's letters. In addition, scholars also doubt Paul's authorship of 2 Timothy and Colossians, which also weakens Irenaeus's argument because he built his case on the assumption that Paul wrote them.

## Date

The author of Luke's gospel knew and used Mark; thus he wrote after 70 CE. He also expanded the "little apocalypse" of Mark 13. Whereas Mark did not mention Jerusalem explicitly, Luke said: "Jerusalem will be tramped on by the Gentiles" (21:24). He apparently knew about the catastrophe of Jerusalem's destruction by the Romans. Mark spoke about the "desolating sacrilege," and this story was repeated by Matthew (Mark 13:14; Matt. 24:15). Luke dropped this reference and instead described the siege of Jerusalem as a "desolation" (21:20).

The author appeared to reckon with the possibility that it might be some time before the end of the age arrived. Of the synoptics, only Luke prefaced the parable of the pounds by saying that Jesus told this parable "because they [his disciples] supposed that the kingdom of God was to appear immediately" (19:11), which indicates that he wrote at a later date when the enthusiastic expectation of the end had cooled down. Luke is usually placed a little later than Matthew is (85 CE).

No one knows where Luke wrote. He was not familiar with Palestine and thus did not live there. In Acts, however, we find a "we" passage that may suggest the author had been to Jerusalem (21:17).

## Language

Luke's vocabulary is richer than that of both Mark and Matthew. He used 261 words not found elsewhere in the New Testament. Luke was also the best stylist of the three. Luke's prologue, the first four verses of his gospel, shows the sophisticated style that accords with formal Greek documents. Here he stated his purpose in writing, "so that you may know the truth concerning the things about which you have been instructed" (1:4) and thus demonstrated his Hellenistic literary style.

## Sources

The problem of Luke's sources is complicated. He used Mark—or rather Ur-Mark and Q—as did Matthew, and his own special source—p-Luke. If we remove the Markan material from Luke, what remains consists of Q and p-Luke. It is intriguing that this material is mixed together, whereas neither Q nor p-Luke is mixed together with Mark. On this basis, some scholars have argued for the existence of a proto-Lukan gospel that consisted of Q and p-Luke mixed together. At a later date Ur-Mark may have been added but not mixed together with Q and p-Luke. Thus, the source may have been as shown in Figure 11.1.

However, Q and p-Luke do not amount to a gospel. These sources do not have a passion narrative. Some p-Luke passion material exists, but we find no passion material from Q, and what p-Luke has (mostly appearances) is not sufficient for a complete passion account. Moreover, the structure of Luke, as well as that of Matthew, is clearly based on Mark.

Yet, some of the p-Luke material, as well as the Q material, may very well have existed in already collected blocks. Luke is the only gospel that contains so-called example stories, such as the story of the good Samaritan (Chapter 10), the story of the rich man and Lazarus (Chapter 16), and the Pharisee and the tax collector (Chapter 18). These stories give varying examples of neighborliness (good, bad, and indifferent). They may originally have existed together, orally or in written form.

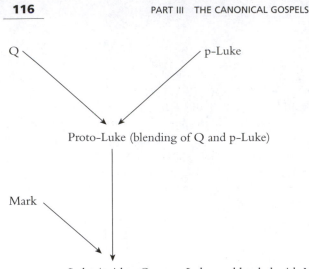

Luke (neither Q nor p–Luke are blended with Mark)     **FIGURE 11.1**

Chapters 1 and 2, or at least parts of them, may also have existed in written form. Their allusions to the Old Testament give them a more characteristically Semitic flavor than the rest of the gospel, and they may have been added later. We find no references to Jesus' birth and childhood in the accounts of Jesus' life given in Acts, and this lack may signal that the birth and childhood stories in Chapters 1 and 2 do not belong to the gospel proper. The material on John the Baptist in Chapter 1 was probably adapted from circles that venerated John as a deliverer figure.

## Structure

Apart from Chapters 1 and 2 where the births and infancies of John and Jesus are narrated as a preface to Jesus' baptism and transfiguration (3:1–4:13), it is clear that Luke turned Mark's basic two-part structure into three parts: (1) journeys in Galilee, 4:14–9:50; (2) a long journey to Jerusalem 9:51–19:27 (Mark has only one chapter on the journey, this being a transition between his two parts: Galilee and Jerusalem); and (3) Jesus in Jerusalem, 19:28–24:53. This final section narrates more extensive resurrection appearances by Jesus in Judea than the other synoptics do. The significance of this structure becomes apparent when Luke's theological interests come into view.

## THE THEOLOGY OF LUKE

### (1) Historical Perspective

The Gospel according to Luke is the first part of one work, Luke-Acts (the order should be Mark, Matthew, Luke-Acts, John). In Acts, Luke continued the story of the evangelists; he was in a way the first historian of the Church. He told his readers about the first community in Jerusalem and the first mission as well as the Jesus story. His readers obviously received a different picture than the readers of Mark and Matthew. Luke and Acts should be read together.

Mark and even Matthew give the impression that the end of the age is near. Soon Jesus will come back to judge the evil. In the versions of the "little apocalypse" in Mark and Matthew, Jesus' return is closely associated with the fall of Jerusalem. Luke, however, inserted a verse. After the fall of the city, Luke said, Jerusalem will be taken over by the Gentiles "until the times of the Gentiles are fulfilled" (21:24). Thus, God stood behind everything that happened. "Until the times that . . ." suggests a longer time span. Luke wrote his work to tell about God's plan, the divine purpose being worked out in history.

The introduction to Luke's gospel is very important (1:1–4). Luke knew that others had written Gospels; still, he felt compelled to write because he wanted to set the record straight. He was not satisfied with his predecessors (Mark was one of them). What about the other Gospels that Luke alluded to with his words, "Since many have undertaken to set down an orderly account . . ." (1:1)? They probably included some Jewish-Christian Gospels. Luke said that he gave the true picture (1:4). Thus, many "accounts" were around at this time. However, these accounts were inadequate for Luke's community, so he had to write.

Luke therefore took great care to place events in an historical setting. Immediately after his introduction, he placed the birth of John the Baptist in a historical context: "In the days of King Herod of Judea, there was a priest named Zechariah" (1:5). And in 3:1, he was very careful to indicate the precise time when John started his work: "In the fifteenth year of the reign of Emperor Tiberius, when Pontius Pilate was governor of Judea, and Herod was ruler of Galilee, and his brother Philip ruler of the region of Ituraea and Trachonitis, and Lysanias ruler of Abilene." Before this Luke linked the birth of Jesus to the historical reign of Caesar Augustus, in particular the decree "that all the world should be registered," and "this was the first registration and was taken while Quirinius was governor of Syria" (2:1–2).

In Acts, Luke mentioned the emperor Claudius. In fact, Luke was the only evangelist to mention the names of the emperors. He can be shown to be mistaken about some of his historical information, but we cannot doubt the fact that he placed weight upon historical material. Why was this important to him?

## (2) Luke's Language

As we already mentioned, Luke wrote good Greek. But what kind of Greek? It was neither classical nor vernacular. He imitated the Greek of the Septuagint, something that other first-century writers also did. Thus, Luke's Greek was saturated with Semitic words and phrases that recalled the Bible of Greek-speaking Jews. What made Luke emulate Biblical Greek?

## (3) Jewish Orientation

Luke was very interested in the Jewish people. So was Matthew, but Luke's interest was different. In Acts, he presented the primitive Jesus community in Jerusalem as a group of law-abiding Jews. This may have been historically correct,[1] but it is easy to see that Luke made a point of it. In Acts, God overruled

---

[1]Some scholars are unsure of Acts' reliability in this instance. According to Josephus, James, the brother of Jesus, as the leader of the Jerusalem Church, was accused of violating the law and condemned to be stoned (*Ant.* 20:200). Whether a person was observant of the law in first-century Jerusalem may have been open to dispute, depending on the Jewish parties involved.

Peter's hesitancy about admitting Gentiles into the Church (Chapter 10). Acts also has summaries of Israel's history (7:13ff.).

Luke underlined the view that Jesus did not work outside the borders of Israel. Luke's emphasis on Jesus in Israel is further demonstrated by his positioning Jesus and his mission in Jerusalem. He began with the announcement of John the Baptist's birth in Jerusalem (1:5–25) and concluded his gospel with Jesus' followers worshipping in Jerusalem's temple (24:52–53). In between, Luke fit Q material to his interest in Jerusalem; he identified Satan's call for Jesus to throw himself off the temple of Jerusalem as Satan's third and final temptation, whereas in Matthew, this temptation was Satan's second (Luke 4:9–12; compare with Matt. 4:8–11).

We find one exception to Luke's focus on Jerusalem and Israel. In 8:26–39 Jesus traveled to the country of the Gerasenes east of Galilee in northern Israel, but Luke dropped Mark's story of Jesus' journeys into gentile territory. Luke omitted the whole of Mark 6:45–8:26, probably because here Jesus crossed the Sea of Galilee, landing in gentile country on the eastern shore. Later Jesus moved north to Tyre and Sidon on the Phoenician coast, and then back south to the Decapolis territory and into Galilee again. Tyre and Sidon were gentile towns; Decapolis was gentile territory. Luke developed Mark's narrative again at the point where Peter confessed Jesus as the Messiah (Mark 8:27ff.). Mark said that this happened on the way to Caesarea Philippi, and again it is significant that Luke dropped the geographical information about where this happened because Caesarea Philippi was a gentile city.

Furthermore, Luke emphasized that Jesus, when working within the borders of the Jewish nation, did not associate with Gentiles. (We must remember that the Romans ruled Palestine and that gentile peoples were living in the territory). Both Matthew and Luke transmitted a Q story about Jesus healing the servant of a Roman officer at Capernaum. In Matthew the centurion approached Jesus and besought him (8:5ff.). In Luke, however, the centurion sent "elders of the Jews" to Jesus, asking him to come to heal the servant (7:1ff.). When Jesus went with them and approached the house of the Roman officer, the officer sent certain "friends" to Jesus. In Luke's version, Jesus never met the centurion himself. How did the original Q story run? If Luke's version is closest to the original, it is hard to find a reason for Matthew's change. However, if we regard Matthew as original, it is easy to find a motive for Luke's change; he didn't want to represent Jesus as associating with Gentiles. Therefore, it is more plausible, given Luke's pattern of omitting gentile references, that Luke changed the original rather than Matthew.

In this connection, we should also note that Luke underlined the view that Jesus worked publicly. Masses of people were present all the time. In Chapter 5, Luke said: "One day, while he was teaching, Pharisees and teachers of the Law were sitting near by (they had come from every village of Galilee and Judea and from Jerusalem); and the power of the Lord was with him to heal" (v. 17). We find the same focus on the masses in the passion narrative—a "great number" followed Jesus as he carried his cross (23:27) and "All the crowds" witnessed the death of Jesus (23:48). Luke preserved Mark's messianic motif in the Markan accounts he reproduced, but we find no secrecy accounts in the material peculiar to Luke. In Luke, all of Israel knew about Jesus.

### (4) The Holy Spirit

Luke noted the way the Spirit of God was active in and through Jesus' mission, beginning with John the Baptist and continuing afterward with Jesus' followers. In contrast with the other synoptics, Luke identified John the Baptist, Jesus' fore-runner according to Luke, as one who was filled by the Holy Spirit (1:15). In addition, Luke's account of Jesus' birth also referred to the Spirit's activity among members of Jesus' family and relatives as they were drawn into the event, like Mary (1:35), Elizabeth (1:41–45), and Zechariah (1:67–79). Luke's unique infancy narrative described how Simeon was "guided by the Spirit" when he entered the temple and identified the child Jesus as God's "salvation" (2:27, 29).

As in Mark and Matthew, Jesus was guided by the Spirit into the wilderness temptations, but only in Luke did Jesus identify himself as the fulfillment of Isaiah's prophecy about a spirit-led herald of the "good news" that the year of God's deliverance had arrived (4:16–21; compare with Isa. 61:1–2). Later, in a Q saying about a prayer of Jesus, only Luke includes a reference to Jesus rejoicing in the Holy Spirit (10:21; Matt. 11:25–27). In another Q saying, which encouraged Jesus' disciples to pray, only Luke referred to the Father's willingness to give his Holy Spirit "to those who ask him" (11:13; Matt. 7:11).

Acts continues Luke's interest in connecting Jesus' mission with the Holy Spirit by explicitly identifying Jesus' followers as spirit-filled and led in their mis-sion. In this fashion, Luke-Acts presents Jesus and his followers as an operation of the Holy Spirit. The text begins with Jesus ordering his apostles not to leave Jerusalem and thus not to begin their mission until they have been baptized with the Holy Spirit (1:4–5). Jesus then predicted that his followers "will receive power when the Holy Spirit has come upon" them, and they will travel as his witnesses to the ends of the earth (1:8). This prophecy of the Spirit was fulfilled in dramatic fashion when the Spirit descended on Jesus' followers and they began to speak in other languages (2:4). Peter interpreted this event as indicative of the "last days" when God would "pour out" his "Spirit upon all flesh" as Joel prophesied (2:16–21). The rest of Acts illustrates how the Spirit led Jesus' followers on their mission (8:29; 11:12; 13:2; 21:4).

### (5) The Resurrection

Luke emphasized the Resurrection and the appearances of the resurrected Jesus. Mark was rather silent on these issues; he mentioned only the empty tomb and the prophesies about Jesus' appearances. Mark included nothing after the empty tomb. Matthew's gospel has eleven verses on what happened after the discovery of the empty tomb, and Luke tripled the number found in Matthew (24:1–53). In Acts, Jesus' Resurrection is also emphasized in the speeches of the apostles.

Luke is the only synoptic who provided "scriptural proof" for the Resurrection. In his gospel, he said, "Thus it is written, that the Messiah is to suffer and rise from the dead on the third day" (24:46). However, this statement is not explicit in the Jewish Bible! To Luke, however, the Resurrection was so important that it had to be prophesied. To Mark, the passion and death were the all important events; he ended his gospel without dealing with the Resurrection and the post-resurrection appearances. To Luke, the Resurrection clearly overshadowed the passion and death of Jesus. The Resurrection had to be proven by the post-resurrection appearances. Why?

### (6) Humane and Social Concern

Luke intensified this common synoptic interest in social issues. In Luke Jesus was a friend of sinners. All the synoptics included the story about the woman who anointed Jesus, but only Luke said that the woman was a sinner (7:39). Moreover, only Luke said that this took place in the house of a Pharisee and that the Pharisee criticized Jesus and was answered by him. He did this to show that Jesus had a different attitude toward sinners than he did toward the pious.

Of all the Gospels, Luke explicitly relates the significance of women to Jesus. Luke's special source, p-Luke, preserved a birth and infancy narrative that emphasized the piety of Elizabeth, Mary, and Anna, the prophetess who celebrated over the news of Jesus (1:39–55; 2:36–38). Whereas Matthew and Luke adopted Mark's reference to the women who traveled with Jesus from Galilee and were present at his crucifixion in Jerusalem (Mark 15:40–41; Matt. 27:55–56; Luke 23:49), only Luke identified how three specific women (Mary Magdalene, Joanna, and Susanna), along with many others, traveled with Jesus throughout Galilee and were Jesus' benefactors, providing for him and his apostles out of their own resources (8:1–3). Luke even presented women as disciples, with Jesus' approval, and Jesus was received into their home (10:38–42). The thrust of Luke's gospel is that women, whose station in Jewish life was well below that of Jewish men, were welcomed as Jesus' followers and were integral to his work.

Both Matthew and Luke related the parable of the sheep. In Matthew 18:10–14, the story is about a sheep that has strayed, and the point is that God's will is that not even one of the believers should be led astray and perish. In Luke 15:3–7, however, the story is about a lost sheep, and the point is that there is more joy in heaven over a sinner who repents than there is over 99 righteous people who do not need to repent. The story justifies Jesus' table-fellowship with sinners. Luke's Chapters 9 through 19 contain several parables from p-Luke that relate to this theme of Jesus' acceptance of sinners (15:11–32; 18:9–14).

In Luke 10 Jesus used the acts of a Samaritan as an example of true neighborliness. The **Samaritans,** however, were not regarded as Jewish and were hated by Jews. Yet, Jesus rebuked his own disciples who wished to call down fire on an inhospitable Samaritan village (9:51–56). In addition, only Luke described how Jesus healed a Samaritan (17:11–19).

Luke was very aggressive against the rich. Jesus threatened the rich in Luke's version of the Sermon on the Mount (6:24–26). Later Jesus warned his disciples about greed in the parable of the rich fool (12:15). At the same time, he blessed the poor, the hungry, and the persecuted. These stories are probably historically correct, but it was Luke more than anyone else who retained this picture of Jesus.

## THEOLOGICAL PURPOSE

Now we can highlight the significance of these six theological characteristics of Luke. Luke was the first Church historian—a forerunner of Eusebius (fourth century) and later historians of the Church. But Luke wanted to write something more than Church history. The language used in the introduction communicates Luke's purpose:

> Luke 1:1–4 1 Since many have undertaken to set down an orderly account of the events that have been fulfilled among us, 2 just as they were handed on to us by those who from the beginning were eyewitnesses and servants of the word, 3 I too decided, after investigating everything carefully from the very first, to write an orderly account for you, most excellent Theophilus, 4 so that you may know the truth concerning the things about which you have been instructed.

The phrase *to set down* was often used in historical writings. Also, Luke wrote that he had investigated "everything *carefully*." *Carefully* is a translation of a Greek adverb meaning "accurately" (Greek: *akribos*). He also said that he wanted to write an "orderly account."

Moreover, alongside these historiographical terms, Luke used theological terms. Luke wrote about things that "have been fulfilled." The verb *fulfill* is closely related to other verbs that Luke used for the fulfillment of Scripture. The contents of Luke's narrative were "handed" to him by eyewitnesses and servants. The word *handed* was regularly used for the transmission of the good news, as in 1 Cor. 15:3. Luke wrote so that "the truth" should be known. The word he used meant literally "firmness," or "certainty." Luke wrote to establish a "firm," "certain" faith.

Luke's way of writing Church history is characterized by promise-fulfillment. This pattern is also found in other New Testament books. Matthew's formula quotations are similar in nature. In Matthew the pattern is promise in the Bible, the Old Testament, and then fulfillment in the Jesus events. Luke's pattern is somewhat peculiar. Once a promise is fulfilled, a new promise is given, which is later fulfilled and then exchanged for a new promise, and so on. This progression is the way Luke understood history. God was behind the course of history. In Luke 1:32, an angel promised Mary that her son would be given the throne of David. This promise was fulfilled by the Resurrection, as we can see from Peter's Pentecost speech in Acts 2:34–36:

> Acts 2:34–36: 34 For David did not ascend into the heavens, but he himself says, "The Lord said to my Lord, 'Sit at my right hand 35 until I make your enemies your footstool.' 36 Therefore, let all the entire house of Israel know with certainty that God has made him both Lord and Messiah, this Jesus whom you crucified."

According to Peter, David was a prophet who spoke of the Resurrection and enthronement (as the Christ [Messiah]) of Jesus in Psalm 110:1: "The Lord says to my lord, 'Sit at my right hand. . . .'" At the time of the Resurrection, a new promise was given. In Luke 24:49, after his Resurrection, Jesus promised to send the Holy Spirit. This promise was fulfilled at the first Pentecost after his Resurrection. In his speech in Acts 2, Peter said that Jesus had now fulfilled his promise (v. 33). In Peter's speech a new promise was made (actually it was already made by David, but the time for its realization came after the Resurrection). The second part of Psalm 110:1 says that all enemies will be placed under the feet of the lord who is seen as Jesus. This promise still had to be fulfilled, but the community could rest assured that it would happen because, as Luke showed, God always fulfilled His promises.

Why did Luke follow this scheme? He wanted to inform his readers that God had a definite plan and that he was bringing his plan to realization. Thus Luke made the Holy Spirit prominent in his presentation of Jesus. He wanted to demonstrate how God was at work in and through Jesus and his people, both predecessors and successors, rescuing Israel as God promised long ago. Luke's history presents God as the empowering and guiding power behind Jesus' mission to Israel.

It was of course not the history of the world that was of importance to Luke; it was the history of Israel. God's promises were given to Israel. Luke did not agree with Matthew that God had rejected Israel, that God had chosen a new people out of "all the nations." Luke wanted to show that there was no break in the history of salvation. The primitive community in Jerusalem, the Jewish Christians led by James in the book of Acts, continued the history that started with Abraham. Luke's purpose was to show where God's Israel could be found. That is why he wrote.

We can also find in Luke a situation that existed in Matthew. Two groups of Christians existed, the Jewish Christians and the gentile Christians. The Jewish Christians demanded that the gentile Christians should be circumcised—that is, made members of Israel. Matthew solved the problem by maintaining that Israelites were rejected as God's people. God had created a new people. Luke provided another solution. He thought there could not be people of God other than Israel. There existed an unbroken line from Abraham to the Christian community in Jerusalem. This community was Israel, and the history of Israel continued. It is clear why he mimicked the Septuagint and wrote biblical Greek. These works, Luke's gospel and the Acts, were meant to be understood as the continuation of the Jewish Bible. Luke-Acts may be considered the New Testament in that it served as a supplement to the Old Testament and continued the story of God and Israel.

Luke's overriding concern for the continuation of Israel also explains the Jewish interest and perspective of his gospel. In Chapters 1 and 2, the beginning of his gospel, we find the following characteristics: Jesus was circumcised on the eighth day, as were all Jewish boys; he proved that he was a bar mitzvah (Hebrew: "son of the commandment"), a religiously responsible person, at the age of twelve, as did all Jewish boys. He even did so in the temple of Jerusalem, which is probably not historical (it does not pass the criteria of authenticity), but it is of great importance exactly for this reason. Jesus was Jewish; he was the Jewish Messiah who initiated the salvation of Israel beginning in Jerusalem (Luke 24:47).

Prophecies and fulfillments of prophecies abound in Chapters 1 and 2. Especially significant is the fact that several charismatic people, even prophets and prophetesses (Simeon and Anna), proclaimed Jesus as the promised redeemer of Israel. Jesus was the Messiah of Israel. The history of Israel continued first of all with the Messiah. Because of this interest in Israel, Luke began his narration of Jesus' ministry with a quote from Isaiah that depicted Jesus as God's agent for the restoration of Israel's downtrodden, implying that her time of suffering was over (4:16–21).

This narration explains why Jesus worked within the borders of the nation of Israel and why everybody knew about him. He was Israel's savior. In the prophecy by the righteous Simeon in Chapter 2 it had already been said that Jesus was "set for the fall and rising of many in Israel" (v. 34). Thus, many Jews also rejected Jesus. These people placed themselves outside Israel. There was no excuse for them to do so because Jesus' ministry was a public ministry. It was made clear to all that he was designated by God as the Messiah, but according to Luke only some of the Jews rejected Jesus.

Luke, more so than Matthew, distinguished between the leaders of the Jews and the people at large. At the cross, only "the rulers" of the Jews scoffed, whereas the people stood silently watching (23:27). In fact, "all the crowds" went home beating their chests—a sign of grief—when Jesus died (23:48). The two disciples on their way to Emmaus said, "our chief priests and leaders handed him over to be condemned to death" (24:20).

In light of these theological interests, we can understand Luke's representation of Jesus as something of an "anti-establishment" figure who favored the downtrodden. The upper classes were responsible for his death; the common people liked Jesus. Among the poor, suffering, and rejected people, Israel's history continued.

We can also understand the importance of the Resurrection in Luke. It was the final proof of Jesus' messiahship, and it signaled the final chance of accepting Jesus. The harvest of the real Israel began after the Resurrection. By the Resurrection of Jesus, God completely fulfilled the promises about the Messiah and vindicated Jesus. In Acts the resurrection of the people of Israel was often called the "hope of Israel." With Jesus, the Messiah was resurrected, as Peter told the Jews (Acts 2:32–37), and Jesus would soon return to bring about the "universal restoration" (Acts 3:20–21). Those who rejected the Messiah could not call themselves "Israel." The gathering of the true Israel occurred through mass conversions of Jews. The first one occurred when Jews from all over the Roman empire gathered in Jerusalem for the festival of the giving of the law (Pentecost), fifty days after Passover, when Jesus died and was resurrected. Thus, many Jews did understand the importance of the Resurrection. The primitive community in Jerusalem was the kernel of the restored Israel.

It was not only Jews who understood. According to Luke, Jesus' mission did not remain restricted to Jews, which did not contradict Luke's view that the people of God could be only Israel. When the Messiah had come and been resurrected from the dead and then enthroned, the gathering and restoration of Israel had begun. The time had also come to expand the rule of the Messiah over the entire world. Gentiles therefore embraced the message. Luke saw this act as prophesied in the words to Abraham. In the posterity of Abraham all the peoples shall be blessed (Acts 3:25). In Luke 2 the righteous Simeon also prophesied that Jesus would be a "light" to the Gentiles (v. 29–32), alluding to Isaiah 42:6 and 49:6.

The thought of Gentiles adopting the religion of Israel was in fact part of Jewish tradition at the time. Luke saw the adoption happening through the Christian mission. The structure of Luke-Acts set forth Luke's idea of the history of salvation in an explicit manner. Luke used the historical-geographical expansion of Jesus' movement and early Christianity to prove his view of the history of Israel. After his two-chapter introduction about John and the early years of Jesus, and the baptism and temptation of Jesus in 3:1–4:13, the gospel describes a movement from Galilee to Jerusalem: (1) gathering witnesses throughout the country, Luke 4:14–9:50; (2) journey to Jerusalem, Luke 9:51–19:27; and (3) triumph in

Jerusalem, Luke 19:28–24:53. In Acts the movement of Christianity continued from Jerusalem to Rome: (1) the Church was born, Acts 1:1–2:47; (2) witnesses in Judea and Samaria, Acts 3:1–12:25; (3) journey to the Gentiles, Acts 13:1–21:14; and (4) Paul's triumph in Rome, Acts 21:15–28:31.

For whom did Luke write all this? For whom was this history of the beginnings of Christianity important? Traditionally, scholars have argued for a gentile readership. For instance, Jesus' designation as "savior" (2:11) can be associated with the imperial cult of the Roman emperor who was hailed as savior. Luke omitted any references to the ritualistic traditions of the Pharisees—something that would be of little interest to Gentiles. Luke even substituted Greek words for some of the Aramaic terms of Mark and Q—that is, teacher for rabbi. Yet, Luke was very well informed about Scripture reading, organization, and discussions within synagogues. And the name of the recipient identified in Luke 1:3 (compare with Acts 1:1), "Theophilus" (Greek: "Lover of God"), was given to Gentiles *and* Jews.

Luke's community may have been Jewish-Christian. These Jewish Christians would have viewed themselves as rejected by their own people, the Jewish nation at large. That would have been no small thing. Salvation was granted only to members of the community. Giving up the old ways meant being a traitor to Israel. Exclusion from the synagogue often involved an economic loss, and so we can understand even more about why Jesus blessed not only the poor but also turned against the rich. Luke turned the perspective of the Jews upside down. His poor and persecuted Jewish-Christian community was the true Israel. The Jews who rejected Jesus placed themselves outside the history of Israel, which ran from Abraham through Jesus to the primitive community and then out into the gentile world.

## SUMMARY

The Gospel according to Luke was written by an unknown follower of Jesus sometime after 70 CE. Its language reflects the Greek Old Testament, and its sources are more extensive than those of the other synoptics. After a brief description of John's and Jesus' births, Luke presented Jesus' ministry in three sections and later added a lengthy account of Jesus' followers that is known as the Acts of the Apostles. Luke's gospel places Jesus within a Jewish setting that portrays him as a Jewish Messiah who fulfilled God's promise of saving Israel and the offering salvation to Gentiles. Although priests and scribes rejected him, Jesus sought out the downtrodden in his effort to establish God's people. His mission began in Jerusalem and went to the heart of the Roman empire, Rome.

## KEY TERMS FOR REVIEW

| | | |
|---|---|---|
| Acts | Septuagint Greek | Resurrection |
| Irenaeus | Jews and Gentiles | Sinners |
| Proto-Luke | Holy Spirit | Promise-fulfillment |

## QUESTIONS FOR REVIEW

1. Why must scholars be careful when they consider Irenaeus' comments about the authorship of Luke?

2. How did Luke demonstrate his interest in writing history?

3. Of what significance is Jesus for Jews and Gentiles in Luke?

## SUGGESTIONS FOR FURTHER READING

Green, J. *The Theology of the Gospel of Luke.* New York: Cambridge University Press, 1995.

Juel, D. *Luke-Acts: The Promise of History.* Atlanta: John Knox, 1983

Maddox, R. *The Purpose of Luke-Acts.* Edinburgh: T & T Clark, 1982.

Powell, M. *What Are They Saying About Luke?* New York: Paulist, 1989.

Shellard, B. *New Light on Luke: Its Purpose, Sources and Literary Context.* London: Sheffield Academic Press, 2002.

# 12

✹

# The Gospel according to John

## INTRODUCTORY QUESTIONS

### Authorship and Related Issues

According to Irenaeus, the disciple John, presumably one of the sons of Zebedee, wrote the Fourth Gospel. Irenaeus also said that John wrote in Ephesus, in Asia Minor, at the time of Trajan (98–117) and that he was the same person who wrote the book of Revelation.

No critical scholar today believes that the Gospel according to John and the book of Revelation were written by the same author. By the middle of the third century, a bishop of Alexandria, Dionysius by name, already doubted that the two books had the same author because the vocabulary, style, and thoughts of the two texts were so different. But what about the other assertion made by Irenaeus—that a disciple of Jesus who lived in Ephesus around 100 CE wrote the gospel? We will postpone the question of provenance and deal with the question of authorship first.

Could John, the son of Zebedee, who was called to be a disciple of Jesus around the year 30, have survived until the year 100? He would have been at least 90 years old, an age that is possible but not likely. However, Irenaeus may have been mistaken about the date. According to an early Christian tradition (already referred to in Mark 10:35–40), John, the son of Zebedee, was killed by the Jews at a very early date. This tradition discredits Irenaeus' information.

Some scholars have argued that John had good geographical and topographical knowledge of Palestine and that his Greek could easily be translated into Aramaic, thus suggesting an Aramaic original. It is true that John was geographically and topographically well oriented, but this fact is not necessarily evidence that the author was an eyewitness. It is difficult to think that he was. John called the Sea of Galilee by the name "Sea of Tiberias," Tiberias being the Greek form of Tebarya, a town on the west coast of the sea. Sea of Tiberias appears to be a late gentile name for the sea. John apparently had access to one or more good geographical and topographical sources.

As for John's Semitisms, they show only that someone who also spoke a Semitic language wrote the gospel. We can demonstrate an Aramaic original only if a Greek text has to be regarded as a translation error, as when an obscure Greek text can be understood only by transposition to an original Aramaic form. No such clear case occurs in John.

Another problem is often cited in this discussion, namely, that of the many differences between John and the synoptics. Are we to see the Gospel according to John as an eyewitness correction of the synoptic Gospels? If so, the question is how to understand this "correction." John's contents are hardly the evidence of an eyewitness. In 18:13 John implied that the high priest held his office for only one year, which is not true.[1]

Irenaeus also stated that the disciple John was the teacher of bishop Polycarp of Smyrna, located just north of Ephesus. In Polycarp's extant letter, we find only one possible allusion to but no certain reference to the Gospel according to John.

The gospel itself makes no claim that it was written by John. However, a claim occurs at the end of the gospel, saying that the so-called "disciple whom Jesus loved" was the author of at least the last chapter of the gospel, or perhaps even of the entire gospel. When Jesus appeared to the disciples in Galilee after his resurrection, he addressed Peter in particular. As the two walked along the shore of the "Sea of Tiberias" and talked, they were followed by "the disciple whom Jesus loved" (21:20). Three verses later, it is said: "This is the disciple who is testifying to these things and has written them, and we know that his testimony is true" (21:24).

Who is this disciple? First we must determine what "these things" refer to. Chapter 21 is clearly an appendix; the original gospel ended with Chapter 20. The last two verses of Chapter 20 read:

> 20:30-31: 30 "Now Jesus did many other signs in the presence of the disciples, which are not written in this book. 31 But these are written so that you may come to believe that Jesus is the Messiah, the Son of God, and that through believing you may have life in his name."

This passage comes after Jesus' appearance to the disciples in Jerusalem. Then Chapter 21 follows, beginning thus: "After these things Jesus showed himself again to the disciples by the Sea of Tiberias. . . . " The appendix brings John more in line with Mark and Matthew, where we have a Galilean appearance of Jesus after the resurrection. Does 21:24 mean that the beloved disciple was the author of only the appendix? Or does "these things" refer to the entire gospel? The editor who added Chapter 21 probably meant the words to refer to the entire gospel.

---

[1] John 18:13 literally reads the "high priest that (Greek, *ekeinou*) year," suggesting that a different year would mean a different high priest. Another problem for John's historicity is that John identified Annas as the high priest in 18:15, 16, 19, and 22. According to Josephus, Annas was high priest from 6 to 15 CE, long before Jesus' public ministry.

Who was the "disciple whom Jesus loved"? According to the gospel he was some sort of rival to Peter. Peter appeared to be annoyed by his presence, asking Jesus, "Lord, what about him?" (21:21). At the beginning of Chapter 20, the two disciples, Peter and the beloved disciple, raced each other to the tomb. Some scholars have interpreted this person as a symbol for the circle of disciples to which the gospel originally belonged. The beloved disciple may have been a symbol of gentile Christianity as opposed to Jewish Christianity represented by Peter. Or he may have been a symbol of the church of the Spirit in contrast to the church of the ecclesiastical offices, the charismatic church in contrast to the church ruled by bishops and priests.

Such an interpretation rests on an **eisegesis** (reading into the text) rather than an **exegesis** (reading out of the text). The end of the gospel implies that the "disciple whom Jesus loved" was an historical person who had died. In answer to Peter's question, "What about him?" Jesus said: "If it is my will that he remain until I come, what is that to you?" (21:21–22). Then the text reads: "So the rumor spread in the community that this disciple would not die. Yet Jesus did not say to him that he would die, but, 'If it is my will that he remain until I come, what is that to you?'" (21:23). Some people probably believed that the "disciple whom Jesus loved" would not die before the return of Jesus, and Jesus corrected that false notion.

Thus, the gospel itself addresses its author as "the disciple whom Jesus loved," a characterization that is no doubt meant to lend credence to John's gospel. But would a Galilean fisherman or artisan be able to create or edit a document as distinctive as the Fourth Gospel? The "disciple whom Jesus loved" came on the scene only in Jerusalem, near the end of Jesus' life (13:23). It is precisely in this section that John appeared trustworthy, although the statement to the effect that the high priest was in office for only one year is erroneous (18:13). Interestingly, John spoke of no trial before the Jewish authorities and maintained that Jesus died on the eve of Passover, both of which appear plausible. Behind the "disciple whom Jesus loved" we can see a tradition about the last events in the life of Jesus going back to a disciple in Jerusalem, but the description of the disciple himself may be fictitious.

## Origin

Irenaeus said that John's gospel was written in Ephesus, which is also connected with the name John in another tradition. Papias said that he had listened to a certain John Presbyter, John the Elder, in that city. Thus we hear about two different Johns in Ephesus. The author of 2 and 3 John referred to himself as "the Elder." Was he John Presbyter in Ephesus? And was this John also the author of the gospel? It seems that 1 John has the same author as the gospel, but the author of 1 John does not refer to himself as "the Elder."

Other locations are candidates for the place of origin. The earliest preserved fragment of the New Testament, P52, or Rylands 457, quoted five verses from John 18. This papyrus stemmed from the early second century. Therefore, at this time the gospel was known in Egypt (where the papyri fragments were discovered). A very interesting papyrus called Egerton 2 was published in 1935. This papyrus, which was also found in Egypt and is to be dated no later than 150, contains some gospel passages that are similar to passages in John. But the gospel text reflected in the papyrus is not identical with John's text. Is it dependent upon John? Or is it the source of John? Or do John and Egerton 2 draw on the same tradition? In any case, the earliest evidence for the Gospel according to John ties it firmly to Egypt. If John was written in Ephesus, the gospel must have traveled between Ephesus and Egypt rather quickly. Of course that is not impossible, but an Egyptian origin seems more likely. In support of this probability, some Christian authors in Alexandria quoted the Gospel according to John around the middle of the second century. On the whole, Egyptian (Alexandria) seems to be a more likely origin than Ephesus.

John's gospel, or at least its basic traditions, could also have originated in Antioch in Syria. Later Syrian theologians claim Antioch as the place of origin. The letters of bishop Ignatius of Antioch, who was martyred under Trajan around 115, evince the same atmosphere as the Gospel according to John, although scholars can identify no clear quotation or allusion. Both Antioch and Alexandria seem to be better candidates for the origin than Ephesus. However, the place of origin may be neither Antioch nor Alexandria but some place in Palestine itself between these cities.

Why was the Gospel according to John linked with Ephesus? The reasons are probably twofold. First, Papias spoke of a John the elder in Ephesus, and 2 and 3 John are the works of a certain "Elder." Second, the book of Revelation, whose author's name is given as John (1:1), was written on the island Patmos, which is not far from Ephesus.

## Date

P52, the fragment of John, dates from the early second century. How early John is, is difficult to say. Most scholars agree on the last decade of the first century on the basis of an evolutionistic argument: John contains a more elaborate Christology than the synoptics. Many scholars assume that an elaborate Christology required time to develop.

## Sources

When we disregard the prologue (the first 18 verses of Chapter 1), John tells essentially the same story as Mark. He describes Jesus and John the Baptist, then depicts Jesus' public ministry, and finally includes Jesus' passion and the events after Easter morning. But we find great differences between John and the synoptics, both in the sequence of the individual events and in the method of representing Jesus. First we consider the sequence of the events. Although a certain amount of narrative material is common to both John and the synoptics, the context is different. Often the reason for the different contexts is that John took into consideration several visits of Jesus to Jerusalem at the three feasts, whereas the synoptics narrated only one (Passover) at the conclusion of Jesus' ministry. The most striking example is that of the so-called cleansing of the temple, which John placed at the beginning of the ministry, whereas the synoptics had it at the end.

Second, as for the method of representing Jesus, in the synoptics Jesus taught in parables whereas in John he gave long discourses and did not relate a single parable. The synoptics have many short sayings that can usually be isolated form critically from the context. A few of these sayings occur in John, too, but there they are mostly incorporated into the long discourses. John's passion narrative, on the other hand, is largely congruous with that of the synoptics.

These observations lead to the question of the relationship between the synoptics and John. The are two possibilities, historically speaking. First, either John is right, or the synoptics are. Or second, neither John nor the synoptics are correct. For the former alternative, either the synoptics are right about the cleansing of the temple and it happened at the end of Jesus' ministry, or John is right and it happened at the beginning. The latter alternative assumes that both John and the synoptics were misinformed, or not at all informed, about the context of a particular event or saying. Thus, some scholars have argued that Jesus' entry into Jerusalem would fit better with the occasion of the Feast of Tabernacles than the Feast of Passover. The pilgrims carried palm branches at the Feast of Tabernacles but not at the Feast of Passover.

Source critical considerations also suggest two basic alternatives: (1) John was familiar with one of the synoptics (here scholars invoke mostly Mark) or with two or all three of them or (2) John did not know any of the synoptic Gospels but drew on certain traditions that had reached the synoptics or he drew on independent traditions.

If we use alternative (1), we must assume that John rewrote his sources to supplement or supplant them, which is not likely. No evidence that John wanted to supplement the synoptics exists, for he did not presuppose that other Gospels ought to be read. His gospel is a full and adequate report that builds to his purpose statement in 20:30–31, the end of the original gospel.

But did John write to correct the synoptics—to replace them—perhaps because he thought that he possessed more authentic material? This view is not likely either because we find no polemical statements against the synoptics in John. The only thing that is certain is that John knew the gospel genre.

What about alternative (2)? If John did not know the synoptics first hand, what are we to make of the similarities? Did he know oral material that was also used by the synoptics? That possibility stands to reason because he knew the gospel genre. For the passion narrative, however, we have to reckon with a written source. The story is too long and well rounded to have been put together from different oral strands. However, John cannot have taken it from any of the synoptics because his version contains some remarkable peculiarities. For instance, in 18:33–38 and again in 19:7–13, we find a strange dialogue between Jesus and Pilate. John also reproduced numerous accounts, like the story of Peter's denial, without using them for a theological purpose, as is the case in the synoptics (although Chapter 21, which was apparently added later, does have a unique threefold "re-commissioning" scene with Peter [21:15–17]). Moreover, the peculiar characteristics of John's theology are not present in John's passion narrative. Finally, the passion story has a peculiar linguistic and stylistic character different from the rest of the gospel.

Thus, John used a synopticlike passion source. Did John also use other sources, written and/or oral? Rudolf Bultmann, through the application of form critical principles, distinguished two other sources in addition to the passion source: (1) a sign, or miracle, source, and (2) a discourse or revelation source. In

2:11 it is said that the turning of water into wine was the first "sign" (miracle) that Jesus did. In 4:54, yet a second "sign" is referred to, but other miracles are to be found between these two stories (2:23; 3:2). For this reason Bultmann concludes that there were insertions from another source.

To refute Bultmann, it may be said that the miracles between these two stories are merely alluded to, not recounted in full. And John did present the healing of the official's son at Capernaum in Chapter 4 as the second sign; he did not change the text as we would expect if he had taken this from a source. Bultmann appears to have been too confident in circumscribing the sign source (he found a source of seven miracles), but he was generally correct because the miracle stories appear to have been written in very simple Greek, without specific Johannine characteristics. The case of the "second sign" is significant in this respect. The pericope is 4:46–54. Verse 48 stands out: "Unless you see signs and wonders you will not believe." This language is typically Johannine. Moreover, it does not fit the context. The official asked Jesus to come to heal his son. Verse 48 is not an adequate answer to the request. The father had faith. He believed that Jesus could cure his son. He did not ask for a miracle as a demonstration of Jesus' power so that he could believe. In verse 49 the father said: "Sir, come down before my little boy dies," which is not a response to Jesus' statement. Verse 48 halts the progress of the narrative. It was inserted into the story about the second sign. It seems as if there may have been a sign source. Despite this insight, the exact details of the source remain a point of discussion, and several scholars since Bultmann have offered several different reconstructions of the sign source.

The existence of the discourse source, which is also argued for by Bultmann, is on even shakier ground. Bultmann argues once again on the basis of an analysis of style, but this analysis is carried out fully only in his discussion of the prologue, 1:1–18. It is clear that in many ways the prologue is different from the rest of the gospel, but is it similar enough to all the segments that Bultmann associates with the discourse source? A discourse source may have existed, but it is difficult to isolate it except with regard to the prologue.

## Rearrangements and Interpolations

At the end of John's gospel, it is said that "we know that his testimony is true" (21:24)—that is, the testimony of the beloved disciple. Thus, Chapter 21 is an appendix ascribed to a "we" who—as a collective, a community of faith—served as an "editorial board." It stands to reason that this editorial board may have altered the text of the gospel.

Even though the Greek copies of John present the same order of events, the text seems to be out of order in several places. Chapters 5 through 7 present a rather clear case. Chapter 6:1 says, "After this Jesus went to the other side of the Sea of Galilee, also called the Sea of Tiberias." According to Chapter 5, however, Jesus was in Jerusalem. If we reverse the order of Chapters 5 and 6, the contents are smoothed out because the end of Chapter 4 has Jesus in Capernaum in Galilee, and the beginning of Chapter 5 relates that he went to Jerusalem. (A couple of other problems in Chapters 5 through 7 would also be solved by placing Chapter 6 between Chapters 4 and 5.)

Something is wrong in Chapters 13 through 17 because the last verse of Chapter 14 is the end of a farewell speech by Jesus and reads, "Rise, let us go hence" (14:31). Chapter 18:1, which describes how Jesus went across the Kidron Valley to the Garden, would follow 14.31 easily. Instead, Chapters 15 through 17 provide a parallel farewell discourse. Did Chapters 15 through 17 originally precede Chapter 14 (or rather 13:36–14:31)? Or did John write two drafts of the farewell discourse and the editors incorporated both of them?

In two cases it is very difficult to explain why the text was rearranged. This rearrangement also makes it difficult to determine the extent of the editors' work. We don't know what editorial criteria they used. In several other cases it is possible to attempt reconstructions that read more smoothly than the text as it now stands, but this fact may be due to John's clumsiness, not the work of the editors. Perhaps the scrolls or pages of John's work were ordered incorrectly and never corrected.

Some scholars also argue for a number of interpolations in John's text. We find an alleged case in Chapter 6. After a speech by Jesus in which he referred to himself as the bread of life, he suddenly started to speak about the bread that he gave and interpreted it as his flesh. (6:51). A couple of verses later Jesus talked about the drinking of his blood (6:53). Thus 6:51–53 interprets Jesus words about being the bread of life as the Eucharist bread and wine. This interpretation may be correct, but it is questionable whether John would speak so openly about it. John did not include an account of the Last Supper as the synoptics did. In its place, John told of Jesus washing his disciple's feet (13:3–12). Perhaps the editors addressed this oversight by adding 6:51–53 to address the meaning of the Eucharist. We should allow room for the possibility of interpolations, but it is difficult to ascertain their extent.

## Purpose

Why was John's gospel written? It was not written as a competitor or as a supplement to the synoptics. An old theory is that John was written to refute the claims of a sect devoted to John the Baptist. Polemical remarks are directed against John the Baptist and the claims that could have been made on his behalf, but John's major concern was not simply to refute them. John also criticized the Jews at large, but the Jews' hatred of the Christians is considered in the general hatred of the world for the Christians. The Jews appeared as representative of the world.

John's purpose in writing was stated clearly at the end of the original gospel; it was written in order that "you may come to believe that Jesus is the Messiah, the Son of God, and that through believing you may have life in his name" (20:31). Is it a missionary writing that seeks to convert Jews or Gentiles, or both? Nothing in the text supports this view. Actually, many passages, such as the farewell discourses, are directed to Christians. John is a book of faith for a Christian community. Whereas it is a theological product of the community it addresses, its theology is rather peculiar when compared with the synoptics.

## Structure

Chapter 1 is an introduction. Chapters 2 through 12, which describe Jesus' ministry among the Jews, can be called "The Revelation of Christ's Glory before the

World." The gospel divides itself at the end of Chapter 12. Chapters 13 through 17 describe the last evening that Jesus spent with his disciples. Chapters 18 through 20 describe the passion and Easter events. These eight chapters (13–20) can be called "The Revelation of Christ's Glory before the Community." Chapter 21 is a later addition of resurrection appearances. In Chapters 2 through 12, Bultmann argues for two sources, a sign source and a discourse source. The existence of a sign or miracle source is probable. Moreover, this source may have been part of a primitive gospel used by John. Perhaps the sign source and the source behind the passion and Easter narratives, which also were originally independent, made up a primitive gospel.

In any event, John interwove the miracles with other material, mostly discourses by Jesus, and he prefixed the passion narrative, Chapters 18 through 20, with the story of what went on between him and his disciples that last evening (Chapters 13–17). Here we find Jesus' act of footwashing, prayers, discourses (for example, instructions and promise of the Paraclete), and final conversations.

## THE THEOLOGY OF JOHN

### (1) Dualism

*Dual* means composed of two parts. The terminological and conceptual world of John is very different from that of the synoptics. John spoke of the opposites of "above" and "below," "light" and "darkness," "truth" and "falsehood." The upper world of light was the source of all truth; the lower world of darkness was the source of falsehood. Jesus came from above. He was "sent" into this world (13:1–3), and he returned to the upper world. Thus he did not belong here. In a way, his disciples—those who believed in him (the Christians)—did not belong here either because the world hated them. In 17:14, Jesus said, ". . .the world has hated them because they do not belong to the world, just as I do not belong to the world." The disciples, however, could not at this time, like Jesus, ascend to the upper world of light. The text continues, "I am not asking you [God] to take them out of the world, but I ask you to protect them from the evil one" (17:15). The evil one, Satan, is the "ruler of this world" (12:31; 14:30; 16:11). The believers were in a frightening situation. They were strangers in a hostile world ruled by Satan.

### (2) Christology

As we already mentioned, Jesus was sent into this world. Originally he had a non-worldly existence. His original and real mode of existence defied the limit of time. In 8:58, Jesus claimed to have existed before Abraham. The very opening of the gospel even ascribed preexistence to him: "In the beginning was the Word" (1:1). The divine sonship of Jesus thus did not date from the ascension, as is the case in Acts 2:36 and the confession formula cited by Paul in Romans 1:3–4. Nor did Jesus' divine sonship date from his baptism, as implied in Mark's gospel (1:11). Nor again did it date from his conception, as was the case in Matthew and Luke (Matt. 1: 20; Luke 1:35). In John, Jesus was the Son of God from eternity.

The divine sonship of Jesus and the fatherhood of God are very important in John. God is called the "Father" 120 times. Jesus is called the "Son of God" 27 times. In the synoptics, Jesus is called the son of God only twice—a clear example of the limitation of the Father-name of God in the original preaching of Jesus. In John, the Son-name of Jesus is associated closely with the Father-name of God some 20 times. This association thereby emphasizes the intimacy between the Father and the Son. In 10:30, Jesus said, "The Father and I are one." Whoever had seen Jesus had seen the Father (14:9). The Son did only what the Father wanted him to do; he was thus a true revelation of the Father (1:18).

But it is difficult to see this association. The prologue states, "We have seen his glory" (1:14). The "we," the collective, is the Church. Or perhaps not even the Church. When Jesus was about to depart, Philip said, "Show us the Father" (14:8). But Philip had seen the Father all the time. He just had not realized it. The ultimate reason for our difficulty is that God manifested himself in a human being (John 1:1, 14). In John, Jesus set himself apart by his claim to represent God. The people of the "world," the Jews in the gospel, understood this claim and took offense at it. They did not understand the miracles (the signs) that proved the identify of Jesus. Obviously Philip had not understood them either. The puzzle continues throughout the gospel. John is a gospel for insiders: "Can anything good come out of Nazareth?" Philip said to them, "Come and see" (1:46). Nazareth in Galilee could not be the home of God's Son, but according to John, external credentials counted for nothing: "Come and see!"

The use of the nominative personal pronoun "I," which occurs in significant utterances of Jesus some 120 times, is a very important way of indicating Jesus' significance. The most important of these utterances are the "I am" statements: "I am the bread of life"; "I am the light of the world"; "I am the good shepherd"; "I am the true vine"; and so on. Each statement consists of a subject and a predicate. But what is the subject and what is the predicate in each statement? Many are apt to say that "I" is the subject and the associated nouns are the predicates, that the latter is predicated by the former (for example, "true vine" is predicated by "I"). But these phrases should really be understood in the sense of "the state—that's I." Here the "state" is really the subject, that which is inquired about. "The state—what is it?" Answer: "The state—that's I." Similarly, the question is asked about the true vine. "Who is the true vine?" "The true vine," said Jesus, "that's I." Thus the translations should really be, "The true vine is I."

It is important to understand this interpretation because it shows that people in John's environment asked questions such as, "Who is the good shepherd?" "Who is the bread of life?" John wanted to convince these people about the identity of the shepherd and the bread. There were obviously other candidates for these titles; John the Baptist may have been one of them.

In one set of "I am" statements, Jesus used "I am" in an absolute sense, without a predicate. He does not say "so and so is I" or even "I am so and so," but simply "I am." In 8:58 he said, "Before Abraham was, I am." This construction is impossible in Greek; in Greek the verb "I am" is used with a predicate. But in Hebrew "I am" was used as an explanatory substitution for the proper name of God (Exod. 3:14: "I am who I am"). Thus, when Jesus said, "I am," he claimed the name of God. Jesus did not have to say "I am who I am." According to the Greek text of Isa. 45:18, the name of God can be phrased by "I am." Jesus' assertion in 8:58 caused the Jews to treat him as a blasphemer and thus they took up stones to throw at him. Stoning was the penalty for blasphemy.

### (3) The Paraclete

Paraclete is a name of the Holy Spirit. Dealing with this concept in connection with Christology is appropriate because John called Jesus by the same name as the Spirit—that is, Paraclete. In 14:16–17, Jesus said, "And I will ask the Father, and He will give you another Advocate [*parakletos*], to be with you forever. This is the Spirit of Truth." Because the Spirit is "another advocate," Jesus must also be an advocate." The Spirit represents Jesus. The **charismatic** aspect of the Spirit found in primitive Christianity and Paul is absent.

*Paraclete* is a Greek word (*parakletos*) that means "advocate" or "intercessor." However, Christ and the Spirit did not pray or plead for believers in John's gospel. In John, the Paraclete is described as a helper who strengthens the faithful. He dwells in the believers and teaches them all things (14:17, 26). The Spirit is incarnated in the Church, the Church is its flesh. Jesus gave the disciples the Spirit before he ascended. Thus, Pentecost (the time of the Spirit's bestowal according to Acts 2) and the *parousia* (a Greek word referring to the return of Jesus) are welded together. Moreover, the day Jesus bestowed the Spirit on his disciples was the very day he arose. John brought the resurrection and *parousia* together. In addition, in John Jesus' crucifixion is referred to as his "glorification" and his being "lifted up." These terms contain clear allusions to the resurrection and ascension. Therefore, in John, the death, resurrection, ascension, coming of the Spirit, and return of Jesus are all brought together.

### (4) Realized Eschatology (and Eternal Life)

Along with the emphasis on the sending of the Son into the world, and then the sending of the Spirit, there goes a revaluation of traditional eschatology. The basic texts are found in Chapters 5 and 11. John reflects traditional Jewish and Christian eschatology. In 5:28–29, Jesus said that the time would come when those who were in the tombs would hear his voice "and will come out—those who have done good, to the resurrection of life, and those who have done evil, to the resurrection of judgment." This passage is quite similar to Daniel 12:2, the starting point for the resurrection doctrine in Judaism: "Many of those who sleep in the dust of the earth shall awake, some to everlasting life, and some to shame and everlasting contempt."

But John revealed a more complex resurrection doctrine. In 11:23, Jesus said to Martha, "Your brother will rise again." Martha answered, "I know that he will rise again in the resurrection on the last day" (11:24). This doctrine is the same one voiced by Jesus in 5:29. It is the conventional doctrine going back to Daniel. But Jesus was not talking about only that doctrine. Here Jesus introduced a new idea. In reply he said to Martha: "I am the resurrection and the life. Those who believe in me, even though they die, will live, and everyone who lives and believes in me will never die" (11:25–26). We can take verse 25 to concur with popular doctrine: The believer will rise. But the next verse says something new: The believer will never die. The resurrection had already taken place. The believer had passed from death to life. The eschatology of the end was realized and yet Jesus spoke about the future resurrection.

Jesus talked about realized eschatology. According to 5:28, those who were in the tombs would hear the voice of Jesus and come forth. In 11:43–44 Jesus "cried with a loud voice, 'Lazarus, come out!' The dead man came out. . . ." Lazarus's resurrection is an anticipation of the resurrection of the dead at the end of time, but that is not the whole story. In 5:24–25 it is said, "Very truly, I tell you, anyone who hears my word and believes him who sent me, has eternal life, and does not come under judgment, but has passed from death to life . . . the hour is coming, and is now here, when the dead will hear the voice of the Son of God, and those who hear will live." These verses speak of the future resurrection.

Thus, Lazarus's resurrection is not simply a miracle and an anticipation of the final resurrection but a symbol of the real resurrection described in 5:24–25 and 11:26. Jesus raised Lazarus to drive home the point that those who believe are already risen. Those who heard the voice of Jesus had already come out of the tomb, which is the meaning of the story about the raising of Lazarus. To discuss whether or not this actually happened is trivial and shows a lack of understanding of John's theology. (In fact, some scholars question whether the references to the future resurrection represent the work of the editors, thus making John's thought divergent from main line Christianity).

## (5) Ecclesiology

As we have already noted, the world hated the Christians. By contrast, Christians loved one another. The synoptic command to love God and one's neighbor does not appear in John. John did not enjoin love of God. The word *neighbor* does not occur at all in John. However, John spoke of love of fellow Christians. "I give you a new commandment, that you love one another" (13:34; 15:12, 17). 1 John, which was probably written by the same author as the Gospel according to John, speaks of loving one's "brother" (2:10).

In John the atmosphere is different from that of the synoptics, where Jesus taught followers to break down the walls between people and to love even one's enemies. There is no teaching to that effect in John. Whereas John teaches that God "loved the world" (3:16), we should love only Christians (13:34). John reflects the idea and existence of a new society based on brotherly love (which was paralleled by the Jewish community at Qumran).

## (6) Belief and Knowledge

John emphasized both belief and knowledge. In fact, in some passages, he seemed to equate the two. To "know" God and Christ, who had been sent from him, is eternal life (17:3). Knowledge effects the salvation and is even a sign of it. The disciples are said to have known that Jesus came from God and to have believed that God had sent him (17:8). The parallelism here between knowing and believing is clear. They both denote the same thing—a nonrational, intuitive experience. How can we understand that claim? It can be experienced only by joining the group: "Come and see!" We need an intuitive, nonrational experience. The verb *know* and the noun *knowledge* are not used in a technical sense in the synoptics. Furthermore, in John the sense of *believe* is different from that in the synoptics, where it means trust and is used much less often.

## (7) Symbolism (Allegory)

John does not contain any parables like those found in the synoptics (stories with allegorical significance), but it has some discourses that are similar to allegories, like the discourse about the good shepherd (10:1ff.). Long before that discourse ends, the shepherd is identified with Jesus. Thus it is not a real allegory. In the discourse on the true vine (15:1ff.), the identity is clear from the very beginning. As a matter of fact, the language changes back and forth between the literal and the metaphorical. The statements all refer to Christ and his disciples; hence, there are some peculiar expressions, like that of the branches "abiding" in the vine. The expression is determined by the fact the evangelist found this an appropriate way of describing the relationship of the believer to Christ.

However, not everything is clear. Thus, we cannot doubt that Jesus' identification of himself as the true vine carries an allusion to the Eucharist although the Eucharist is not mentioned. In this connection, we should also note that many of the stories in the Fourth Gospel, and not only the discourses, may contain such a symbolism. Consider the feeding of the five thousand (Chapter 6). In the same chapter we find the discourse beginning, "I am the bread of life" (6:35). The feeding story must have carried allusions to the Eucharist.

## THE BACKGROUND OF JOHN

Where can we find the key to the interpretation of this unusual gospel? As for the synoptics, knowledge of the Jewish Bible, Josephus's work, and the rabbinic movement helps to explain these Gospels. But this type of knowledge is far from enough to explain John. The dualistic worldview and the myth of the descending-ascending redeemer must be explained against another background.

It is common to read John against a gnostic background. The noun **Gnosticism** and the adjective *gnostic* derive from the Greek word, *gnosis*, "knowledge." Gnosticism is a label used to cover many different religious sects around the turn of the Christian era. Some sects were Christian, some were Jewish, and some were gentile. Common to most of them were a dualistic worldview and a mythological framework within which the savior was a preexistent figure who was commissioned and sent out by his Father, the highest God, to reveal the saving *gnosis*. This knowledge is about the way the soul or spirit, which was really divine, came to be imprisoned in the material world, in the body. Matter did not derive from God but from certain inferior angels, who managed to capture the soul or spirit and imprison it in their material creation. When the savior came and imparted his teaching, people recognized their true identity and were saved. The savior ascended to heaven again, and when people died, their souls or spirits were released and could follow the savior.

We cannot ascertain this myth in full in John. He made no reference to a gnostic creation or preexistent souls. But we find many similarities between the way in which the gnostic savior spoke or was described, especially in **Mandeism,** and the way in which Jesus spoke and was described in John.

Formerly, it was not uncommon to read John against a Greek background. The key to understanding John was found in Plato's philosophy. Plato taught that behind this world of space and time, which was always changing, there was a real, eternal, and changeless world—the world of ideas. Everything in this world is but a faint copy of an idea. Thus when anything is called *good,* it is merely being described as a pale reflection of true goodness, which exists only in the realm of ideas.

This view amounts to a dualistic philosophy with an opposition of above and below, truth and falsehood, not unlike the dualism in John. Moreover, some scholars used to argue that John's characterization of Jesus as the "true light" (1:9) should be explained against the background of the Platonic concept of ideas: Jesus was the idea of light—light in the ancient world being a metaphor of the divine. The sunlight is only a copy of this divine light that Jesus embodied.

There can be little doubt that **Platonism** contributed to John's thought, but we cannot find a direct influence. Plato was extremely influential; Platonic influence was found everywhere. We must go further in our search for the special channel through which this influence reached John, and we must look for a spiritual current with a savior figure. Plato had no personal savior.

Some scholars have pointed to **Hermetism,** the name given to the Alexandrian movement that brought forth the Hermetic literature, so-called because it was attributed to the god Hermes. The Hermetic documents, which show traces of Jewish influence, date from around the third century CE but probably preserve material which is much older. In Hermetism, we find clear parallels to John. Even Martin Luther thought that John had influenced Hermetism, but this could not have been the case because no single trace of Christian influence appears in the bulky body of Hermetic literature.

In Hermetism, salvation is found in the here and now through knowledge of God and the cosmos. This knowledge allows a person to pass through and beyond this world and the heavenly spheres to the divine world. Terms such as *light* and *life* are used of the nature of God and of the gifts that his worshippers were given. We can also find a mediator, often the god Hermes, who could be called the "Word." He revealed the mysteries necessary for salvation, which usually included sacraments.

Gnosticism, whose savior is a mythological figure of great plasticity and vividness, is more like John than Hermetism is. The mediator in Hermetism remained a somewhat pale figure; he was the conveyor of divine mysteries but not the main character in a mythological drama. The gnostic savior is a preexistent figure who was commissioned by God, his Father, and sent down to earth to reveal saving knowledge. This knowledge is about how the soul or the spirit, which is divine, came to be imprisoned in the material world and the body. Matter does not derive from God, but from certain evil angels, who managed to capture the soul or spirit and to imprison it in their material creation. When the savior imparted this teaching, which is given in a full mythological dressing in the texts, people recognized their true identity and were saved. The savior ascended to heaven, making a passage through the vaults of heaven that were controlled by the evil angels. When people died, their spirits were set free and could follow the savior. The ideas of the antidivine origin of matter and of the preexistence and fall, or abduction, of the soul or spirit cannot be found in John's gospel, but everything else seems to fit. Thus, some scholars have argued that John found it appropriate to present his Jesus story by means of a gnostic myth from which he had extracted these particularly mythological ideas.

The Mandean form of Gnosticism represents a fully developed gnostic system and can be used to elucidate John. *Manda* is an Aramaic word that has the same meaning as the Greek *gnosis*, "knowledge." Although Mandean texts postdate the Gospels, they reflect some very early traditions. John the Baptist is a hero in the Mandean writings, and the baptism of John figures prominently in these texts. For the Mandeans, knowledge alone was not sufficient for salvation. The believers also had to receive some sacraments, the most important of which was baptism, which was repeated frequently.

The Mandean savior spoke or was described in a language strongly reminiscent of John's. He was preexistent. It was said of him: "Before even the angels existed, God created and commissioned you." He was sent into the world. He said, "I am the Sent One from the Light whom God has sent into this world." Still he was one with his Father. People said to him, "Who has sent you, new king, who is sitting in the kingdom of God?" The revealer was on earth and in heaven at the same time. God said to the Mandean savior, "Your speech is our speech, be close to us and do not become dissociated." In John, Jesus said, "The Father and I are one" (10:30); "And the one who sent me is with me; he has not left me alone" (8:29). The Mandean savior said, ". . . I brought you life." It was said about him, "He calls and quicken raises the dead." This passage parallels John 5:21: "Indeed, just as the Father raises the dead and gives them life, so also the Son gives life to whomever he wishes."

In the Mandean literature we also find conceptual pairs: life and death, light and darkness, truth and falsehood. It is said of the savior: "You snatched us out of death and placed us in life; you snatched us out of darkness and placed us in light . . . you showed us the way of life and the path of truth and had us walk it." This is reminiscent of the descriptions of the work of Jesus in John 8:12: "Whoever follows me will not walk in darkness but will have the light of life."

We could give several other parallels, but two more will suffice. The Mandean savior was a stranger on earth. The evil ones said, "Who is this stranger, whose speech is not like our speech." Compare this passage with Jesus' discussion with the Jews in John, Chapter 8. The Jews didn't understand Jesus because he had a different origin than they had. "He said to them, 'You are from below, I am from above; you are of this world, I am not of this world'" (8:23). Lastly, the Mandean savior spoke like the Johannine Jesus when the latter said, "I am the good shepherd," "I am the true vine," actually, "The good shepherd is I," "The true vine is I."

Some scholars take the Mandean parallels to mean that John influenced Mandeism. They strongly emphasize that the Mandean writings cannot be shown to be earlier than John. We must bear in mind that the ancestors of the Mandeans came from the Jordan valley. They called all baptismal water "Jordan," and the language of their holy books was a form of Aramaic with many Western elements, although they lived in an environment where eastern Aramaic was spoken before Arabic became dominant. An earlier self-designation was "Nazoreans," which was also a name of the first Christians. The similarities between John and Mandeism are best explained by the fact that they both stem from the same milieu, a Jewish form of religion dissimilar to that evidenced by the Jewish Bible and rabbinism.

Topics in John's theology can be paralleled with teachings of the Qumran-Essenes, a Judaism different from that of the Jewish Bible and Rabbinism. Knowledge among the Qumran-Essenes is not very similar to knowledge in John. In Qumran knowledge consisted of cosmological secrets and the end of times. Their writings reflected a Jewish form of dualism. These people of the new covenant referred to themselves as the "children of light." All others, including non-Qumranic Jews, were considered "children of darkness." The crass denunciation of the Jews in John's gospel (8:44) does not rule out a Jewish origin. Anti-Semitism did not have to be anti-Jewish. John's admonition to love fellow Christians but not others can also be paralleled in Qumran. In a writing from Qumran's library, it was said, "Everyone shall love his brother as himself" (*CD* 6:20). This accords with 1 John, where *brother* serves as a name of the fellow Christian who is to be loved (2:10).

In another Qumran text we find the admonition to love the chosen ones and to hate the children of darkness (*IQS* 1:2–11). This admonition is not found in John, but we cannot doubt that on this issue John is much nearer to Qumran than the synoptics, where love of one's enemies is enjoined. A Qumran dualism of truth and falsehood, corresponding to the dualism of light and darkness, matches that found in John. God appointed two spirits, the spirit of truth and the spirit of error. These spirits were described as different ways of life, or a presiding over these ways. The children of light followed the spirit of truth, whereas the children of darkness followed the spirit of error (*1QS* 2; 4).

The dualism of above and below—an upper and a nether world, a so-called cosmological dualism that is found in John—is not prominent in Qumran. However, the Qumran teaching that this world is ruled by the angel of darkness suggests such a dualism. The angel of darkness tried to lead the children of light astray, but they were helped by God and his angel of truth (*1QS* 3), who was also called the prince of light. But neither John nor Qumran is gnostic in having a being other than God who is the "creator" of the world (Greek: *demiurge*).

The angelology of Qumran also throws light on the Christology of John. An interesting figure in this respect is Melchizedek in one of the texts from Qumran. He was probably identical with the prince of light who appeared in other texts because these two figures were ascribed with the same eschatological functions. What is of interest in this connection, however, is that Melchizedek was called *Elohim* (Hebrew for God). In John, Jesus claimed divine status. Jesus even claimed to share the proper name of God, *Yahweh* (Hebrew), which was paraphrased as "I am." Nothing quite like that appears in Qumran, but other quarters of Judaism have a similar idea. In some later Jewish texts, an angel by the name of Metatron is said to have been called "Little *Yahweh*." This title designated him as divine, although not quite on the same level as *Yahweh*.

Whereas the chief angel in Qumran was called the prince of light, Metatron can be regarded as the light of the world because it was related that God dressed him in glorious garments and a crown whose light reached to the four corners of the world (*3 Enoch* 12:1–2). In John 8:12, Jesus was called the light of the world. In Qumran, God was said to love the spirit of the prince of light, whereas in the Metatron tradition, God was said to love Metatron and to entrust everything to him. John 3:35 says, "the Father loves the Son and has placed all things in his hands." In the Metatron traditions, God was even the "begetter" of the angel Metatron. In John, Jesus was the "only Son" [*monogenes;* begotten] of God his Father (1:18; 3:16). The principal angel in these less known Jewish quarters could also descend to earth, just as Jesus did in John's gospel. In a writing called the *Apocalypse of Abraham,* an angel who was sent down to the patriarch Abraham identified himself as Yaho-El and described himself as a power because the name of God dwelled in him. "Yaho" is an abridgment of *Yahweh,* and El of *Elohim;* thus, Yaho-El translates as *Yahweh-Elohim.*

In the Book of *Tobit,* one of the Old Testament apocrypha texts, the angel Raphael descended to earth and was not recognized as an angel. He revealed his identity to a chosen few, however, and said, "I am ascending to him who sent me" (12:20). This passage is similar to Jesus' words in John: "I will be with you a little while longer, and then I am going to him who sent me" (7:33); "But now I am going to him who sent me" (16:5). If we argue that Jesus was not said to be an angel but the Son of God, we must remember that "Son of God" was also an angelic title. In the Jewish book, *The Prayer of Joseph,* the principal angel who descended to earth characterized himself as "the commander-in-chief among the sons of God."

Finally, we must cite evidence from Philo, the first-century CE Jewish philosopher of Alexandria, in this discussion of Christology. In Philo's philosophy, God was utterly transcendent, and there was a need for an intermediary between God and the world. This intermediary was not a personal being who descended to earth and appeared to people as an angel but a spiritual power with no real personality. The names and biblical passages in which Philo referred to the intermediary show that one of the facets of this intermediary was an adaptation of the principal angel figure. Thus, important biblical passages where a special angel of God was described are taken by Philo as allegorical texts about this spiritual intermediary. What is of particular interest in this connection is that many of Philo's representations of the intermediary are similar to what was said about Jesus in the Gospel according to John, especially the prologue. "Son of God" is one of the names of Philo's intermediary, and that name often occurs in tandem with the name "angel."

We can elucidate even the concept of John's Paraclete, at least in part, by these less known forms of Judaism. To John, the Paraclete was a personal being, not simply the power or function of Christ in the world. The Paraclete could not be seen, but that did not mean that it was not a personal being. John was so positive about this view that he used the personal pronoun "he" with reference to the Spirit, although the noun is neuter in gender. The world cannot receive the Spirit, because it does not know him (14:17); the Holy Spirit, whom God will send, he will teach you all things (14:26).

In John 14:17, the Paraclete is called the "Spirit of Truth," a name that was also found in the Qumran writings. Further, the Spirit of Truth in Qumran was associated closely with the angelic prince of light. We also find the term "Angel of Truth." Are we then justified in concluding that in John, both Jesus and the Paraclete, the Spirit, are angels, the former visible, the latter invisible?

The material from Mandeism, John, the Qumran-Essenes, and Philo points to a shared religious milieu that was Jewish. Drawing from this milieu, all these traditions used common concepts and terminology in expressing their competing theologies. The result was a story of redemption that had elements which corresponded with one another, but not perfectly. Although they reflected the same worldview, they arranged and modified their interpretations differently. John's stands within the Christian tradition.

## SUMMARY

We cannot identify the author of the Gospel according to John, although his association with the "disciple whom Jesus loved" suggests that the narration of the last events of Jesus' life goes back to a disciple in Jerusalem. Because this gospel was credited to John the apostle, its origins were traced to Ephesus, but Alexandria and Antioch, or even some Palestinian site, remain possibilities. Scholars have usually dated John at the end of the first century. John's nonsynoptic structure and contents suggest that he used different sources in its composition. A close examination of the gospel also reveals a structural arrangement around the theme of Jesus' glory, but several sections appear to be out of place and may benefit from rearrangement. John's portrayal of Jesus as a preexistent, divine being who was sent into this world distinguishes his gospel theologically. The themes of dualism and knowledge link this gospel with Jewish traditions identifiable with the Essenes and Mandeism.

## KEY TERMS FOR REVIEW

| | | |
|---|---|---|
| "Disciple whom Jesus loved" | Preexistence | "Love one another" |
| P52 | "I am . . ." | Knowledge |
| Sign source | Paraclete | Gnosticism |
| Dualism | Realized eschatology | Mandeism |

## QUESTIONS FOR REVIEW

1.  Why do scholars question the view that John, the son of Zebedee, wrote John?
2.  What was John's relationship to the synoptics?
3.  What distinguishes John's Christology from that of the synoptics?

# SUGGESTIONS FOR FURTHER READING

Ashton, J. *Understanding the Fourth Gospel.*
New York: Oxford University Press,
1991.

Sloyan, G. *What Are They Saying About John?*
New York: Paulist, 1991.

Smith, D. *John Among The Gospels: The
Relationship in Twentieth-Century
Research.* Minneapolis: Fortress, 1992.

Smith, D. *The Theology of the Gospel of John.*
New York: Cambridge University Press,
1995.

# PART IV

# The Noncanonical Gospels

# 13

✳

# The *Gospel according to Thomas*

## A SAYINGS GOSPEL

As we have already shown, most scholars believe that Matthew and Luke, independently of one another, used a sayings source in their revisions of Mark's gospel. Those sayings that occur in both Matthew and Luke, but not in Mark, derive from that source, commonly called Q. Although many scholars think that Q was a written source, it seems likely that the Q material was part written and part oral. Some of it must have been written because Matthew and Luke often agreed word for word in rather long passages.

No Q document has ever been found, which is the main reason why the two-document theory was not accepted quickly. Scholars doubted the existence of a written source that consisted of only Jesus sayings—no narrative, no passion story, no miracles—just sayings.

The *Gospel according to Thomas* is a sayings (Greek: *logia*) source. Therefore, it is not proper to call it a gospel, at least in the New Testament sense, although it bears this name. It contains no narrative or passion story, which constitutes a New Testament gospel; it is simply a collection of unconnected Jesus sayings, each introduced by the phrase, "Jesus said." Whereas only a handful of scholars argue that the *Gospel according to Thomas* is Q, most scholars agree that *Thomas's* presentation of Jesus demonstrates that a sayings source, such as Q, was entirely possible.

The fascinating story about the discovery of the *Gospel according to Thomas* occurred in several stages and began in 1897, when two British scholars were digging in rubbish heaps in Egypt. On the site of Oxyrhynchus, one of the chief cities of ancient Egypt some 120 miles south of Cairo, they found a very large collection of Greek papyri dating from the first to the seventh centuries CE. Among the numerous texts that were recovered was a page from a book con-

taining Jesus sayings that aroused great interest. It contained eight *logia*,—oracles—
and was published under the title *LOGIA IHCOY*, Greek for "Oracles of Jesus."
As it later turned out, they had discovered eight sayings from the *Gospel according
to Thomas*.

Actually, the first saying of those discovered is only partly preserved; just the end
remains. It reads, "and then you shall see clearly to cast out the mote that is in your
brother's eye." This seems to be the end of a saying preserved in the synoptics:

> Matt. 7:4–5 (cf. Luke 6:42): 4 "Or how can you say to your neighbor, 'Let me take
> the speck out of your eye', while the log is in your own eye? 5 You hypocrite, first
> take the log out of your own eye, and then you will see clearly to take the speck
> out of your neighbor's eye."

What about the other seven *logia*? We can find no real parallel to the words
of Jesus in the canonical Gospels, although some of the new sayings are reminiscent of the canonical words of Jesus. One saying reads, "Jesus said, 'a prophet is
not acceptable in his own country, neither does a physician work cures upon
those who know him.'" The first part of this saying is reminiscent of a passage of
Jesus found in all the synoptics, Luke's form being closest to the new saying:
"Truly I tell you, no prophet is accepted in the prophet's hometown" (4:24). No
parallel to the last part of the Oxyrhynchus sayings exists, but it is interesting to
note that just before the verse quoted, Luke related that Jesus said to the people
in his hometown, "Doubtless you will quote to me this proverb, 'Doctor, cure
yourself!'" Thus the new *logion* (Greek: saying) was at least related to Luke
4:23–24. Luke knew the saying for he included both parts of it. Other *logia* appear
to have no relation at all to the canonical gospel sayings. For instance, one such
saying says, "Jesus said,

> 'I stood in the midst of the world and in the flesh I was seen by them and I found
> all people drunk, and I found no one thirsty, and my soul grieves over the sons of
> men, because they are blind in their heart.'"

Another strange Jesus saying among the new *logia* says, "Raise the stone, and
there you shall find me; cleave the wood, and there I am." Jesus sayings like this
one were simply not known before the discovery of *Thomas*. Still, the papyrus
leaf, which was called Oxyrhynchus 1 (Oxy. 1) was not dated later than the
beginning of the third century CE; thus it was older than the oldest Greek
manuscripts of the New Testament, *Sinaiticus* and *Vaticanus*. Moreover, the sayings
themselves seem to be older because they do not appear to be influenced by the
canonical gospel texts—if we can speak of a canon at so early a date. These new
sayings were independent of the canonical Gospels.

In 1903, the two British scholars returned to Oxyrhynchus and discovered
two more papyri, Oxy. 654 and 655, which also contained more or less unknown
words of Jesus. As in the earlier *logia*, these sayings are introduced by the formula,
"Jesus said." All three papyri, then, seemed to come from the same writing.
Moreover, Oxy. 654 apparently contained the beginning of the work. It begins,
"These are the [wonderful?] words which Jesus the living spoke [. . .] and
Thomas, and he said to them, 'Everyone who hears these words shall never taste
death.'" Here we find the name Thomas. Hippolytus, one of the church fathers,

mentioned a *Gospel according to Thomas* and even gave a short quotation from it (*logion* 4). At about the same time (about 230), Origen mentioned a heretical *Gospel according to Thomas.* In the fourth century, the *Gospel according to Thomas* was said to have been used with great popularity by the Manicheans (a Jewish-Christian sect).

Did these Greek papyri fragments actually stem from the *Gospel according to Thomas*? That was certainly a possibility. Other candidates were the *Gospel according to the Egyptians* and the *Gospel according to the Hebrews,* writings quoted by different church fathers. Scholars generally agreed that no direct influence from the canonical Gospels was found in the recovered sayings.

The next stage in the discovery of the *Gospel according to Thomas* began with the discovery of the Nag Hammadi library in Upper Egypt in 1945. This collection of more than 50 writings is divided among 13 codices, written in Coptic (the last stage of the old Egyptian language). We can tell, however, that the original language for these documents was Greek.

Most, but not all, of the Nag Hammadi writings are gnostic. The Gnostics emphasized knowledge (Greek: *gnosis*), not faith (Greek: *pistis*). The savior came down from heaven and imparted *gnosis*. *Gnosis* about what? About the true nature of human beings and the cosmos. Certain angels—more or less removed from God—made the material world and the human body. In some gnostic systems the angels were evil and opposed to God. God was pure spirit and had nothing to do with material creation. Human beings contained a spark of the divine spirit, which had come down here through a fall that took place in the divine world. When the savior imparted this *gnosis*, people recognized their divine origin and were saved. When they died, their spirits ascended back to their true home. In John's gospel the interest in knowledge was related to Gnosticism. Although the *Gospel according to Thomas* was found in a basically gnostic library, *Thomas* is not gnostic.

A French professor first saw the connection between the Oxyrhynchus papyri and the Coptic *Gospel according to Thomas*. He was sitting at the metro underground railway in Paris, turning over the leaves of some transcriptions from the Nag Hammadi library that had been brought to him by a young French scholar. This scholar had just arrived from Egypt and had been shown the codices by the director of the Coptic Museum in Cairo. The professor, turning over the pages in the subway, saw some lines reading, "These are the secret words which the living Jesus spoke and Didymus Judas Thomas wrote." It occurred to him that he had read that line before. When he arrived home, he took out his copy of the Oxyrhynchus Papyri. Its fragmentary beginning was very similar to what he had read in the metro. It seemed that the *Gospel according to Thomas* was among the writings found at Nag Hammadi and Oxyrhynchus.

An international committee of scholars was soon formed and traveled to Cairo. Gilles Quispel, a Dutch scholar, was a member of the team, and he made the first provisional translation of the *Gospel according to Thomas*. When the English and French declared war on Egypt in 1956, Professor Quispel left Alexandria on an American battleship with a complete photocopy of the Coptic gospel. It was published with a translation in 1959.

The *logia* in Oxy. P.1, 654, and 655 all have parallels in the Coptic *Thomas*, and it is clear that the Coptic writing was based on a Greek original. The important question, of course, is whether this collection of Jesus sayings, which appears to be independent of the New Testament Gospels, has any genuine Jesus sayings.

## THE AUTHORSHIP AND PROVENANCE OF THE *GOSPEL ACCORDING TO THOMAS*

Who is "Didymus Judas Thomas?" The lists of disciples in the New Testament Gospels all include a Thomas. But Didymus Judas Thomas, though unusual as a name, has a specific meaning. *Didymus* is Greek for "twin," as in twin brother. *Thomas* is the Aramaic word with the same meaning. In John, the disciple Thomas is referred to as "Thomas, who was called the Twin (Greek: *Didymus*)" (11:16; 20:24). Was Thomas a nickname, or had it become a personal name?

A number of early Christian sources regarded Thomas to have been a nickname, for they also supplied the real name of the disciple. Thus, Eusebius (fourth century) spoke of "Judas, who is also called Thomas." Eusebius said that his data on this person came from a Syriac document that he discovered in Edessa, now Urfa, in southeastern Turkey. The Syriac source, the *Doctrine of Addai,* spoke of "Judas Thomas," that is, "Judas the Twin."

A problem arises because John did not identify "Thomas, who was called the Twin (*Didymus*)" with Judas, although he identified a certain Judas as one of the followers of Jesus (14:22). Mark 6:3 even recorded that Jesus had a brother by the name of Judas, but Judas was not identified as a twin of Jesus. The sources are confusing!

In summary: (1) Mark (repeated by Matthew 13:55) says that Jesus had a brother named Judas; (2) the New Testament Gospels say that Jesus had a disciple by the name of Thomas, who was called "Didymus"; (3) in the Syrian tradition, these two characters occurred together: "Judas who is also called Thomas;" and (4) the *Gospel according to Thomas* reads "Didymus Judas Thomas." Apparently the brother of Jesus, Judas by name, was identified with the disciple with the name of "Thomas" meaning "twin." Judas Thomas is thus Didymus (the twin brother of Jesus).

Judas Thomas was represented exactly this way in the *Acts of Thomas,* an early third-century Syriac source. Here Judas, Jesus' twin brother, was portrayed as a special apostle. He stood between Jesus and the world of humans as a revealer in his own right, although he was not in the same class of Jesus. Thomas was the apostle to the east. Even today, Christians on the east coast of India are called "Thomas Christians."

The *Gospel according to Thomas,* then, was apparently put together in the Syrian realm, probably in Edessa. This collection of Jesus sayings was probably put under the name of a revered figure so it would reach a wide readership. This practice was common in antiquity (compare the books of **Enoch** with the New Testament letters of Peter). A few scholars date the *Gospel according to Thomas* as early 50 CE and consider it invaluable for understanding the historical Jesus, but because of *Thomas's* sources, most agree that it was written some time in the first half of the second century, perhaps around 140 CE.

# THE SOURCES OF THE *GOSPEL ACCORDING TO THOMAS*

Because the *Gospel according to Thomas* was found among the Nag Hammadi tracts, scholars have been apt to label it as a gnostic source. But *Thomas* is not gnostic. No trace of the specifically gnostic mythology can be detected in it. However, some source sayings are similar to statements found in some gnostic texts, but these are simply part of a certain mystical trend found throughout more-or-less philosophical works in late antiquity. The passage of Jesus already found in Oxyrhynchus 1 belongs to these sayings: "Raise the stone, and there you shall find me; cleave the wood, and there I am." This is *logion* 77 in the Coptic *Thomas*.

This saying is pantheistic: God (Greek: *theos*) is found everywhere (Greek: *pan*); the divine nature pervades the cosmos. This thought is not an Israelite-Jewish one, but stems from a certain Greek philosophical tradition that was adapted by different religious groups in the Hellenistic world.

Another *Thomas logion* that belongs to this tradition is *logion* 67: "Whoever knows the All but fails to know himself lacks everything." We find the same thought in *logion* 3, especially in the Oxyrhynchus version: "Whoever knows himself, will find the Kingdom." The idea is that divine nature, being found everywhere, is also found in human beings. Thus, by knowing oneself, one knows everything, even the godhead. It is hard to believe that Jesus taught this. Thus, tradition in *Thomas* does not help scholars understand Jesus.

The redactor of *Thomas* must have been an Encratite. A strong tendency to **Encratism** (Greek: *Enkrateia*, or [self-continence]) existed in the ancient Church; it called for abstention from sex, wine, and meat. It was especially prominent in Gnosticism, which made it even easier for some scholars to classify *Thomas* as gnostic, but Encratism was found also in the New Testament. According to Matthew 19:12, Jesus appeared to approve of people who had castrated themselves,

> Matt. 19:12: "For there are eunuchs who have been so from birth, and there are eunuchs who have been made eunuchs by others, and there are eunuchs who have made themselves eunuchs for the sake of the kingdom of heaven. Let anyone accept this who can."

And Paul encouraged people not to marry if they felt that they could abstain from sex: "To the unmarried and the widows I say that it is well for them to remain unmarried as I am" (1 Cor. 7:8).

Encratism was very strong in Syrian Christianity. In the beginning there was even a teaching to the effect that the baptized must abstain from sex and remain celibate. This view was taught by Tatian, who came from the east, went to Rome and became a pupil of Justin Martyr, and after Justin's martyrdom, went back east. Tatian's argument was that ever since the coming of Christ sex, even in marriage, had been abolished. Christian abstinence hinged on the idea that the resurrection life of the kingdom, which was free of marriage according to Jesus, was being realized in the lives of Christians. Jesus' controversial words touching on marriage are found in Mark: "For when they rise from the dead, they neither marry nor are given in marriage, but are like angels in heaven" (12:25).

*Logion* 75 of the *Gospel according to Thomas* says, "Many are standing at the door, but only those who were celibate will enter the bridal chamber." This statement means that only those who are solitary would go to heaven. A specific Syrian interpretation of the parable of the ten bridesmaids in Matthew 25 said that all the virgins were actually brides, not merely "bridesmaids," as is said in English translations. The Greek word in the parable is *parthenos* (Greek: virgin). According to the Syrian version, only some of the virgins fell asleep, whereas in Matthew's text they all did. According to the Syrian version, only the ones who stayed awake were celibate.

Other Encratite sayings appear in *Thomas*. They can hardly be attributed to Jesus. In the New Testament Gospels, only the passages about the eunuchs can argue for an Encratite inclination on the part of Jesus. In Luke 18:29–30, Jesus said;

> Luke 18:29–30: 29 "Truly I tell to you, there is no one who has left house or wife or brothers or parents or children, for the sake of the kingdom of God, 30 who will not get back very much more in this age, and in the age to come eternal life, . . ."

These words have an Encratite ring with their reference to the abandonment of wives, but the parallel versions in Mark and Matthew leave out any reference to the abandonment of wives (Mark 10:29; Matt. 19:29).

Quispel convincingly argued for the existence of a third source in *Thomas*— a Jewish-Christian source. When the Oxyryhnchus fragments became known, people started to consider the possibility that the fragments derived from a Jewish-Christian source. How was it possible to prove such a thesis? By comparing the *Thomas* saying in question with versions of the same saying in writings generally agreed to be Jewish-Christian. Actually it was not difficult to prove that *Thomas* and Jewish-Christian writings agreed in wording—not only in themes but also in Jesus sayings. What if a saying in *Thomas*, which was corroborated by a Jewish-Christian source, diverges from a parallel reading in the synoptic Gospels? Then scholars had to employ tradition criticism to determine the more original versions.

On a Sunday not long after he had returned from Egypt with the copy of the *Gospel according to Thomas,* Quispel sat in his living room with a book in his lap, slowly turning the pages. The book was a fourth-century novel, the *Pseudo-Clementine Homilies,* ascribed to a certain Clement, who was a bishop of Rome early in the second century. This pseudo-Christian writing, which stemmed from a Jewish-Christian sect, stated that the Pharisees and the scribes received the key to the kingdom but had not given it to those who wanted to enter (*Hom.* 3:18:3) Instantly Quispel remembered that the same thing was said in *logion* 39: "Jesus said, 'The Pharisees and the scribes have received the keys of knowledge and hidden them. They themselves have not entered, nor have they allowed to enter those who wish.'"

A version of this saying appears in Luke 11:52, but here it is said that the Pharisees stole the key: "Woe to you lawyers! For you have taken away the key of knowledge; you did not enter yourselves, and you hindered those who were entering." In this case, scholars concluded that *Thomas* is a witness to a Jewish-Christian tradition, one also found in the *Pseudo-Clementine Homilies.* Scholars are not sure which version of the saying has priority over the version in Luke.

What if a saying in *Thomas* can also be found in the synoptics? Does that mean the synoptic Gospels influenced *Thomas*? Consider *logion* 47.

> *Logion* 47: "Jesus said, 'It is impossible for a man to mount two horses or to stretch two bows. And it is impossible for a servant to serve two masters; otherwise he will honor the one and treat the other contemptuously. No man drinks old wine and immediately desires to drink new wine. And new wine is not put into old wineskins, lest they burst; nor is old wine put into a new wineskin, lest it spoil it. An old patch is not sewn into a new garment, because a tear would result.' "

Here are five sayings, or *logia*, that show that the numbering system is somewhat arbitrary. The second saying occurs in Matthew 6:24 and Luke 16:13, the fourth and fifth in Mark 2:21–22. If the *Gospel according to Thomas* is dependent on the Gospels, why does it borrow so little from them? Why would it leave out other Jesus sayings in the Gospels? A growing number of scholars argue that *Thomas* did not directly rely on the Gospels as source material.

The first and third sayings, "It is impossible for a man to mount two horses or to stretch two bows. . . . No man drinks old wine and immediately desires to drink new wine," have no parallel in the New Testament. Their style fits many of the Jesus sayings in the Gospels, and we find no telltale signs of theological incongruity with the teachings of Jesus. Are the sayings simply inventions that mimic traditional Jesus sayings? Or are they genuine Jesus sayings preserved only by *Thomas,* without parallels in Jewish-Christian literature?

## SUMMARY

The *Gospel according to Thomas* is a collection of Jesus sayings that originated in Syria and dates to the second century. It is falsely attributed to Jesus' brother, Judas, who was identified with Jesus' disciple named Thomas. The teachings of Jesus in *Thomas* are often labeled as gnostic, but more precisely they represent a tradition of Jewish-Christian asceticism known as Encratism. Although many of the Jesus sayings in *Thomas* have parallels in the canonical Gospels, some do not, which prompts scholars to speculate about their authenticity.

## KEY TERMS FOR REVIEW

| | |
|---|---|
| Oxyrhynchus papyri | Gnostic |
| *logia/logion* | Didymus Judas Thomas |
| Nag Hammadi library | Syria |
| Coptic | Encratism |

## QUESTIONS FOR REVIEW

1. What are the "stages" of the discovery of the *Gospel according to Thomas*'s discovery?

2. What can we say about the reputed author of the *Gospel according to Thomas,* Didymus Judas Thomas?

3. Why is it more accurate to consider the *Gospel according to Thomas* as Encratite rather than gnostic?

## SUGGESTIONS FOR FURTHER READING

Patterson, S. *The Gospel according to Thomas and Jesus.* Sonoma: Polebridge Press, 1993.

Patterson, S. *The Fifth Gospel: The Gospel according to Thomas Comes of Age.* Harrisburg: Trinity Press International, 1998.

Tuckett, C. "Thomas and the Synoptics," *Novum Testamentum* 30 (1988) 132–57.

Uro, R. ed. *Thomas at the Crossroads: Essays on the Gospel according to Thomas.* Edinburgh: T & T Clark, 1998.

# 14

※

# Other Jewish-
# Christian Gospels

## THE HISTORY OF JEWISH CHRISTIANS

*Logion* 68 of the *Gospel according to Thomas* says, "Blessed are you when you are hated and persecuted; and you will find a place where you will not be persecuted." The latter part of the saying has no parallel in the synoptics, but it was probably not invented by the author of *Thomas* because it was also quoted by Clement of Alexandria as a Jesus saying cherished by certain people: "Blessed are the persecuted for my sake, for they will have a place where they will not be persecuted" (*Strom.* 4:6). *Thomas* and Clement bear witness to the same tradition.

This version of Jesus' blessing of his persecuted disciples in Matthew 5:10–11, is extra-canonical:

> Matt. 5:10–11: 10 Blessed are those who are persecuted for righteousness' sake, for theirs is the kingdom of heaven. 11 Blessed are you when people revile you and persecute you and utter all kinds of evil against you falsely on my account. [See also Luke 6:22.]

Thus, this version is similar to the saying that the Pharisaic scribes received the key to the kingdom but concealed it. That saying was found both in *the Gospel according to Thomas* (*logion* 39) and in the Jewish-Christian novel ascribed to Clement of Rome in the second century (*Hom.* 3:18:3). In the latter case, there is a parallel in the synoptics; the scribes stole (did not receive), the key to heaven (Luke 11:52; Matt. 23:13). What was the original version of the saying? Did the scribes receive the key, or steal it? The Jewish-Christian tradition said that they received it but then kept it to themselves, which they should not have done.

In the case of the saying about finding a safe place for Christians, there is no parallel in the New Testament Gospels, but there can be little doubt that the saying is Jewish-Christian. It also occurs, as a matter of fact, not only in Clement of Alexandria but also in the Jewish-Christian novel, *Recognitions,* ascribed to Clement of Rome. Those who believed in Jesus were brought into a "strong place and thus kept safe during the war" (*Rec.* 1:37). This novel contains only the second part of the saying, whereas both *Thomas* and Clement of Alexandria include a version of the first part.

Which "war" was this? Obviously the Jewish insurrection against the Romans in 66 CE, a revolt that ended with the destruction of Jerusalem and its temple in 70 CE. The primitive Christian community in Jerusalem did not join arms with the other Jews. According to a tradition that was preserved by Eusebius, the Christian Jews fled across the Jordan River to the city of Pella in the Decapolis region. This city must be the safe place mentioned in *Thomas,* Clement of Alexandria, and the novel ascribed to Clement of Rome.

A sarcophagus (a stone coffin) was found beneath the ruins of an old church building in Pella. It may have contained the body of James, the brother of Jesus who became the leader of the Christian community in Jerusalem. James suffered martyrdom in 62 CE, four years before the war between the Jews and the Romans broke out. His martyrdom was probably bound up with an intensification of Jewish nationalism. The Christian sect was obviously subjected to pressure. Were the Christians against the Romans or not? The Christians believed that Jesus would return as the Messiah and destroy unbelieving Jews as well as unbelieving Gentiles. When the war broke out, they fled from Jerusalem to Pella. They may have taken the remnants of James with them as they fled. The sarcophagus found beneath the church building in Pella may have contained the remnants of James' body or the remnants of another of Jesus' relatives, because, according to Eusebius, the leadership of the Jewish-Christian communities remained, if at all possible, in the hands of a member of Jesus' family.

From Pella, the Jewish Christians moved farther east and established a center in Edessa, a city on the upper Euphrates. The *Gospel according to Thomas* was probably written here in the second century. Later the center was moved to Baghdad. This church came to be known as Eastern Syrian, or Assyrian, and was once a very powerful church. Its patriarch ruled over the entire area from Antioch in the west to Peking in the east. Most people are accustomed to regarding Christianity as a Western phenomenon, but this view is at the expense of overlooking this once powerful church. Today, however, the Assyrian Church, as it is called, is sadly reduced due to persecutions and suppressions. Its patriarch, the successor of James, now lives in an apartment in San Francisco.

Thus, the conventional picture that Jewish Christianity died out without leaving any significant traces is not true; it still lives on in the Assyrian Church. On the other hand, many Jewish-Christian enclaves in Egypt, Palestine, and Syria did die out. Besides the *Gospel according to Thomas,* which was preserved whole thanks to the Nag Hammadi discovery, we have three other Jewish-Christian Gospels that are associated with Jewish Christianity and may have used a Jewish-Christian source. Only fragments of these gospel texts survive, and these fragments are, in essence, scattered citations found in the works of different Christian writers who had a rather low view of these Jewish-Christian communities. Scholars, therefore, must exercise caution when describing these texts.

## JEWISH-CHRISTIAN GOSPELS

### (1) The *Gospel according to the Nazoreans*

Several church fathers quoted fragments of the *Gospel according to the Nazoreans*. As far as we can learn, it appears to be close to Matthew. Most of the differences between it and Matthew involve additional Jesus sayings. These sayings exhibit a tendency to explain some of Jesus' actions and other sayings. When Jesus' family asked him to receive John's baptism he said, "Wherein have I sinned that I should go and be baptized by him? Unless what I have said is ignorance (a sin of ignorance)." There is no point in enumerating the other differences between the *Gospel according to the Nazoreans* and Matthew, but the divergences cannot be explained simply as arbitrary changes of Matthew.

The name of this gospel is, however, intriguing. *Nazoreans* is a very ancient designation of the Christians; it is in fact the oldest designation of the followers of Jesus, which we can see from the Book of Acts. Paul was accused of being a ringleader of the sect of the Nazoreans (Acts 24:5). "Christians," or "Men of Christ," was a name given to this sect in Antioch (Syria), a Greek-speaking territory (Acts 11:26). The name *Nazorean,* however, is Aramaic and is still applied to the Christians in the east. Thus the members of the Eastern Syrian or Assyrian Church are still referred to as Nazoreans.

What does the name *Nazorean* signify? One possibility comes from Matthew. Among his many formula quotations (quotations from the Jewish Bible purporting to show that Jesus is the Messiah) is Matthew 2:23. There it is said that the parents of Jesus settled in Nazareth, a town in Galilee, in order that "what had been spoken through the prophets might be fulfilled, 'He will be called a Nazorean.' " Two difficulties are connected with this verse. In the first place, no such prophetic passage exists in the Jewish Bible. Why would Matthew fake an explanation? Second, it is philologically impossible to derive the word *Nazorean* from *Nazareth. Nazorean* (Greek: *Nazoraios*) would have to come from *Nazoreth,* but we can find no such spelling of the name of the town Nazareth. A man from Nazareth would have been a *nazaraios* or *nazarenos*, not a *nazoraios*. The obstacle is that the first "o" in *Nazoraios* is long; it cannot come from the second "a" in Nazareth. It would also be unique for a sect to take a name derived from the hometown of its founder, members of the Jesus sect being called "people of Nazareth." Jesus and his disciples did not use Nazareth as their headquarters.

What then does *Nazorean* mean? It derives from the Hebrew verb *nazar,* "keep" or "observe." When *Nazorean* is used as an Aramaic noun, it becomes *nazor* or *nazoraios*. This sect of Jesus was called the "observers." Observers of what? Certain secret traditions, rites, or teachings? Is there some credence to the story in the *Secret Gospel according to Mark* that the Jesus sect had secret rites and teachings?

Different sects referred to themselves as "observers." John the Baptist's sect probably used this name. Jesus followed John the Baptist and may have taken over the name of his sect as well as some of John's disciples when starting on his own.

## (2) The *Gospel according to the Ebionites*

The *Gospel according to the Ebionites* deviates considerably from that of the Nazoreans. It has no virgin birth story. Instead, Jesus is said to have been adopted as the Son of God upon his baptism. When he came up out of the water, the Spirit descended upon him and entered into him. Then the voice from heaven declared him to be God's Son.

Epiphanius, the fourth-century bishop of Salamis in Cyprus who reported on this gospel, also stated that it was because of this account that the Ebionites, a Jewish-Christian sect, said Jesus was begotten like any other human but chosen by God to be the Son of God. According to the bishop, this choice was made when God entered Jesus at baptism. Thus the heavenly Christ and the Spirit were the same being. Epiphanius said that this figure was the highest of the angels created by the Father. Another church father, Tertullian, who lived toward the end of the second century, said that Jewish Christianity taught that an angel was in Jesus. At the baptism of Jesus, then, the highest of the angels, known as both the Messiah and the Spirit, entered into Jesus.

This view seems strange and contrary to the canonical Gospels. What did the synoptics say? Matthew and Luke said that the Spirit descended upon Jesus, but not that it entered into him. Mark is different, however. He used a different preposition from Matthew's and Luke's. Whereas Matthew and Luke said that the Spirit descended upon Jesus, Mark said that it descended "into" (*eis*) him (although English translations downplay this difference). Consider what Jesus cried out on the cross: "At three o'clock Jesus cried out with a loud voice, 'Eloi, Eloi, lema sabachthani?' which means, 'My God, my God, why have you forsaken me?'" (Mark 15:34). Did the divine figure who entered into the man Jesus at his baptism leave him before his death? It seems so according to the *Gospel according to the Ebionites.* The Jewish Christians attached no significance to the death of Jesus; it had no aspect of atonement for them. The past life of Jesus was simply that of a teacher.

According to the *Gospel according to the Ebionites,* one of the reasons Jesus came into the world was to teach that all the passages in the Bible that dealt with the temple and sacrifices were falsifications—the Jewish-Christian way of dealing with the fall of the temple. All Jews were shocked by the fall and sought to explain it. As for the Christians, they had two options. One was to say that the death of Jesus was the sacrifice that put an end to all sacrifices under the old dispensation and ended the need for a temple.

This view was propounded by Paul, the apostle to the Gentiles. Paul wanted to have Gentiles join Christianity without having to convert to Jewish ways—without having to undergo circumcision, bring sacrifices to the temple, and so forth. The Christians in Jerusalem, however, were law-abiding Jews. They could not regard Jesus' sacrifice as the end of the law and the temple, so they preferred another option. Jesus was understood as a teacher who would return as the

Messiah. Why then, was it necessary to destroy the very temple whose worship they had always condoned? Because Jesus had not only criticized the way in which the temple was run and predicted its downfall but also taught that the biblical passages prescribing temple worship were false. Ultimately, the Jewish Christians seemed to have taken certain words literally, such as Jesus' quotation of Hosea 6:6 in Matthew 12:7: "I desire mercy, and not sacrifice" (which probably means "I want more mercy than sacrifice").

Thus, the idea that the divine figure would leave Jesus before he died is only logical because God cannot die. That view would have no meaning to Jewish Christians; it would be absurd. Thus it appears that the Gospel according to Mark is based on an old Jewish-Christian gospel and that the teachings found in the Jewish-Christian sources, which stem from the second century, may indeed be quite old. Others in the first century shared this idea of Jesus. Irenaeus, a second-century church father, described a certain Cerinthus who taught that Jesus was the natural offspring of Joseph and Mary who gained the presence of the Christ at his baptism (*Against the Heresies* 1:26:1).

The Jewish-Christian origin of the *Gospel according to the Ebionites* can be corroborated by its name. *Ebionite* is derived from the Hebrew word, *ebyon*, which means poor. Thus this gospel is the gospel of the poor ones. In Judaism, poor was synonymous with being pious because Jewish collaborators who worked together with occupying peoples, like the Greeks and Romans, got rich, whereas pious Jews who adhered to the old ways suffered economically. In Psalms in the Old Testament, the righteous who suffered were often referred to as "poor ones." In Jesus' time, various groups called themselves "pious ones," which was probably true of Jesus' group. In Matthew's version of the Sermon on the Mount, Jesus began the beatitudes by saying, "Blessed are the poor in spirit" (5:3). Is this a characterization of the righteous among the people, as it was in Psalms in the Old Testament? Or is it a designation of a specific group? In Matthew, Jesus addressed the crowd as well as his disciples, but especially the latter (5:2). Luke was quite specific about Jesus addressing his disciples: "Then he looked up at his disciples and said: 'Blessed are you who are poor . . .'" (6:20). Here the disciples were singled out as the "poor" without Matthew's qualification (poor *in spirit*).

The group behind the *Gospel according to the Ebionites* continued the archaic name of "poor ones" for the disciples. This gospel probably preserved traditions that went back to the Jerusalem community, which does not necessarily mean that Luke preserved the original words of Jesus. The opposite may be true in this case because in Judaism beatitudes were usually expressed in the third person. Luke, though, placed great weight on the primitive community in Jerusalem, and the nucleus of this community was made up of Jesus' disciples.

### (3) The *Gospel according to the Hebrews*

*Hebrews* is simply another designation for Jews. The Jews cherishing the *Gospel according to the Hebrews* probably lived in Egypt because two Alexandrian church fathers quoted different passages from it. It is the most widely attested Jewish-Christian gospel.

The *Gospel according to the Hebrews* seems to be rather different from the other Gospels we have examined so far, both canonical and noncanonical. One passage in particular—that of the baptism of Jesus—illustrates this. As in the *Gospel according to the Ebionites,* it presupposes a permanent union of Jesus with the Spirit. However, whereas the *Gospel according to the Ebionites* affirms that the Spirit "entered into" Jesus; the *Gospel according to the Hebrews* teaches that the Spirit "descended upon him" and came to "rest in" him. The portrayal of the Spirit in the *Gospel according to the Hebrews* is also distinctive. Instead of the voice from heaven acknowledging Jesus, the Spirit who descended spoke and acknowledged him. The Spirit called Jesus "My Son" and stated that "in all the prophets was I waiting for thee that thou shouldest come and I might rest in thee."

Who was this personified Spirit of God? In another fragment of this gospel, Jesus, after his baptism, said, "Even so did my mother, the Holy Spirit, take me by one of my hairs and carry me away on to the great mountain Tabor." Obviously, according to some Jewish Christians, the Spirit of God was a female figure. This view contrasts with the neuter-gendered Spirit of trinitarian dogma in the Western church. The Jewish Christianity of the *Gospel according to the Hebrews* assumes that the trinity consisted of the Father, Mother, and Child—the nuclear family. Jewish tradition has many references to the female gender of God's Spirit. In Hebrew Spirit is a female noun, and during the late **second temple era** God's Spirit was regularly identified as a woman.

This idea may strike many people as strange because most are accustomed to thinking of the Jewish and Christian God of the Bible as a male figure without a female counterpart. But the Bible is a heavily edited book. Ancient inscriptions describe Yahweh, the God of the Jews, as having a spouse named Asherah. Asherah was a female goddess of the Canaanite peoples in Israel. Later, Wisdom (or God's Spirit) took the place of this goddess by being personified and made into an independent being by the side of God. Wisdom can be represented as God's daughter as well as his wife. Wisdom was described as God's daughter in the book of Proverbs. In the noncanonical work, the *Wisdom of Solomon,* Wisdom was depicted as God's wife. This text also equated Wisdom with the Spirit and said that they inspired the prophets.

## SUMMARY

There are three other Jewish–Christian Gospels in addition to the *Gospel according to Thomas,* although they are preserved only in fragmentary form. The *Gospel according to the Nazoreans* appears to be close to the Gospel according to Matthew in content and takes its name from the idea of Jesus' followers "observing" his teachings. The *Gospel according to the Ebionites* presents an adoptionist Christology in which the man Jesus is adopted as the Son of God at his baptism by means of receiving God's Spirit. This gospel is named after the "poor ones," presumably righteous Jews, who followed Jesus. The *Gospel according to the Hebrews* places Jesus within a distinctly Jewish setting by identifying God as his father and God's Spirit

as his mother. As a group, these Gospels bear witness to some of the Jewish interpretations of Jesus that were marginalized by later Christian communities.

## KEY TERMS FOR REVIEW

| | |
|---|---|
| 66 CE–70 CE | Nazorean |
| Pella | *Gospel according to the Ebionites* |
| Edessa | Ebionite |
| Assyrian Church | *Gospel according to the Hebrews* |
| *Gospel according to the Nazoreans* | Asherah/Spirit |

## QUESTIONS FOR REVIEW

1. What happened to the Jerusalem Church after the Jewish war against the
   Romans?
2. How does the *Gospel according to the Nazoreans* modify the Gospel according
   to Matthew?
3. How does the *Gospel according to the Ebionites* present the mission of Jesus?
4. How does the *Gospel according to the Hebrews* describe God's Spirit?

## SUGGESTIONS FOR FURTHER READING

Cameron, R. *The Other Gospels: Non-
Canonical Gospel Texts.* Philadelphia:
Westminster, 1982.

Elliot, J. ed. *The Apocryphal New Testament: A
Collection of Apocryphal Christian
Literature.* Oxford: Clarendon, 1993.

Henneke, E. and Schneemelcher, W., eds.
*New Testament Apocrypha,* 2 vols. Trans.
by A. Higgins, et al. Ed. R. McL.
Wilson. Philadelphia: Westminster, 1991.

Klijn, A. *Jewish-Christian Gospel Tradition.*
Leiden: Brill, 1992.

# PART V

# Jesus and His World

# 15

✵

# The Major
# Religious Groups

## THE RELIGIOUS SITUATION
## OF JESUS' DAY

When Josephus, the first-century Jewish historian, described his religion to the Romans, he said that from the beginning Judaism had been divided into three "philosophies," as he called them: the Sadducees, the Pharisees, and the Essenes. A fourth philosophy was added later, a new party, namely that of the revolutionaries—those who raised insurrections against the Romans. These people were traditionally referred to as the Zealots, "people of zeal" or fanatics.

As Josephus's description of Judaism implied, in Jesus' day Jewish communities may have shared many beliefs, but they did not have the *same* beliefs. The result was a form of religious diversity and a Jewish community that was home to many "Judaisms." Belief in Israel's God and covenant united Jews at large, but there was room for disagreement over the details, and some of the disagreements led to hostile relations among Jews. Jewish sects competed in their efforts to prescribe their brand of Judaism to other Jews.

Although we know that non-Israelite religions were present and active in Israel during Jesus' lifetime (there were pagan shrines in Israel and many Gentiles in the territory of Galilee where Jesus lived), the Gospels never refer to them, nor is Jesus ever presented as discussing them. Some scholars have argued that Jesus needs to be interpreted within a broader context that emphasizes the influence of Greco-Roman religions and philosophies on the Jews. While we must acknowledge that the wide presence of the Greeks and Romans left a mark on Israeli life and culture, the Gospels do not give a clear indication of their religious influence on Jesus. According to the Gospels, Jesus was active among Israelite circles that encouraged a commitment to Israel's religious heritage.

The Gospels describe how Jesus clashed with different Jewish sects of his day and had his "Jewishness" assailed when he was charged with a lax observance of the law, which was Israel's religious standard. Interestingly, no gospel accounts of Jesus debating with Gentiles exist, except for some very brief encounters that exhibit Jesus' reluctance to deal with Gentiles. Nor are there accounts that discuss issues of importance to Gentiles—this despite the fact that Gentiles had been present in and around Israel for centuries and that the Gospels were written when Gentiles were a growing force within the Church. Instead, Jesus was presented as touching on Jewish concerns that were of interest to other Jews as well.

Scholars do not dispute that Jesus was a controversial figure, but it was *as a Jew* that he was controversial. Jesus was even accused by some Jews of being possessed by Beelzebul, the prince of demons, but Jesus' behavior that brought about such a charge was the very *Jewish* act of exorcism. It is therefore unwise to devalue Jesus' Jewishness because of the charges leveled against him; it was not uncommon for a Jewish sect to verbally lock horns with other Jewish sects and leave the impression that it was the only true Judaism. Christianity's earliest writer, Paul, the Christian missionary, came from the ranks of the Pharisees, and he insisted that he did not compromise his Jewish faith. The New Testament also says that Jesus counted a Zealot among his disciples (Luke 6:15, "Simon, who was called the Zealot"). If *Zealot* signified a Jewish revolutionary in Jesus' day—an issue that is still debated by scholars—then this view may be further evidence that Jesus attracted devout Jews from competing sects.

### Second Temple Judaism

Second temple Judaism was the era that shaped the Jewish communities of Jesus' day. It began with the rebuilding of Jerusalem's temple in 515 BCE, after the destruction of the first Jewish temple in 587 BCE by the Babylonians, and ended with the destruction of the second temple by the Romans in 70 CE. Over the span of approximately 600 years, Israel was subjugated by, and in turn influenced by, three major powers.

The Persians gained their authority over Israel when they conquered the Babylonian empire in 539 BCE and thus came to control Israel and other peoples of the Near East. Cyrus, who led the conquest, established a policy of limited local rule through governors (usually indigenous) and granted religious freedom. This method of rule allowed the Jews to rebuild their city and their temple and to reestablish a community devoted to the law of Moses under the leadership of the priests. Biblical texts like Ezra and Nehemiah describe the struggles and tensions that existed among the Jews who lived during this period.

In 333 BCE, Alexander the Great defeated the Persian forces at Issus and gained control of their vast holdings, Israel included. Alexander's victory allowed the export of Hellenistic culture and encouraged the spread of Hellenistic political, religious, and philosophical interests throughout the Near East. His sudden death in 323 BCE resulted in the breakup of his empire among his generals. From 323 to 198 BCE, the Jews were ruled by the Ptolemaic dynasty, founded by Ptolemy; from 198 to 142 BCE, the Jews were ruled by the Seleucid dynasty, founded by Seleucus. It was not until the time of the Seleucid ruler named Antiochus IV Epiphanes that many law-abiding Jews rebelled against the harshness of Greek rule. Antiochus's policy of forced Hellenization (that is, outlawing circumcision) in 167 BCE clashed with their religious interests and triggered the **Maccabean revolt** that brought religious freedom for Jews in 164 BCE, and eventually political freedom for Jerusalem in 142 BCE.

Jewish political independence lasted from 142 BCE to 63 BCE. During this time, Israel was ruled by the **Hasmonean** dynasty, the Jewish descendants of the Maccabean leaders who later went on to establish a period of territorial expansion and economic prosperity. Within the Jewish community, however, differences mounted over the application of Jewish law to daily life, and this issue led to the different religious communities that operated in Jesus' day. Their religious concerns can thus be traced to the Maccabean revolt. These communities operated with religious agendas for Israel that made them de facto political parties with the line between religion and politics being blurred. The Hasmonean rulers were too Hellenistic in their ways for many Jews who were devoted to the law, and some Hasmonean rulers went so far as to oppress and even crucify Jewish dissidents.

Eventually, strife among two Hasmonean princes allowed the Roman general Pompeii, under the pretense of being a peacemaker, to place Israel under Roman control in 63 BCE. Rome granted religious freedom to the Jews and left the high priest of the Jerusalem temple and his council in charge of daily matters for Jews, whereas ultimate civil authority lay in Roman hands. Long before the time of Jesus' birth, Herod the Great, a Jew of questionable lineage, had established a dynasty in Israel as a **client king** of Rome. Herod's rule as king over Israel began in 37 BCE and ended with his death in 4 BCE, shortly after the birth of Jesus (according to the birth narratives of Matthew and Luke). As a Galilean living in northern Israel, Jesus lived almost his entire life under the rule of Herod's son, Antipas, who governed Galilee (4 BCE–39 CE), while a series of Roman **prefects** governed Judea, home to Jerusalem, and Samaria, the southern and central regions of Israel. Five hundred years of tumultuous experiences left the Jewish community of the first century subservient to yet another foreign power.

## THE SOCIAL-POLITICAL SITUATION OF JESUS' DAY

The great problem that Jews faced in the centuries immediately preceding the emergence of Christianity was whether the Jewish community should be led by the progressives or by the conservatives. The former were Hellenizers and open to the culture imposed by the Greeks and Romans, whereas the latter were Jews who resisted foreign influences. The Greek verb *hellenizo* means to speak Greek. With the conquest of the Persian empire by Alexander the Great, Greek became the diplomatic language of the Near East, and it remained the major language even after the Romans arrived on the scene.

After Alexander's death, his great empire was split among his generals who, with their successors, wanted their subjects to adopt Greek ways of life as well as the Greek language. Perhaps the most important facet of Hellenization was the foundation of *poleis* (Greek: cities) with the status of *polis* (Greek: city), the classical Greek city-state. A *polis* was autonomous and democratically governed—that is, governed by the *demos* (Greek), the people or landowners, which excluded women as well as children and slaves. (The region of Decapolis had ten *poleis*— the name Decapolis means ten cities.) The leading men in the *poleis* became rich because the cities were situated at the crossroads where the trade routes intersected one another. The trade between east and west brought great wealth to these cities, which, because they were independent, did not pay taxes to a central government.

The progressives among the Jews wanted Jerusalem to obtain *polis* status and practiced a policy of *inclusion* regarding Hellenistic culture, whereas the conservatives wanted the entire Jewish nation to remain an *ethnos,* to use another Greek term, which means nation or people, and stood for *exclusion* regarding Hellenistic culture. An *ethnos* was a group of people of the same stock, sharing the same history, inhabiting the same area, and speaking the same language. An *ethnos* was usually governed by a monarch or an aristocracy. By Jesus' day Jewish society was an *ethnos* ruled by an aristocracy; the power lay in the hands of the **Sanhedrin,** an assembly of priests and men from the most esteemed lay families under the leadership of the high priest, whose office was hereditary within certain families. The Romans were overlords, but the Jewish people had a certain autonomy of self-government in their assembly and the Romans had granted Jews everywhere the freedom to practice their own religion.

It appears that the progressives, or inclusionists, who made up the new money aristocracy with business in the *poleis,* made their way into this assembly and posed a substantial challenge to the conservatives, or exclusionists. The tension within Jewish society was now also felt within the body governing the Jewish *ethnos.* Any discussion of the major groups within the Jewish society should assess their respective positions in this conflict between *polis* and *ethnos* as well as their religious views. The relationship is dialectical.

## THE SADDUCEES

The Sadducees are the most difficult group to understand because they are known only through the writings of their opponents: Josephus, the New Testament, later Christian authors, and the writings of the later **rabbis,** some of whom represented the Pharisaic party.

Josephus said that the Sadducees were supported by the well-off and enjoyed no support among "the people." If we take this statement together with the derivation of their name from that of Zadok, the priest of David and Solomon, the Sadducees appear to be the dominant party in the Sanhedrin. The circumference of the party of the Sadducees, however, remains as vague as that of the makeup of the assembly.

According to their name, the Sadducees must have originally been a priestly party. Because the priesthood dominated the assembly, we might think they were all conservatives; the Jewish society was an *ethnos.* However, the priesthood consisted of a very large class of society. Some of the lesser priests might have sided with the progressives if Jerusalem had became a *polis.* However, not all of them would have. This was the age of **syncretism** and the mixing of religions. The Jewish deity, Yahweh, could be identified with the high god of the Greeks, Zeus

(Jupiter in Roman religion). Alexander and his Greek followers had introduced both the worship of Zeus and the practice of syncretism in their efforts to Hellenize peoples they considered barbaric. The Maccabean rebellion two centuries before Jesus' birth violently opposed a syncretism that was initiated by a high priest named Jason (*2 Macc.* 4:7–10). If Jerusalem became a *polis,* its temple and cult would thus honor Yahweh and Zeus, which would eventually benefit the priestly classes because more worshippers would support the temple and pay taxes. The temple itself had an enormous treasury.

Such a development would benefit not only the priests but also certain lay members of the Sadducean party, such as the members of the new money aristocracy who had made their way into the assembly and (thereby) became associated with the Sadducees. If Jerusalem became a *polis,* the city would be exempt from taxes, and the leading families could reap large economic harvests.

This situation was very important because the assembly seems to have played a role in apprehending Jesus and handing him over to the Romans. But was their fear of Jesus grounded only in economics? Was he merely a threat to the success of the temple? Many scholars have argued that Jesus' "cleansing of the temple" would have been understood as an attack on the temple. The high priest was in charge, but was he a syncretist? Probably not, but the old, conservative part of the Sadducean party, even the assembly, wanted to retain the status quo and wanted to preserve their temple. They may have been afraid that the Romans would destroy the heart of the Jewish *ethnos* and nation if Jesus was not stopped. Therefore, we can see progressive and conservative powers both struggling with one another *and* joining forces with the Sadducees.

The New Testament Gospels illustrate this very paradox. The Sadducees did not believe in the resurrection of the body. They wanted to make it difficult to accept this belief. Mark 12 tells a story about some Sadducees who challenged Jesus by raising a hypothetical test case involving the resurrection. There was a Jewish law to the effect that if a man died, leaving no children, his brother must marry the widow and make her pregnant; the child would then be the first husband's child and his line would continue (a very important Jewish concept). Now, what if the second husband was sterile? And then if he died, what if the third brother turned out the same way with the same result? This might cause a later problem. What would the relationship be when they all rose from the dead? Which one would be the woman's husband? None of them had produced an heir.

We can see the Sadducees' rejection of the doctrine of the resurrection as an example of religious conservatism. The idea of the resurrection is not found in the law, the oldest part of the Jewish Scriptures. Nor is it found in the Prophets, the next most important part of the Scriptures. It is found only once in the Old Testament, namely in the Book of Daniel (12:2), which belongs to the third and last part of the Jewish Scriptures, the Writings. By rejecting the resurrection, the Sadducees were theological conservatives who lived in strict accordance with the law. This fact is borne out when we notice that Jesus answered the Sadducees by appealing to that portion of the Jewish Scriptures preserving the law (Mark 12:26).

Paradoxically, we can see the rejection of the doctrine of the resurrection as cultural liberalism and as a pro-Roman attitude. In the first place, the Greeks and Romans did not believe in the resurrection of the body, but in the survival of the soul, a doctrine popularized by the writings of Plato. Moreover, the idea of the resurrection was bound up with revolutionary ideas. Daniel 12:2 says that only the martyrs and the collaborators with Israel's enemy would rise, the former to everlasting life, the latter to everlasting contempt. Thus, the idea of resurrection in Israelite religion is originally a political as well as a religious idea. From a liberal point of view, it was not wise to cherish it. Those who opposed syncretism and violently opposed the Roman occupation and its accompanying culture cherished it.

## THE PHARISEES

Whereas some of the Sadducees were positive toward the influence of Greek culture, the Pharisees were not. However, the Pharisees accepted the political situation although they did not associate with the Romans, which even the conservative elements of the Sanhedrin, including the high priest, seemed to have done.

Josephus said that the Pharisees, in contrast to the Sadducees, were popular among the people. We cannot understand him to mean the people at large because the Pharisees were an exclusivist body and withdrew from society at large. Although they accepted the political situation, they tended to withdraw from society, adopting a separatist lifestyle.

The Pharisees tried to awaken the people, to point out the dangers of Hellenism, and to lead the people back to the way of their ancestors, back to the law. They believed that the Torah should be the norm for the daily life of each individual Jew. The majority of the Sadducees also demanded the observance of the law. The Pharisees, however, went much farther. In contrast to the Sadducees, they demanded that the purity rules, which were observed by the priests, should be valid for all Jews. In substantiation of their demand, they referred to God's demand in Exodus 19:6: Israel "shall be for me a priestly kingdom and a holy nation." All Israelites should act as priests of God; all Israelites should be holy.

Also, by assuming priestly purity regulations, the Pharisees did penance because—in their eyes—many of the priests had deserted the God of Israel by welcoming Hellenistic influence. The Pharisees took the place of the priests and summoned all Jews to repent and follow them.

It is extremely difficult to observe the priestly purity regulations, especially for nonpriests who have a secular occupation and live in the society at large. The Pharisees were constantly exposed to the dangers of contact with impure people while trying to live like priests and associating only with priests. The Pharisees thus made rules regarding what to eat, with whom to eat, what and whom they could touch, and so on. The name *Pharisees,* which is derived from the Hebrew word *Perushim,* probably means "those who separate themselves." A saying in the Mishnah, a written account of the Jewish oral law dating to 200 CE, reads, "Purity leads to separation, separation to holiness." This statement can be amended to bring out the essence of Pharisaism: "Separation leads to purity, purity to holiness."

Many Pharisees came together in clubs of *Haberim* (Hebrew), "friends," or "associates." As a *haber* (Hebrew) of such a society, a "friend" could guarantee that he was among equals. He would be assured that the food had been prepared in a certain way and that his *haberim,* "associates," were not unclean. In this way, Pharisees avoided close contacts with nonaffiliated Jews.

These societies developed into schools. This progression was only natural because the law did not cover every aspect of life, and the Torah left much unsaid or implicit. Thus, the Pharisaic schools tried to apply the law to each new situation in life and thus guard against violations of the law. This attempt at expanding the laws in turn led to competing sects among the Pharisees. In Jesus' time there were two main schools—that of Hillel and that of Shammai. The latter was, on the whole, more stern. This judgment is borne out by Jewish tradition. The Babylonian Talmud, a Jewish commentary on the Mishnah dating to the fifth century CE, tells a story about a Gentile who asked both Shammai and Hillel about becoming a Jew. Shammai struck the Gentile when he heard that the Gentile wanted to be converted while standing on one foot. Hillel responded by telling him, "What is hateful to you, do not do to your neighbor. This is the whole Torah, while the rest is commentary thereof; go and learn it." Jesus formulated this rule in a positive way: "In everything do to others as you would have them do to you; for this is the law and the prophets" (Matt. 7:12).

Although Hillel was more lenient than Shammai on most occasions, he was very harsh on at least one issue, namely that of divorce. For Pharisees like Hillel and Shammai, their legal traditions were a "fence around the law" that was a safeguard against violating the law. If a Jew observed their traditions, he could be sure that he was observing the law. According to Matthew, Jesus attacked the Pharisees for elevating their tradition and their teachings about the law above the law (15:1–9).

## THE ESSENES

The third philosophy, as Josephus called it, was that of the Essenes. In addition to Josephus, Philo of Alexandria, who was slightly older than Josephus, and the first-century Roman historian Pliny the Elder reported on them. These three authors agreed in all essential respects. The Essenes were a very ascetic people. They held women in low esteem, and many chose celibacy over marriage. Those who did marry only did so after having watched their wives-to-be for three years to make sure that they were not loose women. The men thought these precautions were necessary because they considered women to be wanton by nature. A similar view is also found in the so-called pastoral letters in the New Testament (1 and 2 Timothy and Titus).

The Essenes shared everything in common. Every member was expected to contribute his possessions to the Essene community. These goods were then under the control of Essene authorities who would use them for the common good. According to the book of Acts, the first Christians also carried out this practice of communal goods.

Josephus reported several interesting aspects concerning the religious practices of the Essenes. He stated that the Essenes said prayers before sunrise as if they were entreating the sun to rise, perhaps because they worshipped the God of their ancestors under the image of the sun. If this was true, it would be evidence of foreign influence. The image of the sun had been discovered in ancient synagogues. The Essenes believed that the soul was preexistent and that the body was a prison for the soul. The soul was liberated upon death and could then return to its heavenly home. The souls of evil people, however, were tormented. Essenes were divided into classes according to their degree of holiness. If one happened to touch someone from a lower class, the former had to purify himself through ritual immersion in water. From Josephus's report it appears that the Essenes took Pharisaic ideas to the extreme; they separated themselves to obtain a purity that led to holiness.

Josephus went on to state that the Essenes were found everywhere. Philo said that they avoided the big cities. Pliny had an interesting observation. He said that they were found on the west coast of the Dead Sea, and right after World War II the Dead Sea Scrolls were discovered at a site called Qumran on the west coast of the Dead Sea.

## THE QUMRAN SECT

Pliny, a Roman who traveled through Palestine, wrote,

> On the west coast of Dead Sea, but out of range of the noxious exhalation of the coast, is the solitary tribe of the Essenes, which is remarkable beyond all other tribes in the entire world, as it has no women and has renounced all sexual desire, has no money, and has only palm trees for company. (*Natural History* 5:73)

Pliny added that the Essenes recruited "people tired of life," so that "a race in which no one is born lives on forever." He then went on to describe the location lying below the Essene quarter—that is, present-day En-gedi in southern Israel.

The caves containing the Qumran Scrolls, or the Dead Sea Scrolls, were found at the very place where Pliny said the Essenes had lived. This discovery contained about 800 documents with a legible text and about 100,000 fragments. Just beneath the caves were the ruins of a large building compound that had contained a dining room, a kitchen, a library, and even a cemetery. Different fields of study all point to a date around 70 CE for the ruins. Scholars tend to agree that this must have been an Essene settlement—the settlement of a special branch of the Essenes—because there is no full agreement among the reports of Josephus, Philo, and Pliny.

No other known group fits the site or the scrolls as well as the Essenes. Several clear similarities between the Essenes and the Qumran sect support this view. Josephus said that the Essenes held a doctrine of fate, or predestination. The *Manual of Discipline,* one of the Qumran writings, said that God preordained everything. Josephus said that the Essenes held common ownership of property. The *Manual of Discipline* said that the new members, after a period of initiation, should hand over their property to the group. Josephus said that the Essenes forbid spitting. The *Manual of Discipline* declared that there should be no spitting in the assembly.

Last, we need to consider the following statistics: 27 clear parallels exist between the Essenes in Josephus and the Qumran Scrolls; 21 probable parallels exist; 10 cases in Josephus exist without parallels in the Scrolls, but the Scrolls may not present the total picture; and 6 discrepancies exist. In 2 of the 6 discrepancies, the scrolls differ among themselves. Thus, according to the *Damascus Document,* another Dead Sea Scroll, the members of the sect seemed to possess private property, which contradicts the *Manual of Discipline.* If the group at Qumran had a history of some 200 years, as most scholars believe, it can easily account for the contradictions among the Dead Sea Scrolls. All in all, scholars cannot avoid this evidence. A close connection seems to exist between the people responsible for the Qumran scrolls and the Essenes reported on by the classical authors.

This connection brings up the question of the origin of the Essenes. The leaders of the Qumran groups were called the "sons of Zadok." The name *Zadok* is, as we pointed out earlier, also behind the name of the Sadducees. Some additional overlaps occur between Essene practices and what is ascribed to the Sadducees in rabbinic sources. They both appear to be priestly dominated groups. As for the name *Essenes* (an English form of the Greek name used by Josephus, Philo, and Pliny), it probably derives from the Hebrew word *Hasidim,* or pious ones. It was the designation of the religious conservatives who supported the Maccabean revolt in rebellion against Israel's Greek rulers (167–142 BCE) but who later walked out when the Maccabees assumed high priestly honors—an act that they believed was unlawful.

It seems that the Pharisees also had their origin in the *Hasidim.* The later rabbinic sources state that the Hasmonean (the dynastic name of the Maccabean rulers, taken from their family name, Hasmon) king Alexander persecuted the predecessor of the Pharisees. Alexander (104–78 BCE) was said to have executed 50,000 Hasidim. Josephus said that he found support for this execution among the Sadducees. It appears that the *Hasidim* split into two wings: a priestly dominated wing, which came to be known as Essenes, especially the Essenes at Qumran, and a lay wing, which was represented later by the Pharisees (see Figure 15.1).

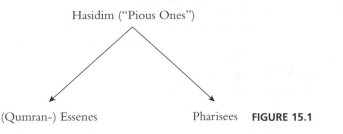

Hasidim ("Pious Ones")

(Qumran-) Essenes                    Pharisees    **FIGURE 15.1**

The *Hasidim* objected to the Hasmonean usurpation of the high priestly office. The Hasmonean rulers paradoxically turned to the Sadducees, an originally priestly party, for support. The Hasmoneans were not Hellenizers, but they did expand the Jewish state and made it wealthier. The upper classes, from which the Sadducees came, became richer and more receptive of Hellenistic ways. Thus, we can account for the seemingly unnatural cooperation between the Hasmoneans and the Sadducees.

The Essenes and the Pharisees can be compared and contrasted. Study of the law, observance of priestly purity rules, and isolation for the sake of holiness characterize both groups. The last point is especially significant. Whereas the Pharisees tried to practice isolation within the society, the Essenes, at least those at Qumran, physically removed themselves; they went out into the desert. The Essenes believed the Pharisees were not stringent observers of the law and labeled them the teachers of "smooth things"—that is, the Pharisees lessened the demands of the law.

A more significant difference between the two groups involves the temple of Jerusalem. The Qumran-Essenes had as little as possible to do with the temple. They said that their community had taken the place of the temple. The life of the Essene community, in strict observance of the law, effected the atonement, which was the purpose of the sacrifices in the temple. They were not opposed to the temple as such but were against the unlawful priests who had defiled the temple. This opposition probably dates to the time of the *Hasidim* and Hasmoneans.

The Qumran settlement was destroyed by the Romans around 70 CE as part of their quenching of the first Jewish revolt. The members of this sect apparently interpreted the assault as the beginning of the final eschatological war between the children of light and the children of darkness. The Essenes practiced a form of prophetic interpretation called *pesher* (Hebrew), or "interpretation." With it they scrutinized the prophetic books with the objective of finding references to the past times in which they thought they lived. Holding the same belief, the Christians did the same with the prophetic books. When the Romans stormed Qumran, the Jewish sect must have thought that the eschatological war had begun. They took up arms in the belief that God would send his army of angels to join them. The Christians, on the other hand, did not take up arms against the Romans but fled Jerusalem. The Qumran-Essenes looked upon themselves as the children of light and all others—even other Jews—as the children of darkness.

Here too we find similarities with early Christian thought. Although the terminology—"children of light" and "children of darkness"—is not found in the Gospel according to Matthew, the gospel contains the idea that the Jewish people were condemned. The light-darkness terminology found in the Qumran Scrolls is found in the Gospel according to John, where Jesus said, "The light is with you for a little longer. Walk while you have the light, so that the darkness may not overtake you; If you walk in the darkness, you do not know where you are going" (12:35).

The Qumran people celebrated ritual meals with bread and wine, which perhaps anticipated the meal with the messiah to be enjoyed in the future Kingdom of God. The Christians celebrated a similar meal, commonly known as the Lord's Supper, or the Last Supper, which they said Jesus had institutionalized the evening before he died. Both the Essenes of Qumran and the early Christians regarded themselves as the people of the new covenant promised by the prophet Jeremiah.

Actually, the Qumran people expected the coming of two messiah figures—one royal messiah who would serve as a new David or ruler and one priestly messiah who would serve as a new Aaron or high priest. The Essenes were a priestly group and cherished the idea of an eschatological high priest who would be a messiah—an anointed one—because the ritual of anointing was part of the installation of the priests. Only one Messiah existed in Christianity, but in the Letter to the Hebrews, Jesus was portrayed as a priestly Messiah as well as a kingly or royal Messiah. Thus, according to Christianity, one person—Jesus—assumed both roles of the Messiah that were delegated to different persons by the Essenes of Qumran.

## THE HERODIANS

Until 1947, we knew nothing about the Qumran-Essenes. The New Testament did not mention the Essenes. Or did it mention this sect by another name? The Herodians, a sect not known from other sources, were mentioned in the New Testament Gospels. They were said to have worked with the Pharisees against Jesus (Mark 3:6; Matt. 22:16). The Herodians were usually regarded as people who supported the family of Herod the Great. One of his sons, Herod Antipas, was the client king of the Romans over Galilee and Perea (4 BCE–39 CE), the land east of the River Jordan. Perhaps the Herodian party intended to reinstate a person from Herod's family as the Roman client king over Judea and Samaria (and Idumea south of Judea), which were ruled directly by Roman prefects (governors) after the failure of Herod's son, Archelaus, as ruler (4 BCE–6 CE). Is it likely that the Pharisees would have been in league with such people?

According to Josephus, the Jewish historian, a certain Essene prophesied that Herod the Great, while still a boy, would one day become "king of the Jews." Josephus said that Herod the Great held the Essenes "in honor." They may have liked him in return because Herod did not usurp the high priestly office as the Hasmoneans had done. Archaeology reveals that the people at Qumran left their settlement around 31 BCE and then returned around 4 BCE. These dates coincide with the reign of Herod the Great (37–4 BCE). Perhaps the Qumran-Essenes went to Jerusalem because they were attracted by Herod's restoration of the temple, a project that began in 20 BCE and ended with the war of 66 CE.

The theory identifying the Herodians with the Essenes is weakened by the idea that Herod was a Hellenizer. The Essenes would hardly have supported him if this was the case because they were xenophobic and devoted to Jewish tradition. The Herodian sect remains a mystery.

## THE FOURTH PHILOSOPHY AND JEWISH RESISTANCE GROUPS

Shortly after the Romans ended 80 years of Jewish independence in 63 BCE, they imposed the puppet-kingship of Herod the Great (37–4 BCE) through military force. From the 30s BCE through 66 CE, Jews raised nonviolent and violent insurrections against the Romans and their foreign imposition of Herodian rule. Many of these Jews came from Galilee, and some of their leaders even came from the same family. Galilee was an agricultural province where the landowners, many of them holding large estates, lived in the cities. They were Hellenizers and pro-Roman, whereas many Galilean peasants who worked the land were tenants. If the peasants did not pay rent, they lost the land. They were thus dependent on the crops. If a harvest failed, they faced hard times and would be unable to both care for their families and pay the taxes that Rome required and that the Herods collected. Josephus described an episode that took place in 4 BCE when Archelaus, Herod's son, put down a tax protest that turned violent as Jews fought with Roman soldiers. That 3,000 people were killed illustrates how struggling Jews might resist Roman rule.

A socio-economic explanation is perhaps insufficient to account for Jewish insurrection. "No king but God!" (*War.* 2:118) is the slogan that Josephus attributed to Judas the Galilean, the leader of the fourth philosophy. Josephus, in another of his histories, associated Judas with a Pharisee named Sadok (*Ant.* 18:4). Thus, a religious program seems to have been behind many of the Jews who revolted. In 6 CE, the Romans removed Archelaus, the son of Herod the Great, who had been the client king over Judea, Samaria, and Idumea. The emperor then ordered that a census be conducted so a proper tax assessment could be made. Galilean Jews rose up under the leadership of Judas the Galilean. No tribute, they claimed, should be paid to anyone but to Israel's God, the only one who owned the land. Their apparently nonviolent tax revolt was crushed, and 2,000 rebels were crucified along the road running from Galilee to Jerusalem. Jesus, a boy about 12 years old, must have witnessed the crucifixions.

Some scholars believe that Jesus may have felt sympathy with violent revolutionaries on the basis of Luke 6:15, which identified Simon, one of Jesus' followers, as a Zealot. (Although this passage may indicate that Jesus sympathized with Zealots, it may also mean that the Zealots were sympathetic toward Jesus.) Scholars have traditionally argued that the term *Zealot* denoted a violent revolutionary group in Jesus' day, even though Josephus used the term to describe a specific band of violent Jewish rebels during the Jewish revolt against Rome (66–73 CE), more than 30 years after Jesus' death. The term may also be a characterizing name that identified Simon as steadfastly devoted to Jewish traditions. Perhaps the author of Luke, writing after the revolt of 66–73 CE, used the term anachronistically to denote a follower of Jesus who had resisted Roman rule (a stance presumably shared by some Jews in Jesus' day).

However, the Gospels contain no explicit passages where Jesus talked with Jews who counseled a revolt of any sort, violent or nonviolent, as he did with the Sadducees and Pharisees—the wealthy and the pious. Yet, scholars agree that the period of direct Roman rule of Judea (6–66 CE) was characterized by Jewish discontent and moments of disturbance. Roman rule and the collusion of the Jewish aristocracy had created difficult living conditions and a high level of discontent. The parable about the wicked tenants in Mark 12 may be directed against the violent methods of the Jewish rebels, and if the parable is authentic (it appears in independent sources), then Jesus cannot be considered a *violent* revolutionary.

From the 20s CE Israel was overrun by many gangs. Many of them were real bandits who robbed Jews as well as Romans. This situation furnished the background of the parable of the good Samaritan (Luke 10). A man went down from Jerusalem to Jericho. He fell among "robbers" *(lestes)*. Josephus used the same Greek word for the leader of the first Zealot uprising in 66 CE. Barabbas, who was set free while Jesus was executed, was called a robber in John's gospel (18:40). Luke called him a rebel (23:19). Barabbas may have been a political insurrectionist, but this is not certain. Whereas bandits may have been upset with Roman rule and its effects on Jews, they did not lead a premeditated revolt.

Were violent revolutionary Jewish groups active during Antipas's rule (4 BCE–39 CE) in Galilee or during Pilate's term (26–36 CE) as prefect of Judea and Samaria? Josephus was silent about troubles in Galilee during Antipas's time, saying nothing about the use of force, either Jewish or Roman, against rebellious subjects (*War.* 3:41–43). As to Pilate's term as prefect, Josephus described a Samaritan Israelite whose speech convinced some Samaritans to collect arms and gather in an Israelite village (*Ant.* 18:85–87). Josephus's comments suggest that this movement was religiously oriented. The Samaritan acted in the guise of a Israelite restorer in the mold of Moses. In response, Pilate's forces attacked these Samaritans, killing some and capturing many.

In the 50s CE, certain *sicarii* (Greek for dagger men) entered the scene. They concealed daggers under their cloaks and stabbed Sadducees in the crowds. The *sicarii* seemed to advocate a program of social equality and a balanced distribution of wealth. At the beginning of the great revolt, they burned the public archives where the records of debts were stored. It is interesting to recall that in the Gospel according to Matthew, Jesus taught his disciples to forgive the debts of others as God had forgiven their debts. The Greek word used for debt is *opheilema,* literally, what is legally due.

When the great revolt against the Romans broke out in 66 CE, a rebel group identified by Josephus as the Zealots managed to drive the Romans out of Jerusalem. Their religious convictions led to a reign of terror in the city. Several messianic pretenders arose among them and at least one of those was killed by other revolutionaries who wanted to prove that he was not the messiah. One of them, Simon bar Giora, publicized his messianic pretensions by surrendering himself to the Romans while dressed in the purple garb of royalty. Actually, this was not the first time a rebel claimed to be the messiah. Josephus said that the leader of the revolt in the year 6 CE, Judas the Galilean, claimed to be the messiah.

Jerusalem fell to the Romans in the year 70. The last bastion of the revolutionaries was Masada, a desert fortress built by Herod in case of popular revolts. Here, above the Dead Sea, some 953 Jews committed mass suicide in 73 CE because they did not want to surrender to the Romans. The cry "never again Masada" is still heard.

## SAMARITANS

The Gospels also refer to the Samaritans. Many people are familiar with the parable of the good Samaritan in Luke's gospel. He identified a Samaritan as a "neighbor" who should be loved (10:29 and 36). In the Gospel according to John, we find a lesser-known story about Jesus conversing with a Samaritan woman at a well in Samaria. There Jesus identified himself as the Messiah for Jews and Samaritans (4:25–26). Samaritans still live in the Holy Land (about a thousand). Who were the Samaritans?

Maps of ancient Palestine show that Samaria was the province between Judea in the south and Galilee in the north. The people who lived there were looked down on by the Jews living in Judea and Galilee. After the death of Solomon in 928 BCE, the kingdom was split in two: the northern kingdom of Israel and the southern kingdom of Judah. In 721 BCE, the kingdom of Israel fell to the Assyrians. 2 Kings 17 says that the entire population was carried away and the country was inhabited by people from other parts of the Assyrian empire. These people continued to practice their own religion, but they also modified their worship to include worship of Yahweh, the God of Israel. According to the Jewish Bible, the Samaritans are the descendants of these colonists. The name *Samaritans* is derived from the name of the capitol in the former northern kingdom (Samaria) and was extended to the entire territory.

However, the account in 2 Kings 17 is not accurate. Only a small percentage of the population was carried away, perhaps as little as ten percent. The Samaritans are basically descendants of the old Israelite population of the northern kingdom. They represent a very conservative form of Yahwistic religion and are in many ways like the old Sadducees, although the Samaritans have no direct ties to the Sadducees and the Samaritans were viewed with disdain by the Jews.

The Samaritans read only the Torah of Moses and rejected additional texts such as the Prophets and the Writings of the Jewish Bible. Like the Sadducees, they rejected the doctrine of the resurrection. Worship for them focused on Mount Gerizim in Samaria, where they had established a temple and priesthood that rivaled that of the Jews in Jerusalem. They held a concept of a prophetic deliverer like Moses, called a *taheb,* in place of a Davidic messiah because the Davidic dynasty was a southern (Jewish) kingdom. Thus, their religious outlook was Israelite but not Jewish.


## THE PEOPLE OF THE LAND

The majority of the Jews in Jesus' day were not affiliated with any of the sects we have discussed here. These "common Jews" were known to the rabbis as the "people of the land" (Hebrew: *am ha-aretz*). Sectarian Jews presumed that these Jews were lax in their knowledge and observation of the law. Perhaps common Jews were given less respect because they did not adhere to the more rigorous observance of the law that many sectarians required. For this reason, Pharisees adopted social practices that limited their contact with this group in an effort to avoid contact with unclean Jews. Scholars usually identify them with the lower classes of Palestinian Jewish society and designate them Jewish peasants, in contrast to the more educated Jews, the learned class, who were thought more likely to join sects.

Despite their less than scrupulous lifestyles, these common Jews were generally viewed by sect members as "true Israelites," although a group like the Qumran-Essenes would have rejected them as they rejected all other Jews. However, there appears to have been some tension between scrupulous and unscrupulous Jews. John 7:49 describes the disdain that some Pharisees had for a crowd of presumably common Jews they deemed to be ignorant of the law and therefore "accursed." This tension between sectarian and common Jews may have been reciprocal. Rabbi Akiva, a rabbi of the early second century, said, "When I was an *am ha-aretz,* I used to say, 'I wish I had one of those scholars, I would bite him like an ass.' His disciples said, 'You mean like a dog.' He replied, 'An ass's bite breaks the bone; a dog's does not'" (*bPes.* 49b).

We should not confuse common Jews with those Jews known as "sinners" (Greek: *hamartoloi*) in the Gospels. The latter were Jews who, by their behavior, made *no* effort to observe the law and thereby had renounced it. The tax-collectors of the Gospels fit this category and were associated with "sinners" (Mark 2:16) because they willfully collected more than the taxes required of Jews, and this act was considered usury, a violation of the law (Lev. 25:36–37). By contrast, common Jews in Jesus' day were not dismissive of the law and observed it in varying degrees; they circumcised their sons, kept the Sabbath, observed some purity regulations, and celebrated the feasts—the temple area could accommodate thousands and thousands of Jews who made the pilgrimage for feasts like Passover. In the public sphere, Josephus has several accounts of the people at large strongly protesting acts by either Antipas or Pilate because the latter were deemed to be unlawful and thus offensive to Jews (*Ant.* 18:36–38; 55–59; *War.* 2:169–177).

## SUMMARY

The world of Jesus was dominated by social and religious conflicts that were heightened by Israel's foreign occupation. The Persians allowed the Jews to live under local rule, according to their own faith. Beginning with Alexander, Israel had to live under Hellenistic influences that continued under the Romans. The Sadducees tried to balance their position of authority as Jewish priests with an accommodation to Roman ways. The Pharisees called Israelites to a life of devotion to the law and a priestly lifestyle. The Essenes were ascetic and separationist in their observance of the law. The Qumran sect, which can be identified as Essene, openly critiqued other Jewish sects, seeing itself as God's true people who properly kept the law. The fourth philosophy of Josephus was a generally nonviolent group of Jews who protested Roman policies, but there were Jews who took up arms against the Romans. The Samaritans were northern Israelites who were viewed with disdain by the Jews of Judea. They held fast to Israelite traditions that competed with those of Jerusalem. The majority of Jews were nonsectarian and in general were observant of the law. According to gospel traditions, Jesus had contact with many, but not all, of these groups.

## KEY TERMS FOR REVIEW

| | | |
|---|---|---|
| Second temple Judaism | Essenes | Qumran-Essenes |
| Alexander the Great | Zealots | Herodians |
| Hellenization | *Polis/Ethnos* | *Sicarii* |
| Sadducees | Sanhedrin | Samaritans |
| Pharisees | Hillel/Shammai | *Am ha-aretz* |

## QUESTIONS FOR REVIEW

**1.** How did Alexander and the Greeks influence Jewish life in Palestine?

**2.** Why can we describe the Sadducees as both progressive and conservative?

**3.** Why was purity a major interest of the Pharisees?

**4.** Why do many scholars associate the Essenes with the Qumran community?

**5.** Why is a socio-economic explanation insufficient to account for Zealotism?

**6.** How does a Samaritan differ from a Jew?

## SUGGESTIONS FOR FURTHER READING

Cohen, S. *From the Maccabees to the Mishnah.* Philadelphia: Westminster, 1987.

Horsley, R. and Hanson, J. *Bandits, Prophets, and Messiahs: Popular Movements at the Time of Jesus.* San Francisco: Harper & Row, 1985.

Saldarini, A. *Pharisees, Scribes, and Sadducees in Palestinian Society.* Grand Rapids: Eerdmans, 2001.

Stemberger, G. *Jewish Contemporaries of Jesus: Pharisees, Sadducees, Essenes.* Minneapolis: Fortress, 1995.

Thiessen, G. *The Gospels in Context: Social and Political History in the Synoptic Tradition.* Minneapolis: Fortress, 1992.

# 16

# John the Baptist

## THE AMBIGUITY OF JOHN THE BAPTIST

Some readers of the New Testament wonder why there are so many contrasting references to John the Baptist. Some passages emphasize John's importance whereas others stress his inferiority to Jesus. The key to this inconsistency is the insight that John is "Christianized" in the New Testament writings. He is considered significant for the story of Jesus but not significant as a person in his own right. Although some people think of him as a forerunner of Jesus, some New Testament traditions about John may not fit this picture of John.

## JOHN AND THE GOSPELS

A composite picture emerges when we examine the Gospels. John the Baptist is referred to in the prologue to the Gospel according to John, 1:1–18. After having described the preexistent Word—Jesus Christ—as the light, the prologue states, rather abruptly,

> John 1:6–8: 6 There was a man sent from God, whose name was John. 7 He came as a witness to testify to the light so that all might believe through him. 8 He himself was not the light, but he came to testify to the light.

Then the prologue goes on to speak of "the true light"—that is, Jesus Christ. Why is this section on John the Baptist included in the prologue? Did some people believe that John was "the true light"? In verses 19–21 John emphatically denied that he was the holder of any eschatological office,

John 1:19–21: 19 This is the testimony given by John when the Jews sent priests and
Levites from Jerusalem to ask him, "Who are you?" 20 He confessed and did not
deny it, but confessed, "I am not the Messiah." 21 And they asked him, "What then?"
"Are you Elijah?" He said, "I am not." "Are you the prophet?" He answered, "No."

Why was this stated so emphatically in John's gospel? Was John the Baptist
held to be the Messiah, Elijah, or the Prophet? All three titles had great eschatological significance in the first century. The title Messiah referred to the
"anointed" deliverer who would rescue Israel. Elijah the prophet was expected to
return as the forerunner of the messiah. A Moses-like prophet (Deut. 18:15) was
anticipated by many Jews, especially Samaritans. Did people see John the Baptist
as any of these figures, or perhaps as all three?

Verses 6–8 say that John the Baptist was only a witness to Jesus. This statement
is repeated in verse 15: "John testified to him and cried out, "This was he of
whom I said, 'He who comes after me ranks ahead of me because he was before
me.' " This emphasis on John's role as a prophet of Jesus is found in other places
in the Gospel according to John. Later Christian literature, stemming from about
200 CE, refers to groups that held John to be their savior. Thus it seems likely that
John's gospel may already be arguing against this view.

Why should the contemporaries of John the Baptist not regard him as the savior? No one can deny that John's baptisms attracted huge numbers of Jews; they are
even described in the Gospel according to John. But John's gospel does not relate
the actual event wherein John baptized Jesus, as the synoptic Gospels do. Why isn't
Jesus' baptism described in John's gospel? At best it is only alluded to (1:32–34). Was
Jesus' baptism an act that suggested the superiority of John over Jesus? The Gospel
according to John manifestly knows of the baptism because it says that the Baptist
testified that he had seen the dove come down and remain on Jesus.

John's gospel and the synoptics go separate ways on one other important
issue. In the synoptics, Jesus began to teach and heal after John the Baptist was
imprisoned, which is not the case in the Fourth Gospel. According to John's
gospel, there was an overlap in the ministries of John and Jesus, and the two of
them are even described as having contact with one another through their disciples (3:22–30). This overlap may also be seen as an indication of the independence and superiority of Jesus over John the Baptist. Showing this dominance is
obviously one of the aims of the Gospel according to John.

The way John the Baptist is portrayed in the other Gospels is also significant.
There the representation of John is more a picture of a figure who is important
in his own right, which is made clear in the accounts of Jesus' baptism. According
to Mark's gospel, Jesus went from Galilee to Judea "and was baptized by John in
the Jordan" (1:9). Why did Jesus seek to be baptized by John? Mark 1:4 may provide an answer: John administered "a baptism of repentance for the forgiveness of
sins." Thus, according to the earliest gospel, Jesus may have felt that he needed this
type of baptism. It is at least implied that Jesus was a sinner. That is the natural
way to read this story in Mark.

We can argue that Mark's silence about Jesus "confessing his sins" at his baptism—as the people did when they were baptized (1:5)—implies Jesus' sinlessness.
The *Gospel according to the Nazoreans* sheds an interesting light on John's baptism

of Jesus. It reinforces this view. In this gospel Jesus opposed the proposal of his
family to go and be baptized by John because he considered himself sinless.

> The *Gospel according to the Nazoreans:* behold, the mother of the Lord and his
> brethren said to him: John the Baptist baptizes unto the remission of sins, let us go
> and be baptized by him. But he said to them: Wherein have I sinned that I should go
> and be baptized by him? Unless what I have said is ignorance (a sin of ignorance).

The Gospel according to Matthew implicitly presents the theme of Jesus' sinlessness. Here John the Baptist refused to baptize Jesus with the words, "I need to
be baptized by you, and do you come to me?" (3:14). Jesus replied, "Let it be so
now; for it is proper for us in this way to fulfill all righteousness" (3:15). What
does Jesus' baptism mean according to Matthew? It is hard for us to tell, and our
difficulty in finding an answer may actually indicate that Matthew had a hard
time providing one. Matthew appears to teach that because John was a prophet
(11:7–9), and because Jesus fulfilled the law and the prophets (5:17), Jesus was
baptized by John as an act of obedience to the prophets (righteousness).
Matthew's modification of Mark is clear.

Luke's account of Jesus' baptism differs from that of both Mark and Matthew.
Luke relates that Jesus was baptized but does not say that John baptized him. Luke
describes John's ministry of baptism, and then he says that John was put into
prison (3:15–20). The story about the baptism of Jesus follows (3:21–22).
Although we may infer that John baptized Jesus, Luke's gospel does not say so.

> Luke 3:18–21: 18 So, with many other exhortations, he proclaimed the good news
> to the people. 19 But Herod the ruler, who had been rebuked by him because of
> Herodias, his brother's wife, and because of all the evil things that Herod had done,
> 20 added to them all by shutting up John in prison. 21 Now when all the people
> were baptized, and when Jesus also had been baptized and was praying, the heaven
> was opened,

If you had not read Mark and Matthew would you conclude that John baptized Jesus? Imagine having only Luke's report. We might think: Luke does not
mention another baptizer so John must have baptized Jesus before he was imprisoned. Perhaps it is important that Luke is not explicit. Remember that both
Matthew and Luke used Mark, and they obviously modified his account of Jesus'
baptism. The last gospel is John's and his gospel does not even say that Jesus was
baptized (1:29–34).

Moving from Mark and the way John the Baptist was treated by Matthew and
Luke to the source known as Q sheds further light on John's significance.
Matthew 11:11 and Luke 7:28 preserve a Jesus saying drawn from Q: "Truly, I tell
you, among those born of women no one has risen greater than John the
Baptist." This sentence is followed by the clause: "yet the least in the kingdom of
heaven is greater than he." These two passages do not concur. In the first, Jesus
praises John as the greatest of all people. In the second, Jesus seems to deny him
a place in the kingdom.

Are these two passages logical? Jesus was born of a woman, and so were Peter
and the rest of the disciples. Were they all inferior to John the Baptist? It is probable that the Church added the second part. Why? Because the first sentence

ranked John higher than Jesus. The added clause does not have to mean that John would have no part in the kingdom. Perhaps we should consider it in a futuristic sense. Everyone who will be an inhabitant of the kingdom to come is greater than John is now on earth. If we apply form criticism's criterion of dissimilarity to this saying in an effort to find out what Jesus said, the first sentence passes the test. No Christian or Jew would say that John the Baptist was the greatest of all born of a woman. The whole saying, of course, may go back to Jesus. Still, John remains the greatest "among those born of women."

The story that precedes this Jesus saying implies that there was an overlapping in the works of John and Jesus (Matt. 11:2–10; Luke 7:18–27). Some time after Jesus was baptized by John—an event that demonstrates Jesus' acceptance of John's legitimacy and his own role as a disciple of John—John was imprisoned. However, although John was in prison he was not totally out of the picture, and he was not at all sure about Jesus' identity. This view runs counter to the synoptic tradition that John was the forerunner of Jesus. John the Baptist's disciples did not all follow Jesus (according to John's gospel some of them did [1:35–42]). John's sect remained alongside Jesus' sect. According to the Q tradition in Matthew 11 and Luke 7, John the Baptist was not at all certain about Jesus' identity and asked if he was the one who was to come.

## THE HISTORICAL JOHN THE BAPTIST

Josephus, in his history *Antiquities,* described John the Baptist as a popular figure known simply as "the Baptist," who baptized Jews and commanded them to "practice virtue." Josephus, Mark, and p-Matthew all say that Herod Antipas executed John. Mark's gospel says that Herod's motive was John's criticism of Herod's marriage to his sister-in-law, Herodias (6:17). For Josephus, Herod's motive was his fear that John would start a rebellion. Unfortunately for historians, Josephus is not clear about Herod's "fear." Mark and Q depict John as an eschatological preacher-prophet (Mark 1:4–8; Matt. 3:11–12; Luke 3:15–17), whereas Josephus presents him as a teacher of virtue, which may be due to Josephus' tendency to downplay eschatological traditions. That John appeared in the desert is significant (Mark 1:4). God's first saving act was in the desert with the exodus of Israel, and his last saving act was to be there too. Josephus described many self-styled prophets who led people out into the desert, even across the River Jordan, promising their followers miracles and deliverance—the latter in at least one case being connected to a return and an attack on the Roman garrison at Jerusalem (*War.* 2:258–260; *Ant.* 20:167–172). We can discern a Moses typology here:

| *Moses* | *Prophets* |
| --- | --- |
| 1. Crossing of the Red Sea | 1. Crossing the Jordan |
| 2. Desert wanderings | 2. Time in the desert |
| 3. Miracles | 3. The promise of miracles |
| 4. Entry into the Promised Land | 4. Return to Judea |
| 5. Victory over enemies | 5. Victory over enemies (in one case) |

These "prophets" obviously viewed themselves as the Moses-like prophet of Deuteronomy 18:15, 18.

> Deut. 18:15, 18:18 "The LORD your God will raise up for you a prophet like me from among your own people; you shall heed such a prophet. —18 I will raise up for them a prophet like you from among their people; I will put my words in the mouth of the prophet, who shall speak to them everything that I command."

Here God promised that in the future he would raise up a Moses-like prophet whom the people must obey. A Moses-like prophet was thus one of the eschatological figures of Judaism—one of the figures who was expected to appear at the end of the age. According to the *Community Rule* of the Qumran Essenes, two messiahs were expected as well as a prophet.

John the Baptist fit this model. He was no mere forerunner of Jesus. He was no mere preacher of repentance. Josephus related that Herod Antipas put John to death because he feared that John would raise an insurrection among the people (*Ant.* 18:116–119). According to the Gospels, it was rumored that John had been raised from the dead—that Jesus was the Baptist raised to new life (Mark 6:14). John had disciples of his own with their own special practices; the gospel tradition says that they differed from the disciples of Jesus over the question of fasting.

The hymns in honor of John the Baptist in Luke Chapter 1 seem to be derived from his disciples. One hymn appears in verses 14–17 and another in verses 67–79, the latter being called the "Benedictus" from the first word of the Latin translation meaning blessed. There is nothing specifically Christian in these hymns. Moreover, John seems to be the forerunner of God himself, not of the messiah. Verse 76 says, "And you, child, will be called the prophet of the Most High; for you will go before the Lord to prepare his ways." If John the Baptist saw himself as the forerunner of the messiah, his followers seem to have regarded him as the forerunner of God himself. We can see this view in the tradition that John prophesied the coming of one who would baptize with fire, that is—a heavenly figure.

John the Baptist was probably seen as a savior figure on the model of Moses. Admittedly, John did not lead people out into the desert (and then back) as did the so-called false prophets reported on by Josephus. John appeared in the desert, but this fact seems to be only a variation of the motif of the Moses-like prophet.

> Matt. 24:23–26: 23 Then if anyone says to you, 'Look! Here is the Messiah!' or 'There he is!'— do not believe it. 24 For false Messiahs and false prophets will appear and produce great signs and omens, to lead astray, if possible, even the elect. 25 Take note, I have told you beforehand. 26 So, if they say to you, 'Look! He is in the wilderness,' do not go out. If they say, 'Look! He is in the inner rooms,' do not believe it.

The idea of the hidden messiah is present here. Jesus warned his disciples about seeking out messiahs in the "wilderness" or "inner rooms." Thus the false prophets of Josephus were not savior figures but men who led people out to find the messiah. Still, the analogy to John the Baptist applies because he appeared in the desert, he was a savior.

What about the baptism that John performed? Can it be explained against a Moses background? In 1 Cor. 10:1–2, Paul said: "I do not want you to be unaware, brothers and sisters, that our ancestors were all under the cloud, and all passed through the sea, and all were baptized into Moses in the cloud and in the sea." Thus there was a tradition that Moses had been instrumental in conferring a baptism upon the Hebrews when they crossed the Red Sea. In the scheme of the false prophets reported on by Josephus, the crossing of the sea plays a prominent part. John baptized people in the Jordan, so the Moses typology continues to be valid.

How should we understand John's baptism? What was its significance? The Essenes practiced frequent ritual immersions or baptisms. Baptismal tanks were found at Qumran. But John's baptism was performed once whereas Essene baptisms were frequent so they could maintain a continual state of purity. However, the confession of sin, which accompanied John's baptism, does not seem to have been a part of Essene baptisms. Josephus related that he spent a period of three years with a hermit named Bannus who immersed himself everyday. No parallel to John's baptism exists with these self-administered, repeated baptisms of the Qumran community.

Other groups and sects also practiced baptism in the River Jordan. The Mandeans, one such sect whose teachings reach back to the origins of Christianity, looked on John the Baptist as a prophet and rejected Jesus as one who falsified John's teachings. Their baptism was repeated. They used running water in their baptisms and called it "Jordan." They have survived down to the present and can be found in Iraq and Iran. They also go by the name "Nazoreans," which we have already shown to be a name of the first Christians.

The proselyte baptism of Gentiles took place only once. Anyone who wanted to convert to Judaism had to be circumcised, to bring a sacrifice to the temple, and to be baptized. For women, only the last rite applied. Scholars are not certain that proselytes were baptized in the first century CE. Moreover, it seems that at this time baptisms were undertaken by the people themselves and not administered by someone else. Also, unlike John's baptism, where people were immersed, proselyte baptisms were not accompanied by a confession of sins. A final difference is that proselyte baptism was not an eschatological rite as John's was.

Several Old Testament texts contain an admonition to wash and thereby be cleansed from sin (for example, Isa. 1:16; Jer. 4:14). Water was a symbolic means of removing sins. This general idea, of course, was behind the lustrations of the Qumran community, the hermits, the baptizing sects in the Jordan valley (including the Mandeans), and proselyte baptism. The final cleansing would be made at the end of the age. Ezekiel 36:25 says that God will sprinkle water upon the people and cleanse them from all uncleanness, which helps to explain John's baptism because the Baptist obviously thought that the end was at hand.

What about the report that people had to repent and confess their sins when John baptized them? The Israelite feast known as the Day of Atonement (Lev. 16) was the day when all Jews were forgiven and impurity was removed from the people and the temple. During this festival, Tishri 10 (approximately October), the high priest performed sacrifices on behalf of all of the people after he, on behalf of Israel, confessed their sins. Before that, he had to wash ritually (Lev.

16:24), even immersing himself several times (according to the Mishnah). Only then could he act as a representative of the people.

Perhaps John the Baptist combined the idea of the eschatological cleansing with that of the confessional cleansing done by the high priest at the Day of Atonement ceremony. The Day of Atonement stood at the beginning of a new year. John's baptism stood at the beginning of a new age. His baptism was a one-time substitute for the ritual carried out on the Day of Atonement. With John's baptism the individuals had to confess their sins. No priest did it on their behalf. With John's baptism the individuals were immersed. None baptized themselves. John's baptism thus served as an efficacious rite for Jews seeking the kingdom. The Christians took their own baptism as a forgiveness of sins. Would they have ascribed the same efficacy to John's baptism?

## SUMMARY

John the Baptist's existence was affirmed by Josephus and the Gospels. John appeared in the first century CE and presented himself as a Moses-like prophet in an age of competing deliverer figures. He administered an eschatological sacrament of water baptism that was made necessary by the prophecy of an end-of-the-age cleansing and the ritual cleansing of the Day of Atonement. This "sacrament" made it possible for the baptized community to enter the Kingdom of God. Like many other Jews, Jesus accepted the ministry of John, was baptized by him, and thus served for a time as one of his disciples. Later, Jesus separated himself from John to lead his own community. After John the Baptist was executed by Herod Antipas, some followers believed that Jesus was John raised from the dead.

## KEY TERMS FOR REVIEW

Christianized                    Mandeans

Moses-like prophet               Proselyte baptisms

Luke's hymns of John             Day of Atonement

John's baptism

## QUESTIONS FOR REVIEW

1. Why do some people think the portrayal of John the Baptist in the Gospels is ambiguous?

2. How does John the Baptist compare with the self-styled prophets described by Josephus?

3. How does John's baptism differ from Essene baptisms and proselyte baptisms?

# SUGGESTIONS FOR FURTHER READING

Tatum, W. *John the Baptist and Jesus: A Report of the Jesus Seminar.* Sonoma: Polebridge Press, 1994.

Taylor, J. *The Immerser: John the Baptist within Second Temple Judaism.* Grand Rapids: Eerdmans, 1997.

Webb, R. *John the Baptizer and Prophet: A Socio-Historical Study.* JSNTSup 62. Sheffield: JSOT, 1991.

Wink, W. *John the Baptist in the Gospel Tradition.* Cambridge: Cambridge University Press, 1968.

# PART VI

# Jesus and His Life

# 17

✳

# The Nativity and Childhood Legends

## THE EARLY YEARS OF JESUS

Two of the four Gospels, Matthew and Luke, address the subject of Jesus' birth. Only one gospel, Luke, describes him as a child. All together, the subject of Jesus' early years amounts to approximately five percent of the Gospels, yet its theological significance is far greater than the space it takes up. By the late second century, converts were reciting early Christian creeds that included references to the virgin conception and birth of Jesus, ideas that are found only in the accounts of Matthew and Luke.

The accounts of Matthew and Luke both agree and disagree (Matt. 1–2; Luke 1–2). Both agree that Jesus was born of a virgin, Mary, and that Joseph was his adoptive father. Both teach that Jesus was born in Bethlehem during Herod the Great's reign and raised in Nazareth. (John's gospel says nothing about Jesus' birth, but it does appear to disavow Jesus' origin in Bethlehem (7:26–27, 41–43). Beyond these agreements, however, are some clear differences. Matthew appears to have presented his material in a format that answers a series of questions. Who was Jesus (1:1–17)? How was he conceived (1:18–25)? Where and when was he born (2:1–12)? What was his destiny (2:13–23)? As Matthew told the story, readers were introduced to Joseph's dreams, the magi, Herod the Great's slaughter of the infants, and Jesus' sojourn in Egypt. All these items are distinctive to Matthew.

Luke's account compares and contrasts Jesus and John the Baptist. Both enjoyed special births, but Jesus' birth was through a virgin conception whereas John's birth was more in keeping with the births of Isaac, Samson, and Samuel: A barren couple was blessed with a child. Both were circumcised, named, and praised, but only Jesus was praised as the Savior of Israel. It was Luke who introduced readers to the angel Gabriel, John's parents, Mary and Joseph's trip to

Bethlehem for a census, the shepherds, and Jesus' visit to Jerusalem's temple as a young boy. If Matthew and Luke both used Q as a source, they greatly modified it with their own special sources, p–Matthew and p–Luke.

## THE GENEALOGY OF JESUS

Both Matthew's and Luke's Gospels give a record of the ancestry of Jesus (Matt. 1:1–17; Luke 3:23–38). The authors included genealogies that traced, through the paternal line, the ancestors of Joseph, to show that Jesus was the "son of David." However, the two records are different and were not derived from Q. The number of generations between David and Joseph was 41 in Luke but only 27 in Matthew. The name of Joseph's father was not the same in the two Gospels. These accounts included material from p–Matthew and p–Luke. Matthew traced the genealogy back to Abraham and emphasized Jesus' Hebrew identity, whereas Luke went all the way back to Adam. By going back this far Luke said that Jesus was not only the son of David, or even that the history of Israel was fulfilled in him, but also that the history of all humankind was realized in him.

But why did Mathew and Luke trace the ancestors of Joseph when it was believed that Jesus did not have a human father, especially when both their Gospels contain a story of the virgin conception and birth? The probable answer is that these genealogies were compiled by Christians who did not believe in the virgin birth of Jesus. Around the year 150 Justin Martyr reported on Christians who believed that Jesus was the "son of Joseph and Mary according to the ordinary course of human generation." These people that Justin Martyr described were Jewish Christians. The *Gospel according to the Ebionites* says that "Jesus was begotten of human seed, and chosen, and thus by election called the Son of God, Christ having come upon him from on high in the form of a dove." That Jesus was begotten of human seed was apparently assumed in Mark because he said nothing about a special birth.

Matthew's genealogy says that "Abraham was the father of Isaac, and Isaac the father of Jacob," and so on. When the record comes to Joseph, the wording changes: "Jacob the father of Joseph the husband of Mary, of whom Jesus was born, who is called the Messiah" (1:16). This change was necessary because, according to Matthew, Jesus was not the natural son of Joseph.

One of the Syriac translations of the New Testament says that Joseph *begat* (was the father of) Jesus. The Syrian (or Assyrian) Church is heavily indebted to Jewish-Christian ideas and practices, and a reading such as this may have been the original in the genealogy. Matthew, then, may have changed the genealogy at this point because he thought Jesus was born of a virgin. However, in the other parts of the version of Matthew 1 and 2 that appear in the Syriac version, we find no polemic against the virgin birth. Perhaps the translator wanted to stress that Jesus was the legal son of Joseph. Thus, he changed the text to say that Joseph begat Jesus, thereby saying that Joseph was the legal father of Jesus.

Luke, too, made a change in his list. Luke started with Joseph and worked backward, so his change appears at the beginning. Luke says, "Jesus was about thirty years old when he began his work. He was the son (as was thought) of

Joseph, the son of Heli," and so on (3:23). The words "as was thought" are probably Luke's addition. Their purpose was to remind the readers that Jesus was not the real son of Joseph—that this view was held only by some.

Why did Mathew and Luke include these genealogical lists? They wanted to have it both ways. They wanted Jesus to be both the son of a virgin and a descendant of David. Through Joseph, Jesus was traced to the house of David. The Jews reckoned the descent of a child through the mother's first husband. Thus, if a man died childless, his brother had to marry the widow and give her a child who would then be reckoned as the child of the dead man (Deut. 25:5–6). Thus Jesus was made a legal descendant of David because Joseph was of David's house. It goes without saying that many non-Christian Jews would not have been satisfied with a Messiah who was not a real descendant of David. There was no teaching to the effect that the Messiah would be born of a virgin.

The first chapters of Matthew and Luke contain a fascinating picture of no less than four different groups of Christians. Two of them were alike in that they both wanted a messiah with a Davidic ancestry. Their interest in such a messiah suggests that they were Jewish Christians and that they constructed the genealogies to prove Jesus' Davidic lineage. Because these genealogies are not alike, there must have been two groups. Then there were two gentile Christian groups whose members believed that Jesus was born of a virgin without a human father; divine paternity was a common interest in the Hellenistic world. Once again, Matthew and Luke are independent of Mark and Q—their common source—in their accounts of Jesus' birth. Mark does not have a virgin birth story, and Matthew and Luke cannot have used the same source.

## THE VIRGIN BIRTH OF JESUS

By introducing Jesus at the time of his baptism, Mark's gospel gives the impression that Jesus was adopted as the Son of God upon his baptism. Jesus' baptism was seen as his anointing, his installation as the messianic king. Baptism and genealogy go together; they are derived from Jewish Christianity. The virgin birth is not so derived. Justin Martyr said that the Christians who rejected the virgin birth of Jesus said they thought it resembled pagan mythology.

The notion of a divine conception of a remarkable individual can take one of two basic forms. First, it can be said that a god can impregnate a woman by means of a nonhuman form. One tradition has Zeus impregnating the mother of Alexander the Great, when Zeus, in the form of a snake, coupled with her. The emperor Augustus was said to be the son of Apollo in the same manner. This idea is not a good parallel to the Christian notion of the virgin birth of Jesus. Second, it can also be said that a deity in the form of a human being impregnates a woman. In old Egyptian religion it was already thought that the high god assumed the form of a Pharaoh (a god-king) and had intercourse with the queen, who was called "god's wife." Before he left her, he predicted that she would give birth to a son who would become king. A similar prophecy was given by the angel who announced the birth of Jesus to Mary in Luke's gospel (1:31–33).

According to legend, Apollo was the father of the philosopher Plato (fourth century BCE). It was said that Apollo appeared in a dream to Plato's father and bid him not to have sexual intercourse with his wife. Apollo therefore kept her "pure of the relation of wedlock until she had brought forth Plato." This story is similar to the one related in Matthew's gospel (1:25). After the angel had appeared to Joseph in a dream, Joseph "had no marital relations with her until she had borne a son" ("marital relations" means to have intercourse).

We can find no close parallel to the Christian notion of the virgin birth, according to which the Spirit of God effected the conception. Plutarch, a philosopher and historian who died about 120 CE, said that the Egyptians believed that the spirit of a god could work the beginnings of a new life in a woman (*Numa. 4*), but there are no stories about individuals being born as a result.

Matthew wanted his readers to believe that the virgin birth of the Messiah was prophesied in the Bible. He quoted Isaiah 7:14: "Look, the virgin shall conceive and bear a son, and they shall call him Emmanuel, which means, 'God is with us' " (1:23). Matthew quoted the Greek text of Isaiah. The Hebrew text says "young woman" instead of "virgin." Also, whereas the Greek version used the verb in the future tense, "shall conceive," the Hebrew version used the present tense—"the young woman is with child." Isaiah 7:14 dealt with events of the prophet's own time and was really based on Near Eastern oracles about the birth of the royal child of the queen. The Greek text shows that the translators, who worked in Alexandria, were influenced by general Near Eastern notions. In a later period, the church father Epiphanius reported that every year on the sixth of January, the people of Alexandria celebrated the birth of the god Aion from the "virgin." (In the Eastern churches, the sixth of January is Christmas, the date when Jesus' birth is celebrated).

Virgin was one of the titles of the great mother and love goddess in the Near East. The goddess Anath, who was worshipped as Yahweh's spouse by the Jews at Elephantine, was known as the Virgin Anath. The designation Virgin signified that the goddess was the source of life. It was primarily a religious term; it did not mean that Anath did not engage in sex. Interestingly, Whore was also the name of the mother and love goddess. Virgin and Whore are two sides of the same coin—the coin of femaleness as understood in the ancient Near East: the origin of life. The Virgin contains life; the Whore practices life. The Christians chose the aspect of Virgin.

The passage from Isaiah may not have been the source of the Christian concept of the virgin birth because Luke does not cite it in his virgin birth account. Matthew appears to have found a scriptural proof of an already existing notion.

## THE MAGI AND THE STAR

Matthew contains a peculiar story about some "wise men" from the East being led by a star to the place where Jesus was born. The Greek text calls them *magoi;* the Latin calls them *magi*. This name belonged to a certain class of Persian priests who occupied themselves with astrology. Every year on the 24th of December, they gathered on their holy mountain and awaited the birth of the savior god **Mithras,** which was supposed to have been heralded by a star. (It was Mithras's birthday, the 25th of December, that became the date for Christmas in the Western church).

Magi, or at least native astrologers, appeared in different Western stories about the births of the saviors. A Roman author related that a certain Eastern ruler once came to pay homage to the emperor Nero (the emperor was seen as a savior of humankind). The king brought with him some magi, and they all knelt before the emperor and called him "master" and made obeisance to him. Matthew 2:11 says that the magi "knelt down and paid him [Jesus] homage." When Augustus was born, an astrologer cried out, "The ruler of the world has been born!" The Roman historian who told this story went on to relate that when Augustus once entered the house of a certain astrologer, the latter threw himself at Augustus's feet.

The "star" followed by the magi has parallels in Jewish literature. A Jewish legend said that Abraham's birth was heralded by a star that swallowed up four other stars. This enormous star was observed in the sky. This sighting was interpreted by certain soothsayers to mean that a conqueror was about to be born. Every year before Christmas some newspapers print stories about what kind of phenomenon the star of Bethlehem might have been. One theory is that it was a comet that moved about the sun in a certain orbit. It had a starlike center and a tail pointing away from the sun. Halley's Comet was visible in the year 11 BCE. (It is called Halley's Comet because it was observed for the first time by an astronomer named Halley). Another theory is that the star of Bethlehem was a nova, a new star, actually a rekindling of a star that will soon fade away.

The most popular of these scientific theories was formulated by astronomer Johannes Kepler in 1603. He learned that Jupiter and Saturn had no less than three conjunctions under the sign of Pisces in the year 7 BCE. Jupiter was the planet of the ruler, Saturn was the planet star of Palestine, and the Pisces (fish) was the sign of the final age. Thus, it was supposed that when Jupiter and Saturn met in Pisces, the king of the final age would appear in Palestine. Kepler knew that Jewish astrologers had said that the Messiah would be born when such a conjunction took place. The conjunction of the two planets under Pisces appeared in the year 7 BCE and attracted a great deal of attention; it was mentioned in archives from Sippar, a center for astronomy and astrology located near Baghdad.

An American astronomer, Michael Molnar, has challenged Kepler's explanation, arguing that scholars should consider the astrological sign Aries, which symbolized Judea in Roman times, instead of Pisces. He discovered that there was a lunar eclipse of Jupiter during the time that people think Jesus was born. With the help of a computer program, Molnar was able to chart an eclipse of Jupiter in Aries on April 17, 6 BCE. He also found that a Roman astrologer had described the conditions on that date (that is, the sun, moon, and several planets in favorable positions) as fitting the birth of a "divine and immortal" person. Molnar believes that such a sight would have drawn the magi, whom he describes as Hellenistic astrologers who were away from their homes in search of a special birth in Judea.

Either 6 or 7 BCE would fit as the year that Jesus was born because both Matthew and Luke say that Jesus was born when Herod still was alive, and the latter died in 4 BCE. This date also fits both Kepler's and Molnar's explanations of the star of Bethlehem. Are these explanations of the star reasonable?

We should resist the temptation to consider every scientific explanation of the star. No comet, nova, or stellar conjunction behaves the way the star was said to behave. Matthew wanted to show that this sighting was a miracle. Scientists often set aside all religious sense and want to explain such phenomena rationally. Matthew drew on traditions about the magi and ancient astrology in general. Christianity continued to draw on popular traditions and practices.

## THE PERSECUTION OF MALE CHILDREN

Some months before the birth of Augustus, a public portent warned the people of Rome that a king was soon to be born. This omen provoked the Senate to issue a decree that forbade the rearing of any male child for a whole year. Augustus, however, was born, raised, and became the ruler of the Roman empire. The legend about Abraham's birth says that his father had to hide Abraham because he was afraid that the king would kill his son. According to the Moses legend, which is found in Exodus, the Pharaoh commanded that every male child of his Hebrew slaves should be killed. But Moses was hidden away and escaped the wrath of the Pharaoh. Later Jewish literature says that the Pharaoh feared a prophecy about the birth of a Hebrew deliverer.

In the Jesus legend as told by Matthew, Herod, like the Pharaoh, ordered all the male children under two years of age in and around Bethlehem to be killed (2:16). In this way Matthew portrayed Jesus as a Moses-like deliverer (Matthew also cited Jer. 31:15: "A voice was heard in Ramah, . . . Rachel weeping for her children" [2:18]). He was so eager to find scriptural proofs for Jesus' life that he forgot that Ramah is not anywhere near Bethlehem). Like the other heroes, Jesus was saved. Joseph and Mary took him to Egypt. Only when Herod died could they return. Matthew then found Hosea 11:1 fulfilled: "Out of Egypt I have called My son" (2:15). Whereas this verse says that the son of God is Israel, Matthew interpreted it as a prophecy of Jesus.

## BETHLEHEM AND NAZARETH

Matthew says Jesus' family settled in Nazareth, which is in Galilee. They could not go back to their home in Bethlehem because one of Herod's sons, Archaelaus, ruled in Judea. But another son of Herod, Antipas, was in power in Galilee. By Matthew's own criterion, that province, too, was dangerous because both Archaelaus and Antipas were the descendants of Herod the Great. On this basis it appears that Matthew contradicted himself. But Matthew had to settle Jesus there because Jesus came from Nazareth (Archaelaus was infamous for his harsh rule of the Jews). As for Matthew's scriptural proof, "He will be called a Nazorean" (2:23), we have already shown that no such prophecy appears in the Old Testament and that the name "Nazorean" cannot be derived from the name of the town of Nazareth. Nazorean was the name of the first followers of Jesus (Acts 24:5). "Christian" was a later name based on the Greek word for messiah, *christos* (Acts 11:26). The name *Nazorean* means "keepers" or "observers," from *nazor,* and probably denoted Jesus and his followers as having special teachings or practices. Christians in the East are still called Nazoreans.

Matthew could not let Jesus be born in Nazareth because the messiah was not expected to come from Galilee. The Galileans were viewed with suspicion because they were surrounded by Samaritans and Gentiles. An old characterization was "Galilee of the nations [gentiles]" (Isa. 9:1). David, however, was born in Bethlehem in Judea, and so it was considered appropriate that Jesus, the last king, should be born in Bethlehem. According to Matthew, Mary and Joseph lived there.

Luke narrated that Mary and Joseph lived in Nazareth when Jesus was conceived. Thus, Joseph had to transfer Mary from Nazareth to Bethlehem in the last days of her pregnancy. That is a journey of 70 miles, and Mary could not have made this journey, either on foot or on a donkey. The entire story of the census appears to have been fabricated. A census was taken under Quirinius, the governor of Syria, but that was in the year 6 or 7 CE, and it was only for Judea. Moreover, it was nothing like what Luke related. The Romans, who were very efficient, would never require large numbers of people to journey many miles to the villages of millennium-old ancestors to enroll. They simply had people sign tax forms.

Luke 2:7 relates that Jesus was wrapped in infant clothes and placed in a manger because there was no room in the inn. In the *Wisdom of Solomon,* one of the apocryphal writings of the Jewish Bible, King Solomon said that he was nursed in infant clothes like everybody else (7:4–5). Jesus thus had a royal, yet common, beginning. The Greek version of 2 Samuel 7:8 says that David was taken by God from the "stables of the sheep" and made king. According to Luke the new David also had his beginnings in a stable. Isaiah 1:3 says that the donkey knew its manger, but Israel did not know God. This verse, too, throws light on Luke. The Messiah was born among animals because the people of God did not know him. There was no room for the Messiah in the town of David. The people of Israel failed to understand God's work.

## SUMMARY

In Matthew and Luke the nativity and childhood legends of Jesus bear witness to each gospel writer's intent to theologize about the man believed to be the Messiah. Their genealogies rooted Jesus in Israelite and human communities, yet they argued for a divine origin that showed some influence from pagan myths. Jesus' virgin birth appears to be an expression of gentile communities and their interest in the circumstances surrounding the birth of great men. We can connect the story of the magi with ancient astrologers who traditionally prophesied about Roman rulers, and we can identify the star that guided the magi but not the census that dates Jesus' birth. Like Moses, Jesus was persecuted when he was an infant. Bethlehem, as the birthplace of Jesus, fits with David the great deliverer of Israel, whereas his infant clothes associated him with both Solomon and the common Israelites.

## KEY TERMS FOR REVIEW

| | | |
|---|---|---|
| Genealogy | Isaiah 7:14 | 7 BCE |
| Virgin birth | Magi | Bethlehem |
| Plato and Apollo | The "star" | Nazareth |

## QUESTIONS FOR REVIEW

1. How do the descriptions of Jesus' early years in Matthew and Luke agree?
2. What purpose do the genealogies in Matthew and Luke serve?
3. How does the virgin birth of Jesus compare with ancient accounts of virgin births?
4. How do scholars explain the "star" of Jesus' birth that is related in Matthew?
5. How do Matthew and Luke relate Bethlehem and Nazareth in their birth accounts?

## SUGGESTIONS FOR FURTHER READING

Brooke, G. ed. *The Birth of Jesus: Biblical and Theological Reflections*. London: T & T Clark, 2001.

Brown, R. *The Birth of the Messiah: A Commentary on the Infancy Narratives in Matthew and Luke*. Garden City: Doubleday & Company, 1977.

Brown, R. "Gospel Infancy Narrative Research from 1976–86: Part I (Matthew)" and "Gospel Infancy Narrative Research from 1976–86: Part II (Luke)," *CBQ* 48 (1986) 468–83 and 660–80.

Fuller, R. *He That Cometh: The Birth of Jesus in the New Testament*. Harrisburg: Morehouse, 1990.

Hendrickx, H. *The Infancy Narratives*. London: Geoffrey Chapman, 1984.

# 18

# Passion Narrative

## A DISTINCTIVE NARRATIVE

The passion narrative is different from the rest of the Gospels. Form criticism argues that the evangelists or maybe gospel writers can rearrange the order of the various miracle stories, parables, and teaching sections. The crucial events in the passion narrative—entry into Jerusalem, cleansing of the temple, arrest, trial, and execution—cannot be recorded in any other sequence. The continuation of the passion narrative—burial, resurrection, and post-resurrection appearances—also follows a standard sequence.

This arrangement does not mean that the passion narratives of the synoptics are simple historical records. The Gospels are dominated by christological concerns throughout. In Mark 10:33–34 we find a condensed story of the events of the passion narrative, a "prophecy after the occurrence."

> Mark 10:33–34: 33 saying, "See, we are going up to Jerusalem, and the Son of Man will be handed over to the chief priests and the scribes, and they will condemn him to death; then they will hand him over to the Gentiles; 34 they will mock him, and spit upon him, and flog him, and kill him; and after three days he will rise again."

People frequently ask why Jesus, who was able to heal, could not predict the future. Healing and predicting the future are not comparable. There were healers in Jesus' day. Today there are still people who claim to be healers. They do not predict the future. The point is not whether or not Jesus could predict the future. People have been able to do that from time to time. There were "prophets" in Jesus' day. The point is that the passion predictions, as they are told in the Gospels, present a problem for historians because they run counter to probability. The view that Jesus anticipated opposition and conflict, perhaps even his own death, is possible given John the Baptist's arrest and execution by Herod. However, historians of Jesus, or of Socrates for that matter, can establish only what probably happened in the past. The probability of such precise predictions, like those of the passion narratives, is extremely remote. In fact, many scholars argue that the passion predictions reveal the hand of the community—that is, they believe the Church added these Jesus sayings.

The earliest account of Jesus' passion was related by Paul more than twenty years after Jesus' death and almost twenty years before Mark wrote his gospel. Paul recounted Jesus' final meal, betrayal, death, burial, and post-resurrection appearances very briefly (1 Cor. 11:23–26; 15:3–8). Thus, it is probable that the original narrative of the last events of Jesus' life was rather short, consisting of a few events, and later embellished by the different evangelists. The much longer accounts in the Gospels cause scholars to debate the historicity of their passion stories. That several of the events are identified by the evangelists as fulfillments of Old Testament prophecies raises the possibility that some passion events were invented to fulfill the prophecies.

Some scholars argue that the evangelists were influenced by the prophecies when they narrated actual events. They wanted to cast light on the events' significance. It is also possible that Jesus intentionally acted out prophetic actions, as some first-century Jewish figures did according to Josephus (*Ant.* 20:97–98; 169–171). The question then becomes whether a passion event represented a prophecy that was "historicized" or an historical event that was "prophecized" when it was acted out or recorded. In any case, each evangelist made different points in his passion narrative, and beyond the chief events, the details of the passion narrative vary from one version to another (Mark 11:1–15:47; Matt. 21:1–27:66; Luke 19:28–23:56; John 12:12–19:42).

In general, the Gospels share two main story lines. One concerns Jesus' entanglement with the Jewish and Roman authorities. Here we find the entry into Jerusalem, the cleansing of the temple (John moved this event to the beginning of his gospel), the arrest, the trial, and the execution. Then we have a largely separate story that concerns Jesus' relationship with the disciples. Here we have the Last Supper, Peter's denials, the discovery of the empty tomb, and the appearances of the resurrected Jesus. There may also be a third focus—Jesus' relationship to God. In this case we have the prayer in Gethsemane and the words of Jesus from the cross.

## THE ENTRY INTO JERUSALEM

Why did Jesus go to Jerusalem? Theologically, Jesus went to Jerusalem because of his predictions about suffering in Jerusalem. He had to go there and suffer. Mark taught that the way to glory was one of suffering.

Historically, the answer is that Jesus went to Jerusalem because the Passover festival drew near. Every adult Jew kept the Passover in Jerusalem unless prevented from doing so by having to travel too far. Of course, Jesus may also have welcomed the idea of reaching so many people with his message of the imminence of the Kingdom of God and his call for repentance. During Passover,

100,000 Jews gathered in Jerusalem so Jesus would have had a large audience for his message. But of course we know nothing of what went on in Jesus' mind, so this reason remains speculation.

The story of Jesus' entry into Jerusalem is legendary. It is, of course, possible that Jesus entered Jerusalem riding on a donkey, but the form of the story in Mark 11:1–10 is not that of an historical report but rather one of a legend. It is based on Zechariah 9:9, which was a prophecy about the coming of the "messianic" king: "Rejoice greatly, O daughter Zion! Shout aloud, O daughter Jerusalem! Lo, your king comes to you; triumphant and victorious is he, humble and riding on a donkey. . . ." This passage is often taken to mean that Jesus demonstrated his humility by riding on an ass. That view may not be accurate. The king in Zechariah 9:9 won the victory: "triumphant and victorious is he." The next verse says that God will destroy war chariots and war horses. There was no need for them anymore. In Zechariah 9:9, the king rode a mule because the victory had been won. Thus, Mark 11:1–10 regards Jesus as the messianic king, although he had yet to win his victory. This view was brought out clearly in the cry of the people: "Blessed is the coming kingdom of our ancestor David!" According to this story, Jesus brought the messianic kingdom.

This rejoicing was preceded by another greeting: "Blessed is the one who comes in the name of the Lord!" This passage was taken from Psalm 118:26 and was simply the greeting of any pilgrim who came to Jerusalem. Mark, however, took it in a messianic, christological, sense, amplifying it with the next greeting and the reference to Zechariah 9:9.

## THE "CLEANSING" OF THE TEMPLE

The center of the story about the cleansing of the temple is the saying in Mark 11:17: "'My house shall be called a house of prayer for all nations.'? But you have made it a den of robbers." This verse was taken from two prophets (Isa. 56:7 and Jer. 7:11). Form critically, the story presents a biographical apophthegm; the story relates an incident in the life of Jesus with a pregnant word as the climax. Thus, it is possible that the community formed the story to serve as a setting for the saying. Even so, it is difficult to escape the impression that the story has an historical core. We find no precedent or basis for Jesus' action in the Old Testament. Some scholars doubt that the story was part of the passion narrative because there are no such indications in the story itself, and John was able to move it to the beginning of Jesus' ministry. But it is hard to escape the conclusion that such a provocative action on the part of Jesus' would not have gone unchecked. Such an event satisfies the historian's need to identify a cause for Jesus' arrest and crucifixion in Jerusalem. Many scholars now argue that this action—the cleansing of the temple—led to his arrest, trial, and execution.

As the story now stands, it is a little puzzling. Buying and selling were necessary to maintain temple worship. Sacrificial animals were bought and sold. Foreign money had to be changed so that Diaspora Jews could obtain the right kind of money to buy sacrificial animals. Therefore Jesus' act may symbolize the destruction of the temple **cult** itself. Without the changing of money and buying and selling there would be no cult. The traditional explanation—that Jesus wanted to cleanse (or reform) the temple by getting rid of some abuses—may miss this point. An ancient temple without a sacrificial cult would not be a temple. Jesus drove out buyers, who would offer sacrifices, as well as sellers (Mark 11:15).

In addition, the part of the quote in italics from Jeremiah 7:11 in Mark 11:17 ("But you have made it [the temple] a *den of robbers*") does not bear out the conventional interpretation that Jesus was interested only in reforming temple practices. Jeremiah criticized his people's morality in general (they stole, committed adultery, swore falsely, practiced idolatry, and then came to the temple and worshipped **Yahweh**). This lack of morality is why Jeremiah called the temple a den of robbers. Jeremiah went on to promise that the temple would be destroyed because of the people's wickedness (Jer. 7:13–14). We can probably understand Jesus' behavior best as continuing the prophetic criticism of the people. He asserted that they were not worthy of having the temple and therefore the temple had to be destroyed.

Did Jesus intend to spark a full-scale revolutionary uprising against the Romans, who usually stationed troops in Jerusalem during the Passover festival? This is one theory of the so-called cleansing of the temple. Some scholars believe that Jesus was sympathetic to revolutionary Jewish interests, but it is difficult to find clear evidence to the effect that he shared their violent methods. In the parable of the wicked husbandmen, violent measures failed (Mark 12:1–12; *Gospel according to Thomas logion* 65). Moreover, Mark greatly exaggerated the scope of the so-called cleansing. It took place in the outer court of the temple, the Court of Gentiles, which was an immense area. Tradition has it that one person brought 3,000 sheep into the gentile court. It is out of the question that Jesus could have swept this entire place clean. Finally, if he had tried to do so in an attempt to get the masses to join him, he would have been stopped. There were temple police, and, as we have already noted, the Romans reinforced their garrison in Jerusalem at Passover time. A large number of Roman troops were stationed just north of the outer court. The cleansing incident, if historical, was probably a very short one, restricted to a small area of the outer court. It could not have been an attempt at sparking a full-scale insurrection; it was rather a symbolic act for his followers and later played a role in Jesus' trial.

## THE LAST SUPPER

### (1) The Question of Priority among the Sources

Within the framework of the passion story, Jesus' final meal with his followers—the Last Supper (Lord's Supper)—was a Passover meal. In Mark's account of the meal itself, there is no reference to the Passover, which is also the case in 1 Corinthians 11:23—the oldest tradition about the Lord's Supper. (We will discuss the supper's Passover association later). In Paul and Mark, the two oldest sources, the Lord's Supper is a cult legend. Such accounts were meant to be read and heeded when the Christians celebrated the **Eucharist** in remembrance of Jesus' death. These accounts therefore focus on the *significance* of Jesus' death. The setting in life (*Sitz im Leben*) was **sacramental;** the sociological setting in the life of the community was part of the cult and early Christian ritual. It is doubtful that the story said anything about what really went on at the last meal Jesus shared with his disciples. Some suggest that Mark 14:25 may contain an historical element: "Truly I tell you, I will never again drink of the fruit of the vine until that day when I drink it new in the kingdom of God." This passage appears in Luke 22:14–18.

> Luke 22:14–18: 14 When the hour came, he took his place at the table, and the apostles with him. 15 He said to them, "I have eagerly desired to eat this Passover with you before I suffer; 16 for I tell you I will not eat it until it is fulfilled in the kingdom of God." 17 Then he took a cup, and after giving thanks he said, "Take this, and divide it among yourselves; 18 for I tell you that from now on I will not drink of the fruit of the vine until the kingdom of God comes."

Luke's version of the Last Supper says that it was a Passover meal, and this version does not appear to be a cult legend (biographical legend). Is this section historical? Probably not, because this passage refers to Jesus' suffering (prophecy after the event). Perhaps this tradition about the Last Supper made it into a Passover meal. (Note that there is no reference to a Passover lamb).

Mark's account is followed by Matthew's, but the latter expanded the former by additions that represented liturgical practice: (1) "Take, eat, this is my body" (Matt. 26:26), the command to eat was added; (2) "Drink from it, all of you" (Matt. 26:27), Mark's text was changed into a command; and (3) "for this is my blood of the covenant, which is poured out for many for the forgiveness of sins" (Matt. 26:28). Matthew interpreted the death of Jesus as an atonement for sins. This view had already been expressed in Mark, but Matthew made it clearer.

In general, we can say that the texts represent two traditions. The first tradition emphasizes the **atoning** death of Jesus. Mark and Matthew represent this view. Luke and Paul represent a second tradition in which the new covenant is the dominant theme (1 Cor. 11:25; Luke 22:20). However, Luke was also influenced by Mark because he spoke of the blood "poured out for you" (Luke 22:20) and thus showed some influence from the atonement tradition (see Figure 18.1).

Atonement Tradition                     Covenant Tradition

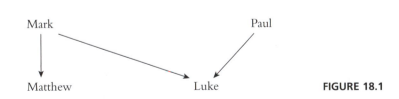

FIGURE 18.1

Paul's account in 1 Corinthians 11:23–25 appears to represent the more original tradition.

> 1 Cor. 11:23–25: 23 For I received from the Lord what I also handed on to you, that the Lord Jesus on the night when he was betrayed took a loaf of bread, 24 and when he had given thanks, he broke it and said, "This is my body that is for you. Do this in remembrance of me." 25 In the same way he took the cup also, after

supper, saying, "This cup is the new covenant in my blood. Do this, as often as you drink it, in remembrance of me."

Three arguments support the priority of Paul's account. First, in Paul the words Jesus spoke over the cup were separated from the words that he spoke over the bread; the meal separated them. ("After the supper," the Lord took the cup). In Mark, on the other hand, the words Jesus spoke over the cup followed immediately after the words he spoke over the bread. It is more plausible that Mark brought together what was originally separated than it is that Paul separated what was originally united. Mark's gospel also contains a thanksgiving over the cup as well as a blessing over the bread, whereas Paul has only the latter. Mark tried to create a parallelism.

This view leads us to the second argument in favor of Pauline priority. There is a strange symbolism in Paul:

Bread is body.

Cup is covenant.

That bread symbolizes the body reads well, but the cup symbolizes the covenant does not. Mark put it differently:

Bread is body.

Cup is blood.

Cup symbolizing blood makes more sense than cup symbolizing covenant. Mark clearly tried to present a consistent symbolism, but he did not create a good parallelism because body does not correspond to blood. Instead he should have used flesh. Flesh and blood are what John used in his allusions to the Eucharist (John 6:51–58). No problem occurs in Paul because he has no intentional parallelism (covenant does not correspond to body).

The third and final argument for Pauline priority is that Paul has no passage about drinking blood. An admonition to drink blood would have sounded utterly abhorrent to a Jew because the law forbids Jews to use blood as a food. Mark appears to have been influenced by the mystery religions of the Hellenistic world, where people obtained salvation by being initiated with certain rituals, including sacramental meals where they partook of sacramental representations of the flesh and/or blood of the savior god. This ideology was fully adopted by the Gospel according to John, as we can see from reading John 6:51–58. By eating the flesh and drinking the blood of the deity, people obtained divine nature.

In Paul, the cup represented some sort of a seal of the covenant made "in or through the blood" of Jesus, which was based on the death of Jesus. The term *blood* could stand for *death*. In verse 26 Paul says that every time the Eucharist was celebrated, the death of the Lord was proclaimed: "For as often as you eat this bread and drink the cup, you proclaim the Lord's death until he comes." The Eucharist is a *kerygma* (Greek), a proclamation, through an act, of the death of Jesus.

As for Paul's reference to the body, we should not think of it in the sense that it was used in Mark and John. In 1 Corinthians *body* stands for *person, self, I,* which is taken to mean that Jesus himself is present at the meal. His broken body is present—that is, his sacrificed body. The point is not that people eat the bread. The point is that Jesus, as the sacrifice, is present at the meal.

The idea of a covenant between God and the people was of course important in Judaism. The Qumran-Essenes regarded themselves as the people of the new covenant. They shared a regular meal with bread and wine; it was some kind of seal of this new covenant. When the covenant between God and the people was established at Mt. Sinai, a meal marked its conclusion (Exod. 24). It was related that Moses took the blood of the sacrificed animal and sprinkled it upon the people as a seal of the covenant being established (the meaning probably being: If I break the covenant, I will suffer the fate of this animal). Paul's words, "the new covenant in or through my blood," seem to have their background here. Christ was the sacrifice that marked the beginning of the new covenant.

## (2) What Happened at the Last Supper?

The Eucharist was a meal commemorating the new covenant in the early Church in Paul's basically Jewish-Christian congregations as well as in the gentile congregations of Mark and John. Can we find out what happened at the Last Supper?

The Acts of the Apostles has several references to bread breaking in the early Church. Apparently this bread breaking did not refer to the observance of the Eucharist because wine was not mentioned. However, it is clear that the meal was a religious one. "They devoted themselves to the apostles' teachings and fellowship, to the breaking of bread, and the prayers" (2:42). Attending the temple together and breaking bread in their homes, people "ate their food with glad and generous hearts" (2:46). The joy characterizing these meals appears to be an eschatologically motivated joy; the Christians looked forward to the end of the age and anticipated the meals of the kingdom to come. This dimension is also found in the accounts of the Last Supper, as we can see from Mark 14:25 and Matthew 26:29: "Truly, I tell you, I will never again drink of the fruit of the vine until that day when I drink it new in the kingdom of God," and especially Luke 22:16–18.

> Luke 22:16–18: 16 for I tell you, I will not eat it until it is fulfilled in the kingdom of God." 17 Then he took a cup, and after giving thanks he said, "Take this and divide it among yourselves; 18 for I tell you that from now on I will not drink of the fruit of the vine until the kingdom of God comes."

This dimension also appears in Paul's account because Paul says that every time the Eucharist was celebrated, Christians proclaimed the death of the Lord "until he comes" (1 Cor. 11:26).

The Christian meal with this eschatological dimension seems to be a continuation of the meal that Jesus shared with his disciples. Did he introduce a new aspect at the Last Supper? Did he give himself a significant role at this meal? We can see that the deaths of martyrs had an atoning function. In 4 Maccabees 17 it is said that the deaths of the martyrs purified the nation, that they were a ransom for the sins of the people, and that God would deliver Israel because of their blood (v. 21–22). If Jesus had a premonition that he would be apprehended and executed because of what he did in the temple court, he could have interpreted his fate in the light of such ideas.

However, we must first point out that the covenantal sacrifice, which appears to have been the basis for the version in Paul's and Luke's accounts, did not have an atoning function. We cannot read one into Paul's text, which contains a tradition older than Mark's and Matthew's accounts. This lack means that in the earliest tradition of the Last Supper (Paul's account), Jesus' death was not considered to have an atoning significance. Secondly, no one knows what went on in Jesus' mind. For that reason, it would be foolhardy to assume that Jesus had a premonition of his death and interpreted it as an atoning sacrifice, or as a covenantal sacrifice for that matter.

In conclusion, (1) the first Christians continued the meals that they had shared with Jesus—meals at which the eschatological perspective was always present. This fact is evident from the book of Acts. (2) The last meal that Jesus shared with his disciples acquired a special significance; it was not commemorated every day. It was seen as a sign of the new covenant instituted by God. The Christians were the new Israel (as shown by Paul, and to a certain extent, Luke). Later, the ideas of mysterious Hellenistic religions entered into the picture, and Jesus appears to have become a cult divinity sacramentally consumed.

## THE APPREHENSION OF JESUS

After the account of the Last Supper, we find the story about Jesus praying in Gethsemane. This account also appears to be a legend. No witnesses could have reported what happened when Jesus prayed. The point of the legend is to show that Jesus, lonely and afraid, remained obedient to the will of God. The story was meant to provide a paradigm for believers. It was here that the unique address of God as *abba,* "Dad or Daddy," was used in Jesus' prayer. Jesus, the persecuted martyr, was cared for by God the way a small child is cared for by her father.

The arrest of Jesus followed his prayer at Gethsemane. The goal of this story is to show the fulfillment of the prophecy of Zechariah 13:7, ". . . Strike the shepherd, that the sheep may be scattered." Jesus spoke those words in Mark 14:27 after the Last Supper, and the account of Jesus' arrest ended with the words: "All of them deserted him and fled" (v. 50). The story of his arrest is basically a legend. There were not two groups—Jesus and the disciples on the one hand and Jesus' enemies on the other. There was one person and two groups. Jesus was alone. His enemies were led by a former friend, and his disciples were confused, helpless, and running away. That the disciples left Jesus is probably historical because the Church would not be inclined to depict its founding apostles as cowards.

One of Jesus' disciples may have been instrumental in his apprehension because it is unlikely that the Church would have made up a story that one of Jesus' followers was a traitor. The story is well attested to in several independent sources (Mark 14:10–11, 43–45; John 18:2–3; Acts 1:16). If such a betrayal was true, the Gospels are strangely silent about the betrayer's motives. (The reference to Jesus' betrayal by Judas, within the narrative of the Last Supper, is legendary because it was based on Psalm 41:9: "Even my bosom friend in whom I trusted, who ate of my bread, has lifted the heel against me.")

Who gave the orders to arrest Jesus? Mark says that people "from the chief priest and the scribes and the elders" apprehended him (14:43). However, John 18:12 says that Jesus was apprehended by "soldiers" (presumably Romans) as well as by Jews. John tried very hard to play down the part the Romans played in the process against Jesus, so his account is peculiar and possibly rests on an authentic tradition. This version of the arrest implies some type of corroboration: Jesus was executed by Romans with the help of some Jews.

According to Mark, Jesus was tried and found guilty before the Sanhedrin during the night. The next morning there was a consultation, and then Jesus was handed over to the Roman prefect (governor) for execution. This story is probably not true. In the first place, it is debatable whether the assembly, here called the Sanhedrin, had the right to pronounce the death sentence. John 18:31 says that the Jews did not have this right. If John is wrong, Jesus would have been stoned by Jews, not crucified by Romans. Stoning was the Jewish way of execution, crucifixion the Roman way.

Secondly, according to rabbinic sources, capital charges could not be dealt with during the night. Moreover, there would have to be a new trial the next day. Because the Jewish day began at sundown, the consultation in the morning would not be seen as a new trial. Admittedly, the Mishnah, a late second-century CE text of rabbinic law, reflects the view of Pharisaic rabbinism, whereas a Sadducean judicial practice in the first century may have been different. But we know little about Sadducean law. The Sadducees left no writings. Scholars have also argued that the case of Jesus was an exception to the rule—that the Jewish authorities found Jesus so dangerous that they allowed the judicial practices to be set aside. This view is implausible. If the synoptic chronology is correct, the day was a feast day, which was like a Sabbath in that no death sentence could be pronounced on that day because it would be considered work.

It is thus more logical to accept Luke's version. Luke 22:54 and 66 relate that Jesus was detained in the quarters of the high priest during the night and then interrogated in the morning. The high priest did not pronounce a death sentence but had Jesus taken to Pilate. John 18 is in essential agreement with Luke 22— the high priest did not pronounce a death sentence.

The fixed point in all the accounts is that Jesus was executed in Roman fashion on the order of Pilate. This event is one that scholars agree on, although there is some debate over the circumstances surrounding it. In this connection, we should also remember that the name of the high priest is not firmly established in the sources, whereas that of the Roman prefect is. Mark did not name the high priest. Matthew and Luke provided two different names (Caiaphas in Matt. 26:57 and Annas in Luke 3:2 and Acts 4:6). John gave both these names, one as the name of the high priest and the other as the name of the high priest's father-in-law, who was also a priest (John 18:13). It seems that the first Christians should have been better informed about the identity of the person responsible for the death of Jesus.

One weakness occurs in Luke's account of Jesus' apprehension. Luke did not talk about a formal trial, but in his account the assembly did seem to be involved in more activity than would have been allowed on a feast day, which was similar to the Sabbath. This difficulty can be overcome if the Last Supper was not a Passover meal. The Passover lamb was sacrificed in the afternoon of Nisan 14, and the meal was eaten after sundown—that is, when Nisan 15 began. Passover was merged into the Feast of Unleavened Bread, which was celebrated for one week.

Nisan 15 was the first day of the Feast of Unleavened Bread. Mark 14:1–2 says that the chief priest and the scribes agreed not to kill Jesus during Passover and the Feast of Unleavened Bread, but this was exactly what happened according to Mark's next chapter. Because the Jewish day began at sundown, Jesus was executed on the same day he had his last meal. Was it a Passover meal? Nothing in the description of the meal indicates that it was. On the contrary, essential elements of a Passover meal were lacking. The meal should have included lamb, unleavened bread, and additional cups, and women should have been present (*all* Israel). No one reading only Mark 14:22–25 would conclude that the Last Supper was a Passover meal. John differs from the synoptics by saying that Jesus died on Nisan 14, the day before Passover began.

## THE INTERROGATION

### (1) Jesus before the Sanhedrin

Consider Jesus' so-called cleansing of the temple just before Passover. It stands to reason that Jesus' attitude toward the temple would be an issue, if indeed not the main issue, during his interrogation by the Jewish authorities. However, Mark's account is legendary and shaped from the perspective of the believing post-Easter community. For that reason we are surprised to see how clumsily he dealt with the temple issue. He asserted that false witnesses said, "we heard him say, 'I will destroy this temple that is made with hands, and in three days I will build another, not made with hands' " (14:58). To Mark, the latter part of the saying was not a false testimony. Rather it was an allegory that referred to Jesus' resurrection. For Mark, only the first part of the saying was false, yet he did not make this clear.

In John's gospel, the whole saying was attributed to Jesus, and an allegorical interpretation was extended to all of it: "Jesus answered them, 'Destroy this temple, and in three days I will raise it up' " (2:19). The allegorical interpretation reveals the hand of the Church; it is a "prophecy after the event"—after the resurrection. The question remains whether the text represents a Christian apologetic (defense of Christianity). Did Jesus predict the downfall of the temple? Did he do so when he "cleansed" the temple? According to John this was when Jesus spoke his words about the temple. In John the cleansing occurred at the start of Jesus' ministry, which was the same time of year as the synoptics' Passover. A cleansing at the beginning of Jesus' ministry would not have gone unchecked by the authorities. As it was, Jerusalem's authorities were only suspiciously interested and did not openly oppose Jesus or attempt to apprehend him. Instead, John emphasized the opposition between Jesus and the Jews at the beginning of his ministry.

It is easy to find a reason to explain such a prediction of the Temple's destruction. The first Christians lived in Jerusalem and took part in the temple service. Both Matthew and Luke changed Mark's text. Matthew said that Jesus only claimed to be able to destroy the temple (Matt. 26:61), whereas Luke went further and left the statement out (Luke 22:54–71). On this basis we can reasonably conclude that Jesus spoke against the temple.

Can we corroborate this construction? Although many of the first Christians were part of the temple cult, some of them appeared to have been critical of the temple. In Acts Chapter 6, the Jews charged one of Jesus' followers, Stephen, with having said that Jesus would come back to destroy the temple, "we have heard him say that this Jesus of Nazareth will destroy this place [temple]" (v. 14). Was Stephen adapting the words of Jesus? Stephen did not deny this charge. In his speech of defense, he said that God did not dwell in a house made by hands (Acts 7:48).

We can find important evidence in the *Gospel according to Thomas logion* 71: "Jesus said, 'I shall destroy this house, and no one shall be able to rebuild it.' " *Thomas* is often independent of the synoptics and in some instances more original. Is this the case here? *Thomas* certainly is not dependent on the synoptics. In the first place, *Thomas* affirms what the Gospels deny, namely that Jesus said that he would destroy the temple. Secondly, *Thomas* has no allegorical explanation as the Gospels do.

Jesus probably spoke words as such as those found in *Thomas logion* 71. He spoke in the name of God, like the prophets in the Old Testament. When the prophets said "I," they meant the divine "I." Thus Jeremiah was bidden by God to go and take his stand at the gate of the temple and proclaim in the name of God that God would destroy the house "that is called by my name" (Jer. 7:14). Note the similar name of the temple in *Thomas logion* 71—"this house"—a thoroughly Semitic designation.

This statement does not mean that Jeremiah and Jesus were opposed to the temple as such, but that they found something wrong with the people responsible for the temple and the people worshipping there. The destruction of the temple would imply the removal of the divine presence as a punishment for the sins of the people. God dwelt in the temple, and his presence would be removed with its destruction.

Other people, too, prophesied the downfall of the temple in Jesus' time. Josephus reported on a certain illiterate peasant, also called Jesus (a common name), who claimed to represent a "voice against Jerusalem and the temple" . . . "a voice from the east, a voice from the west, a voice from the four winds, a voice against Jerusalem and the sanctuary." He probably caused a great disturbance because the Jewish authorities handed him over to the Roman governor, who had him scourged.

According to Mark, Jesus was sentenced to death by the Sanhedrin because of blasphemy (14:64). This charge required the mention of the name of God, which was too holy to be uttered. This prohibition is probably the reason that some Greek manuscripts of Mark read "I am" in Jesus' answer to the high priest's question of whether he was the Messiah. "I AM" was a substitute for the name of God. The substitute was almost as holy as the proper name itself because it was taken to be an explanation of the name. Thus, if we accept this reading, Jesus did not simply claim messianic status but divine honor. We might say that Jesus should then have said, "I am I AM," but there is some evidence to the effect that this statement can be abridged to simply "I am."

When dealing with the question of the personal claims of Jesus, scholars have argued that "I am" was probably not the original reading of Mark; the original reading was probably a noncommittal answer such as the one found in both Matthew and Luke. The whole scene was not based on an eyewitness report (because according to the Gospels no followers were present at Jesus' trial; all had abandoned him) but was shaped from the perspective of the post-Easter community, which expected Jesus to return as the Son of man on the clouds of heaven. The high priest's question and Jesus' answer amount to a compendium in Christology. Thus, the question is not "What charge did the high priest bring against Jesus?" but rather "What did the Christian narrator allow Jesus to say?"

Early Christians were occasionally harassed, persecuted, and put to death by the Jews in Jerusalem. That happened to Stephen, who was stoned by an angry mob, and that happened later to James, the leader of the community, who was executed with a sword on Herod Agrippa's orders (Acts 7:58; 12:2). Stoning was the penalty for blasphemy. Their confession of Jesus as the Messiah seemed to the first Christians to qualify for the charge of blasphemy and to require a death sentence. This explanation for Mark's account of Jesus' reply and subsequent sentencing by the Sanhedrin remains conjecture.

It seems that what happened before the assembly was an interrogation of Jesus on the issue of the temple against the background of Jesus'"cleansing" of the outer court, and, possibly, an utterance of Jesus against the temple. Then the assembly handed Jesus over to the Romans. On what premise did the Jews hand Jesus over to the Romans? It must have been a political accusation because the Romans took such charges very seriously but did not concern themselves with purely religious matters. Jesus' actions in the outer court and his words against the temple could easily be adapted to a political accusation. (Remember that the Roman authorities punished the other Jesus who spoke against the temple—the one about whom Josephus wrote.) Jesus would have then been charged with creating a disturbance among the people by his declaration that the temple should be destroyed because of sin, the critical declaration being that the "sin" was the Roman presence and its resulting defilement. Jesus' supposed solution was insurrection.

## (2) Who Was Guilty of Jesus' Death?

Too many times in history the Jews have been called "murderers of God." We find the evidence for this accusation in the Gospels where certain Jews, probably Sadducees, were instrumental in bringing about the death of Jesus. The Jews have often been defended, and have defended themselves, against this charge. The evidence for the defense also appears in the Gospels: Jesus was executed by the Romans. Are the Italians, the descendants of the Romans, considered "murderers of God"? Neither the Jews nor the Italians need defending. The Italians of today had nothing to do with the execution of Jesus in Palestine by Pilate two thousand years ago. The Jews of today had nothing to do with the Saducean-dominated Sanhedrin in the first century.

## JESUS BEFORE PILATE

Early Christian, Jewish, and Roman sources agree that Jesus appeared before Pilate and was executed according to Roman law. What happened? The trial before Pilate was no simple review of the "trial" before the Sanhedrin. Actually, Mark 15 does not say anything about a previous trial.

Pilate's question, "Are you the king of the Jews?," was the Greco-Roman formulation of what the high priest asked. This entire encounter may therefore have been shaped by the perspective of the post–Easter community, which expected Jesus to return as the Son of man on the clouds of heaven to establish his rule. Yet, it makes historical sense that Jesus would have been charged before Pilate with a crime that was political in nature, a crime that undermined Roman rule. It was Roman practice to leave religious matters to the locals but to safeguard Roman rule over the provinces. Pilate's charge also passes the criteria of dissimilarity because neither Jews nor early Christians gave Jesus this title.

Jesus' answer to Pilate was noncommittal. "You say so" meant "the statement is yours" (Mark 15:2). Therefore, other unspecified charges were pressed by the Jewish authorities, and later Pilate even thought that Jesus was innocent and asked Jesus to defend himself. Had Jesus admitted that he was the Messiah, there would have been no need to press other charges.

Mark placed Pilate's question in the foreground before he presented the account of Jesus being sentenced as the Messiah, specifically the King of the Jews, which term is used six times in Mark 15 but not earlier in his gospel. Mark could not have Jesus answer affirmatively because then the scene would have come to a close. Of course, one motive for not having Jesus affirm messiahship is that the time had not yet come to reveal Jesus' identity in Mark's gospel. That revelation can come only after his death (as the "messianic secret" of Mark dictates). But Mark had something else to say here, and that is why Pilate asked Jesus to defend himself and entered into a dialogue with the Jews.

In Chapter 15, one of Mark's concerns was to represent the Romans as having no essential quarrel with Jesus and his movement. The Christians lived and preached in a Roman environment. If there was no harm in its founder, there would be no harm in his followers. Mark represented Pilate as finding no harm in Jesus. Pilate was pressured into yielding to the demand of the Jews to release Barabbas instead of Jesus. In Mark, Pilate did not condemn Jesus; he acted against his better judgment. In the later Gospels, this motif becomes increasingly prominent. In Luke, Pilate sent Jesus to Herod Antipas, the Roman client ruler in Galilee who was in Jerusalem for Passover (Luke 23:7). Here Jesus said nothing. In John, Pilate was subtly threatened by the Jews: "If you release this man, you are no friend of the emperor" (19:12).

History recorded a few things about Pilate. He was not a saint. Jewish sources depicted him as cruel and inflexible toward the Jews, even raiding the temple treasury to fund an aqueduct. Pilate did not appear to be the type of person who would have allowed a Jewish mob to influence him, and this view causes historians to pause as they read the accounts of Pilate in the Gospels. After ten years as governor of Judea, he was recalled for poor administration in 36 CE by the emperor Tiberius.

## BARABBAS AND THE CROSS

The story of Barabbas calls for a brief comment. Ancient records make no mention of a Roman custom of releasing a prisoner at Passover (Mark 15:6). It is also implausible that the crowd could name one individual to be freed no matter what his offense, and Jesus had not yet been convicted. In addition, nothing prevented

Pilate from acquitting Jesus as well as Barabbas. Up until now the crowd had been in favor of Jesus. Then they turned against him. What could be the motive for such a construction except to blame the Jews for rejecting Jesus? Still, though, we need to explain the Barabbas story.

Philo related that the people of his city (Alexandria) once had fun with an imbecile. They put a paper crown on his head, clothed him with a mat for a robe, and put a papyrus reed in his hand. They seated this fool in a public place and saluted him as "king" and "lord." They then asked him questions regarding public matters. Note the parallel of this story to the Roman soldiers' treatment of Jesus.

> Mark 15:16–20: 16 Then the soldiers led him into the courtyard of the palace (that is, the governor's headquarters); and they called together the whole cohort. 17 And they clothed him in a purple cloak; and after twisting some thorns into a crown they put it on him. 18 And they began saluting him, "Hail, King of the Jews!" 19 They struck his head with a reed, spat upon him, and knelt down in homage to him. 20 After mocking him, they stripped him of the purple cloak and put his own clothes on him. Then they led him out to crucify him.

Matthew even says that Jesus was given a reed (Matt. 27:29). This may have been dropped from Mark's account.

The imbecile in Alexandria was called Carabas. Should it have been Barabbas ("the Son of the Father")? Was it a title? Philo probably related a profane emulation of a ritual drama in which a character named "the Son of the Father" played a part. Such ritual dramas were actually staged. They pointed to the ancient practice of putting the king (the Son of the Father—that is, the Son of God) himself to death to obtain abundant crops. Later they used a substitute for the king. One of these dramas was staged during the Babylonian-Persian sacral festival in the spring. A condemned prisoner was arrayed in royal attire and admitted to the palace of the king. The king had to abdicate for five days. The substitute king enjoyed the king's harem, and all his orders had to be obeyed. In the end, however, he was stripped, whipped, and crucified. The parallelism with the treatment of Jesus is unmistakable.

The Roman festival of the god Saturn, known as Saturnalia, was similar to ancient Mesopotamian practices like the Babylonian-Persian sacral festival. It was presided over by a mock king, often a slave, who played the part of Saturn, ruler of the Golden Age at the beginning of time. After a short but merry reign, he committed suicide on the altar of the god. The Roman soldiers seem to have staged a secular version of an ancient ritual drama. A certain prisoner was picked to play the mock king, Barabbas, the Son of the Father. Why Jesus took his place is a mystery, and perhaps Barabbas was not released. He may have been one of the "bandits" crucified with Jesus (Mark 15:27). John says that Barabbas was a bandit (John 18:40).

## THE CRUCIFIXION

The story of the crucifixion of Jesus contains many legendary features that were probably fashioned after Old Testament passages. After this account we have the story of the tearing of the temple veil (which symbolized the removal of the barrier between God and the people), and before it there is an interesting reference to a certain Simon being forced to carry Jesus' cross. The identification of Simon suggests that this reference was probably historical. At the same time, Mark says that Simon was "compelled . . . to carry his [Jesus'] cross" (Mark 15:21). Luke wrote that Simon carried the cross behind Jesus (Luke 23:26). These differences represent different theological interpretations. Mark refers to Jesus' demand that any one who followed him must "take up his cross" (Mark 8:34).

Crucifixion itself was an ancient form of execution, dating back a thousand years to the Assyrians. The Hasmonean (Jewish) rulers of the second and first centuries BCE even used it on their Jewish subjects. Whereas the Romans made it a practice to crucify criminals, especially rebels, they viewed crucifixion as so humiliating a way to die—hanging on a cross until one died of thirst—that they never crucified Roman citizens, and crucifixion became a form of imperial terrorism used only against rebels. For Jews it was especially repugnant because Jews identified the person who was crucified as being cursed by God because he was hanged on a tree (Gal. 3:13; compare with Deut. 21:23). The Mishnah confirms this view by teaching that the hanged or crucified man was guilty of blaspheming God's name (*Sanh.* 6:4). Paul alluded to the scandal that Jesus' crucifixion created among Jews when he wrote: "Christ crucified, a stumbling block to Jews" (1 Cor. 1:22).

The dividing up of Jesus' clothes was based on Psalm 22: "they divide my cloths among themselves, and for my clothing they cast lots" (v. 18). The hostile verbal attacks against Jesus were also drawn from the Psalms; "Insults have broken my heart, so that I am in despair. I looked for pity, but there was none; and for comforters, but I found none" (Ps. 69:20), as was the despairing cry of Jesus, "My God, my God, why have you forsaken me?" (Ps. 22:1). No one who knew Aramaic would have misunderstood Jesus to speak of Elijah as Mark recounted (Mark 15:35). And no one who did not know Aramaic could find any mention of Elijah in his words. The eclipse of the sun that immediately preceded Jesus' cry from the cross was impossible because it was the Passover, when there had to be a full moon. The effort to give Jesus a sponge filled with sour wine came from Psalm 69:21: "They gave me poison for food, and for my thirst they gave me vinegar to drink." Lastly, the confession of the centurion that "Truly this man was God's Son!" fit with Mark's messianic secret theme and Jesus' identity as the crucified Messiah (Mark 15:39).

## SUMMARY

The passion narratives describe Jesus' final visit to Jerusalem and his eventual death. The sequence of events is rather uniform and suggests that the events are historical. However, we need to keep in mind the theological motives of the evangelists. History and faith were blended by the early Church. Jesus' entrance into Jerusalem was borrowed from Zechariah. Jesus' cleansing of the temple may have provided an historical explanation for his arrest. The Last Supper stories provided the early Church with important guidance for the observance of the Eucharist. Jesus' trial before the Sanhedrin at night is contrary to what we know of Jewish practices. The charge that Jesus spoke against the temple has some support from noncanonical sources. The type of mistreatment Jesus faced by Roman soldiers has some parallels in the first century, and it is probable that the story of Simon being enlisted to help Jesus is authentic.

## KEY TERMS FOR REVIEW

| | | |
|---|---|---|
| Passion narrative | Cleansing of the temple | Pilate |
| Jerusalem | Last Supper | Sanhedrin |
| Passover | Bread and cup | Blasphemy |
| Prophecy after the event | Gethsemane | Barabbas |
| Entry into Jerusalem | Arrest of Jesus | |

## QUESTIONS FOR REVIEW

1. What sets the passion narrative apart from the rest of the Gospels?
2. For what reasons did Jesus travel to Jerusalem?
3. What meaning do the Gospels give to Jesus' cleansing of the temple?
4. Why is Paul important for understanding Jesus' Last Supper?
5. How do rabbinic sources affect the study of Jesus' trial?
6. What role did the temple play in Jesus' trial?
7. What role did the Old Testament play in the passion narrative?

## SUGGESTIONS FOR FURTHER READING

Brown, R. *The Death of the Messiah.* 2 vols. Garden City: Doubleday, 1994.

Crossan, J. *The Cross That Spoke: The Origins of the Passion Narrative.* San Francisco: Harper & Row, 1988.

Matera, F. *Passion Narratives and Gospel Theologies.* New York: Paulist, 1986.

# 19

# Easter and After

## THE RESURRECTION OF JESUS

Did Jesus rise from the dead? This question isn't the one we should ask. His followers believed that he did, and Jesus' resurrection was the foundational message of early Christianity. Despite this being the case, whether or not Jesus actually rose from the dead is a question that cannot be studied historically nor can it be answered by historians. Why? Because the best sources (the Gospels and Paul) do not describe Jesus' resurrection,[1] and even if they did, historians would have to evaluate all the events in the light of probability. The resurrection of Jesus, being an extreme miracle—raising a dead man to everlasting life—defies probability, so historians must view it with skepticism. In this case, historians are restricted by their sources and methods, and they cannot with certainty establish or discredit the resurrection. (Historians argue in degrees of probability.) What, then, do the Gospels relate? They relate the appearances of Jesus after his resurrection (Matt. 28:1–20; Luke 24:1–53; John 20:1–31; 21:1–25).

According to the synoptic accounts, the followers of Jesus, who were Galileans, fled to Galilee when Jesus was crucified then moved to Jerusalem with their families and settled there. They probably moved because they expected God to intervene in history and do something in Jerusalem. They may have expected God to establish the Kingdom of God in Jerusalem, preceded by the judgment and resurrection. Remember that many Jews believed that the Creation began where Jerusalem was founded because they thought it was the center of the

[1] The second-century noncanonical gospel known as the *Gospel according to Peter* describes the resurrection of Jesus, but it appears to be imaginative and largely derivative. The overwhelming majority of scholars view it as having little historical value.

world. The rock that broke through in the Holy of Holies in the temple of Jerusalem was the first dry land that arose out of the waters of chaos when God created the world. The new creation would also take place in Jerusalem. In Jewish **apocalypticism,** the belief was that paradise would be established in Jerusalem, or that a heavenly Jerusalem would descend on earth where the old Jerusalem had been (Rev. 21–22).

The reason for the Galileans' belief that the end of the age was near must have been their belief that Jesus had been resurrected. The resurrection was a sign of the imminent end of the world. In 1 Thessalonians (the oldest document in the New Testament), Paul wrote that according to the "Lord" (Jesus), Christ would descend from heaven and all the dead would arise and ascend into the air to meet Christ, together with those who were alive (4:15–18). Here the resurrection of the dead was closely associated with the coming of a resurrected Christ.

**Easter** as the beginning of the new age is conspicuous in Matthew 27:50–54, where it is said that after Jesus' death, many strange events took place, the most strange being that many who were dead rose from their graves and wandered about in Jerusalem.

> Matt. 27:50–54: 50 Then Jesus cried again with a loud voice and breathed his last. 51 At that moment the curtain of the temple was torn in two, from top to bottom. The earth shook, and the rocks were split. 52 The tombs also were opened, and many bodies of the saints who had fallen asleep were raised. 53 After his resurrection they came out of the tombs and entered the holy city and appeared to many. 54 Now the centurion and those with him, who were keeping watch over Jesus, saw the earthquake and what took place, they were terrified, and said, "Truly this man was God's Son!"

At this point Matthew inserted the declaration of the centurion that Jesus "was God's Son." Clearly, Jesus' death and ensuing resurrection mark a decisive shift according to the Gospels. These events signaled the beginnings of the end of the age and the resurrection of the dead. Thus Easter was the start of something significant. Something had happened. What do the sources say?

## THE POST-RESURRECTION APPEARANCES

In 1 Corinthians 15:1–8 Paul gives the earliest testimony about Jesus' resurrection. His comments date to around 55 CE:

> 1 Cor. 15:1–8: 1 Now I would remind you, brothers and sisters, of the good news that I proclaimed to you, which you in turn received, in which also you stand, 2 through which also you are being saved, if you hold firmly to the message that I proclaimed to you—unless you have come to believe in vain 3 For I handed on to you as of first importance what I in turn had received, that Christ died for our sins in accordance with the scriptures, 4 and that he was buried, and he was raised on the third day in accordance with the scriptures, 5 and that he appeared to Cephas, then to the twelve. 6 Then he appeared to more than five hundred brothers and

sisters at one time, most of whom are still alive, though some have died. 7 Then he appeared to James, then to all the apostles. 8 Last of all, as to one untimely born, he appeared also to me.

This section is a formulation of the gospel of the first Christians. At this stage the word *gospel,* meaning "good news," was used of the proclamation on which Christians based their faith—Jesus' death and resurrection. Later it was used of the books that told about Jesus' works and words, as well as his death and resurrection. Paul said that this proclamation was something he had "received"—thus his claim that he did not preach something different from the apostles. He delivered it "as of first importance" to the Christian communities of his day. This proclamation was that (1) Jesus had died for our sins, (2) he was buried and rose, and (3) he appeared to his followers afterward.

Paul says that Jesus appeared first to Peter, then to the twelve (apostles), then to more than five hundred believers, then to James, the brother of Jesus, then to all the apostles, which must have been a larger circle than the twelve, and finally to Paul himself. As Paul stated, he had received this traditional material from those directly affected. Paul emphasized that most of the people who witnessed Jesus' appearances were still alive. Both Peter and James were alive when Paul wrote, but Paul did not say what actually took place regarding the manner of Jesus' appearances and where they occurred.

Luke 24:34 tells of an appearance to Peter: "The Lord has risen indeed, and he has appeared to Simon!" Two disciples who were returning from a journey made this announcement. On that journey they had met Jesus but did not recognize him at first. Nothing more was written about this meeting. Luke obviously did not know more about it. Luke went on to relate an appearance of Jesus to all the disciples in Jerusalem. This description was rather realistic because the disciples touched Jesus and ate with him (24:36–43).

John 20 contains a similar story, but here the evangelist did not know about an earlier appearance to Peter. However, John did know about an appearance to Mary. Both Luke and John say that Jesus' appearance to the disciples (according to Luke, there were two: one to Peter and one to all the disciples) took place in Jerusalem on Easter Sunday. John 21 also mentions an appearance in Galilee, but that chapter was added later.

According to Matthew 28, however, Jesus appeared to all the disciples in Galilee. Mark also presupposes this. The young man at the tomb (possibly an angel) said to the women: "But go, tell his disciples and Peter that he is going ahead of you to Galilee; there you will see him, just as he told you" (16:7). And in Mark 14:28, a prophecy of Jesus was that, after the resurrection, he would go before the disciples to Galilee. Mark's gospel ends with verse 8, which says that the women fled and said nothing. Verses 9–20 were added; they were lacking in the oldest manuscripts. Also, these verses do not fit as a continuation of Mark. In Mark's gospel Jesus was said to have appeared to Mary Magdalene on the same day as he arose, which is similar to John's gospel. He was also said to have appeared to two of his disciples. This version is similar to Luke's. Matthew did not describe an appearance to Peter, only one to all the disciples. Here the disciples were commissioned to teach in a manner similar to the one expressed by Matthew.

Mark 16:7, however, seems to necessitate appearances to Peter and all the apostles, as Paul stated.

It is impossible to harmonize the various sources chronologically. Matthew described one appearance of Jesus to Mary Magdalene and Mary when they were on their way to tell the disciples about the empty tomb (28:1–10) and one appearance of Jesus to his disciples (28:17). It is unlikely that some of the disciples would have doubted the resurrection when they saw Jesus after the crucifixion, even though Matthew said some doubted. Both Luke and John related that all the disciples became convinced of the resurrection when they met with Jesus. Moreover, in Luke 24:49, Jesus commanded his disciples to stay in Jerusalem. Thus according to Luke they had no business being in Galilee. John 21, which was a later addition to his gospel, told of an appearance in Galilee, but John's redactor probably added this material to bring John more into line with Mark and Matthew.

In addition to the impossibility of harmonizing the sources chronologically, there is a discrepancy in the nature of Jesus' appearance in the various sources. We noted that Luke and John conceived of Jesus' body in a realistic manner, although this body of flesh and blood could walk through closed doors. Paul and Matthew, however, conceived of Jesus' appearance differently. Paul probably thought that the appearances to Peter, the Twelve Apostles, and the others were like Jesus' appearance to himself on the road to Damascus (Acts 9).

> Acts 9:3–6: 3 Now as he was going along and approaching Damascus, suddenly a light from heaven flashed around him. 4 He fell to the ground and heard a voice saying to him, "Saul, Saul, why do you persecute me?" 5 He asked, "Who are you, Lord?" The reply came, "I am Jesus, whom you are persecuting. 6 But get up and enter the city, and you will be told what you are to do."

It is hard to say how much this section reflects Paul's own experience. Some references to a vision of Christ appear in Paul's own letters. These descriptions are of a mystical vision, which is nothing like what we find in Luke and John. The vision was something that only Paul saw. Acts 9 says that Paul's companions did not see the heavenly light but only heard a voice. When Paul spoke of the future body of believers, he emphasized that it was a "spiritual body" (1 Cor. 15:44).

Matthew, too, assumed an appearance from heaven because the risen Christ said he had been given all authority in heaven and on earth, which presupposed Jesus' being elevated to God's right hand. Jesus also sent his disciples out, saying that he would be with them until the end of the age. He made no distinction between his presence with his disciples now and the presence that the community would experience in the future.

Chronologically, we must regard Paul as the most trustworthy source for the reasons already stated. Paul did not say where the different appearances occurred. However, he did mention appearances to Peter, to the disciples, and to James. All were Galileans. There would have been no reason for James to go to Jerusalem if Jesus had not appeared to him.

Thus it seems that Jesus' appearances were first seen as appearances of the heavenly Christ in Galilee. What was the purpose of these appearances? According to

Luke and John, they were to convince the disciples that the resurrection had taken place. According to Paul and Matthew, they were to urge people to go out as missionaries. Again, Matthew is close to Paul, the oldest source. Thus the different locations of the appearances correspond to different functions.

We can conclude that the first appearances of the risen Jesus occurred in Galilee and were appearances from heaven—appearances of the heavenly Christ. The purpose of the appearances was to commission missionaries of the Christian movement. The promise that the disciples would see Jesus in Galilee, as found in Mark, was probably an attempt to combine the tradition of the empty tomb with that of the appearances in Galilee. The promises also served the purpose of excusing the disciples for having fled. According to Mark, the disciples were not present at the crucifixion, the burial, or the tomb. They had fled at Jesus' arrest. They must have gone to Galilee, for later they were found in Jerusalem with their families, whom they must have brought with them.

Conversely, we can see the tradition about the appearances in Jerusalem, as found in Luke and John, as an attempt to exonerate the disciples. At the same time, Luke at least used that tradition in his missionary program, which extended from Galilee through Judea to Jerusalem, then from Jerusalem through Judea and Samaria (half-heathen territory), and finally to the ends of the world. There was no time here for the disciples to move from Jerusalem to Galilee and then back to Jerusalem before their missionary activity started.

## THE EMPTY TOMB

The various versions of the story of the empty tomb differ considerably. Following the sequence of the Gospels in the New Testament, two women, or three women, or several women, or one woman discovered that Jesus' tomb was empty. The different Gospels speak about either one or two angels being present and giving some directions; they do not agree with one another.

We can start with Paul and work back to the Gospels when we study Jesus' appearances. Appearances to Peter, and especially to the Twelve Apostles, are central in both Paul's account and in the Gospels. But we cannot work this way with the empty tomb story. Paul does not mention it, nor does any other early Christian writing.

Scholars have often discussed Paul's silence on the matter of the empty tomb. Some say that the sequence of verbs Paul used—died, buried, and raised—implied an empty tomb. If someone had asked Paul if the tomb was empty, he would of course have said yes. But it is not at all certain that he would have heard stories like the ones told in the Gospels. He did not cite witnesses to the empty tomb. To Paul, the tomb would have been empty only because Jesus had been raised from the dead. Are we certain that Paul would have insisted that the tomb was empty?

Paul's silence about the empty tomb is corroborated by the fact that all the creedal statements—the confessionlike statements in Paul's letters—lack references to the empty tomb. The formula Paul quoted in the beginning of 1 Corinthians 15 is only one among several. Others appear in Romans 1:3–4, Philippians 2:9, and 1 Timothy 3:16. These texts all focus on the raising of Jesus by God, and they predate Paul. As for the creedal statement in 1 Corinthians 15:3–7, here Paul spoke for himself, which means that Christian belief in the resurrection of Jesus was not based on the story about the empty tomb.

Evidently we have two streams of tradition—one centering on the empty tomb and the other centering on the appearances of Jesus. Moreover, the first tradition was derived from Jerusalem whereas the second one had its origins in Galilee. When the appearance tradition transferred to Jerusalem, its function changed. It no longer served the purpose of commissioning disciples to teach but rather that of convincing people of the truth of the resurrection. What about the tradition of the empty tomb? Which purpose did that serve? Here we have nothing about commissioning disciples to spread Jesus' word. Some scholars have concluded that the tradition of the empty tomb was a late addition by Christian apologetics—an attempt to prove the resurrection of Jesus that was proclaimed by the Christians.

The explanation is not that simple. The empty tomb tradition is secondary, but possibly only in the sense that it did not impress itself on early creedal statements. It is found in all the synoptics and in John, so it passes the test of multiple attestation. It was clearly not derived from Mark alone; it must have been found in several sources because the names of the women differ. The reason that it is not found in the confessionlike formulas may be simply that the tradition went back to women. Among Jews and Gentiles, women were not considered trustworthy. According to Jewish legal practice, women could not serve as witnesses. Women fared no better in the gentile world. In the second century, Celsus, a philosopher who wrote against Christianity, mocked the belief in the resurrection of Jesus. "Who saw it?" he asked. He also provided the answer: "A hysterical woman." (According to the gospel, Mary did not see the resurrection, but that is not important in this connection. The point is Celsus's opinion of women, which is implied by his comments.)

The way men regarded women also shows that the primitive community could not have produced the empty tomb tradition to prove Jesus' resurrection because women could not prove anything. This fact is actually admitted in the Gospels. According to Mark, the women did not even bother to try to tell anyone about the empty tomb but ran away "for terror and amazement had seized them" (Mark 16:8). Matthew related that the women met Jesus while they were on their way to tell the disciples about the empty tomb. Jesus bid them to tell his disciples to go to Galilee, and the disciples did meet him there, but it was not stated explicitly that the disciples went there because the women told them what Jesus said. In Luke, the women told the disciples about the empty tomb, but the women were not believed. One of the disciples went to see whether the tomb was empty, but Luke emphasized that he did not see Jesus. Jesus himself must have appeared to his male disciples. In John, the beloved disciple and Peter had to go to see the empty tomb although Mary Magdalene had found the tomb first. Jesus later appeared to Mary and told her to inform the disciples, but no report of Mary doing so was recorded.

Thus, the tradition that survived is a somewhat fragile one about some women, or even about only one woman, who found an empty tomb. The part about the empty tomb cannot have been made up. The story could have been checked. The empty tomb was a Jerusalem tradition, and Jesus was buried in Jerusalem. There must have been an empty tomb. But must there have been a resurrection? Not necessarily. Celsus may have been right in a way. Mary may have been an hysterical woman, and she may have convinced Jesus' followers, who were returning from Galilee, that Jesus' tomb was empty. The women or Mary (if she was alone) may have gone to the wrong tomb. The Gospels say that the women were witnesses to Jesus' final moments from some distance.

It is also possible that the body had been removed before the women (or Mary) arrived at the tomb because Jesus died when the Sabbath drew near and could not be buried properly. John, who appeared to be well informed about the last events, said that Jesus was buried in a hurry in a tomb close by Golgotha. This hurried burial was actually implied by the synoptics, who all emphasized that the Sabbath was about to begin when Jesus was buried (Mark 15:42). The burial may have been provisional.

We should keep in mind that the belief in the resurrection of Jesus was not dependent on the tradition of the empty tomb. Neither Paul nor the synoptics said it was. (John 20:8 is different. The beloved disciple believed something when he saw the empty tomb, but what?) What was fundamental was the belief that Jesus met people, according to the oldest tradition, and called them to apostleship.

## JESUS AND THE WOMEN

The Gospels all relate that Jesus was followed around by a great number of women and that women were among the witnesses to the risen Christ. He must have appealed to women, which in itself is unique—no other Jewish teacher or prophet was followed by women, perhaps because of purity concerns. What function did they have? Luke 8:3 says that Jesus and the disciples were followed by many women, some of them coming from prominent families, "who provided for them out of their resources." Matthew says quite clearly that Jesus associated with "tax-collectors and prostitutes" (21:31–32). Mark and Luke add "sinners" to the list (Mark 2:16; Luke 5:30). Without doubt Jesus ate with "tax-collectors and sinners." These sinners probably included prostitutes. Matthew was probably right in this regard. Tax collectors often trafficked in prostitution so it makes sense that prostitutes would be among the sinners. Jesus' meals with tax collectors and sinners were criticized by his opponents, and he was labeled a "glutton and a drunkard" (Luke 7:34; Mark 2:15–16). This kind of description created a certain image of a meal well known in the literature of that time—an image of a banquet revelry with prostitutes. Women usually ate separately from men if they were not prostitutes. Jesus ate with women. If a man ate with women, the conclusion was inevitable; the women were prostitutes. Although Jesus' enemies attacked him for the company he kept, Jesus' behavior demonstrated his attitude toward people in general. He welcomed them all, regardless of their backgrounds, experiences, or gender.

## ACCORDING TO THE SCRIPTURES

In 1 Corinthians 15 Paul says that Jesus "died for our sins in accordance with the Scriptures" and was raised "on the third day, in accordance with the Scriptures." Which passages did Paul have in mind? Scholars usually refer to Isaiah 53, with its "suffering servant" imagery, and to Hosea 6:2: "After two days he will revive us; on the third day he will raise us up, that we may live before him." This statement refers to the people of Israel, and the condition for their being raised up is that they return to the Lord, God. Hosea 6:2 does not fit the case of Jesus, an individual who had not strayed. Then why do scholars refer to Hosea?

   The Gospel according to Matthew portrays Jesus as a type of righteous Israelite. In 2:15 Matthew applied Hosea 11:1 ("Out of Egypt I called my son") to Jesus when describing his return from Egypt as a child. Paul may thus have applied Hosea 6:2 to Jesus as a prophetic passage of Jesus' resurrection. However, in the ancient world there were stories about gods who died and were raised after just three days, and that may be why we find the number three in Hosea. Originally, this period of time was not meant literally. "Three days" was a mythological expression for a short time. Christianity was one of many religions in the Hellenistic age, and it had to compete with the others. To do that well, its proponents had to present the message in certain well-known forms. Thus, the death and resurrection of Jesus may have been modeled after a well-known mythical pattern.

## SUMMARY

The Gospels do not describe the resurrection of Jesus, but they do describe Jesus' post-resurrection appearances. In this regard, Paul's references to the post-resurrection appearances of Jesus are important because Paul was the earliest Christian author. Although we cannot harmonize the resurrection accounts, as a whole they uphold the tradition of an appearance of Jesus to Peter and to the disciples in Galilee. The accounts of the empty tomb associated with Mary Magdalene and other women who followed Jesus appear to be authentic, but in themselves they do not prove the resurrection. The belief in the resurrection rests on the story that Jesus personally met with his disciples after his crucifixion.

## KEY TERMS FOR REVIEW

| | | |
|---|---|---|
| Galilee | Easter | Paul |
| Jerusalem | Peter/Cephas | Empty tomb tradition |
| Apocalypticism | Mary Magdalene | |

# QUESTIONS FOR REVIEW

1. Why is the study of the resurrection of Jesus difficult for historians?
2. To whom did Jesus appear according to Paul? According to the Gospels?
3. How do Galilee and Jerusalem figure into the resurrection narratives?
4. What is the historical value of the empty tomb accounts?

# SUGGESTIONS FOR FURTHER READING

Davis, S., Kendall, D. and O'Collins, G. eds. *The Resurrection*. Oxford: Oxford University Press, 1997.

Fuller, R. *The Formation of the Resurrection Narratives.* New York: MacMillan, 1971.

Ludemann, G. *The Resurrection of Jesus.* Minneapolis: Fortress, 1994.

Perrin, N. *The Resurrection according to Matthew, Mark, and Luke.* Philadelphia: Fortress, 1977.

# PART VII

# Jesus and His Teachings

# 20

✳

# Jesus and the Kingdom of God

## THE MESSAGE OF JESUS

The synoptic Gospels teach that after Jesus was baptized by John and tempted in the wilderness, he began to preach about the Kingdom of God. Mark described Jesus as saying, "The time is fulfilled, and the **kingdom of God** has come near; repent, and believe in the good news" (Mark 1:15). Except for the words, "believe in the good news" (*good news* became a term that belonged to the later Christian mission), this passage seems to have been Jesus' fundamental message. In Matthew 4:17 Jesus said, "Repent, for the kingdom of heaven has come near!" Matthew's phrase does not mean that the kingdom is a heavenly place. (The word *heaven* was a substitute for *God,* which many Jews avoided.) In Matthew Jesus' message is exactly the same one ascribed to John the Baptist in Matthew 3:2, "Repent, for the kingdom of heaven has come near!" According to Matthew, John the Baptist and Jesus had basically the same message; both preached that the Kingdom of God was near and called on the people to repent.

It is not strange that Jesus and John should preach the same message. After all, Jesus had accepted John's ministry, serving as a disciple of John (as demonstrated by submitting to baptism by John), and according to the Gospels, Jesus never repudiated John or his message. Looking at the stories of Jesus' baptism and temptation form critically, we can see that the link between these two stories was artificial and can be accounted for by the redactional concerns of the evangelists. Jesus did not go into the desert immediately after his baptism and thus quickly and permanently separate himself from John. The Gospel according to John says that John the Baptist and Jesus were associates for a while and that when Jesus left he took with him some of John's disciples. This view seems to be historically correct because it is improbable that Jesus' followers would have made up an account like the one found in John. Jesus appears to have decided to travel about and to spread John's message in Galilee while John the Baptist himself apparently remained in Judea.[1]

That John remained in one place while Jesus traveled about was not the only difference between the two. Preaching about the kingdom and healing went hand-in-hand for Jesus. Both Matthew and Luke linked Jesus' preaching of the kingdom to his healing activity: "proclaiming the good news of the kingdom and curing every disease and every sickness among the people" (Matt. 4:23). When Jesus commissioned his disciples to spread his word, he said that they were to heal and proclaim the kingdom (Matt. 10:7–8; Luke 9:2). In this way (and there are other ways), Jesus was different from John the Baptist because there are no references to John healing people.

Preaching of the nearness of the Kingdom of God was central to Jesus. What does this phrase mean? A Jesus scholar once said, "Jesus preached the Kingdom of God, but the Church came." If we assume that the kingdom and the Church are different entities, then the claim that the Church was established instead of the kingdom is true. The Roman Catholic Church traditionally does not see any conflict here because Catholic theology understands the Church to be the kingdom. By entering the Catholic Church, people enter the Kingdom of God where they find divine love and forgiveness.

A popular Protestant view, which dates to the nineteenth century and was popularized by Albrecht Ritschl, interprets the kingdom as human society organized through actions inspired by love. This interpretation emphasizes human activity and the gradual building up of the kingdom by means of loving attitudes and behavior.

In 1892, Johannes Weiss, in his famous book *Jesus' Proclamation of the Kingdom of God,* vigorously repudiated these views by arguing that on the basis of Jesus' kingdom sayings, the kingdom was an eschatological reality to be initiated by God in the near future. He denied that it was subjective or internal but rather an event involving the judgment of the world and the glorification of Israel. Human beings could do nothing to bring about its realization. Neither a Christian community nor a Christian society could pass as the kingdom. Weiss' interpretation saw Jesus as an apocalypticist, announcing the kingdom's imminent appearance through God's intervention. The kingdom had to be prepared for (people must repent) because it would soon be dramatically established on earth (see Figure 20.1).

Creation                              Jesus          Kingdom ──────────────────────────→
                        History

**FIGURE 20.1**

---

[1]According to the synoptics and Josephus, John the Baptist was arrested and put to death on Herod Antipas's order, so John the Baptist must have eventually left Judea and traveled to Galilee where Herod Antipas ruled.

A question that remains for this futuristic view is whether the kingdom will be a kind of earthly political state in which the messiah rules or a completely otherworldly kind of existence ruled directly by God. During the era of the second temple Jews bore witness to several views. One view was based on the prophetic books of the Bible like Isaiah and was found in works such as the *Psalms of Solomon* that date from the first century BCE. A second view was found in apocalyptic works that date from the second century BCE. Texts of this type often dealt with the events leading up to and including the end of the age (the time of God's judgment), the *eschatos* (Greek: last). In Greek, the Revelation of John, the last book of the New Testament, is called the *apocalupsis* (unveiling). A vision of the future state of affairs, called a "new heaven and a new earth" (21.1), is unveiled there. John says that the whole cosmos would be recreated and ruled by God. However, it was possible to have it both ways because Revelation prophesies both a millennial kingdom ruled by saints and a new age ruled by God.

In 1935 the British scholar Charles Harold Dodd introduced still another view of the kingdom that was something of a reaction to the futuristic interpretation. He said that although Jewish writings from the time of Jesus envisaged the kingdom as a future reality, Jesus himself moved the end-of-time from the future to the present, from expectation to realized experience (see Figure 20.2).

Creation                                Jesus & Kingdom ⟶
                    History

**FIGURE 20.2**

What Dodd meant is not that the kingdom is a blissful state of mind, which has been and still is a popular view. He meant that Jesus' words and works themselves realized the kingdom. What many Jews had hoped for in the kingdom was being actualized whenever Jesus forgave a sin or healed a sick person. Jesus' kingdom sayings, which others read as eschatological and apocalyptic in nature, were interpreted by Dodd as metaphors that described a present kingdom. Dodd then argued that several sayings taught about a present kingdom.

Dodd's argument for what became known as realized eschatology (in contrast to consistent or thoroughgoing eschatology) caused several scholars to propose a mediating position that interpreted the kingdom as both present *and* future. In 1945 Werner Kümmel was one of the first scholars to offer a synthesis of the two views when he argued that God was already establishing his rule in Jesus' actions and preaching, but that God's rule would be fully manifested only in the future.

At the close of the twentieth century, several prominent scholars proposed other noneschatological interpretations of the kingdom, many similar to Dodd's. John Dominic Crossan, in his work *The Historical Jesus, The Life of a Mediterranean Jewish Peasant* (1991), argued for one such view. He presented an interpretation of the kingdom that shared Dodd's view of a realized kingdom, but he added the view that Jesus was a cyniclike social reformer who sought to institute an egalitarian kingdom among his followers. Crossan argued that the futuristic kingdom passages in the synoptics reflected the hand of Jesus' followers, whereas earlier, noncanonical texts supported a realized kingdom.

## THE FUTURE KINGDOM

One of the petitions in the Lord's Prayer, which was preserved in two independent sources (Q [Matt. 6:9–13; Luke 11:1–4]; *Didache* 8:2) reads, "Your Kingdom come" (Matt. 6:10; Luke 11:2; *Didache* 8:2). This petition is strongly reminiscent of a Jewish prayer, the Kaddish, that dates to the synagogues of ancient Israel: "May He establish His Kingdom in your lifetime and in your days and in the lifetime of all the house of Israel, even speedily and at a near time." This prayer clearly expresses the Jewish anticipation of the kingdom. Jews prayed for it in Jesus' time and, as a Jew, Jesus would have been familiar with this hope. According to the Gospels, the enthusiastic reception that John the Baptist's preaching about the kingdom received fit with the kingdom teaching of the Kaddish. The *Psalms of Solomon,* a Palestinian Jewish text written shortly after the Roman takeover (63 BCE), describes a future kingdom to be established by a son of David (17:21–34).

According to Mark, Jesus taught that the kingdom would soon come dramatically in an apocalyptic sense: "Truly I tell you, there are some standing here who will not taste death until they see that the Kingdom of God has come with power" (Mark 9:1). Luke reproduced Mark 9:1 but left out the last few words: "But truly I tell you, there are some who are standing here who will not taste death until they see the Kingdom of God" (Luke 9:27). Luke's deletion of "with power" mutes the apocalyptic aspect of Mark while preserving its eschatological interest. Matthew did the same (16:28), and this modification of the Jesus tradition appears to be a tendency of later gospel texts.[2] For many scholars these sayings pass the criterion of dissimilarity because the Church would not have created predictions that appear to have been falsified; Jesus did not return during his disciples' lifetime. (Some scholars say that these verses also pass a criterion of "embarrassment" in that the Church would have to explain the kingdom's failure to appear.)

According to Jesus, the "Son of Man" (compare with Dan. 7:13–14) was an eschatological figure closely associated with the establishment of the kingdom. As a group, the Gospels refer to the Messiah, the returning Elijah, and the Moses-like prophet. The Son of Man is another Jewish eschatological figure referred to by Jesus. In his speech commissioning his apostles in Matthew, Jesus said, " . . . you will not have gone through all the towns of Israel before the Son of Man comes" (Matt. 10:23). Many synoptic Jesus sayings refer to the coming of the Son of Man in an apocalyptic sense (Mark [Mark 8:38–9:1; 13:24–27; 14:62]; Q [Matt. 24:27, 37–39; Luke 17:24, 26–27]; p-Matthew [Matt. 13:40–43]; p-Luke [Luke 21:34–36]). Whereas the kingdom is not always mentioned in these Son of Man sayings, they

---

[2]It appears that the delay of Jesus' return led to appropriate changes in the Jesus tradition as it was preserved in later Gospels. Luke and Matthew tone down but do not remove the apocalyptic element whereas John's gospel goes even further and places kingdom events, like the judgment and bestowal of eternal life, in the present (John 3:3, 5; 5:24–29). What some scholars have called the "de-apocalypticizing" of the Jesus tradition is consistently carried out in the second-century text, *The Gospel according to Thomas.* Here eschatological-apocalyptic thinking is attacked (*logion* 3) in favor of a "realized" kingdom (*logion* 113).

are undoubtedly related to the kingdom sayings. For instance, the kingdom saying in Mark 9:1 follows a saying about the coming of the Son of Man. Matthew even modified Mark 9:1 and connected the Son of Man with the kingdom, "Truly, I tell you, there are some standing here who will not taste death before they see the Son of Man coming in his kingdom" (16:28).

If there are some Jesus sayings in which the kingdom is part of a sphere of realized experience, as argued by Dodd, applying the criterion of dissimilarity leads to the conclusion that the sayings about the kingdom as a future state were the creations of the Church. The Jesus Seminar, a group of scholars who weighed the authenticity of Jesus' sayings in the Gospels, reached the conclusion that these sayings were the creation of the Church. It appears that the early Church, as a whole, believed in the imminence of a future kingdom. The earliest Christian writer, Paul, comforted persecuted believers by teaching them that they were suffering for the kingdom that would soon appear with the return of Jesus (1 Thess. 1:5–10; 4:15–17). It is also possible that the saying in Matthew 10:23 was a production of the Church because the context provided a glimpse into a period when the Christians were in conflict with the authorities. The preceding verses in Matthew speak of the disciples being flogged in the synagogues and brought before governors, which was not what happened to those whom Jesus sent out during his ministry and probably reflected a later period.

Would the early Church have so completely misunderstood Jesus? After all, some of its members were close to Jesus historically and must have been familiar with *some* Jesus traditions. Did they deliberately change Jesus' teachings about the kingdom as the Jesus Seminar argued?

One dilemma for scholars who reject a futuristic interpretation of Jesus' kingdom involves Jesus' historical/religious context and his association with John the Baptist. Did Jesus, who was reared in an eschatological setting and accepted the future kingdom as preached by John the Baptist, eventually break with John's view of the kingdom? Did he then, after dying, become the focal point of an early community of followers who hoped for a future kingdom and ascribed to him a view of the kingdom that he himself had rejected? This kind of scenario is, of course, possible, but not probable in light of the synoptics.[3]

Although there is a sense in which the kingdom is a present reality, this does not necessarily conflict with the expectation of the future coming of the kingdom. The parables of the kingdom, which use the image of growth and development when describing the kingdom, may offer a means of reconciling both views. The parable of the mustard seed, which is attested to in three sources, teaches that the mustard seed begins as the smallest of all seeds but develops into

---

[3] Some scholars have argued that Jesus repudiated John's apocalyptic preaching on the basis of a Q passage (Matt. 11:11; Luke 7:28): "Truly I say to you, among those born of women, there has arisen no one greater than John the Baptist; yet he who is least in the kingdom of heaven is greater than he." As we pointed out in Chapter 16, these two clauses do not agree. The first clause that praises John passes the test of dissimilarity, whereas the second one that devalues John does not. Devaluing John's significance was characteristic of Matthew and Luke's Gospels as they portray the baptism of Jesus. An alternate reading of the second clause, other than reading it as a repudiation of John, sees it as using hyperbole to describe the value of entering into the kingdom. The lowliest person in the kingdom is superior to the greatest prophet.

a huge shrub (Mark 4:30–32; Q [Matt. 13:31–32; Luke 13:18–19]; *Gospel accord-ing to Thomas logion* 20). What is the point of comparing this difference between the seed and the shrub to the kingdom? Until the seed becomes a huge shrub, something remains to be realized. Something is still in the future. Thus, even if some of the sayings about the future kingdom may have been derived from the Church, they were fabricated on the authority of Jesus.

According to the Gospels, Jesus never stated when the kingdom would arrive. He gave none of the calculations that are commonly found in apocalyptic texts and claimed to have no knowledge of the exact time of the end of the age (Mark 13:32). Luke 17:20–21 is one of several texts in the Gospels that addresses the kingdom's arrival and is often used to defend a noneschatological view of the kingdom.

> Luke 17:20–21: 20 Once Jesus was asked by the Pharisees when the kingdom of God was coming, and he answered, "The kingdom of God is not coming with things that can be observed; 21 nor will they say, 'Look, here it is!' or 'There it is!' For, in fact, the kingdom of God is among you."

The words of verse 21b have been taken to mean that the kingdom is present or will suddenly and openly appear. Scholars arguing for the former interpretation say that Jesus was either telling the Pharisees that the kingdom was *present* to the degree that they could see it at work and even receive it, or that the kingdom was *established,* but in a fashion that they did not recognize or expect. The first option, supported by most scholars, is often compared with Luke 11:20 where Jesus taught that his exorcisms demonstrated how the kingdom had come near to people, per-haps in the sense that its power was active. The *Gospel according to Thomas* has a Jesus saying, similar to Luke 17:20–21, that supports the second option:

> *Logion* 113: His disciples said to Him, "When will the Kingdom come?" [Jesus said,] "It will not come by waiting for it. It will not be a matter of saying 'Here it is' or 'There it is.' Rather, the Kingdom of the Father is spread out upon the earth, and men do not see it."

Here the kingdom is portrayed as seemingly established ("spread out upon the earth"), but humans were oblivious to it—a view in keeping with the realized eschatology of the *Gospel according to Thomas* and its tendency to diminish the eschatological orientation of Jesus' kingdom sayings.

The latter interpretation of Luke 17:20–21 contends that because 17:20–21a rebuts the idea that the kingdom comes with anticipatory signs or needs some-one to locate it for others, 17:21b may mean that the kingdom's arrival will be sudden (without signs) and obvious to all (without any need of declaration): "for in fact, the kingdom of God is among you." The immediate context of verses 22–24 about the coming of the Son of Man supports this interpretation.

> Luke 17:22–24: 22 Then he said to the disciples, "The days are coming when you will long to see one of the days of the Son of Man, and you will not see it. 23 They will say to you, 'Look there!' or 'Look here!' Do not go, do not set off in pursuit. 24 For as the lightning flashes and lights up the sky from one side to the other, so will the Son of Man be in his day.

The Son of Man will appear suddenly and publicly; thus the kingdom will also have to appear suddenly and publicly. Jesus was saying that his disciples must not listen to those who claim to have found the Son of Man. No one needs to search for him (and the kingdom), for when the Son of Man (and the kingdom) appears it will be as dramatic and evident as lightning that flashes across the sky.

The words *among you* in verse 21 can also be translated *within you*. The word translated *within* (Greek: *entos*) is an adverb of place and has both meanings. Some people choose the latter sense and thus are able to support the old popular opinion that the kingdom is an inward reality. Two observations demonstrate why this interpretation is incorrect. First, note that Jesus spoke to his opponents, the Pharisees. He could not mean that they have the kingdom within them. It would be very awkward for Luke to have added this reference. Second, no other text in the Gospels can be taken to mean that the kingdom is in the hearts of individuals. In fact, to argue that this meaning occurs in Luke 17:20–21 is to ignore important evidence that cannot be made to conform to such an interpretation. In all likelihood the Greek word means "in the midst of you" rather than "within you."

## THE PRESENT KINGDOM

Some evidence exists that Jesus thought that the Kingdom of God was already present (although not as an inner reality). If we regard the Son of Man saying in Luke 17:22–24 as originally independent, we can take verses 20 and 21 to mean that the kingdom was already "in the midst" of Jesus' contemporaries—active and within their reach. This view seems to have been the original element in Jesus' preaching about the kingdom in contrast to John the Baptist's preaching; the future kingdom is also present. One Q text touches on the idea of a kingdom that is present and future:

> Matt. 11:12–13: 12 From the days of John the Baptist until now the kingdom of heaven has suffered violence, and the violent take it by force. 13 For all the prophets and the law prophesied until John came;

> Luke 16:16: 16 "The law and the prophets were in effect until John came; since then the good news of the kingdom of God is proclaimed, and everyone tries to enter it by force.

Both versions of Q raise the question of the relationship between Jesus and John the Baptist. Luke's version seems to separate the two. John the Baptist belonged to the old order, Jesus to the new. Matthew appears to be more original. As for the rest of the saying, Luke is more straightforward. "Everyone tries to enter it by force" must refer to the enthusiastic response to the preaching of the imminence of the kingdom. Perhaps it should be translated, "Everyone is pressed to enter the kingdom." Thus, the saying refers to Jesus' urgent invitation. Matthew's version is very difficult. We can translate the Greek in different ways. Matthew's meaning may be the same as Luke's: The kingdom has been forcing its way forward, and tax collectors and sinners storm the kingdom. However, it may also mean that the kingdom has been opposed with violence. Both interpretations of the Q saying link Jesus and John the Baptist closely. In addition, both interpretations imply that the kingdom is in some sense already present in the proclamation of Jesus. How can the view of the kingdom as a present reality be related to that of the kingdom as a future reality?

Why did Jesus refuse to say when the kingdom would dawn? If he had done so, perhaps he would have given people a chance to remain outsiders, even indifferent for a while. He did not give them this chance. He could not because the kingdom was already here in a strange way. In an important Q story, Jesus answered the Baptist's question, "Are you the one who is to come, or are we to wait for another?" (Matt. 11:3; Luke 7:19). Jesus did not answer directly, which seemed to be a habit of his. (Jesus' use of the parable of the good Samaritan illustrates this point.) Jesus told John's disciples, who communicated John's question to him, to tell their master what they witnessed: The blind saw, the lame walked, the lepers were cleansed, the deaf heard, and dead people were raised. Jesus did all these deeds. The fact that Jesus did them does not necessarily mean that Jesus was the Messiah because the Messiah was not typically expected to be a miracle worker, but these miracles would happen in the Messiah's time. The answer to John's question ("Are you the one who is to come . . . ?") alludes to several passages in Isaiah that describe the age of salvation (Isa. 35:5–6). How can a future reality be present? The clue to understanding this seeming contradiction is found at the very end of Jesus' answer to the Baptist: "And blessed is anyone who takes no offense at me" (Matt. 11:6). In Jesus' work, the kingdom was present, and this presence was the new element in Jesus' teaching about the kingdom.

Several other texts say, or at least imply, the same thing. In a Q passage (Matt. 12:28; Luke 11:20) Jesus said, "But if it is by the Spirit ["finger" in Luke] of God that I cast out demons, then the kingdom of God has come to you." An intimate connection existed between Jesus' preaching of the kingdom and his healing. This connection is evidence that the kingdom is a future affair because, if not, Jesus' healings would be only inconsequential drops in an ocean of suffering. Something more is to come because the kingdom is still not realized.

On the other hand, Jesus did say that the kingdom "has come to you." The verb *has come* is strange. It means "come before the time" but is usually used in the sense of "come near to." Thus, in Jesus' healings and exorcisms, we get a foretaste of the kingdom. Whenever and wherever Jesus healed someone, then and there the kingdom was active and present. When the disciples returned after having been sent out to preach about the kingdom and drive out demons, Jesus exclaimed: "I watched Satan fall from heaven like a flash of lightning!" (Luke 10:18)

We can now see the parable of the mustard seed in a new light, or more correctly, we can cast additional light on it. Clearly, the kingdom is a future reality, which is what was expressed by the time aspect: at the beginning, a seed; at the end, a huge shrub. But consider also the contrast between the seed and the shrub: something small and something big. Applied to the work of Jesus, this meant that what was present in Jesus' work would be completely realized in the establishment of the kingdom. We find a contrast and a connection between the present work of Jesus and the future establishment of the kingdom.

It is easier to understand that the kingdom was a present reality, as well as a future reality, when we consider that *kingdom* is not a good translation of the

Hebrew term that lies behind the Greek word *basileia*. The Hebrew term, *malkuth,* is dynamic; it denotes God's kingly rule and reign. *Kingdom* has an association with a spatial locality, a realm, whereas in the Jewish Bible *malkuth* denotes the rule that God exercised among his people. Thus, the Kingdom of God was God's kingly rule, the place and time where God's power will hold sway. Yet, according to Q and p–Matthew, Jesus taught that God's kingly rule would be centered on earth, presumably in Israel (Q [Matt. 19:28; Luke 22:30]; Matt. 5:5), and would be an era when the lowly and oppressed would be rescued (Q [Matt. 5:3, 6; Luke 6:20–21] and the *Gospel according to Thomas logia* 54, 68–69). Jesus' miracles bear out this restorationist aspect of Jesus' kingdom message.

At the same time, this kingdom would be a universal kingdom in the end, and some sayings describe a cosmic judgment by the Son of Man who would come as a judge to determine who could enter the kingdom and who would be punished (Mark 8:38; p-Matt. 25:31–46). In this connection, Jesus implied that many Gentiles would come and sit at table with the patriarchs and the prophets in the kingdom (Q [Matt. 8:11; Luke 13:28–29]). The kingdom was therefore not a right solely for Israelites, and some sayings speak of the effort needed to enter into this blessed realm: ". . . it is better for you to enter the kingdom of God with one eye than to have two eyes and to be thrown into hell" (Mark 9:47; Matt. 18.9; p-Matt. 5:29). The effort needed to enter the kingdom was heightened by the imminence that Jesus attached to it—the kingdom was near and would catch many by surprise when it arrived (Q [Matt. 24:43–44; Luke 12:39–40]; p-Matt. 25:13).

The synoptics go on to say that Jesus shocked sectarian Jews by reaching out to "sinners" and offering them the kingdom (Mark 2:17; p-Matt. 21:31–32), while at the same time questioning the repentance of righteous Jews (p-Matt. 21:28–32; p-Luke 18:9–14). The repentance that Jesus demanded in preparation for the kingdom (Mark 1:15; p-Matt. 4:17) called on people to love God and their neighbors, as was taught originally in Israel's law (Mark 12:28–34; Matt. 22:34–40; Luke 10:25–28; p-Matt. 25:31–46). This interpretation of the law appears to be the reason Jesus insisted that his followers serve others and love unconditionally (Mark 9:35; Q [Matt. 5:43–48; Luke 6:27–36]).

## SUMMARY

Jesus, along with many other first-century Jews, shared the hope of a future kingdom, but Jesus offered a distinct view. One of the rabbis said, "If all Israel made penance for only one day, God would establish his Kingdom." The Zealots took up arms to usher in God's kingdom. The Essenes waited for God to make the first move and to intervene with his heavenly army. They believed that this event was close, and they prepared themselves for God's intervention by keeping the law scrupulously. Like John the Baptist, they wanted Israel to be cleansed and ready for the kingdom's appearance. Jesus' perspective, however, was different. He, like the rabbis, spoke of repentance, but he did not say that repentance, or keeping the law, was *required* for the kingdom to be established. He said the Kingdom of God was at hand; therefore you must repent. Jesus also seems to have gone beyond John the Baptist and the Essenes by linking the presence of the kingdom to his own person. With Jesus, the kingdom drew near in the form of his healings and exorcisms, and it was already there in a way. Moreover, it was there for those who did not deserve it, not for those who obeyed the law, but for those who repented. However, as Jesus emphasized, the kingdom's fullness would be achieved only when the Son of Man appeared.

## KEY TERMS FOR REVIEW

| | | |
|---|---|---|
| Kingdom of God | Johannes Weiss | Realized eschatology |
| John the Baptist | Charles Harold Dodd | Son of Man |
| Healings and exorcisms | Werner Kümmel | Jesus Seminar |
| Albrecht Ritschl | Consistent eschatology | *Basileia/Malkuth* |

## QUESTIONS FOR REVIEW

1. How do Jesus' kingdom messages compare and contrast with John the Baptist's?
2. What support is there for a futuristic interpretation of the Kingdom of God as preached by Jesus?
3. How does the parable of the mustard seed relate to Jesus' view of the kingdom?

## SUGGESTIONS FOR FURTHER READING

Allison, D. *Jesus of Nazareth: Millenarian Prophet*. Minneapolis: Fortress, 1998.

Borg, M. "A Temperate Case for a Non-Eschatological Jesus" and "Jesus and Eschatology: Current Reflections," in M. Borg, *Jesus in Contemporary Scholarship*. Valley Forge: Trinity Press International, 1994, pp. 47–68, 69–96.

Ehrman, B. *Jesus: Apocalyptic Prophet of the New Millennium*. New York: Oxford University Press, 1999.

Funk, R. ed. *The Apocalyptic Jesus: A Debate*. Sonoma: Polebridge Press, 2002.

Willis, W. ed. *The Kingdom of God in 20th-Century Interpretation*. Peabody: Hendrickson, 1987.

# 21

✤

# Jesus and the Parables

## JESUS AND PARABLES

Jesus' did much of his teaching about the Kingdom of God in the form of parables. They were undoubtedly the most important part of the dominical sayings according to a form-critical analysis of the sayings material in the Gospels. Many of Jesus' parables contain the words, "The kingdom of God is like . . . ." Matthew 13:31 begins with "The kingdom of heaven is like a mustard seed. . . ." This statement does not mean that the kingdom is being compared with a mustard seed. In other parables the kingdom is not being compared with a merchant, a fishing net, the owner of a vineyard, and so on. A more helpful translation would read, "The matter of the Kingdom of God is like that of . . . ." Thus, the kingdom is compared with the entire process or story described in the parable, not with a particular thing or person.

Parables are associated with Jesus in several early and independent sources (Mark, Q, p-Matthew, p-Luke) and in a later source (the *Gospel according to Thomas*), so scholars assume that Jesus spoke in parables and that he spoke about the kingdom in parables. Besides being well known as tools for instruction by Jewish rabbis—and Jesus was called a rabbi—parables are so characteristic of Jesus' teaching that it would have been difficult, if not impossible, for the Church to have created this feature. If Jesus did not use parables, why would the Church impute this way of teaching to him? If this argument is not convincing, we can appeal to the criterion of dissimilarity. The parables do not contain any explicit information about Jesus as a person. In addition, very few parables address problems in the early Church. The first Christians, however, were very concerned about Christology and Ecclesiology.

We can thus understand the parables best as coming from the period of Jesus' own life. The material in the parables comes from the rural milieu of Palestine and has an authentic ring: peasants, servants, the baking housewife, house construction, fishing, and children playing. Thus, the parables also pass the test of the criterion of Palestinian coloring. One danger with this criterion is that a saying or story may have developed at an early stage among Galilean Christians, but this cannot be true for all the parables. Applying these criteria will help us to determine when a parable is not authentic. Some parables were created by the Church, or at least adapted by the Church.

Students of the parables should also be aware of another problem. All the parables about the kingdom may not have originally been about the kingdom. That is, the Church may have been responsible for the introductory phrase, "The matter of the kingdom of God is like that of . . . ." We can think of other applications for some of the kingdom parables, like that of the seed growing secretly or that of the leaven. It is also possible that some parables were handed down without their original applications and the Church supplied them.

## ALLEGORY

What is a parable? First we should determine what a parable is not. It is not simply an allegory, although parables have traditionally been treated like allegories, starting with the text of the New Testament. What is an allegory? An allegory is a story in which each and every element is a cryptogram—that is, a message whose meaning is hidden and has to be decoded by its hearers. A famous example of this approach to the parables can be found in the church father Augustine, who died in 430. His interpretation of the parable of the good Samaritan in Luke 10 treated it like an allegory. The parable begins: "A man was going down from Jerusalem to Jericho. . . ." Augustine said that the man was Adam who, as the primal man, incorporated humankind. *Jerusalem* represented the heavenly Jerusalem, which was identical with paradise. *Jericho* stood for mortal existence. Note that the parable says that the man "went down." According to Augustine, these words indicated the fall of Adam. The parable says he "fell into the hands of robbers. . . ." Augustine said that the "robbers" were Satan and his angels who robbed the man of his immortality. Who was the good Samaritan? It was Jesus. The inn where he placed the poor man was the Church. And the innkeeper was none other than Paul, who was a great theologian in Augustine's opinion.

From this example we can see that an allegory is a string of metaphors. What is a metaphor? It is a truncated, abbreviated comparison. Parables and allegories have the same root, a simple comparison. The Hebrew word *mashal,* which lies behind the Greek word for parable, *parabole,* means comparison, and it does not refer to any particular type of comparison. Matthew 10:16 is an example of a comparison that counts as a parable: "See, I am sending you out like sheep into the midst of wolves; so be wise as serpents and innocent as doves." The disciples to whom Jesus spoke are figuratively compared to serpents and doves by the use of a simile (a comparison using *like* or *as*).

An allegory is developed by way of a metaphor. When a comparison is truncated, a metaphor results. Matthew 7:13–14 is another parable and can serve as an example of a metaphor: "Enter through the narrow gate; for the gate is wide and the road is easy that leads to destruction, and there are many who take it. For the gate is narrow and the road is hard that leads to life, and there are few who find it." Here the second link of the comparison is missing. To what are the narrow gate and the wide gate compared? In a simple comparison like Matthew 10:16, this link is present; the disciples are compared to doves and snakes. In this metaphor, the listener has to supply the link. The narrow gate is the Christian way of life; the wide gate is the non-Christian way of life. This link is made more or less clear by the context, but still it is not made explicit. In some cases there is no clue at all in the context.

Who would come up with Augustine's interpretation of the good Samaritan without having been given some clue? And who would hit on the allegorical interpretation of the parable of the sower in Mark 4:1–9 if the text of that chapter did not provide an interpretation in Mark 4:13–20? Here the sower was Jesus, or, perhaps, any preacher of the word; the seed was the word of God; the soil was the world of human beings; the birds that picked up some of the seeds were Satan (and presumably his angels). The formula for the allegory is $a = A, b = B$. When the text says one thing, it means this other thing. As we have said, the hearers have to supply the second link for allegories.

An allegory is therefore more difficult to interpret than a metaphor. When we string metaphors together, making a story, it is difficult to give clues to the interpretation of the various elements without distorting the story as such. The aim of the allegory is often to conceal the true meaning of the story, and as a result we have to decode (or decipher) the story for the intended audience. Outsiders are not meant to understand it; that is why a metaphor is not always an allegory, where we often find a clue in the text itself.

In wartime, messages from ally to ally often take the form of allegories. The messages are sent in code; the recipients possess the code so they can decipher the messages; enemies try to obtain access to the code. The Revelation of John, one of the most allegorical books of the New Testament, was written during a period when the Christians were more or less at war with the state. There was no war in a literal sense, but some Christians were being persecuted. The contents of the book refer to that persecution and were written in an allegorical language. Thus, the persecutor of the Christians was said to have a name that was also the number 666 (13:18). The code in this case was based on the ancient idea that letters also had numerical values, and 666 was the numerical value of the separate letters of the name "Emperor Nero" in Aramaic. Thus, $a = A$: $a =$ the number of (the name of) the beast; $A =$ "Emperor Nero."

Why, then, do we find allegorical interpretations of Jesus' parables in the Gospels? There are several reasons. First, some of Jesus' parables probably relied on characters or elements that encouraged the early Christian community to make allegories of some of the parables. Cues, like the words *father* or *king,* might have given ancient listeners all the reasons they needed to allegorize a parable. Second, allegory was a common method of interpretation, being popular among both

Jews and Greeks during Jesus' day. Philo, a first-century CE Alexandrian Jew, treated much of the Jewish Bible as an allegory. Finally, an allegory can help make obscure or dated accounts relevant for Christian communities. Jesus' parables could be clarified by means of an allegorical interpretation or made to speak to pressing Christian concerns.

An allegorical explanation of the parable of the sower appears in Mark 4. How can people say that this parable is not derived from Jesus when the text asserts just the opposite? There are four good reasons. But first we must consider the context. After the narration of the parable, we find the following story in Mark 4:10–12:

> Mark 4:10–12: 10 When he was alone, those who were around him along with the twelve asked him about the parables. 11 And he said to them, "To you has been given the secret of the kingdom of God, but for those outside, everything comes in parables; 12 in order that 'they may indeed look but not perceive, and may indeed listen, but not understand; so that they may not turn again and be forgiven.'"

Then follows the allegorical exposition: "And he said to them, 'Do you not understand this parable? Then how will you understand all the parables?'" (v. 13). Then, in verse 14, we have: "The sower sows the word." The allegorical interpretation follows after that.

The four good reasons for questioning the authenticity of the allegorical interpretation follow.

1. Verses 11 and 12 are strikingly different in language and style from the Jesus sayings elsewhere in the Gospels. In these two verses, we have several words that are not used in the rest of the Gospels. These words are characteristic of the vocabulary of Paul. The word *secret* (Greek: *musterion*) appears nowhere else in the synoptics (Mark 4:11; Matt. 13:11; Luke 8:10), but it appears frequently in Paul. These verses are not a part of the primitive Jesus tradition but come from later teachings produced by Jesus' followers.

2. In the allegorization we find terms that point to a later age, as in verse 14: "The sower sows the word." The term *the word* is a technical one used in the Church's proclamation language.

3. The allegorizing interpretation is confused, even forced. The interpretation says that the seed is the word, and the field is the world of people hearing the message. But then the seed, when it sprouts up suddenly, is interpreted as being various classes of men. Thus, the seed is both the word being sown and the resulting crop, the people who hear the word.

4. The allegorical explanation of the purpose of the parable is given to answer a question that arose after Jesus' death. Verses 10 through 12 say that parables were told to prevent those who were not chosen for salvation from understanding the teaching of Jesus. What was the motive for this? The Church had to explain why Jesus was not received by his community, the Jews, God's own people. The answer given was that they were blinded by divine providence. Some mysterious purpose of God was fulfilled through their rejection of Jesus. This answer was given at the time when Jesus' followers tried to convince other Jews that Jesus was the Messiah.

# PARABLE

What, then, are Jesus' parables if they are not allegories? As we pointed out, the root is the same for both parables and allegories. A comparison is always involved. A comparison can be expressed in a similitude as well as in a figure of speech like a metaphor. What is a similitude? Matthew 5:14 is an example of a similitude: "You are the light of the world. A city built on a hill cannot be hid." Thus, just as a town on top of a hill could not be hidden, so the disciples had to be shining examples for all people. A similitude is an extended comparison, not a simple one such as you must be "like snakes and doves"—a simile. A similitude is a comparison consisting of two parts. The disciples are compared to light in the way that a city on a hill is visible. Thus, the visibility of the city on the top of the hill is compared to the shining example of the disciples.

Comparisons can also take the form of stories. Such parables are plot-driven and often have an element of surprise even though they may be very short: "Once more Jesus spoke to them in parables, saying: 'The kingdom of heaven may be compared to a king who gave a wedding banquet for his son . . .' " (Matt. 22:1–14). This story has a plot that revolves around a king's efforts to invite guests to his son's wedding. It concludes with a surprise—his willingness to invite strangers, both good and bad, and then to condemn those who were not dressed properly. In length and complexity it is different from a similitude, but it still involves a comparison. Matthew Black and James Drury pointed out in their study, *The Parables and Allegory* (1960), that story parables may have allegorical features. In Matthew 22 some characters served as standard symbols in the Hebrew Bible and thus may have served as encoded figures in the minds of Jesus' listeners, such as the words *king* or *father* served as symbols for Israel's God. Such allegorical features probably encouraged early Christians to allegorize some of Jesus' parables.

Several scholars have singled out comparisons that function as example or illustration stories. In these parables, a nonallegorical story is used to illustrate a point or to give an answer, as in the parable of the good Samaritan where Jesus answered the Jewish lawyer's question: "who is my neighbor?" Luke's parable answered the question by depicting the Samaritan as the neighbor (10:30–37). Such parables are not to be treated like allegories but rather like concrete examples of Jesus' teachings (see also Luke 12:13–21).

The most important principle in interpreting parables is the point of comparison intended by the speaker. In 1899, Adolf Jülicher championed the view that parables are not simply allegories; they need to be interpreted as intending a single point of comparison. Parables pursue this goal. This approach leads to an emphasis on the conclusion of the parable, and for this reason parables should be deciphered in reverse. The significance of parables is found in the "weight of the stern." In this light, details have no independent significance and are there simply to build up the story and enhance the parable's central interest.

## THE PARABLES OF THE WICKED HUSBANDMEN AND THE SOWER

The first parable we will interpret is the parable of the wicked husbandmen or tenants. Then we will interpret the one of the sower.

### (1) The Parable of the Wicked Husbandmen

The parable of the wicked husbandmen is found in all three synoptics, and a version also appears in the *Gospel according to Thomas*. We consider the synoptic version first before *Thomas*'s. We give Mark's version priority among the synoptics (Mark 12:1–12; Matt. 21:33–44; Luke 20:9–19).

> Mark 12:1–12:1 Then he began to speak to them in parables. "A man planted a vineyard, and put a fence around it, dug a pit for the wine press, and built a watchtower; then he leased it to tenants and went to another country. 2 When the season came, he sent a slave to the tenants to collect from them his share of the produce of the vineyard. 3 But they seized him, and beat him, and sent him away empty-handed. 4 And again he sent another slave to them; this one they beat over the head, and insulted. 5 Then he sent another, and that one they killed. And so it was with many others; some they beat, and others they killed. 6 He had still one other, a beloved son. Finally he sent him to them, saying, 'They will respect my son.' 7 But those tenants said to one another, 'This is the heir; come, let us kill him, and the inheritance will be ours.' 8 So they seized him, and killed him, and threw him out of the vineyard. 9 What then will the owner of the vineyard do? He will come and destroy the tenants, and give the vineyard to others. 10 Have you not read this scripture: 'The stone that the builders rejected has become the cornerstone; 11 this was the Lord's doing, and it is amazing in our eyes'?" 12 When they realized that he had told this parable against them, they wanted to arrest him, but they feared the crowd. So they left him and went away.

This parable has explicit allegorical features that may betray the hand of a Christian author or **interpolator.** What is allegorical about it? Mark begins: "A man planted a vineyard, put a fence around it. . . . " (12:1). This passage is a quote from Isaiah 5:2 in the Greek translation of the Jewish Bible. *Vineyard* was a familiar symbol of Israel. Isaiah 5:1–7 says that Israel is God's vineyard and should produce grapes. Interestingly, the Hebrew text does not say that a hedge was made around the vineyard. The meaning of the Greek text is that Israel had been set apart from other peoples. It was important to stress this fact because the Greek translators worked in Alexandria, Egypt, where social intercourse with non-Jews threatened to corrupt Israel.

Jesus probably did not read his Bible in Greek, whereas the Greek version of the Old Testament was the text read by the Jews who lived outside of Palestine. Even in Jerusalem some Jewish Christians from the Diaspora did not fully understand Hebrew and used the Greek version. Thus, Mark's text may not be derived from Jesus.

Beginning students have little chance of knowing this fact, but by simply looking at a translation we should be able to find other allegorical elements. In 12:6 Mark says that the owner finally sent his "beloved son." "He had still one other, a beloved son. Finally he sent him to them, saying, 'They will respect my son.'" That statement should make readers think of the voice at the baptism of Jesus: "You are my Son, the Beloved; with you I am well pleased" (Mark 1:11). Thus Jesus was the beloved Son, and the owner of the vineyard was his Father, God. There is some Christology in the "parable," so it does not pass the test of the criterion of dissimilarity.

The fate of the son of the owner is the same as that of Jesus. Both were killed. Compare verse 8 in Mark with the corresponding verses in Matthew and Luke. Mark says, "So they seized him, killed him and threw him out of the vineyard" (12:8). Matthew and Luke say, "threw him out of the vineyard, and killed him" (Matt. 21:39; Luke 20:15). Why did they change Mark's order? Well, Jesus was crucified outside Jerusalem, which was the capitol of the Jewish nation and can be seen in a special sense as the vineyard. It is quite clear that Matthew and Luke understood the son to be Jesus.

The end of the story is now clear. The owner will come and destroy the tenants and give the vineyard to others. That is, God will come, destroy the Jews, and raise up a new Israel. Note, especially, that Matthew 21:41 and 43 have added that the new tenants, even a "people" (Greek: *ethnos* [nation]), will give the owner fruit. This duty refers to the Sermon on the Mount, where Matthew says that bad trees which produced no good fruit would be cut down and burned (7:20). Matthew interpreted the story in his last verse: "the kingdom of God will be taken away from you" (you being Jews; Jesus directed the parable to the Jewish authorities) and given to a "people" (21:43). Thus, the new tenants would be the gentile Christians. This parable also contains Ecclesiology.

Who are the servants who were beaten and killed? Obviously they were the prophets. In contrast to Mark and Luke, Matthew 21:34–36 says that the owner sent his servants in two groups: "When the harvest time had come, he sent his slaves to the tenants to collect his produce. But the tenants seized his slaves and beat one, killed another, and stoned another. Again he sent other slaves. . . ." This passage may be an allusion to the earlier and later prophets. The prophets were divided into two groups, depending on whether they appeared before or after the exile.

Thus, the parable of the wicked husbandmen is essentially an allegory, where the formula is $a = A$, $b = B$, and so on. This formula was already present in Mark and made clearer in Matthew and Luke, but especially in Matthew. It is possible that Jesus told a parable that was allegorized later.

The same parable, which also appears in the *Gospel according to Thomas,* is not such a clear allegory. There it is a real parable.

> *Thomas logion* 65: He said, "There was a good man who owned a vineyard. He leased it to tenant farmers so that they might work it and he might collect the produce from them. He sent his servant so that the tenants might give him the produce of the vineyard. They seized his servant and beat him, all but killing him. The servant went back and told his master. The master said, 'Perhaps [they] did not recognize [him].'

He sent another servant. The tenants beat this one as well. Then the owner sent his son and said, 'Perhaps they will show respect to my son.' Because the tenants knew that it was he who was the heir to the vineyard, they seized him and killed him. Let him who has ears hear." *Thomas logion* 66: Jesus said, "Show me the stone which the builders have rejected. That one is the cornerstone."

The *Gospel according to Thomas* has no reference to the Greek text of the Old Testament. *Thomas* says, "A man had a vineyard." It does not include the passage about the hedge being set up. In this version we have no "beloved son," only a "son." No murder takes place outside the vineyard. No word is uttered about the tenants being destroyed and the vineyard given to others. Fewer servants are involved. Instead we have three people, with an emphasis on the third: a servant, a second servant, and the son. This type of presentation is typical in folklore. This parable is comparable to the parable of the good Samaritan. A priest came along, then a Levite, and finally a Samaritan. Literary scholars note that storytellers often focus on three people.

The author of *Thomas* neither knew the synoptic versions nor functioned as a critical scholar who deleted the allegorical traits. Therefore he must have had a version that was closer to the original. However, because *Thomas,* like the synoptics, included the verse about the rejected stone having become the cornerstone, we can see that an allegorizing process had already been started. The vineyard was, after all, a well-known symbol of Israel, and the description of the son as the "heir of the vineyard" certainly lends itself to a christological interpretation. But *Thomas* is more original than the synoptics. The end of the parable in *Thomas,* "Let him who has ears hear," seems to round it off. The part about the cornerstone appears to have been added later. Still "heir of the vineyard" remains and suggests allegory.

What is the point of the story? The story presupposes a social setting in Galilee. The owner of the vineyard was a rich man; he could afford to live abroad. Perhaps he was a foreigner. The tenants were people who had everything to lose if they could not pay the owner. A similar revolutionary situation was the background for the later insurrections of the Zealots. It seems that Jesus, a Galilean, could have used such a setting for a parable. Was the message a warning directed against revolutionary-minded Jews to whom Jesus was sympathetic although he did not side with them? Assuming that the story is a parable, its point might be: As the tenants do to the servants and the son, so rebellious Jews might do to innocent people. Jesus called upon the judgment of his hearers.

One thing does not agree with this interpretation, namely, that the last envoy of the owner was the "heir of the vineyard." This part sounds like a later allegorical addition.

### (2) The Parable of the Sower

We find the parable of the sower in four full versions—three among the synoptic Gospels and one in the *Gospel according to Thomas.* We give Mark's account synoptic priority (Mark 4:1–9). The added explanations for speaking in parables and the following allegorical interpretations of the parable (Mark 4:10–20) are secondary and should be neglected when we try to understand the parable.

> Mark 4:1–9: 1 Again he began to teach beside the sea. Such a very large crowd gathered around him that he got into a boat on the sea and sat there, while the whole crowd was beside the sea on the land. 2 He began to teach them many things in parables, and in his teaching he said to them: 3 "Listen! A sower went out to sow. 4 And as he sowed, some seed fell on the path, and the birds came and ate it up. 5 Other seed fell on rocky ground, where it did not have much soil, and it sprang up quickly, since it had no depth of soil. 6 And when the sun rose, it was scorched; and since it had no root, it withered away. 7 Other seed fell among thorns, and the thorns grew up and choked it, and it yielded no grain. 8 Other seed fell into good soil and brought forth grain, growing up and increasing and yielding thirty and sixty and a hundredfold." 9 And he said, "Let anyone with ears to hear listen!"

We should regard the introduction in verses 1 and 2 as the redactional work of the author. Here we find the characteristic link with the previous story by a reference to time and space: "Again he began to teach beside the sea." These links often say that Jesus taught a crowd. The introduction to the story about the call of Levi in Mark 2:13 is similar: "Jesus went out again beside the sea; the whole crowd gathered around him, and he taught them."

The parables were thus handed down without reference to the situations in which they were originally told. Therefore, it is not acceptable to try to explain them in connection with a particular situation in the life of Jesus. They can be understood only in the light of the totality of Jesus' teaching. Mark begins with an imperative, "Listen!" Thus the hearers were asked to be alert, to be prepared to make a decision. Compare this imperative with the end in verse 9: "Let anyone with ears to hear listen!" The hearers were summoned to understand and act in accordance with their understanding.

What is the meaning of the parable? What was Jesus trying to say? To get to the main point to which the whole narrative is directed, we should start with the end, because the emphasis rests on the conclusion of the parable, "the weight of the stern." The conclusion, in verse 8, says that the harvest will be an abundant one. Everything that went before served this rather startling point. Jesus dwelt on the failures in verses 4 through 7. Then he described the success in just one verse.

This parable belongs to a group of parables called the growth parables. Two more appear in Mark 4—the seed growing secretly and the mustard seed. In the parallel chapter in Matthew (Chapter 13) we find additional growth parables—for example, the weeds in the wheat. These parables deal with the Kingdom of God; they are introduced by the phrase, "The Kingdom of God is like. . . ." This introductory phrase does not introduce the parable of the sower, but we can safely assume that the theme is the same. To speak about the kingdom by using the image of growth, or development, as in the parable of the leaven, appears to have been characteristic of Jesus. Thus, we can assume the second link in the comparison. It is the Kingdom of God. The matter of the kingdom is compared with the story about the sower. What is its point? Like those who heard Jesus' parables, readers have to search for the application—the relevance of the story to the matter of the kingdom. How did this story teach people anything about the way Jesus viewed the kingdom?

Here we should not dwell on the idea of growth—on the development itself. These parables do not describe the organic and continuous development of the kingdom. Misconceptions, such as the idea that the kingdom grows within human beings or is gradually built up in society, would result. Not even the eschatological interpretation is entirely right, although it correctly focuses on the ends of these parables. This eschatological interpretation suggests itself in the parable of the sower, which ends with a harvest, because the harvest is a common symbol of the end of an age. Yet this ending is not the point of the parable. The point is the contrast—the contrast between the early failures and the success in the end. Although much of the seed was lost, the harvest was a miraculously abundant one. This fact leaves the hearers astonished. By mentioning all the failures, Jesus prepared his listeners for the conclusion that God's purpose would be worked out no matter what.

The parable formula, *a* is like *b* in the way that *A* is like *B*, fits the parable of the sower. The sowing of the seed is related to the harvest in the way that the preaching about the kingdom is related to the coming of the kingdom. Although much of the preaching must be regarded as a failure, the kingdom will come anyway.

Now we can answer the question about the setting in life *(Sitz im Leben)*. Is the intention of the parable to console and give encouragement in the face of the many disappointments and setbacks? Or is it to warn, to make clear to the hearers that a great responsibility lies upon them? Put another way, are the parables promises of salvation or warnings of judgment? Do not regard these alternatives as mutually exclusive. The parables are positive illustrations of the promise, "The Kingdom of God is at hand." However, when people do not accept this message, when people do not repent, the message becomes one of judgment. Thus the parables are both consolation and admonition.

When we consider the parable's allegorical exposition in verses 13 through 20, we can see that the order of importance has been changed.

> Mark 4:13–20 13 And he said to them, "Do you not understand this parable? Then how will you understand all the parables? 14 The sower sows the word. 15 These are the ones on the path where the word is sown: when they hear, Satan immediately comes and takes away the word that is sown in them. 16 And these are the ones sown on rocky ground: when they hear the word, they immediately receive it with joy. 17 But they have no root, and endure only for a while; then, when trouble or persecution arises on account of the word, immediately they fall away. 18 And others are those sown among thorns: these are the ones who hear the word, 19 but the cares of the world, and the lure of wealth, and the desire for other things come in and choke the word, and it yields nothing. 20 And these are the ones sown on the good soil; they hear the word and accept it and bear fruit, thirty and sixty and a hundredfold."

In the parable, the plentiful harvest is the point. The allegory elaborates on the failure of the seed. Evidently the experience of the Church is mirrored in the allegorization of parables. The reason given for Jesus' speaking in parables in verses 10 through 12 attempts to explain this lack of response to the gospel.

> Mark 4:10–12: 10 When he was alone, those who were around him along with the twelve asked him about the parables. 11 And he said to them, "To you has been given the secret of the kingdom of God, but for those outside, everything comes in parables; 12 in order that 'they may indeed look, but not perceive, and may indeed listen but not understand; so that they may not turn again and be forgiven.'"

What is the relationship between the synoptic version and that of the *Gospel according to Thomas*? In one sense, *Thomas* is quite close to the synoptics, especially to Matthew. If we make a table of agreement in wording between the synoptic versions and *Thomas,* we find that there are fifteen agreements: eight with Mark and Matthew, five with Matthew alone, one with Matthew and Luke, and one with Luke alone. Thus, in fourteen out of fifteen cases, *Thomas* agrees with Matthew. It is impossible for English readers to notice some of these agreements because the different translations do not bear them out. We can point to one clear agreement. The end of Matthew 13:4 says that the birds came and ate "them"— that is, the seed. Both Mark and Luke read "it," singular. But *Thomas* has the plural—"the birds came and gathered them up" (*logion* 9).

Because *Thomas* was written around 140 CE, and Matthew was written around 80 CE, scholars conclude that the author of *Thomas* was witness to the same tradition as the one found in Matthew. He was not simply dependent on Matthew's text because there are differences between *Thomas* and Matthew that cannot be explained simply by saying that *Thomas* changed Matthew. We can illustrate this relationship as shown in Figure 21.1.

Matthew ◀——————— Jesus Tradition ——————▶ Thomas

**FIGURE 21.1**

An examination of the parable's structure may help us to understand the relationship between Matthew and the *Gospel according to Thomas*. The parable in the synoptics is a pearl of a story. It has a beautiful structure. Some of the seed fell along a path and the birds came and ate it; some fell on stony ground and the sun scorched it; and some fell among thorns and was choked. There were three failures. Then there were three successes. Some seed fell into good soil and bore fruit—some thirtyfold, some sixtyfold, and some one hundredfold. The three successes obviously correspond to the three failures. One part is striking—the seed that fell on stony ground sprang up immediately because it did not have deep soil and was destroyed by the sun because it did not have deep roots. This picture is vivid and realistic.

Comparing the *Gospel according to Thomas* with the synoptics, we can easily see that *Thomas* is less poetic. Also *Thomas* has only two successes—"sixty per measure and a hundred and twenty per measure." The third success is missing. However, a sequence of three is customary in oral law, manifesting itself in parables as well as in folktales. Take, for instance, the parable of the good Samaritan where we have a priest, a Levite (temple official), and a Samaritan. If *Thomas* was dependent on the synoptic tradition, why would he change this formal characteristic? *Thomas* is independent as well as dependent.

*Thomas* also says that the seed that fell on rock did not send roots down into the earth and did not sprout up out of the earth: "it did not take roots in the soil, and it did not produce ears" (*logion* 9). In *Thomas,* not much difference occurs between the seed that fell on the road and the seed that fell on the rock; both were lying around—the first being eaten and the second being unproductive. The point of the synoptic text was that the farmer also sowed where the stony ground was covered with a thin layer of soil. The farmer did not simply throw the seed on rocks. *Thomas* cannot have developed from only the synoptics.

Is it possible to establish that the *Gospel according to Thomas* used other sources? *Thomas* begins by saying, "A sower went out, he filled his hand, he threw." Here we find two differences between it and the synoptics: (1) "he filled his hand" and (2) "he threw." All the synoptics read: "The sower went out to sow." Here *Thomas* depicts the situation more vividly: "he filled his hand, he threw."

We cannot argue that the author of *Thomas* arbitrarily changed Matthew because *I Clement,* a Christian writing from the beginning of the second century, says that the sower "threw" (24). Note also that *I Clement* does not say, "The sower went out to sow," as do the synoptics. Like *Thomas* he says, "The sower went out." *Thomas* and *I Clement* both bear witness to a tradition independent of the one found in the synoptics. As many have noted, *I Clement* does not have "he filled his hand," as does Thomas. But the following reading is found in the Syrian Church. Aphraates (fourth century) said: "The sower filled his hand and threw on his land" (*Dem.* 14:46). Aphraates "filled his hand," as did Thomas, and he used the word *threw* as did both *Thomas* and *I Clement.* Aphraates was not simply dependent on *Thomas,* for he wrote "threw on his land," a statement that *Thomas* does not have. But *I Clement* contains something similar: "threw each of the seeds into the ground." Aphraates, as well as *I Clement,* were witnesses to the same independent tradition as Thomas (see Figure 21.2).

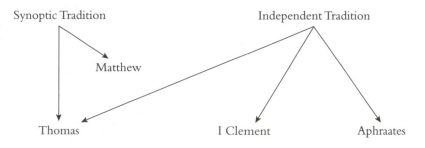

**FIGURE 21.2**

Does the independent tradition go back to Jesus himself? The author of *Thomas* said that some of the seed fell *on* the road. All the synoptics literally read "along the road" (Greek: *para ten hodon*). The point is that the farmer sowed the seed where it could be seen and where the birds could pick it up. Moreover, in the Middle East, seed was sowed before the field was plowed. The farmer knew that the plow would turn over the earth that had been stamped down into a path across the field. The farmer was not careless; no farmer is.

We must keep this image in mind—a path through a farmer's field. The plow will turn over the earth of this path. The preposition "para" (along) in the synoptic version does not make sense. The point must be that the seed is clearly visible to the birds. The seed must be *on* the path. The reason for the incorrect reading of the synoptics is that the Aramaic preposition, *al,* means "on" and "by" and "along." The Greek translator chose the wrong sense because he was not familiar with farming in Palestine. *Thomas* apparently preserved the original word.

In this case is the preposition used in the *Gospel according to Thomas* ("on" the road) a correction of the synoptic tradition? Should *Thomas's* use of the preposition "on" be used to amend the synoptic version? (The author of *Thomas* was familiar with the synoptics.) Or does his version simply demonstrate more familiarity with Galilee? The latter is possible—and also important—because in this one case *Thomas* is certainly closer to the milieu of Jesus than the synoptics are. In addition, we can conclude that *Thomas* (1) was a witness to a Matthew-like tradition and (2) was also a witness to an independent tradition. These points are illustrated (a) by the fact that some phrases cannot be derived from the Gospels, like the beginning of the parable ("Look, a sower went out, he filled his hand he threw") and the words about the seed that fell on the stony ground and (b) by the fact that the allegorical interpretation is lacking. Why would Thomas have deleted it if it was in the tradition he received?

## SUMMARY

Many of Jesus' sayings were in the form of comparisons known as parables, and many of the parables—whether they were figures of speech, similitudes, or stories—satisfy the criteria of authenticity provided by form criticism. Unfortunately, some of Jesus' parables were treated like allegories, and as a result Christian interpolators altered their original meanings. We find this phenomenon in the Gospels where the gospel writers allegorized some of Jesus' parables. Allegories and parables both involve a comparison of some sort. In the case of an allegory, the comparison is that of $a = A,$ whereas in a parable, the comparison is $a$ is like $A.$ Comparing the synoptics with the *Gospel according to Thomas* helps to illustrate the way the parables were allegorized—taken from $a$ is like $A$ to $a = A.$ In interpreting parables it is important to work backward from the conclusion of the parable. It is at the end that the point of comparison appears.

## KEY TERMS FOR REVIEW

| | | |
|---|---|---|
| Parable | Metaphor | Example story |
| Criterion of dissimilarity | *Mashal/Parabole* | Adolf Jülicher |
| Criterion of Palestinian coloring | Simile | Interpolator |
| Allegory | Similitude | *Gospel according to Thomas* |
| | Story | |

## QUESTIONS FOR REVIEW

1. Why are Jesus' parables usually considered authentic?
2. What is a parable and how does it differ from an allegory?
3. What kinds of parables can we find among the sayings of Jesus?
4. Why is the *Gospel according to Thomas* useful in studying the parables of Jesus?

## SUGGESTIONS FOR FURTHER READING

Donahue, J. *The Gospel in Parable: Metaphor, Narrative, and Theology in the Synoptic Gospels.* Philadelphia: Fortress, 1988.

Gowler, D. *What Are they Saying about the Parables?* New York: Paulist, 2000.

Hultgren, A. *The Parables of Jesus: A Commentary.* Grand Rapids: Eerdmans, 2000.

Jeremias, J. *The Parables of Jesus.* 3rd ed. London, SCM Press, 1972.

Longnecker, R. ed. *The Challenge of Jesus' Parables.* Grand Rapids: Eerdmans, 2000.

# 22

✴

# Jesus and the Miracles

## MIRACLES IN THE ANCIENT WORLD

Miracle stories and stories about miracle workers are found in many religions and are not peculiar to Christianity. The New Testament authors were well aware of this fact when they described Jesus as a miracle worker. In their age, miracles were not out of the ordinary. The overwhelming majority of people everywhere believed that miracles could and did happen and that some individuals could and did work miracles. Miracles were not everyday phenomena, but they did not contradict people's understanding of the workings of the laws of nature.

We find miracle workers in both the Greco-Roman world and in the Jewish world. Apollonius of Tyana, a city in Asia Minor, was a famous gentile miracle worker. He was a contemporary of Jesus, living at the close of the first century. According to tradition he traveled widely, visiting both India and Rome. In his biography, which has been preserved, he is seen as a kind of rival to Jesus.

The Jews also had miracle workers. The Old Testament talks about miracle workers. Moses was able to perform miracles. At about Jesus' time, Honi "the rain-maker" was famous. He was also known as Honi "the circle-drawer." He drew a circle, placed himself within it, and declared to God that he would not move until God let it rain. Honi was a Galilean. So was Hanina ben Dosa, a famous healer who could heal from a distance. Centuries before Honi and Hanina lived, Elijah and Elisha, two prophets of Israel's northern kingdom in what came to be known as Galilee, worked miracles according to 1 and 2 Kings. Jesus appeared to be part of this tradition of Galilean healers.

Josephus related that one of his countrymen, an exorcist by the name of Eleazar, cast a demon out of a man in the presence of the emperor Vespasian himself. (Vespasian, by the way, was a miracle worker himself. Suetonius, a second-century CE Roman historian, reported that Vespasian restored the sight of a blind man with spittle and healed a lame man with his touch.) Josephus said that Eleazar drew the demon out of the possessed person by means of a ring like the one King Solomon had owned. (According to Jewish tradition, King Solomon was known to have been a great exorcist.) Josephus related that Eleazar, in order to prove that he had cast the demon out, commanded the demon to overturn a bowl filled with water that Eleazar had placed nearby. Thus everyone would be able to see that the demon had left the man.

Something similar was told about Apollonius of Tyana. When Apollonius charged a demon to leave a certain young man, the demon, through the man, pointed to a statue nearby and said, "I will throw down that statue." When the statue fell, after having rocked for a short while, people applauded. The demon had been driven out.

Thus miracles were not ascribed to Jesus alone (they are associated with Jesus in every important gospel source [Mark, Q, p-Matthew, p-Luke, John, the *Gospel according to Thomas logion* 14), and according to a Q tradition Jesus actually admitted that others also performed miracles. When Jesus' opponents said that he cast out demons in the name of Satan—that is, with the help of Satan—Jesus retorted, "If I cast out demons by Beelzebul, by whom do your own exorcists cast them out?" (Matt. 12:27; Luke 11:19). This passage is important for two reasons: (1) Jesus' opponents admitted that he could exorcise demons (in Jewish writings Jesus was portrayed as a magician who led Israel astray), and (2) Jesus admitted that his opponents could do the same. The important question is by whose power and help did Jesus perform the miracles? Was God or Satan behind the miracle in question? In the competitive world of religion, one person's miracle is another person's magic.

Form criticism sees the healing miracles as examples of how certain stories were told in the same way. Healing miracles were related in more or less the same way. First, the illness was described. The description often included the length and seriousness of the illness and sometimes mentioned the inability of doctors to cure it. Second, the cure itself was described. In several stories the cure was effected by means of strange gestures, like the use of spittle. Third, the proof of healing was noted. The lame started to walk; the blind could see. In a healing story in Mark 5:1–20, the demons possessing a poor fellow asked to be sent into a herd of pigs feeding nearby. Jesus gave the demons permission, and the pigs, upon being possessed by the demons, rushed into the sea and drowned. Pigs did not behave like that. This feature was meant to illustrate that the demons had indeed left the man. We can compare the stampede of the pigs to the stories about the Jewish exorcists Eleazar and Apollonius of Tyana, who both offered proof of their exorcisms. Last, the impression of the cure on those present was sometimes related. They all marveled, "they were afraid" (Mark 5:15). In the story about Apollonius the witnesses applauded.

Redaction criticism shows that some of the healing stories were changed. Mark's story about the healing of the epileptic boy (Mark 9:14–29) was drastically shortened by Matthew and Luke. Mark was interested in describing the illness and its symptoms. Matthew and Luke did not think they were important and edited the account, even adding some words they considered important (Matt. 17:14–21; Luke 9:37–43).

Another example involves the synoptic account about Jesus healing a man with a withered hand on the Sabbath. Matthew said that on that occasion Jesus explained his miracle with a story about a sheep falling into a pit on the Sabbath (Matt. 12:11–12). Mark did not include this story, whereas Luke quoted it in another context (Luke 14:5). Note that Matthew and Luke also left out stories about Jesus healing people when they thought that Mark represented Jesus as a miracle worker who depended on magical rituals involving gestures such as spitting, touching, and the reciting of special phrases (Mark 7:32–35; 8:22–25).

Thus far we can state our conclusions. (1) Miracle stories were common in the ancient world. People did not dispute the fact that Jesus performed miracles, nor did the Christians dispute that other people performed miracles. The issue was by whose power the miracle was performed. (2) The miracle stories conformed to a certain pattern, which shows that the early Church gave them their form. The Church adopted a common literary form. (3) The miracle stories underwent some changes during the course of time. Matthew and Luke changed Mark to make redactional points and thus edited the miracle stories.

We can add a final point to the previous one. (4) We observe an increase in the number of Jesus' healings. The stories about Jesus healing specific individuals number around 25. The picture is different when we add the summarizing statements about his healing activity. Mark 1 relates that Jesus healed a possessed man in the synagogue and then went to Peter's house and healed Peter's mother-in-law. When evening fell, they brought all the sick people to him and he healed many (Mark 1:34). This is a summarizing story. Here it is easy to discern the hand of the community. Moving to Matthew's parallel account (Chapter 8), Jesus is described as healing "all" (Matt. 8:16). Therefore, we find an increase in the number of Jesus' healings from Mark to Matthew.

## DEFINING *MIRACLE* IN THE GOSPELS

In the Gospels miracles can be defined as events that transcend ordinary human experiences and are viewed as a result of supernatural power. Ancients did not view them as contrary to the laws of nature but as events that went beyond nature or natural circumstances—thus the term *super natural*. However, which supernatural power was behind the miracle or miracle worker was not clear because for Jews, as well as for Gentiles, different supernatural beings were active among human beings. Miracles, as proof of God's involvement, were therefore ambiguous in many instances. This situation was evident in the Gospels when Jesus' opponents acknowledged his miracles but questioned the source of his power (Mark 3: 22; Matt. 12:24; Luke 11:15; Matt. 9:34). Still, according to the gospel writers, the meanings of Jesus' miracles could be grasped by those with faith.

Accounts of miracles are particularly difficult for historians. Scholars admit that, according to their written sources, Jesus was identified as a miracle worker, but they are unable to confirm or deny that Jesus actually performed miracles (or that God was directly involved in Jesus' miracles) because confirmation would call for a philosophical or theological judgment beyond the scope of their historical methods. Nevertheless, scholars go on to question the stories of Jesus' miracles on the basis of their critical assumptions about reality (that is, dead people stay dead), identify them as improbable, and then explain them on another basis (that is, exaggeration, fabrication, psychosomatic phenomena, and so on).

The most common synoptic gospel term for a miracle is the Greek word *dunamis,* which means "mighty work" or "power" but is often translated as "miracle" in older English translations of the Bible (see Mark 9:39 in the King James version). The term suggests that a supernatural power is at work, and this view may help to explain why the word *miracle,* with its connotation of the supernatural, is used to translate it. In many instances, the synoptic Gospels simply describe Jesus as healing or casting out a demon without using the word *dunamis* (Mark 1:32–34). John's gospel uses the word *semeion* or "sign" (2:11). As signs, Jesus' miracles are part of John's effort to explain Jesus' spiritual significance to his readers, and they point beyond themselves as they disclose Jesus' identity. In the synoptics, sign takes on the idea of proof and is used negatively; Jesus won't perform signs for everyone who demands them (Mark 8:11–13). Both the synoptics and John imply that Jesus' ability to perform miracles resulted from his reception of the Spirit following his baptism.[1] This view is in keeping with ancient Jewish and gentile notions that human limitations can be overcome through divine intervention.

## TYPES OF MIRACLES
## PERFORMED BY JESUS

Jesus' miracles can be divided into nature miracles and healing miracles. This division is a modern, convenient way of making a distinction among them. The Gospels did not divide the miracles in this way. Jesus could address a demon possessing a person and a storm in the same way: "Be silent" (Mark 1:25; 4:39). This rebuke showed that there was a demoniac power behind the storm.

Whereas it may be helpful to distinguish among healing miracles proper and exorcisms, the first Christians did not seem to make such a distinction. There was no distinction between mental and physical illnesses in the Gospels. On a couple of occasions Jesus raised the dead. This type of event was simply an instance of a healing miracle. Healing leprosy was regarded as equivalent to getting a person up from a deathbed. There was no significant difference between the two acts.

### Nature Miracles

We can divide nature miracles into (1) demonstrations of power over nature (for example, the stilling of the storm), and (2) the feeding of multitudes (for example, the multiplication of the bread and the fishes). But there is no major distinction here. There is, however, a significant distinction between these two types of miracles—the nature miracles and the healing miracles. The healing miracles were public miracles, so to speak. The nature miracles were not. Only the disciples witnessed

---

[1] *The Infancy Gospel of Thomas,* which dates to the middle of the second century and describes Jesus' childhood and youth up to his twelfth year, says that Jesus performed miracles as a child. Scholars view this text as something of an imaginative propaganda text for Christian missionaries.

the nature miracles. This distinction also holds true for the feeding of the multi-tudes. The people neither knew where the food came from nor saw a miracle, nor did they respond to a miracle. Only Jesus' disciples witnessed this miracle in the synoptic Gospels. John's gospel highlights the crowd's recognition of Jesus' miracle and suggests a redactional modification of the miracles in light of John's purpose (6:14–15 and 20:30–31). Jesus never referred to his nature miracles and never even claimed that he had powers over nature. He did refer to his ability to cure people (here we include the raising of the dead). He did so in the answer to the Baptist's question, "Are you the one who is to come, or are we to wait for another?" (Matt. 11:3; Luke 7:19).

The feeding miracles are similar to the nature miracles proper in that Jesus exercised his power over physical substances, in this case bread and fish. The early Church sensed difficulties with these miracles. Hilary of Poitiers (fourth century) asked where the bread and fish were multiplied. In the hand of Jesus or in the mouths of those who ate? A rationalistic explanation might be that even a tiny bit of bread and fish seemed substantial to people under Jesus' spell. This expla-nation loses its persuasiveness when five loaves of bread and two fish were divided by 5,000—the number of people Jesus fed. Perhaps the number 5,000 was exag-gerated, but that is a rationalization.

We need to recognize the allusion of the miracle to the Eucharist. Mark's account is similar to that of the Last Supper (6:32–44 and 14:22–25): Jesus took the bread, blessed it, broke it, and distributed it among his disciples. All ate of the bread and fish as they all ate and drank at the Last Supper. We find an eschato-logical motif in addition to the eucharistic allusion. The feeding corresponds to God's feeding of the children of Israel in the desert. That feeding was regarded as a prefiguration of the "messianic banquet" of the kingdom to come. The sitting down of the people in groups of fifties and hundreds alluded to how Moses instructed people to assemble in groups of 1000s, 100s, and 50s (Num. 1:17–47).

More than one hundred and fifty years ago, David Strauss, in his two-volume book, *The Life of Jesus Critically Examined* (1835–36), argued that some of the mir-acle stories were myths, by which he meant that they were symbolic and not his-torical. Whereas scholars today generally admit that Jesus was recognized by his contemporaries as a miracle worker, Strauss's argument that the Gospels convey religious truth rather than history lessons, particularly with reference to the nature miracles, is insightful. The private, nonpublic characteristic of the nature miracles and their allusions to biblical events or later Christian practices, as with the feeding of the 5,000 and its possible allusion to the manna and/or the Eucharist, suggests the possibility that some may be the Church's literary cre-ations that bear out early Christian beliefs. Despite what readers make of the his-toricity of the nature miracles, they do have a symbolic element. The picture of Jesus feeding the multitudes symbolically expresses the conviction that the new age arrived with the appearance of Jesus.

## Healing Miracles

**(1) Unsuccessful Attempts at Healing** There can be no doubt that Jesus per-formed healings. Equally certain is that the Gospels say he was not always suc-cessful. In Mark 6:1–6, Jesus' lack of success was ascribed to a lack of faith on the part of the people. In the parallel in Luke 4:16–30, Jesus' failure was explained by a reference to the great miracle workers Elijah and his disciple, Elisha. They were not sent to all who needed help in Israel, which implied that God is sovereign and decides whom he will help. No one has any *right* to be helped.

A third explanation for Jesus' lack of success in some cases was that Satan's power had not been entirely broken. Satan could still win some battles against God, although people believed that he would lose in the end. In Matthew 8:29, when the demons recognized Jesus they cried, "Have you come here to torment us before the time?" The demons had their time for judgment. The evil powers were believed to be more or less in control until the Kingdom of God would finally be established. According to Matthew 8:29, what the demons did not know was that the kingdom is already in the process of being established.

**(2) The Meaning of the Miracle Stories** In general, Jesus' miracles meant that the kingdom was being established. This meaning was expressed through the words of Jesus in Luke 10:18, "I watched Satan fall from heaven like a flash of lightning." Jesus had a vision of the imminent defeat of Satan. This statement was made in response to the account of the successful exorcisms of the disciples.

That the kingdom was in the process of being established was also the message in Jesus' answer to John the Baptist in Matthew 11:2–6. He did not answer the Baptist's question of whether he was the Messiah, or the Moses-like prophet, or the returning Elijah. The phrase "the one who is to come" used in Matthew 11:3 could have denoted the Moses-like prophet or Elijah, two figures who were anticipated by many Jews in Jesus' day, as well as the Messiah. In any event the Baptist asked whether Jesus was an eschatological figure—one of the figures who was to be part of the events at the end of the age. John must have had his doubts as his question ("Are you the one who is to come . . . ?") implied. According to Matthew 11:2 John had his doubts because he had heard about the deeds of the so-called Messiah. John may have been doubtful because none of the three eschatological figures was expected to come as a healer.

Jesus did not answer John directly but cited some miracles that people believed would occur in the golden age. Thus, the new age—the Kingdom of God—was about to dawn. The blessings of the kingdom had already been experienced. Why, then, did not John and all others immediately believe? Because these miracles were performed by an ambiguous figure—Jesus. Miracles can be ambiguous and need to be properly interpreted, and this ambiguous quality is enhanced when the miracle worker is also tinged with ambiguity. Those who believed interpreted differently from those who did not believe. Note the rest of Jesus' answer. After having pointed to the eschatological miracles he performed, Jesus said, "and blessed is anyone who takes no offense at me" (Matt. 11:6). Those who wanted to understand the miracles must understand Jesus himself. For those people the miracles were eschatological; they indicated that the kingdom was about to dawn. For all others, the miracles were plain wonders.

It appears that Jesus avoided an attempt to perform miracles that could remove all doubts about his professed authority from God. The inability of Jesus' miracles to convince some people of his messiahship is revealed quite clearly by the accusation that he drove out demons with the help of Satan. This story is found in all the synoptics, but Matthew 12 and Luke 11 give the story in a more elaborate and interesting form. The Pharisees did not doubt that Jesus performed miracles, but they questioned whose power was behind them. Was God or Satan behind them? Also in this connection, Jesus explained the meaning of his healings: "But if it is by the finger of God that I cast out the demons, then the Kingdom of God has come to you" (Luke 11:20). This explanation is the same one that was given to the Baptist: Jesus brought the Kingdom of God through the performance of miracles. They were part of his message about the imminence of the kingdom. But, seen as mere miracles, his exorcisms were no different from those of the Pharisees. Who then could understand the secret of Jesus' miracles? The ones who believed in Jesus.

**(3) Faith and Miracles** We often speak of faith in connection with the miracles. To have faith can mean several things. What does faith mean in connection with Jesus' miracles? It does not mean a belief that miracles can happen. Almost all people shared that belief at the time. Furthermore, it is clear that a miracle was not a means of generating faith. The rejection of Jesus in Nazareth makes that clear. People in Nazareth did not doubt that Jesus could perform miracles. They exclaimed "What deeds of power are being done by his hands!" (Mark 6:2), but they were not convinced that this carpenter, the son of Mary, performed miracles with the help of God himself. Thus faith was the *condition* for working miracles in the synoptics, not the *result* of witnessing miracles, although John's gospel teaches that faith may result from miracles (John 2:11). Because people in Nazareth did not believe in Jesus, he could not work miracles there (Mark 6:5–6).

What, then, is faith? Two miracles that are closely connected in Mark—the healing of the woman with a hemorrhage and the raising of the daughter of Jairus (Mark 5:22–43)—reveal something about it. Both the woman and the girl were hopeless cases. The woman had been ill for twelve years and had been seen by many physicians, but she continued to get worse. This type of description of the length and seriousness of an illness was often found in ancient miracle stories. One ancient miracle account told a story about a woman who desperately sought to deliver her child after having been pregnant for five years. That is a ridiculously long time, but it made the point of the condition being serious. As for the seriousness of the conditions of those who sought out Jesus for healing, we find references to crippled hands, blindness, and so on. The point of Mark 5 is that any effort to help this woman would transcend all human capacities. Luke's version says that the woman could not be healed by anyone (Luke 8:43). In the account of Jairus' daughter, the girl was dead—that of course being the most serious situation. Some people apparently told her father that there was no point in bothering Jesus; even he could not do anything for her (Mark 5:35).

Against this background it becomes clear what faith is. Faith is the belief that only Jesus could help those whose situation was hopeless. Consider the woman with the hemorrhage. The woman was convinced that if she could touch Jesus' garment, she would become well (Mark 5:28).

It is interesting that Mark's story was more one of magic than of miracle. By grasping Jesus' garment while his back was turned, the woman drew power from him without his volition. She was healed immediately, and Jesus asked who touched him (Mark 5:30). Matthew refused to portray the miracle in this fashion and changed it by changing Mark's description (Matt. 9:20–22). In Matthew, Jesus saw the woman after she had touched him, and he never asked who it was that touched him. At the moment when Jesus pronounced "Your faith has made you well," the woman became well. Thus Matthew said that Jesus' words healed. He left out Mark's reference to a transference of power. But the basic point is the same in both stories—faith was the condition for the healing.

We can gain an even deeper understanding of the story when we examine the kind of illness the woman suffered from. She had a continuous flow, or hemorrhage, of blood. According to Jewish law, women were unclean when they menstruated, not only during the menstruation cycle but for seven days starting with the first day of the discharge (Lev. 15:19). This law appears to have been in effect in Jesus' time. Later the rabbis ruled that a woman should also count seven days from the cessation of the discharge. This results in a menstruating woman being ritually unclean for a long time each month. If the woman experienced a bloody discharge, however small, between two menstruation periods—which can happen—she immediately became unclean again. She was unclean as long as she bled and had to count seven days after the cessation of the bleeding, regardless of whether or not the bleeding was just a drop on one day.

Now consider the woman in Mark' story in the light of the laws regarding menstruation and bloody discharges. She was considered continuously unclean. What did that mean? She was not allowed to touch other people. If she did she would render them unclean. Therefore she sneaked up on Jesus from behind. The Christian authors of the Gospels portrayed Jesus as having supernatural powers. He would have recognized her situation if she had come so that he could see her. But he did not because she approached him from behind. Mark's story fits a Jewish milieu and is well told. By touching Jesus' garment, she broke the law of God and made Jesus unclean. According to the law, he should have washed his clothes and remained unclean until sundown.

Moreover, unclean people, like this woman, were also isolated from God because God is holy. The Pharisees isolated themselves from others to practice the laws of purity that would lead to holiness—to adapt a word from a Mishnah saying that purity leads to isolation and isolation to holiness. Only those who kept the purity law and were clean could have communion with Israel's holy God. Therefore, this woman was excluded from communion with God as well as people.

Thus the words of Jesus have a double meaning. His words, "Your faith has made you well," can also be translated, "Your faith has saved you." When she was healed, she was also saved; she was taken into communion with God again. Again we see that God was brought near in Jesus' miracles. The condition for that is faith; only Jesus can help.

Another story in Mark repeats this theme. We find the same concept of faith in the story of the daughter of Jairus. The father did not give up hope even though his daughter was dead. His faith showed in his effort to seek out Jesus and then fall at his feet, begging for help. Here Jesus appeared as God himself, as he did in the case of the nature miracles. Only God should be treated this way. Only God could raise the dead.

It is interesting and important to note that in the miracle stories the concept of faith is not dogma as it is in later ecclesiastical speech, starting with the preaching about the resurrected Jesus. In ecclesiastical language, faith is to receive, or take over, and accept a formulated message; to have faith is to believe. In the miracle stories, faith is not the acceptance that Jesus is the Messiah. In the miracle stories, faith is the belief that Jesus has the will and power to help when no other possibilities for help seem to exist. This definition is important because it says something about the age of the miracle stories. Although the miracle stories were formally preserved in the Church, they predate the Church and thus precede the christological developments of early Christianity.

Thus, in summary (1) the miracles were meant to tell people that Jesus brought the Kingdom of God near and made its powers effective. We must consider the miracles together with Jesus' preaching, and this preaching was characterized by the conviction of the imminence of the dawn of the new age. (2) The miracle stories were meant to say something about faith. They were not meant to be proof on the basis of which faith could be established. Instead, they showed that faith is belief in the power of Jesus, even in desperate situations.

**(4) The Person of Jesus in the Miracle Stories**  What do the miracle stories tell about Jesus as a person? That he was a miracle worker is not the point. There were many miracle workers. What kind of person was Jesus in the miracle stories?

Those who wrote the miracle stories and those for whom they were written believed that Jesus was the Messiah. The miracle stories were not intended to prove that Jesus was the Messiah—the Son of God or the Son of Man, or even the Son of David—to mention the well-known messianic titles. The term *Messiah* does not occur as a title in a single miracle story. This does not mean that the Christians did not believe that Jesus was the Messiah but rather that their Messiah was different from the one people longed for. Thus, if the miracle stories were not meant to prove that Jesus was the Messiah, they are meant to show something else—the kind of Messiah Jesus was.

In this connection we need to consider the story of Jesus healing a leper (Mark 1:40–45). Leprosy was thought to be more or less incurable. A saying ran: "To heal a leper is as difficult as raising a human from the dead." Leprosy also rendered its victims unclean. The illness was deemed to be punishment for sin; a leper was a public testimony of God's punishment. He or she was called "the firstborn child of death." The leper was of course excluded from the temple and the synagogue—from communion with God as well as from communion with people.

The gospel writers assumed this understanding of leprosy. Thus, when they related that Jesus freed people from this terrible illness, they implied that he restored communion between these people and God. Jesus said to the healed leper: "See that you say nothing to anyone [Mark's messianic secret], but go, show yourself to the priest, and offer for your cleansing what Moses commanded, as a testimony to them" (Mark 1:44). This passage is taken to mean that Jesus was obedient to the law, which required a cultic cleansing when a leper was healed. This story is in keeping with Mark's bias. In this story Jesus was an obedient Jew. But there is more to the account of this command in Mark 1:44. The judgment of the leper was abrogated by the law. The story showed that a leper could be reckoned as cleansed in the eyes of God, and that Jesus was able to cleanse him. Jesus had power over this terrible illness, which was seen as God's punishment for sins. This meant Jesus had power over sin; he was the agent of God.

Jesus was thus far more than the Jewish Messiah. The Messiah was not supposed to cleanse people's sins; he was not supposed to cleanse people like lepers and take them again into communion with God. Thus, Jesus manifested divine mercy, not human mercy. The Messiah, as he was understood by first-century Jews, was essentially a human figure.

Another example is the story of Jesus' healing on the Sabbath. To observe the Sabbath was a command of God. There were stringent rules, and no work whatsoever was allowed on this day with one exception—that of saving a life. The rabbis said that if a human being was in danger of dying, a person was allowed to step in to save her (do some work). What did Jesus say? Mark 3:1–6, says that Jesus healed a man with a withered hand on the Sabbath. Why didn't he wait until the next day? The man with the withered hand was not in danger of losing his life. Jesus could have waited until the next day to heal him. Thus Jesus certainly broke the Sabbath law, the law of the society, the law of God. He was a criminal.

Why did he break the law? He could not be merely the Messiah because the Messiah was not expected to come to break, change, or renew the law. In some quarters, however, people believed that a Moses-like prophet would come and introduce certain changes in the law and that Elijah would also set right certain misconceptions in the understanding of the law. However, not much was known about what the Moses-like prophet and the returning Elijah would actually do. The Gospels tell us what Jesus did, and that is important. The belief about messianic figures coming to change the law was vague, but the Gospels were explicit about the way Jesus changed the law. He asked, "Is it lawful to do good or do harm on the Sabbath, to save life or to kill?" (3:4). The parallelism is clear: "do good or do harm, to save life or to kill?" The rabbis would of course say that it was unlawful to kill but lawful to save life. What Jesus did was to equate killing with doing harm, and what is more important, he equated saving life with doing good. Saving life, which was the only work allowed on the Sabbath, was interpreted by Jesus as doing good.

Moreover, the way Jesus' words were formulated makes it clear that he did not appear here simply as a Moses-like prophet or the returning Elijah, giving a new law or changing the old. The way his words were formulated implied that to do good is and had always been God's will.

## SUMMARY

Miracle stories and miracle workers were familiar to both Gentiles and Jews, and they provided the context for Jesus' own miracles. Whereas both friends and foes spoke of Jesus' miracles, their ambiguity raised the question of their origin. Was it God or Satan? Jesus' miracles can be divided into nature miracles, which were done in private, and healing miracles, which were performed publicly. According to the Gospels, Jesus' miracles reflected on the kingdom, faith, and Jesus himself.

The kingdom's presence was demonstrated through miracles. Those who experienced miracles learned that faith in Jesus, believing that only he could help in hopeless situations, was required. Christologically, whenever Jesus performed a miracle, he was communicating something about the nature of his messiahship.

## KEY TERMS FOR REVIEW

| | | |
|---|---|---|
| Apollonius of Tyana | Vespasian | Nature miracles |
| Honi the "rain-maker" | Miracle/magic | Healing miracles |
| Elijah and Elisha | Form criticism | Kingdom |
| Eleazar | Redaction criticism | Faith |

## QUESTIONS FOR REVIEW

1. How did Jesus compare and contrast with other miracle workers?
2. What insights do form criticism and redaction criticism bring to an understanding of Jesus' miracles?
3. According to the Gospels, what do the miracles mean?
4. What is the relationship between *miracle* and *faith* in the Gospels?

## SUGGESTIONS FOR FURTHER READING

Kee, H. *Medicine, Miracle, and Magic in New Testament Times.* New York: Cambridge University Press, 1986.

Pilch, J. *Healing in the New Testament: insights from Medical and Mediterranean Anthropology.* Minneapolis: Fortress, 2000.

Remus, H. *Jesus as Healer.* Cambridge: Cambridge University Press, 1997.

Theissen, G. *The Miracle Stories of the Early Christian Tradition.* Philadelphia: Fortress, 1983.

Twelftree, G. *Jesus the Miracle Worker: A Historical and Theological Study.* Downers Grove: InterVarsity, 1999.

# 23

## ❊

# Jesus and the Law

### THE SERMON ON THE MOUNT

Augustine was the first person to call Jesus' words in Matthew Chapters 5 through 7 the Sermon on the Mount. Since then this portion of Matthew has become the most popular guide for Church life. This section's popularity is due to its succinct teaching of the law. The body of the sermon is 5:1–7:28, which falls into two parts. The first part runs from 5:1 to 5:48 and deals with the fulfillment of the law, which was taken to mean the true observation of the law. The second part, beginning with 6:1, does not contain an interpretation of the law but rather teachings on practical **piety.** It is the first part of the corpus, which has been called the Sermon within the Sermon, that is crucial for understanding Jesus' view of the law.

Matthew's Sermon on the Mount was not delivered by Jesus on one occasion. Instead Matthew edited Jesus' words by collecting many of them and creating a section in which he presented Jesus as addressing issues pertaining to the law. That Jesus dealt with the law is evident by the number of independent sources in which Jesus referred to the law (Mark, Q, p-Matthew, p-Luke, and John). Much of the material in the Sermon on the Mount came from Q, the hypothetical source used by source criticism to explain the common material in Matthew and Luke, as well as some sayings from Matthew's own source, p-Matthew (5:7–10). Some material can be paralleled by Jesus sayings in Mark (Mark 9:43; compare with Matt. 5:30).

We can see common material in Matthew and Luke quite clearly when we compare Matthew with Luke, whose version of the sermon is called Jesus' Sermon on the Plain. (In Luke Jesus spoke from a level place or plain, whereas in Matthew Jesus was on a mountain.) Luke's version, found in 6:17–49, is much shorter than Matthew's and does not explicitly address issues of the law as Matthew's sermon does. Luke does use many of the words in Matthew's sermon in other contexts. For example, Matthew's version of the sermon includes the prayer that is known as the Lord's Prayer (Matt. 6:9–13). Luke also knew that Jesus taught his disciples this prayer, but contrary to Matthew, he did not include the prayer in his version of the sermon. Luke related that Jesus taught his disciples that prayer on another occasion and gave his text of the prayer (Luke 11:2–4). Luke also included Jesus sayings that came from his own source, p-Luke (6:24–26). Both Matthew and Luke appear to have presented Jesus' teachings in a way that addressed the needs of their particular readers.

The authority that Jesus displayed in teaching the law, especially in Matthew's sermon, often strikes readers as bold, argumentative, and even quarrelsome. He called his legal adversaries "blind guides of the blind" (Q [Matt. 15:14; Luke 6:39]; *Gospel according to Thomas logion* 34). However, Jesus' manner when asserting his view of the law was not out of keeping with the importance that other Jews placed on the interpretations of the law. Open, sometimes biting, criticism of competing Torah interpretations came to light with the discovery of the Dead Sea Scrolls. By Jesus' day, there were several competing interpretations of the law, and among the Pharisees alone there were at least two well-established schools, each with its own favored teacher (Shammai and Hillel) and interpretations of the law. It was a rabbinic duty to teach the law, and it should come as no surprise that that there are Jesus sayings on the law because as a rabbi Jesus would be expected to address it. Sections of Matthew's account may display a later Christian emphasis on the exaltedness of Jesus (5:11, 17b), and this emphasis should caution scholars against a simple assumption that all the Jesus sayings are authentic. However, because many of the Jesus sayings on the law, like many of the parables, lack a christological interest, scholars are duly cautious about presuming that they are secondary.

## (1) Beatitudes: 5:3–12

Jesus' view of the law is given in Matthew 5:17–48, but it is important to look briefly at what went on earlier. Matthew 5:1–2 sets the scene. Then, verses 3 through 12 present the **beatitudes** as a prologue to the Sermon on the Mount. Often the sermon is thought of as a series of radical demands, but it begins with radical mercy. Its prologue, the beatitudes, identifies those to whom the Kingdom of Heaven belongs, as we can see by looking at the first and the last (eighth) beatitudes, verse 3 and verses 11 and 12, which derive from Q (Matt. 5:3, 11–12; Luke 6:20b, 22–23). Matthew referred to the beatitudes in verses 11 and 12, and implicitly all the beatitudes, to Jesus' disciples—that is, to the Church. (Matthew 5:11 has "on my account" and makes the beatitudes' connection with Jesus' disciples obvious whereas Luke preserved what appears to be the more authentic "on account of the Son of Man" [6:22], which suggests that Jesus was talking about a third party.)

The beatitudes identify the people who will get into the Kingdom of Heaven. Here the conditions for obtaining citizenship in the Kingdom of Heaven are spelled out. There are no conditions. The people who were promised the kingdom were characterized by distress—an emptiness that only God could fill. Verses 7, 8, and 9 mention the positive characteristics of these people, so the promises in these beatitudes are really promises of rewards. The first, second, fourth, and eighth beatitudes are addressed to people who suffer deprivation. Only these beatitudes—or verses 3, 4, 6, 11, and 12 have parallels in Luke, and they appear to constitute the core of Jesus tradition.

Matthew, in contrast to Luke, emphasized more the spiritual aspect of the suffering by speaking about the "poor [destitute] in spirit" and those who "hunger and thirst for righteousness" (5:3, 6). In Luke's version, however, it is simply the poor, hungry, crying, and persecuted who are pronounced blessed because the Kingdom of Heaven belongs to them (6:20–22). When we take Matthew's tendency to spiritualize Jesus' beatitudes into consideration, it becomes evident that Jesus did not put forth ethical demands that people must fulfill in order to be admitted into the kingdom. He proclaimed that the kingdom belonged to the poor and the oppressed. Jesus' announcement of the kingdom was directed to these people.

## (2) Thematic Statements: 5:13–16

After the prologue and the beatitudes, Matthew includes thematic statements in verses 13–16, in which the poor and oppressed are called the salt of the earth and the light of the world. Salt was—and is—a necessity in the Near East. It prevents food from spoiling. Salt does not exist without saltiness, which is the point. Salt has only one function—namely to be salt. If it has no saltiness, it is not salt. The meaning thus is that those who are citizens of the Kingdom of Heaven must live accordingly. Any other way is impossible for them. If they do not live as citizens of the kingdom, they are not citizens of the kingdom.

The meaning is expressed more clearly in the statement about the light. Light has only one function: to shine, to spread light so people can see. The people of the beatitudes spread light so others can see themselves and God. Readers should not think of missionary activity but of what makes the world endure. The rabbis discussed the things that prevented the world from falling back into darkness and chaos. They were the Torah, divine services, good deeds, Israel, and the righteousness of the people. All these things can be called the light of the world. In Christianity, Jesus' community (the disciples) serves as the light of the world. His disciples are as necessary for the world as salt is for food and light is for seeing.

It is important to note the inner continuity of the sermon. Jesus' words were not directed to everyone. First, the Kingdom of Heaven was promised to certain people—those addressed in the beatitudes. Then Jesus explained to these people what their new situation implied and what their future state would be. Finally, he spelled out the demands. The thematic statements in verses 13–16 focus on the transition between the pure gospel, the glad tidings of the beatitudes, and the demands for the new righteousness, which is the fulfillment of the law, the Sermon within the Sermon.

## (3) Introduction to the Antitheses: Matthew 5:17–19

These verses in Matthew are from p–Matthew and serve to prevent a misunderstanding. There is no new revelation. Here Jesus said, "Do not think that I have come to abolish the Law or the prophets" (5:17). According to Matthew, Jesus interpreted God's law the way God wanted it to be interpreted—in a way that required his followers to fulfill the law even better than the Pharisees did. In contrast to Luke's sermon, Matthew's sermon made explicit the necessity of observing the law in accordance with Jesus' **midrash.**

## (4) The Antitheses: Matthew 5:20–48

The following verses in the sermon (5:20–48) are called the **antitheses** because of Matthew's strong polemical form in this section. Several of these Jesus sayings are traceable to Q. When they appear in Luke they usually turn up elsewhere in his gospel, and only a few have a strong antithetical element (Matt. 5:25–26; Luke 12:58–59; Matt. 5:44; Luke 6:27). In Matthew, Jesus first described the conventional understanding of God's will: "you have heard that it was said . . . ." This statement is the thesis. Against this, Jesus set an antithesis: "But I say to you . . . ." Jesus was not portrayed as contradicting the law but rather as contradicting the prevailing understanding of the law. In essence, these sayings are not christological and thus do not necessarily betray the hand of the Church's theologizing about Jesus. Only one of the five legal topics covered in Matthew's sermon (oaths [5:33–37] from p-Matthew) is without some kind of parallel in either Luke or Mark. For this reason, many scholars have generally accepted these teachings of Jesus as authentic.

The form of these Jesus sayings is important. It shows that at the same time as Jesus put forth his own opinion, he wanted to break down another opinion, which he presented as a false interpretation of the law. Against the authorities, Jesus set his opinion: "I say to you." What authority could he invoke in support of his position? Apparently none. His opponents, the scribes, could cite that they carried a tradition that reached back to Moses, and that they had been educated to interpret God's will. Jesus had only his own authority, which he placed above that of the scribes—even above that of Moses. This must have been the way people understood his words. However, Jesus did not need any authority from men because, according to Matthew, he spoke with God's authority. He assumed that those who listened to his words would say: "Yes, this is right; this is God's will; this is what God means."

Verse 20 functions as a caption of the antitheses. The citizens of the kingdom must show a righteousness that exceeds even that of the scribes and the Pharisees. There was no need to look down on these people. The popular Christian image of the Pharisees is a combination of historical ignorance and a casual reading of the New Testament. There is no reason to doubt the sincerity of the Pharisees. They formed a party (with several different factions) that aimed to fulfill God's will in every detail. To be able to do that, the Pharisees separated themselves from others so they would not contract ritual impurity. Still, Jesus said they would not enter the kingdom. According to Matthew's and Luke's sermons, Jesus demanded more of his disciples than was done by the most pious people of his time.

We must keep one thing in mind to understand what follows. First-century Palestinian society consisted of both church and state. The scribes, most of whom were Pharisees, were both theologians and lawyers. The Roman empire granted that the law of God found in the Torah was also the law that regulated the conduct among the members of Israelite communities. Although the land of Israel was under the authority of Rome, the Jews enjoyed a great amount of freedom and local autonomy; the interpretations of the scribes were also juridical resolutions. Thus, the laws of society expressed God's will. No distinction was made between religious law and secular law.

The first of the antitheses is found in verses 21 through 26. The theme is murder. The scribes said that murder was forbidden in the law and that he who killed another was "liable to judgment"—that is, he would have to appear in a local court of law and be judged. This was both God's will and the law of Israelite society.

Jesus' antithesis seems strange. He spoke like a scribe. One characteristic of the scribal formulation of God's will was that it consisted of **casuistry.** For every violation there existed one special rule. Jesus named three cases (v. 21–22). If you became angry with your neighbor, then you were obligated to appear in a local court of law; if you insulted someone, then you were "liable to the council," which meant that you had to appear before the assembly in Jerusalem, the "supreme court"; and if you called your neighbor a fool, you would face hell's fires.

How is it possible to drag someone to court because he or she is angry with you? Or to serve him or her with a summons to the assembly because you have been insulted—literally called by the Aramaic word *Raka*—which probably means something like "squirt"? It is impossible, and this is the point. God's will is not fulfilled just because murder is avoided. Therefore, people should not think that they fulfill God's will simply by keeping the laws. If God's will should also be the law for society, people will have to make compromises. God's will would have to be adapted. Laws are generally formulated with negatives (that is, you shall not), and so it was in Jesus' time. The Ten Commandments take this form: Do not kill, do not commit adultery, do not steal, do not covet anything that belongs to your neighbor. (The exception is to honor your parents.) Jesus said that God's will could not be expressed in that way. The commandment forbidding murder really meant that God's will was that no one should do anything harmful to another person, and harm included even anger and words of abuse.

Then Jesus formulated the commandment in positive form (v. 23–26). When God said that you should not kill, he implied that you should have an absolute will to become reconciled with others (enemies are implied). This will to reconciliation should precede even the most important of all religious acts, the bringing of a sacrifice to the altar (and therefore all religious acts). In Jesus' view, the Temple, its sacrifices, and presumably Israel's whole ritual calendar were in force. If someone was in the temple with an offering meant to atone for his sins and suddenly remembered that he had a dissension with another person, he should leave the temple and settle the matter before making the sacrifice. Jesus thus appeared to have interpreted the law's requirement of ritual purity (in order to enter the temple) in a moral sense. It is not important whether the grudge was justified. Hostility and enmity had to be done away with before a cultic act could be performed. Hostility and enmity were against the law.

What kind of society can demand that people become reconciled with one another? No society can enforce such a law, and in many instances the observance of the law in ancient Israel was a personal matter. In addition, when implacability was placed on the same level as murder, Jesus was saying something additional about God's will. God demanded not only acts but also the proper disposition of the mind. God demanded the total person.

This demand is shown by the next two antitheses, which deal with adultery (v. 27–30) and divorce (v. 31–32). These words were addressed to men—Jesus talked about looking at a woman (v. 28) and divorcing a wife (v. 31). (The first antithesis was also directed to men because only men could bring sacrifices to the temple.) This audience is understandable in the context of the society in which Jesus lived. A man could not break his own marriage, only another's. There were no prohibitions against extramarital relations provided they were not with the wife of a Jew. If a Jew had an affair with the wife of a man of his own people, he would be guilty of stealing another man's property because a wife was the property of her husband. Adultery and theft were more or less on the same level (see Exod. 20:17). For a woman the situation was different. No extramarital relations were allowed. If she had an affair, she broke her own marriage.

Jesus said that a man's looking at a woman with the intention or even the desire of taking her from her husband was adultery. The same idea seems to be implied by the Greek text of Jesus' words, and there are rabbinic parallels to this interpretation. Some rabbis said that men should not even look at women but should pass by them looking the other way. There are also rabbinic parallels to Jesus' continuation. We can easily understand the mention of the eye leading to sin in light of the preceding verse (5:28). If a man looked at a woman, he might desire her, and that desire would constitute adultery.

It may not be clear why Jesus talked about a man's right hand in verse 30. The subject is adultery. Jesus did not suddenly start to talk about theft. Jesus spoke about what may go before adultery, namely, masturbation. The hand may minister to the same sin as the eye. In such cases the rabbis could demand that the hand be cut off. According to the Talmud, one rabbi even said that the hand should be cut off during the act. When a pupil said that this timing might cause a gash in the belly, he retorted, "Better to have a split belly than to go down into the pit of perdition." The words do not refer to masturbation per se but to masturbation with another man's woman in mind—thus the connection with adultery. Jesus' words about the eye and the hand should not be taken literally. That would be absurd because the sin is not located in the eye or in the hand. The point of these hyperbolic words is that it is worse to end up in hell than to lose something that is regarded as important.

In his antithesis in the statement against divorce (v. 31–32), however, Jesus' words cannot be paralleled by the rabbis. In fact, Jesus turned not only against the rabbinic expounding of the law but also against the law itself. He cited the law prescribed in Deuteronomy 24:1: "Suppose a man enters into a marriage with a woman, but she does not please him because he finds something objectionable about her, and so he writes her a certificate of divorce, puts it in her hand, and sends her out of his house. . . ." Again, it was the man who acted. It was practically impossible for the woman to obtain a divorce. What constituted "something objectionable"? For one rabbinic school, it was adultery. For another school, sufficient grounds for divorce could be as simple as the wife spoiling the man's dinner.

Jesus said that divorce was not an option. He broke with the legal practice of his society, which can be considered the same as breaking with God's law. It sounds strange to say that if a man divorced his wife, he made her an adulteress. The meaning was that if a man divorced his wife and she remarried, he had forced her to break the marriage. Because her first marriage could not be dissolved, her second marriage was adulterous. The first husband was to blame because he had no right to divorce his wife in the first place. To write a bill of divorce was the same as breaking the marriage, and Jesus said both were against God's will. The woman may have served spoiled dinners or even slept around, but it was not God's will that her husband should divorce her.

Furthermore, the man who married a divorced woman broke the marriage. The divorcee was really still married, even if her first husband had dissolved the marriage. Thus the second man married a woman who was already married—one who belonged to another man. Jesus protected women who were really at their husbands' mercy. God's will was not fulfilled if a husband wrote a divorce certificate. God's will was fulfilled when a husband's disposition and acts were such divorce became impossible. In Jesus' day divorce was a lawful act for Jews, but Jesus spoke against it.

In Matthew Jesus said, "anyone who divorces his wife, *except on the ground of unchastity,* causes her to commit adultery . . . " Did Jesus hold this possibility open? Was it thus possible for a husband to get a divorce? We see that Jesus was against divorce in Mark, Chapter 10. It describes a controversy between Jesus and his opponents over the question of divorce. Jesus' last words to them were "what God has joined together, let no one separate" (v. 9). Verses 10 through 12 are words to the disciples. A spouse who divorced and remarried committed adultery.

Mark gives no grounds for divorce. In the parallel in Matthew 19:9, however, the Church inserted an opening for the possibility of divorce and remarriage when adultery had occurred. Is it the same teaching we find in Matthew 5:31–32? It is not the same thing in the Sermon on the Mount. In the sermon the words were only meant to show that a man could not be blamed for causing his wife to commit adultery if she had already made herself an adulteress before the divorce. There was no question of remarriage in the clause. Thus, if a man divorced his wife on the ground of her adultery, then he did not make her an adulteress. Remarriage was not allowed in Matthew 5:32, however. In the Sermon on the Mount, this clause in 5:32 was an addition because the parallel in Luke 16:18 does not say anything about a justification for divorce. There was no justification for divorce (see also 1 Cor. 7:10–11). (It is even possible that the word *unchastity* referred to a premarital act because the Greek word *porneia,* not *moicheia* [adultery], is used).

The next antithesis (v. 33–37) deals with the question of swearing and has no counterpart in the Gospels. Swearing was permitted to guarantee the truthfulness of one's words as long as it was not in God's name. Thus swearing was by "heaven and earth," by the "temple," and so forth. To swear by Jerusalem, however, was not acceptable. Jesus said that this practice did not make much difference because everything belonged to God anyway, and he forbade all swearing. Here Jesus' teaching may have been directed against the Qumran-Essenes, who encouraged swearing and oaths when someone entered their community.

The real reason for not swearing was that people should be trustworthy. If someone is trustworthy, oaths become superfluous. Anything more than *yes* and *no* is evil. Swearing implies that people are not usually honest and do not usually tell the truth. According to Jesus, God's will was not fulfilled when a person spoke the truth only occasionally, such as in court. God's will was fulfilled when all spoken words were true.

The next to last antithesis (v. 38–42) deals with retaliation. "An eye for an eye" sounds terrible, but the principle is found in legal practice everywhere in the Near East. The ancients believed that there had to be some kind of correspondence between crime and punishment. The crime must be repaired by some compensation. The one who suffered, however, must not demand more than what is reasonable. The punishment (or compensation) must fit the crime (or injury). In Jesus' time, the law was not followed literally. If someone damaged someone else's eye, he had to pay a sum of money. The one whose eye was injured had the right to demand compensation. That was God's will.

Jesus did not turn against this practice as an especially cruel form of punishment or retaliation but rather against the principle behind it—the demand for compensation by the offended. People should not demand their rights. People follow God's will when they let injustices go without retaliation. It is not a matter of passive resistance because passive resistance is also a kind of resistance, and Jesus said that people have to suffer more than their enemy intends them to suffer. Jesus was against compensation on principle. However, he also said whatever people requested should be given twofold. Thus Jesus enjoined his followers to honor all requests asked of them with generosity and to hold nothing back, personally or materially.

The last antithesis (v. 43–48) deals with the subject of loving one's enemies. The law commands that you should love your neighbor. The law does not command that you should hate your enemies, and there is no rabbinic saying to that effect. However, Jesus was not as unfair to his opponents as it might seem. The law read: "You shall not hate in your heart anyone of your kin. . . . You shall not take vengeance or bear a grudge against any of your people, but you shall love your neighbor as yourself" (Lev. 19:17–18). By implication, at least, you may hate others. The Qumran sect hated "the Children of Darkness," by which they meant everybody else, even Jews who did not belong to their sect. The Pharisees did not go that far, but they did separate themselves from others. God's will was considered fulfilled when people separated themselves from the evil, the impious, and the ungodly. The motive of the Qumran sectarians and the Pharisees was not aggression or malice; they wanted to guard the purity and holiness of the chosen people. This was how they understood God's will.

The question, however, is "who is my neighbor?" The answer is the "children of my own people." Was it lawful to hate the Samaritans or the Gentiles? Jesus forbade it and demanded that his followers love their enemies. In such cases love had nothing to do with feelings. In the Bible love was seen from the perspective of will and action. Jesus spoke about an attitude. To love others meant to show the will to live together peacefully with others. If people lived in solidarity and community with others, they loved them. Jesus' words may have sounded meaningless because people did not live together with the evil, the impious, and the ungodly—"your enemies" as the text called them. If you lived together with people, they were not your enemies. And this appears to have been Jesus' point—to tear down the wall between the holy people and the others. There are no people other than the ones you are obliged to live with. There are no outsiders.

What was the purpose of "loving" everybody? The purpose was to be children of God—to be like God (v. 45). Here we may see a contradiction to the beatitudes. In the beatitudes, the Kingdom of Heaven was promised to those to whom the sermon was directed. The sermon said that people have to show love in order to be God's children. However, the meaning of the verb *be* here was not *develop into* but *show to be and be recognized as.* The text says that when people demonstrated this love, it was clear that they had been made God's children. God's children act like God. This view recalls the thematic statements between the beatitudes and the introduction to Matthew 5:20–48. Admittedly, there is some tension here because Matthew wrote for a church that did not exist when Jesus spoke these words. People were promised the kingdom but could not be admitted into it unless they practiced God's will.

Jesus made one last point in verses 46 through 48 when he said, "if you love those who love you, what reward do you have?" Everyone does that. The chosen ones would thus have no advantage over others if they loved only people who loved them because the ones they despised would do exactly the same thing. Then piety would become hypocrisy. Jesus taught that God's will was not fulfilled where there were boundaries because God wanted his people to love everyone. Everything that has been said about love was summed up in the command that Jesus' disciples should be "perfect" as God was perfect (v. 48). Here we must not think of moral perfection—for instance, freedom from sin. The term *perfect* is a word meaning whole, undivided, without reservations, without boundaries (Greek: *teleios*). Jesus demanded unconditional, universal love from his followers. Luke 6:36 has *merciful* (Greek, *oiktirmon*) instead of *perfect* and makes clear Jesus' demand for an indiscriminate compassion for all people.

## LOVE AND THE LAW

Jesus' demand for love is reiterated in several other independent sources (Mark 12:28–34; John 13:35; 15:12–13; *Gospel according to Thomas logion* 25) and appears to undergird his understanding of the law, shaping his very exposition of the law. It is love of God and neighbor that radicalizes the commands and transforms the legal notions of murder, adultery, divorce, swearing, retaliation, and neighbor in Matthew's Sermon on the Mount. In each instance, the significance of other human beings and God in the lives of Jesus' followers is so great that it affects their observance of the law. Devotion to God and neighbor—redefined as all human beings (the evil and the good, the just and the unjust)—outweighs every personal concern and right. Luke's Sermon on the Plain presents Jesus' midrash of Leviticus 19:18, the command to love your neighbor as yourself, as its sole legal interest (6:27–36). This command in itself testifies to the centrality of love in Jesus' view of the law according to Luke's gospel.

## THE PROBLEM OF THE SERMON: A SURVEY OF INTERPRETATIONS

The phrase *the problem of the sermon* refers to the understanding of the antitheses in Matthew 5:20–48, which function as something of a Sermon within the Sermon and give Jesus' view of the law. Interpreters have offered differing ideas about their meaning. Here we list ten interpretations, which may or may not be at odds with one another.

1. The sermon was directed to those disciples who wanted to be perfect. This interpretation has been popular in the Roman Catholic Church, which distinguishes between commandments and evangelical advices. In the thirteenth century Thomas Aquinas argued that all Christians did not have to follow the advices but that all must follow the commandments. It is correct that the sermon was addressed to the disciples and no one else, but it does not follow that its range of validity is limited. All Christians are called on to be disciples.

2. Martin Luther also limited the sermon's range of validity. According to Luther the sermon had validity for an individual in his or her personal life but not in the individual's official or public life—not in roles like subject, ruler, father, child, and so on. In these official relations, people must follow the laws and rules of society. Christians might have to swear in court but not at home. It is correct that the antitheses were not aimed at the official life, per se, but we cannot find Luther's distinction between two life spheres, one public and one private, in Judaism at the time of Jesus, and Jesus did not make such a distinction.

3. In the Calvinist tradition, the sermon is an interpretation of the Old Testament law. It is correct that in the Sermon on the Mount Jesus commented on the Mosaic law, but John Calvin was not correct when he sought to reduce the prohibitive interest of the sermon. Calvin argued that only the anger that led to murder was forbidden. Anger in itself, even words of abuse, were forbidden in the sermon. Calvin's use of the **"analogy of faith"** placed the commands alongside all other scriptural commands with the result that the radical flavor of the sermon was toned down.

4. The sermon set forth an ethic of disposition, or frame-of-mind (Wilhelm Hermann, a teacher of Karl Barth). The sermon was not a new law; Jesus was no legalist. The precepts of the sermon were illustrations of a new set of attitudes for the mind and will. This interpretation correctly lifts the sermon out of all legalism and, again correctly, stresses the importance of a person's intention and inner attitude. However, Jesus not only demanded a new frame-of-mind but also deeds. The end of the sermon, Matthew 7:15–27, made that clear.

5. The sermon set forth an ethic of repentance (Gerhard Kittel). This view is not uncommon among modern Lutherans. The sermon is understood as awakening the consciousness of sin. Its moral demands cannot be fulfilled and guilt

results. Realizing that they are sinners, people are driven to the foot of the cross, where they find a theological way out of their difficulties (guilt and condemnation). They have only to accept divine grace. It may be true that people feel sinful when they hear the words of the sermon, but nothing in Jesus' words justifies the interpretation that the purpose of the sermon is to awaken this feeling of personal need and to drive people to repentance. Jesus' moral demands did not constitute an introduction to a gospel for sinners. And, once more, Jesus demanded works and expected them to be performed.

6. The existentialist interpretation of the sermon detects an existential call for decision. Rudolf Bultmann argued that in the sermon Jesus emphasized the demand for radical obedience to God. Every situation demanded a new decision, and the words of Jesus in the sermon were reminders of that fact. This interpretation is certainly correct, but it tends to become somewhat vague. Bultmann does not see Jesus' words as formal authority and does not emphasize that the sermon demanded specific works. In saying that the sermon demanded a response, he is unwilling to say that the sermon dictated concrete models of behavior.

7. The sermon describes an ethic of grace, or rather a response to grace (in various ways, Martin Dibelius and Joachim Jeremias). The sermon was a design for life; it described the new life of the disciples. The antitheses, or demands, were preceded by the beatitudes, the proclamation that the kingdom to come would belong to the disciples who now had a new relationship to God. The antitheses outlined the response of the citizens of the kingdom to the experienced grace of God. This interpretation correctly sees the continuity in the sermon. Its weakness is that the grace can be seen as "cheap grace" (divine favor that is taken for granted). Grace must result in concrete works, and all the explanations up to this point fail to address this issue.

8. The Russian novelist Leo Tolstoy took the antitheses literally (as did Hans Windisch). According to Tolstoy, the antitheses are a blueprint for a new and righteous society. The antitheses constitute a political program. The truth that Jesus gave his commandments in order that they should be obeyed is preserved here. But if we understand the words as a political program, we put them into a foreign context. The words cannot be seen as a new law because they do not cover every situation. What about other moral questions? The antitheses are examples of how we should interpret the existing law. Thus we must realize that the existing laws should not be overturned. What Jesus attacked was the conventional understanding that the will of God could be expressed by a set of rules.

9. The antitheses constitute "an ethic of the interim" (Johannes Weiss and especially Albert Schweitzer). Jesus' ethic must be seen as part of his eschatological message of the imminent kingdom. Just as laws are hurriedly promulgated in wartime to cover the time of crisis, so Jesus' ethic was an emergency ethic for the short period before the coming of the kingdom. Of course, there was some connection between the sermon and Jesus' teachings about the imminent kingdom. The sermon opened with the proclamation that the kingdom belonged to a certain kind of people—those who were then made disciples. But Jesus did not doubt that what he preached had always been God's will and should always be practiced. Moreover, he did not motivate the people to obey his demands by saying that the time was short and the kingdom was near.

10. Gerd Thiessen interprets Jesus' ethic in the Sermon on the Mount as the expression of a radical, itinerant, charismatic life. In contrast to Weiss and Schweitzer, who saw Jesus' antitheses as emergency ethics that had no real place in this world, Thiessen argues that Jesus' view of the law could have been credibly embodied in marginal groups that were outside the mainstream of Palestinian life. Jesus' disciples, freed from the demands of social and civic responsibilities when they followed Jesus and "left all else behind," would be capable of living out such a demanding ethic as an emerging community. Yet, whereas there have been communities in Church history that have lived outside the establishment, such as Anabaptists, Mennonites, and Quakers, Jesus' ethic did not encourage separation for the sake of righteousness. Despite this weakness, however, Thiessen's interpretation appears to be more in keeping with the sociological dimensions of first-century life.

## SUMMARY

Two perspectives are important concerning Jesus' view of the law in the Sermon on the Mount: (1) the contrast with the Pharisaic righteousness by means of their interpretation of the law, and (2) the connection between the "greater righteousness" demanded of the disciples and the kingdom according to Jesus' interpretation.

(1) As depicted in Matthew's gospel, Jesus' demands were tougher than those of the Pharisees. But this is not the main point, which is that obedience to God's will could not be expressed by simply obeying the letter of the law. The spirit or true intent of the law was more demanding and was obligatory for Jesus' followers. Jesus demanded a radical, sacrificial, unconditionally loving obedience—the whole human being, both mind and body, thoughts and actions.

(2) We must consider Jesus' radical demands against the background of the beatitudes. The antitheses do not contain the minimum that Jesus demanded of those who wanted to enter the kingdom but rather examples of the maximum demanded of those who were promised the coming kingdom. Because of Q, both Matthew and Luke positioned Jesus' demands as expectations of those who were promised the kingdom.

The Sermon on the Mount is different from Jewish law as found in the Torah. Jesus' followers were bidden to do things that were not required by law. In fact, the additional duties Jesus required were his criteria for people to become children of God. Only those who did so would be the salt of the earth and the light of the world.

# KEY TERMS FOR REVIEW

Sermon on the Mount          Pharisees and scribes

Sermon on the Plain          Casuistry

Sermon within the Sermon     Love

Beatitudes                   The problem of the sermon

Antitheses                   Analogy of faith


# QUESTIONS FOR REVIEW

1.  How do Luke and Matthew differ in their presentations of Jesus' sermons on the law?

2.  What role do the beatitudes serve in the Sermon on the Mount?

3.  How do the antitheses display the polemical nature of Jesus' Sermon on the Mount?

4.  How does Jesus' view of the law in the Sermon on the Mount differ from that of the Pharisees and scribes?

5.  Why is Jesus' view of the law in the Sermon of the Mount so difficult for the Church to follow?


# SUGGESTIONS FOR FURTHER READING

Betz, H. *Essays on the Sermon on the Mount.* Philadelphia: Fortress, 1985.

Guelich, R. *The Sermon on the Mount: A Foundation for Understanding.* Waco: Word, 1982.

Loader, W. *Jesus' Attitude Towards the Law: A Study of the Gospels.* Tübingen: Mohr Siebeck, 1997.

Strecker, G. *The Sermon on the Mount: An Exegetical Commentary.* Nashville: Abingdon, 1988.

# 24

✳

# Jesus on Jesus

## WHO DID JESUS THINK HE WAS?

The honorific titles bestowed on Jesus raise the issue of whether Jesus actually claimed any of them for himself. Thus, there are two questions. (1) What do the individual honorific titles mean? (2) Did Jesus claim any of them? Historians generally focus on the synoptic Gospels in trying to answering these questions, and of the synoptic Gospels, they consider the Gospel according to Mark the focal point because of its age and central role among the synoptics.

## THE MESSIAH

The title Messiah means anointed one. In the Semitic world, kings and priests were anointed when they were installed in their offices. In the Old Testament, the anointed one, or the Messiah, was the ruling king. The Old Testament also spoke about a future king who would usher in a golden age, but he was never called the Messiah. In one unusual passage in Isaiah, Cyrus, the Median ruler who defeated the Babylonians and indirectly liberated the Judeans from oppression, was called the Messiah (Isa. 45:1). This usage highlights the notion of the Messiah as a deliverer. In several Jewish writings closer in the time to the New Testament, the awaited king was called Messiah. In the Qumran texts we find the expectation of both a royal and a priestly Messiah, an eschatological king and an eschatological high priest.

In a body of writings called the *Testaments of the Twelve Patriarchs,* which may be as early as the second century BCE, we find a description of the installation of the royal Messiah from the house of Judah and a priestly Messiah from the house of Levi. What is particularly interesting is that the *Testaments of the Twelve Patriarchs* described these messianic installations in a way that is strongly reminiscent of the account of the baptism of Jesus. We have the opening of heaven, the heavenly voice, the pouring out of the spirit on the one being installed, and the idea that the latter was the Son of God. Thus, we can argue that the Christians took the baptism of Jesus to be the installation of Jesus as the eschatological Messiah.

The *Testaments of the Twelve Patriarchs* showed that there was a pattern for describing the installation of the eschatological Messiah. The Gospel according to Mark follows that pattern. The descent of the spirit upon the Messiah was part of this pattern because the **unction** was seen to convey the Spirit of God. In the description of the anointing of David, 1 Samuel 16:13 says, "Samuel [the priest] took the horn of oil, and anointed him in the presence of his brothers, and the spirit of the Lord came mightily upon David from that day forward." Thus the descent of the spirit on Jesus was his anointing as the Messiah. The Messiah was the anointed eschatological king.

In the New Testament, the word *Christ* is the Greek translation of the Hebrew word for *Messiah;* accordingly, it often takes an article—the Christ, but it also occurs without an article and is seen as a proper name. The Greeks and Romans did not anoint their kings, and the title "the Christ" was meaningless to them. Christ became a name for Jesus among gentile Christians, but it was not used this way at first.

Did Jesus think he was the Messiah? It is clear that the Gospels conceived of him as the Messiah, but what about the historical Jesus? We need to examine the evidence carefully. Jesus was confessed as the Messiah by Peter (Mark 8:29). Did Jesus affirm the confession? Not at all, for the text reads, "And he sternly ordered them not to tell anyone about him" (Mark 8:30). Mark assumed that Jesus thereby implicitly accepted the title. This assumption is connected with the motif of the "messianic secret" in Mark's gospel; Jesus could not be acknowledged openly as the Messiah until after his death and resurrection. Thus, Mark's account of the confession of Peter in its present form appears to derive from Mark's editorial bias, which makes it hard to establish an historical core.

Mark's bias became even clearer when Jesus began to teach the disciples about his passion, death, and resurrection. These episodes are not historical; they are what scholars call "prophecies after the event, after the occurrence." The exactitude of these prophecies encourages this conclusion. Scholars admit that Jesus may have anticipated opposition and conflict in Jerusalem, but they take the details of his death and resurrection after three days to reflect Mark's hindsight. These prophecies were also part of Mark's messianic secret motif. Jesus was a suffering Messiah; he could not be declared the Messiah openly until after his suffering. Here he prepared his disciples for what he had to go through. He taught them what kind of Messiah he was.

Peter rebuked Jesus when Jesus predicted what would happen in Jerusalem. Why would Peter rebuke Jesus for this prediction? Jesus predicted not only his passion and death but also his resurrection. Thus, he said that he would be vindicated, and why would Peter rebuke him for that? Jesus in turn rebuked Peter: "Get behind me, Satan!" (Mark 8:33). This verse marks the end of the story, and it may be helpful to start at the end. Jesus' rebuke of Peter seems to be historical according to the criterion of dissimilarity. Peter was held in high esteem in the early Church; such an incident would not have been created (Luke left it out).

Why did Jesus rebuke Peter? As we said earlier, Peter's rebuke of Jesus does not seem sensible. Moreover, Jesus' prediction of his passion, death, and resurrection was probably not historical but instead bound up with the messianic secret motif of Mark—the passion (death) and the resurrection had to occur before the fact that Jesus was the Messiah was made public. Thus, these verses could be removed, along with Jesus' charge to remain silent about Peter's confession, because this is also a messianic secret text. What would be left? A confession by Peter that Jesus was the Messiah and Jesus' rebuke of Peter: "Get behind me, Satan!" Is this what happened? If this reconstruction appears too speculative (and some people think it is), perhaps the text is too difficult for historical reconstruction. What certainly remain are Peter's confession and Jesus' prohibition about telling anyone. The messianic secret was a literary device of Mark.

The next story is about Jesus before the Sanhedrin, the assembly, under the leadership of the high priest (Mark 14:53–65). Does the story say anything about how Jesus looked upon himself? It says nothing about that. For one thing, we must regard the whole scene as unhistorical because no followers of Jesus were present. The suggestion that members of the assembly told the Christians what happened is not plausible because the whole story was narrated from a Christian perspective—that is, false witnesses being brought against Jesus. The members of the Sanhedrin would not have admitted that to the Christians. Thus we should consider Mark's version to be the result of his adopting the style of an omniscient author in his account of Jesus' arrest and trial. It is likely that he filled in what he thought happened.

Moreover, the story does not say that Jesus affirmed that he was the Messiah. The high priest asked: "Are you the Messiah, the Son of the Blessed One?" According to Matthew, Jesus answered, "You have said so" (Matt. 26:64). Luke said: "If I tell you, you will not believe" (Luke 22:67). These answers are ambiguous. Most translations of Mark read "I am" (Mark 14:62). But several Greek manuscripts read: "You say that I am." Matthew and Luke would have had no reason to change Mark if Mark reported an affirmative answer. That leaves only one conclusion: Jesus did not affirm his messiahship in Mark's account.

Of course, the evangelists believed that Jesus was the Messiah, as we can see from the continuation of Jesus' answer, "and 'you will see the Son of Man seated at the right hand of the Power,' and 'coming with the clouds of heaven' " (Mark 14:62). To the evangelists, Jesus was the Son of Man, the title that was used to amplify that of the Messiah in the text. But it appears that the evangelists, by presenting Jesus as uncommitted on the question of whether or not he was the Messiah, reflected the fact that Jesus denied it if asked.

The next place where the messianic question comes up is in the question of Pilate: "Are you the king of the Jews?" (Mark 15:2). Jesus answered, "You say so" (Mark 15:2). Again Jesus gave a noncommittal answer.

We need to consider one last text under this heading even though it does not use the title Messiah. That is the familiar Q text beginning with the question of John the Baptist, "Are you the one who is to come?" (Matt. 11:3; Luke 7:19).

Here "who is to come" does not necessarily mean the Messiah. It may refer to Elijah, who had been taken up to heaven alive and was expected to return before the end of the age (Mal. 4:5). Or it may be the Moses-like prophet whose advent was foretold in Deuteronomy 18:15, 18. However, there is some evidence that the phrase carried messianic significance. Although it was not used as a messianic title in Jewish texts, the verse "he will come to Zion as Redeemer" (Isa. 59:20) was used in a messianic sense in synagogue services.

In any case, Jesus did not answer yes or no but pointed to his healing miracles. His answer was based partly on certain verses in Isaiah describing the "golden age." Thus the kingdom was there, or at least at hand. But who was Jesus? Did he claim to be any of these three figures? The Messiah, Elijah, or the Moses-like prophet? Jesus did not claim any specific title. We can say that because, by answering the way he did, Jesus implicitly admitted that he was the one who was expected. It is remarkable that the text does not say that he openly admitted that he was the Messiah when he replied to a question by none other than John the Baptist. Here we have another instance when Jesus did not put forward a messianic claim. The gospel writers and their traditions believed that Jesus was the Messiah, so it is noteworthy that they did not report that he openly claimed to be the Messiah.[1]

We have to conclude that Jesus did not identify himself as the Messiah. Some may argue that whereas Jesus was reluctant to call himself the Messiah, his actions made that claim for him. In light of some of the messianic beliefs that circulated in Jesus' day, Jesus' actions do not meet the criteria of messiahship. Even his most flagrant act, that of cleansing the temple, comes across not as messianic but as a prophetic gesture symbolizing judgment. If the Q text preserved by Matthew 11:3 and Luke 7:19 is authentic (it passes the criterion of dissimilarity), then it is clear that John the Baptist did not recognize Jesus as the Messiah by his words or actions. That Jesus was crucified as a messianic pretender appears to be certain on the basis of the posted charge at his crucifixion; it passes the tests of dissimilarity and multiple attestation (Mark 15:26; Matt. 27:37; Luke 23:38; John 19:19–22). But his crucifixion, according to the evangelists, followed as a result of his answers to the authorities, not his actions.

Because Jesus did not identify himself as the Messiah, the belief that he was the Messiah probably arose in the Church after his resurrection. That belief is evident in the answer to the high priest that Mark attributed to Jesus. Jesus would be recognized as the Messiah when he returned from heaven at the right hand of God. Peter's Pentecost speech said that Jesus was made "both Lord and Messiah" when he was seated at the right hand of God after his ascension (Acts 2:34–36). The seat at the right of God refers to Psalm 110.1, which speaks of the king being seated at the right of God. This message was taken as a messianic text by the Christians.

---

[1] The Gospel according to John lists several passages where Jesus openly declared that he was the Messiah or received without dispute the declaration that he was the Messiah (4:25–26; 11:27). Historians are reluctant to use John because it gives clear indications of explicitly "theologizing" its account of Jesus in a way that fails the test of dissimilarity and lacks multiple attestation. Although there are, without question, elements in John that are authentic, its message about Jesus bears the marks of being a Christian meditation on Jesus' theological significance.

Another messianic proof-text in the early Church was Psalm 2:7, where God said to the king at the latter's installation, "You are My son; today I have begotten you." This text was part of the enthronement ritual; the king was declared as God's son when he was installed in his office. In the entire Near East, the king was the Son of God. Paul's speech in Acts 13:33 quotes Psalm 2:7 in reference to the resurrection/ascension of Jesus. The resurrection/ascension was thus the occasion when he was recognized as the Messiah.

Later Jesus was seen as being installed as the Messiah during his life. In the story of his baptism, the heavenly voice spoke to Jesus quoting Psalm 2:7. The installation text now had a new application; Jesus was installed at his baptism.

## THE SON OF GOD

In the beginning of Romans, Paul quoted an early confession formula stating that Jesus was descended from David according to the flesh but made the Son of God upon his resurrection. Son of God was also a messianic title. It was originally a title of the king as we can see from Psalm 2:7: "You are my son; today I have begotten you." This was an adoption formula spoken by God when a king was installed. Later it was used for the eschatological king, the Messiah, as we can see from the question of the high priest: "Are you the Messiah, the son of the Blessed One?" (Mark 14:61). It is thus natural that in Romans 1:3–4 Paul said that Jesus was made Son of God upon his ascension (compare with Acts 13:33).

Like the title Messiah (or Christ), Son of God came to be used with reference to the earthly life of Jesus. Therefore, the words of God in Psalm 2:7 referred to Jesus' baptism, not his ascension, as in Acts 13. What about Jesus himself? Did he use this title? As we showed when we discussed the Lord's Prayer, Jesus spoke of God as *abba*, "Dad(dy)," thereby revealing a remarkable sense of intimacy with God. But he held God to be the "Dad(dy)" of all people, so we need other evidence to decide whether Jesus claimed a unique relationship with God.

We need to consider two texts. The first is a Q text found in Matthew 11:27 and Luke 10:22: "All things have been handed over to me by my Father; and no one knows the Son except the Father and no one knows the Father except the Son. . . . " This text is unique in the synoptics. Jesus did not put forward similar claims elsewhere. On this basis it does not pass the test of multiple attestation. Its content and form fit best in the Gospel according to John (John 3:35; 7:29; 13:3), not Q. It does not pass the criterion of dissimilarity either because the first Christians believed that Jesus was the Son of God and enjoyed a privileged relationship with the Father.

The second text is found in Mark 13:32. Jesus said, "But about that day or hour no one knows, neither the angels in heaven, nor the Son, but only the Father." Scholars have argued that this Jesus saying must be genuine because the Christians would not fabricate a saying that stated that Jesus lacked knowledge of important things. Luke omitted it. But we must reverse the argument. The point is that Jesus knew more than the angels; he was closer to God than the angels were. There was an implied intimacy in the relationship between the Father and the Son. This implication introduced a tension between this usage of *the Father* which corresponds to that of *the Son* and the words of Jesus about God as the Father of all. Both these texts show a clear limitation on the title of Father as a name of God. This limitation was made in a christological appeal on Jesus' behalf. Jesus was closer to God, his own Father, than people in general were to God their Father.

## THE SON OF DAVID

Many Jews believed that the Messiah would come from the lineage of David, the founder of the Israelite dynasty. The confession formula quoted by Paul in Romans 1:3–4 said that Jesus was descended from David. That made him the designated Messiah during his life; at the ascension he was installed in his office. Did Jesus think that he was designated as the Messiah? Was he waiting for his installation as the ruling Messiah?

In Mark 12:35 Jesus said, "How can the scribes say that the Messiah is the son of David?" Then he quoted Psalm 110:1: "The Lord said to my Lord, 'Sit at my right hand.' " It was believed that David had written this psalm, and Jesus apparently shared that belief. He asked how the Messiah could be the son of David when the latter called the former "Lord" in this place?

Did Jesus himself claim to be the designated Messiah with reference to the title Son of David? This is not the point of the story in Mark 12:35–37, where Jesus criticized a scribal notion. According to 12:35, the scribes taught that the Messiah is from the house of David and is thus the son of David. The point Jesus raised was: What does it mean that the "Lord" of David also is his "son"? Mark is showing how Jesus questioned the Messiah's Davidic connection in favor of the Messiah being "Lord." The story thus has Jesus addressing messianic beliefs and not his self-understanding. Mark believed that Jesus was the Messiah, and "Lord" was the title claimed for Jesus in Mark's account. Messiah as both "Lord" and "Son of David" became a Christian issue. The early Christians had to explain why the Messiah could be called the Son of David when David himself called him his "Lord." Here Jesus says nothing to resolve this issue, and in fact he distinguishes the terms while remaining silent about his own significance.

## THE SERVANT OF GOD

In the second part of the Book of Isaiah, Chapters 40 through 55, we find a series of songs (or passages) about a figure called God's servant (42:1–4; 49:1–6; 50:4–11; 52:13–53:12). The last song, beginning in Isaiah 52:13, is especially important. Here the servant is described as one who willingly accepted all the suffering that God allowed to be put upon him. The servant was despised by all the people. In the end, however, he was exalted by God. Isaiah Chapters 40 through 55 derive from the time of the exile of the Judeans, and scholars generally agree that the servant is a symbol of the deported section of the population. In any case, the servant was not a future figure. However, in some, but not many, New Testament texts the servant songs are seen as prophecies of Jesus. Does this view go back to Jesus himself?

This idea does not seem entirely implausible because Isaiah Chapter 53 appears to have contributed to the general idea of the suffering of the righteous, which is found in a couple of the *Books of the Maccabees* and the *Wisdom of Solomon,* which in turn are found in the Apocrypha of the Old Testament and predate Christianity. This idea has an historical connection with the situation of the pious during the time before the Maccabean revolt. The Christians drew on this tradition. Matthew 27:43 says, "He trusts in God; let God deliver him now, if he wants to; for he said, 'I am God's Son.' " This passage shows the influence of the *Wisdom of Solomon,* 2:12–20, where it is related that the righteous "man," the "servant" of God, was oppressed, tortured, and killed by the ungodly. However, the "man" believed that God would vindicate him in the end. In Matthew 27:43, the leaders of the Jews mockingly asked why God did not deliver Jesus from the cross, since Jesus claimed to be the Son of God. This question is seen as a literary influence from the *Wisdom of Solomon,* 2:12–20.

Did Jesus conceive of himself in this way? We can make two observations with regard to the suffering servant. (1) There is evidence from a later period, which reflects the unsuccessful messianic insurrection of **bar Kochba,** that the suffering servant was seen as the Messiah. However, we find no clear evidence to the effect that the suffering servant was seen as the Messiah in Jesus' time, or that the Messiah was a suffering figure. (Some scholars argue for a messianic precursor of Jesus who was described as the suffering servant in recently published fragments of the Dead Sea Scrolls, but this interpretation has been disputed by other scholars.) Thus if Jesus claimed to be this figure, his claim would not have implied messianic status but would have to be understood in the category of the suffering of the righteous. (2) It is improbable that Jesus claimed to be the suffering servant. Only twice in the synoptics is there a passage ascribed to Jesus that may allude, or even positively refer, to the servant. The first is in Mark 10:45: "the Son of Man came not to be served but to serve, and to give his life a ransom for many." The servant was also a person who carried the guilt of the entire people, but the exact wording used by Mark is not found in Isaiah. The second is in Luke 22:37: "He was counted among the lawless." This passage from the passion narrative is a quotation of Isaiah 53:12, but the atonement is not mentioned here, and it was always mentioned in later Christian literature.

These two passages do not pass the test of the criterion of dissimilarity because the early church believed that Jesus was the servant. In this light, it is surprising how seldom this idea is expressed in the Gospels. It is worth noting that a reference to Jesus as the servant taking away the punishment of people (10:45) is found only once in the New Testament outside of the words ascribed to Jesus himself (Matt. 8:17; compare with Isa. 53:4). If Jesus viewed himself as the suffering servant of Isaiah 53, we would expect much more evidence to that effect to be present, both in Jesus' words about himself and in the rest of the New Testament passages that speak about him. Even the prophecies "after the event" of Jesus' passion and death do not cite Isaiah 53, and it would have been natural for them to do so if Jesus had referred that text to himself.

# THE SON OF MAN

There is a lot of textual evidence for the title Son of Man, but the title itself is difficult to interpret. We must keep two questions in mind. (1) What is its historical derivation? That is, what does it signify? (2) What is Jesus' relation to it?

It is clear that the first Christians viewed Jesus as the Son of Man, but what about the historical Jesus? Thus, students face the same problem as they did with the titles Messiah and Son of God. But the question about the Son of Man is different. The phrase *Son of Man* occurs some eighty times in the words of Jesus, and it occurs in all the traditions (Mark, Q, p-Matthew, p-Luke, and John), but it never occurs in the words of others. The word *Messiah* is never employed by Jesus and occurs only in the words of others, whereas *Son of God* occurs twice in the words of Jesus and more often in the words of others. Thus, it seems that Jesus spoke of the Son of Man, but this third person reference is not clear. In what context did he use these words? Was he speaking about himself? Or was he speaking about some other person? Were these his words or were they attributed to him by the evangelists?

First we have to probe the historical derivation of the figure. The term may mean simply *man.* Psalm 8:4 reads, "what are human beings [Hebrew: *enosh,* man or mortal] that you are mindful of them, mortals [Hebrew: *ben adam,* son of man] that you care for them?" Note the use of Semitic parallelism. The two sentences say essentially the same thing with "son of man" paralleling "man" (a son of man is of course also a man).

Another usage is found in Mark 14:62 when Jesus, in answer to the high priest's question about whether he was the Messiah, said that people would see the Son of Man seated at the right hand of God and coming with the clouds of heaven. The seat at the right of God refers to Psalm 110.1, but that text does not deal with the Son of Man, nor does it refer to his coming with the clouds. Jesus' answer also refers to a vision in Daniel 7. That vision falls into two parts: (1) the vision itself (v. 1–14) and (2) the interpretation of the vision (v. 15–28). The apocalyptic seer had a vision of four beasts rising out of the sea. They represented four successive world powers. The last of the beasts represented the Greek kingdom in Syria against which the Hasmoneans or Maccabees revolted. Daniel 7:22 said that God would come and judge the last beast and give the world dominion to the "holy ones of the Most High," God's "holy ones." This reference may mean the leaders of the revolt or perhaps especially the revolt's martyrs. Daniel 7:27 says "the people of the holy ones of the Most High," which may mean the entire people of Israel would be given world dominion. Some interpreters suggest that "holy ones" refers to angels and "people" refers to the people of Israel.

In the vision itself, however, the dominion over the world was given to "one like a *human being*" (Aramaic: *bar enash,* son of man) who came before God's throne with the clouds of heaven (7:13). Thus the interpretation of the vision took this manlike figure, the "one like a son of man," to be a collective, the holy ones of God, or even the people—a second usage beyond "man." This vision, however, suggests a third usage when it speaks of an individual. Originally, the "one like a human being" (that is, son of man) seems to have been an angel. Angels were described as manlike in the Old Testament and elsewhere in Daniel, where the angel Gabriel had a manlike appearance (8:15–16). It appears then, that as an addition to the vision, the manlike angel—probably Gabriel—was interpreted as the saints of God, the people of God. He was apparently given a throne beside the throne of God, because verse 9 says that before the judgment of the beast, thrones were placed. However, only God was said to have taken his seat. When the "one like a son of man" arrived later, he was not described as sitting down on one of the thrones, but he was described as being given "dominion" and "kingship," which implied enthronement.

An individual interpretation of the Son of Man is also found in *1 Enoch,* where the phrase *Son of Man* is found in reference to a figure, but not yet in a titulary sense, because it is always qualified—for example, "the son of man who has righteousness," or "that man" (about whom it was spoken earlier). In *1 Enoch* the son of man, who was said to be the Messiah, was a heavenly judge who was sitting on a throne. In at least one text he shared God's own throne (51.3 [variant reading]; 61:8 [where he is called the "Elect One" on the throne of Glory]). The uncertain date of *1 Enoch*'s parables, where the Son of Man sayings occur, complicates their value for understanding Jesus' Son of Man sayings. The sayings are not found in copies of *1 Enoch* that predate the Gospels, and some scholars view them as postdating the Gospels and perhaps even being influenced by them.

Some Jewish texts, a few of which date from the turn of the common era, mention an especially exalted angel, a manlike being in heaven, as God's proxy. In Jewish mystical literature this angel was called Metatron, who was said to be enthroned next to God and to share his name (nature). Metatron went by the name "Little Yahweh" *(3 Enoch).* In another text known as the *Apocalypse of Abraham,* an angel called Yaho-El, a name derived from the divine names *Yahweh* and *El,* appeared to Abraham. It was said that Yaho-El looked like a man. In the Qumran texts there is the figure of Melchizedek, who was known as the mysterious priest of Genesis 14. He was described as an angel who was called God *(Elohim)* and exercised divine functions such as announcing the expiation of sin and passing judgment on evil angels, which functions, according to Psalm 82:1, were reserved for God at the end of time. He, like Metatron, possessed God's name (nature). In the *Prayer of Joseph,* a Jewish text preserved in the writings of Origen (third century), an angel named Israel was incarnated as the patriarch Jacob. Thus the angelic figure could also appear on earth in human form. These examples help us to understand the source of the Christian doctrine of the incarnation.

We find the origin of the manlike figure enthroned in heaven in the first chapter of Ezekiel. Here the prophet had a vision of a heavenly throne, and on that throne he saw "something that seemed like a human form" (v. 26). This manlike figure was identified as the Glory of the Lord, *Kabod* (Hebrew: glory) *Yahweh.*

> Ezek. 1:26–29 26 And above the dome over their heads there was something like a throne, in appearance like sapphire; and seated above the likeness of a throne was something that seemed like a human form. 27 Upward from what appeared like the loins I saw something like gleaming amber, something that looked like fire enclosed all around; and downward from what looked like the loins I saw something that looked like fire, and there was a splendor all around. 28 Like the bow in a cloud on

a rainy day, such was the appearance of the splendor all around. This was the appearance of the likeness of the glory of the LORD. When I saw it, I fell on my face, and I heard the voice of someone speaking.

Before Ezekiel's time the Glory of the Lord was conceived of as a shining cloud through which God was both concealed and revealed. As such it was found in the Exodus traditions. In Exodus 24:17 the Glory of *Yahweh* "was like a devouring fire on the top of the mountain." No one could see God, because he was wrapped in this glorious cloud. Thus, Ezekiel said that God did not reveal himself by means of a fiery cloud but through the figure of a man. Here is a pre-Christian, Jewish notion of the manifestation of God in human form.

In the book of Daniel, the "one like a son of man" appears to be identical with the angel Gabriel. This angel appeared to Daniel in Chapters 8 and 9. In 8:15 he was said to have "the appearance of a man." In 9:21 he was called "the man Gabriel." The anonymous angel in Chapters 10 and 12 was probably also Gabriel. He had the same functions as those of Gabriel in Chapters 8 and 9 and was described similarly. In 10:5 and 12:6 he was said to be a "man." In both 10:16 and 18 he was said to have a "human form" (Hebrew: *adam:* man).

Some Jewish Christians believed that the "one like the son of man" in Daniel 7 was an angel. They apparently identified this figure as Jesus and thus admitted that Jesus was an angel. We can see this belief quite clearly in the Revelation of John, which is replete with Jewish-Christian terms and concepts. In Revelation, Chapter 1, there is a description of the "one like the son of man" (1:13)—that is, Jesus—which clearly draws on the description of the "man," the angel Gabriel, in Daniel 10.

> Dan. 10:5–6: 5 I looked up and saw a man clothed in linen, with a belt of gold from Uphaz around his waist. 6 His body was like beryl, his face like lightning, his eyes like flaming torches, his arms and legs like the gleam of burnished bronze, and the sound of his words like the roar of a multitude.

> Rev. 1:12–15 12 Then I turned to see whose voice it was that spoke to me, and on turning I saw seven golden lamp stands, 13 and in the midst of the lamp stands I saw one like the Son of Man, clothed with a long robe and with a golden sash round his chest. 14 His head and his hair were white as white wool, white as snow; his eyes were like a flame of fire, 15 his feet were like burnished bronze, refined as in a furnace, and his voice was like the sound of many waters.[2]

What is Jesus' relation to this phrase and the figure that it entails? As a whole, the Son of Man sayings fall into three groups. (1) Some refer to the earthly activity of the Son of Man, such as a Q passage like Matthew 8:20 or Luke 9:58, where Jesus said, "Foxes have holes, and birds of the air have nests; but the Son of Man has nowhere to lay his head." (2) A second, larger group of sayings, none of which are found in Q, refers to the Son of Man suffering, dying, and rising again. One example from Mark 8:31 describes Jesus as teaching "that the Son of Man must undergo great suffering, and be rejected by the elders, the chief priests, and the scribes, and be killed, and after three days rise again." (3) The last group of sayings

---

[2]Later in Revelation 14:14 it is implied that the "one like a son of man" is an angel.

has to do with the future coming and glory of the Son of Man. Q says that Jesus taught that "For as the lightning comes from the east and flashes as far as the west, so will be the coming of the Son of Man" (Matt. 24:27; Luke 17:24). Interestingly, these categories are never mixed so no saying has a mixture of two or three groups (that is, no earthly activity saying is combined with a suffering, dying, rising saying).

Some scholars have argued that the phrase *Son of Man* served as a type of pronoun (I, me)—a fourth usage. This usage was rabbinic, and Jesus would have been understood as simply referring to himself, but not in a titular sense. Unfortunately, rabbinic evidence for this usage does not predate the Gospels and cannot be used to establish with certainty its usage in Jesus' time. Those Son of Man sayings that serve as predictions of Jesus' suffering, death, and resurrection after three days raise the issue of historical probability. Their explicitness renders them historically improbable for historians if these sayings are taken as predictions uttered by Jesus about himself, and they are usually viewed as secondary creations of the Church that were attributed to Jesus. The Son of Man sayings that are associated with Jesus' future appearance and glory generally fail the criterion of dissimilarity because they reflect what the early Church believed and taught about Jesus, although some, like Mark 9:1, pass the test of dissimilarity.

Was the titular sense of Son of Man, as a heavenly figure, known in Jesus' day? It may be significant that the use of Son of Man did not arouse controversy or conflict among Jesus' hearers as we might expect it to if it was in circulation. Nor do we find any direct evidence that Jesus was talking about a figure who was well known to his audience. In John 12:34 the crowd asked Jesus, when he spoke of the Son of Man, "Who is this Son of Man?" However, none of his disciples found his talk about the Son of Man nonsensical. Nor did the disciples identify Jesus as the Son of Man when he asked them who they thought he was. Is this because a titular meaning of Son of Man, as some type of specific deliverer, was not well known among the Jews of his day? Scholars debate whether or not Son of Man was used in a titular sense in Jesus' day. This issue is complicated by the fact that the parable section in *1 Enoch,* where "Son of Man" is used with reference to a heavenly figure, may have been written after Jesus' lifetime—and even there it is not used as a title.

If Jesus' use of the words *Messiah* and *Son of God* serve as a guide, he did not use *Son of Man* in an honorific sense for himself. In fact, its absence as a title for Jesus among later Christian writings can be used to argue against a titular sense in Jesus' day. That absence would at least help to explain why Jesus' followers never used Son of Man as a title for him. That the phrase is essentially absent from other Christian writings shows that it was not an enduring means of describing or identifying Jesus for Christians.

Why, then, does Son of Man appear in connection with Jesus in the Gospels? Jesus may have used it with the sense of human being, as in Mark 2:27–28: "The sabbath was made for humankind, and not humankind for the sabbath; so the Son of Man is lord even of the sabbath." Here it appears that Jesus was arguing that human beings had authority over the Sabbath. Although the literary evidence does not go back that far, Son of Man may also have functioned as a pronoun in the first century and Jesus may have used it as such on occasion (Matt. 8:20; Luke 9:58).

If Jesus preached an apocalyptic message about the Kingdom of God, it is possible that he offered an interpretation of an apocalyptic text like Daniel 7 and its Son of Man vision. Some sayings imply (although the evangelists intend otherwise) that Jesus spoke of someone other than himself when he spoke of the Son of Man (Mark 8:38; Luke 9:26). All the sayings are in the third person, and Jesus never identified himself as the Son of Man. This lack of identification allows the possibility of a titular use of the Son of Man in Jesus' day, and some Jews, Jesus being among them, taught about such a figure (Matt. 10:23).

In this connection, Jesus may also have spoken of suffering and of God glorifying his suffering people, himself included—a teaching that fits the interpretation of the Son of Man vision in Daniel 7. (We also find this teaching of suffering and exaltation in the Jewish literature of Jesus' day). Such possibilities, coupled with the Church's belief that Jesus was God's deliverer, help to explain why the evangelists could so readily connect Jesus with the phrase *Son of Man* as it was found in the Gospels. Therefore, this very Jewish phrase, which was probably used by Jesus in some capacity, was used to communicate early Church beliefs about Jesus' mission as the Messiah—suffering, death, resurrection, and future glory.

## SUMMARY

The historical Jesus did not openly refer to himself with honorific titles like Messiah, Son of God, Servant of God, or Son of Man. If students of the Gospels take these negative conclusions to entail that Jesus wanted to be less than the Messiah, no more than an ordinary human being, then they have forgotten the preceding chapters on his preaching about the kingdom, his healings, and his interpretation of the law. These sources do not permit the conclusion that Jesus did not regard himself as special. He was not simply a teacher of the fatherhood of God and the brother/sisterhood of all people. If he were, then we could not understand his conflict with the Jewish authorities that ultimately led to his execution by the Romans as a messianic pretender. Did Jesus therefore imply, but not make explicit, that he was an exalted figure? Historians working with critical methodology are hard pressed to make this claim. The sources illustrate that Jesus stood forth with God's own authority. Prophet is a title for Jesus that passes the test of dissimilarity. And God, in Jesus' interpretation, was different from the conventional interpretation of God. The fact that Jesus was found at a table with sinners, not with the righteous, illustrates that God sought out the wicked, not the righteous. The categories of Messiah, Son of God, Servant of God, Son of Man, and other titles are thus exploded. Now, did Jesus have any right to act this way? Or was he crazy? There is certainly no evidence of madness, although he was accused of insanity by some. Unfortunately for students of historical documents, we cannot know the inner dynamic of Jesus' consciousness.

# KEY TERMS FOR REVIEW

| | | |
|---|---|---|
| Messiah | Son of David | Son of Man |
| Christ | Servant of God | Prophet |
| Son of God | Suffering servant | |

# QUESTIONS FOR REVIEW

1. Why are scholars hesitant to claim that Jesus adopted titles like Messiah and Son of God for himself?
2. What is the significance of the title Servant of God?
3. Why is the title Son of Man difficult to define?
4. How is the title Son of Man associated with Jesus in the Gospels?

# SUGGESTIONS FOR FURTHER READING

Brown, R. *An Introduction to New Testament Christology.* New York: Paulist, 1994.

Hahn, F. *The Titles of Jesus in Christology.* London: Lutterworth, 1969.

Fredricksen, P. *From Jesus to Christ: The Origins of New Testament Images of Jesus.* Second edition. New Haven: Yale University Press, 2000.

Powell, M. and Bauer, D. eds. *Who Do You Say That I Am?: Essays on Christology.* Louisville: Westminster John Knox, 1999.

Tuckett, C. *Christology and the New Testament: Jesus and His Earliest Followers.* Louisville: Westminster John Knox, 2001.

# Maps

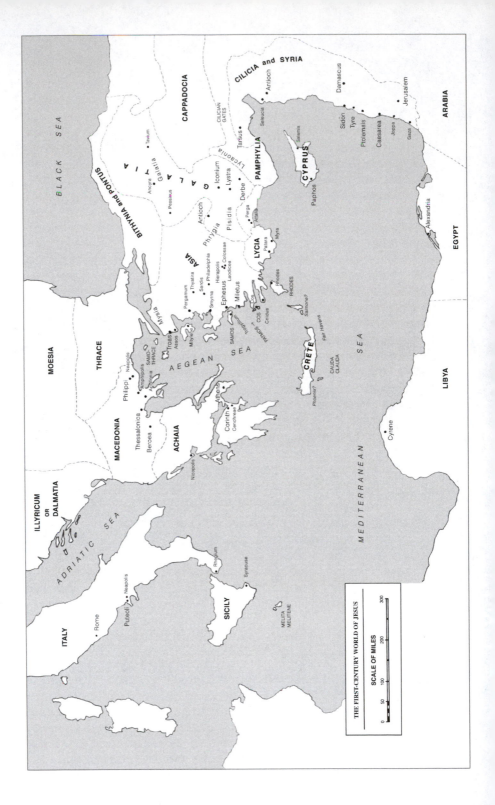

THE FIRST-CENTURY WORLD OF JESUS

SCALE OF MILES

0    50    100         200              300

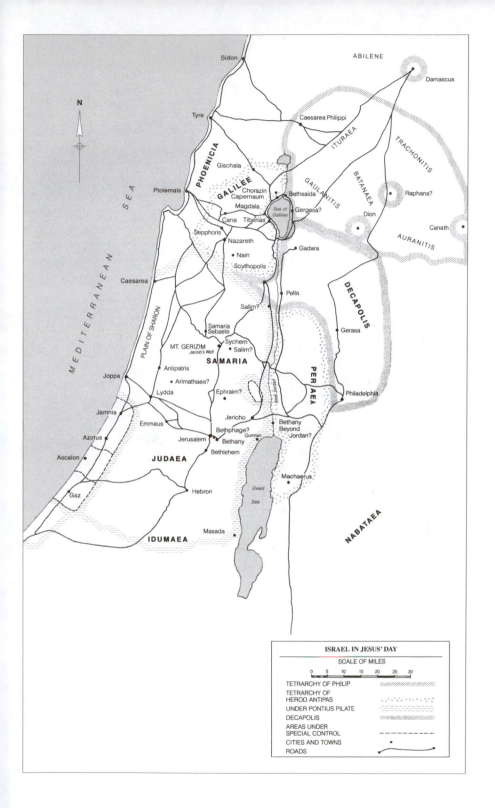

ISRAEL IN JESUS' DAY

SCALE OF MILES

0  5  10  15  20  25  30

TETRARCHY OF PHILIP

TETRARCHY OF
HEROD ANTIPAS

UNDER PONTIUS PILATE

DECAPOLIS

AREAS UNDER
SPECIAL CONTROL

CITIES AND TOWNS

ROADS

N

ABILENE

Sidon

Damascus

Tyre

PHOENICIA

Caesarea Philippi

ITURAEA

TRACHONITIS

Gischala

GALILEE

Chorazin
Capernaum

Bethsaida

GAULANITIS

BATANAEA

Raphana?

Magdala

Sea of
Galilee

Gergesa?

Dion

Canath

Cana  Tiberias

AURANITIS

Sepphoris

Nazareth

Gadara

Nain

DECAPOLIS

MEDITERRANEAN  SEA

Ptolemais

Scythopolis

Caesarea

Pella

PLAIN OF SHARON

Salim?

Gerasa

Samaria
Sebaste

Sychem

Salim?

MT. GERIZIM
Jacob's Well

SAMARIA

PERAEA

Antipatris

Joppa

Arimathaea?

Lydda

Ephraim?

Philadelphia

River Jordan

Jamnia

Jericho

Emmaus

Bethany
Beyond
Jordan?

Azotus

Bethphage?

Jerusalem

Qumran

Ascalon

Bethany

Bethlehem

JUDAEA

Machaerus

Gaz

Dead
Sea

Hebron

NABATAEA

Masada

IDUMAEA

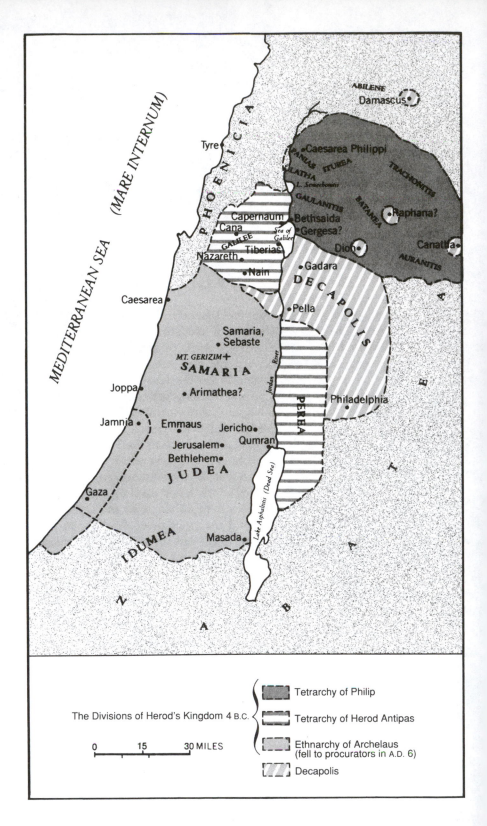

MEDITERRANEAN SEA    (MARE INTERNUM)

ABILENE
Damascus

Tyre

PHOENICIA

Caesarea Philippi
PANIAS ITUREA
GAULATHA
L. Semechonus

TRACHONITIS

Capernaum
Cana
Sea of Galilee
Nazareth
Tiberias
Nain

GALILEE

GAULANITIS
BATANEA
Bethsaida
Gergesa?
Raphana?

Dion
Canatha
AURANITIS

Caesarea

Gadara

DECAPOLIS

Pella

Samaria,
Sebaste

MT. GERIZIM

SAMARIA

Jordan River

Joppa

Arimathea?

PEREA

Philadelphia

Jamnia

Emmaus

Jericho

Jerusalem
Bethlehem

Qumran

JUDEA

Lake Asphaltitis (Dead Sea)

Gaza

IDUMEA

Masada

N          A          B          A          T          E          A

The Divisions of Herod's Kingdom 4 B.C.

0     15     30 MILES

Tetrarchy of Philip

Tetrarchy of Herod Antipas

Ethnarchy of Archelaus
(fell to procurators in A.D. 6)

Decapolis

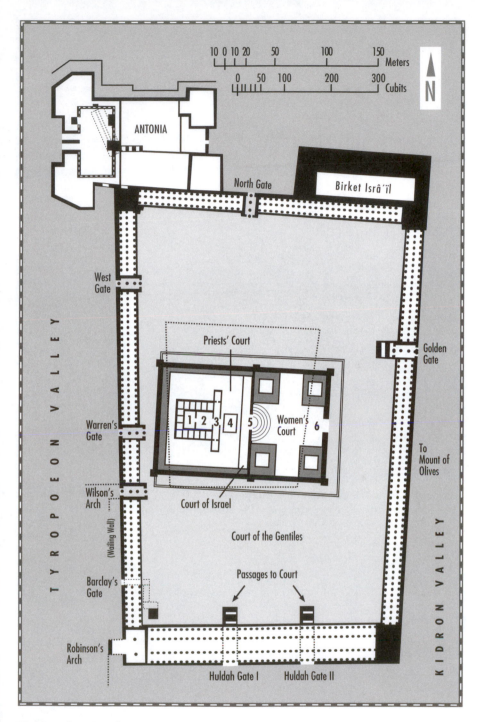

The Jerusalem Temple in Jesus' Day. Floor plan of Herod's Temple and courts: (1) Holy of Holies, (2) Holy Place (Nave), (3) Porch, (4) Altar, (5) Nicanor Gate, (6) Beautiful Gate? (Based on Vincent-Steve [W. F. Stinespring, *IDB* R–Z, p. 556] and C. L. Meyers [*Harpers Bible Dictionary*, p. 1028, Maplewood NJ: Hammond Incorporated]).

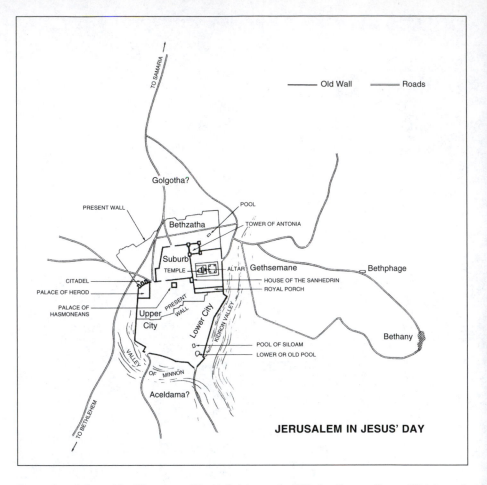

Reproduced from *The Westminster Historical Atlas to the Bible* by George Ernest Wright and Floyd Vivian Wilson. Used by permission of Westminster John Knox Press.

# Glossary

The number in parentheses identifies the chapter where the term is printed in bold type.

**Agraphon (4)**—taken from the Greek word meaning "unwritten." It denotes a Jesus saying not found in the canonical Gospels.

**Analogy of faith (23)**—a principle of interpretation popularized during the Protestant Reformation by which Scripture is used to interpret Scripture. The underlying principle is that no biblical passage can be interpreted in such a way that it conflicts with what is taught elsewhere in the Bible.

**Antitheses (23)**—derived from a Latin word meaning "contrary." The antitheses are those sayings of the Sermon on the Mount where Jesus' teachings differ from what his followers have previously heard (Matt. 5:21–48).

**Apocalypse (1)**—taken from the Greek word meaning "unveil." It denotes a literary form that focuses on disclosure, usually involving some aspect of Israel's future. The Revelation of John is a New Testament apocalypse that intends to disclose the events leading up to the Kingdom of Jesus. Daniel is an Old Testament apocalypse that discloses events leading up to the Kingdom of God.

**Apocalypticism (19)**—taken from the Greek word meaning "unveil." It is used to describe a Jewish and Christian ideology that was very popular from 200 BCE to 200 CE. This ideology was rooted in the belief that the final judgment and kingdom, through God's intervention, was imminent and would soon come about. Writers representing this outlook were responsible for apocalyptic literature (apocalypses) that promoted this view.

**Apocryphal (1)**—taken from the Greek word meaning "hidden things." It designates writings that were left out of the canon. This category includes both Jewish texts and Christian texts. The Roman Catholic Church and the Orthodox Church have included in their canons texts that both Protestants and Jews have excluded from their Bibles.

**Apologetic (3)**—derived from the Greek word meaning "a speech in defense." An apology is a defense of the Christian faith.

**Apophthegms (7)**—a transliteration of a Greek word meaning "saying." It refers to short, instructive Jesus sayings. *See* Form criticism.

**Apostle (1)**—a person who has been sent out as an emissary or representative. *See* Disciple.

**Archaeology (2)**—the scientific study of the life and culture of ancient people and places. Excavation of ancient sites is the chief method used.

**Atoning (18)**—a sacrificial action that, by restoring purity, removes guilt incurred by sin and the threat of God's judgment.

**Authentic (7)**—a term used in form criticism to indicate that a saying or event goes back to Jesus.

**Autograph (4)**—the original copy of an author's work.

**Baptism (1)**—a ritual involving a washing with water.

**Bar Kochba (24)**—known as Simon bar Kochba and heralded by many Jews as the messiah. He led a revolt against the Romans in 132 CE. It ended disastrously in 135 CE when the Romans conquered Jerusalem, slaughtered the Jewish rebels, and transformed the city into a Roman town, devoid of Judaism.

**BCE/CE (1)**—abbreviations for "before the common era" and the "common era." Scholars use them in place of BC (before Christ) and AD (*anno domini,* Latin for "year of our Lord") because they are free of religious overtones.

**Beatitudes (23)**—a term derived from a Latin word meaning "blessing." It refers to the Jesus sayings that pronounce a blessing, as in the Sermon on the Mount (Matt. 5:3–12) or the Sermon on the Plain (Luke 6:20–22).

**Canon (1)**—a transliteration of the Greek word meaning "rule" or "guide." It is used to identify the collection of books accepted as sacred or authoritative by Christians.

**Casuistry (23)**—derived from a Latin word meaning "lawsuit." It refers to the type of scribal argument that Jesus used in Matthew 5: 21–26. Here Jesus uses a general rule to settle several violations of the law.

**Catholicity (1)**—derived from the Latin word meaning "universal." It signifies universality.

**Charismatic (12)**—taken from the Greek word meaning "gift of grace." It denotes the extraordinary operations of the spirit (speaking in tongues, healing powers, and so on) as described in the Book of Acts and Paul's First Letter to the Corinthians.

**Christ (2)**—a transliteration of the Greek word meaning "anointed," which is itself a translation of the Hebrew word *messiah* (anointed). Christ or Anointed One refers to a deliverer expected by some Jewish communities. Anointing denotes God's favor or selection. Israelite priests and kings were inducted into their offices by being anointed with oil.

**Christ of faith (3)**—Jesus as he is worshipped by the Church and defined by its creeds and confessions.

**Christology (2)**—one's beliefs about Jesus. The New Testament Gospels present the Christologies of Jesus' followers.

**Church fathers (4)**—early Christian leaders (second to fourth centuries CE) whose writings have been preserved.

**Client king (15)**—a ruler who was granted local authority by the Roman government and served only as long as Rome allowed. Herod the Great was a client king who ruled Israel from 37–4 BCE, and his sons ruled different portions of his divided kingdom after his death.

**Codex (4)**—derived from the Latin word meaning "book." It came to designate a text that had bound pages as opposed to a scroll.

**Composition analysis (6)**—an analysis of an evangelist's overriding ideas in writing his gospel. *See* Redaction criticism.

**Confessions (3)**—statements of faith that developed during the Protestant Reformation.

**Creed (2) (3)**—taken from the Latin word meaning "I believe." It refers to a statement of faith. Many early Christian creeds were written in conjunction with theological meetings (councils).

**Criteria of authenticity (3)**—principles used to evaluate Jesus traditions for their authenticity. *See* Form criticism.

**Critical (3)**—in the context of biblical studies, the use of scholarly methodologies in the study of the Bible. **(4)**—in the context of textual criticism, a conjectural reconstruction of an autograph that only survives in varying copies.

**Cult (18)**—the way by which communities or individuals give outward expression (liturgy) to their religious life.

**Cultic functionaries (1)**—the personnel (usually priests) who were responsible for the exercise of a community's religious obligations.

**Cynic (3)**—a follower of Cynicism, a Greco-Roman philosophy that was critical of social conventions and encouraged a life in adherence with nature.

**Diaspora (10)**—a transliteration of a Greek word meaning "dispersion." It refers to the dispersion of Israelites outside of Israel that began with the Assyrian conquest of Samaria in 721 BCE.

**Disciple (1)**—a follower who is a teacher's student. *See* Apostle.

**Dominical sayings (7)**—derived from the Latin word meaning "Lord." The term refers to authoritative pronouncements given by Jesus. *See* Form criticism.

**Doublets (5)**—the same Jesus sayings that occur in two different places in the same gospel.

**Dualism (12)**—a perspective that distinguishes between contrasting phenomena, such as good and evil, matter and spirit.

**Early Church (7)**—a term designating the followers of Jesus in the first century, in what may be called the apostolic era.

**Easter (19)**—a term referring to the resurrection of Jesus, particularly the day of his resurrection. The term *Easter* is from an Old English word meaning a festival of spring. It is traceable to the Hebrew meaning "Passover."

**Ecclesiastical (6)**—derived from the word *Ecclesiology*. It refers to matters pertaining to the Church.

**Ecclesiology (10)**—derived from the Greek word meaning "called out." It refers to one's beliefs about the Church.

**Eighteen benedictions (8)**—a series of formal prayers that Jews began to use by at least the late first-century CE. Several of the benedictions may have been known to Jews in Jesus' day.

**Eisegesis**—*See* Exegesis.

**Emendation analysis (6)**—an analysis of how an evangelist used his sources in writing his gospel. *See* Redaction criticism.

**Encratism (13)**—derived from the Greek word meaning "self-control." It refers to an ascetic movement among Jewish Christians of the first and second centuries.

**Enlightenment (3)**—a period of history in Western thought (seventeenth-eighteenth centuries) when reason was championed as the means of knowledge over religious authority.

**Enoch (13)**—the name of one of Adam's near descendants according to Genesis 5:21ff. It is also used as the title of several Jewish writings that date from the first century BCE through the fifth century CE (*1 Enoch, 2 Enoch, 3 Enoch*).

**Eschatology (7)**—a transliteration of the Greek words meaning "last day" and "study." It refers to study of the last things (death, judgment, kingdom, and so forth).

**Essenes (3)**—apocalyptic and ascetic Jews who are often connected with the Dead Sea Scrolls.

**Eucharist (18)**—derived from the Greek word for thanksgiving and a traditional name for the Lord's Supper. According to the Gospels, the term alludes to the thanks that Jesus gave at his last meal (Mark 14:22–24).

**Exegesis/eisegesis (12)**—terms that relate to Biblical interpretation. These terms are distinguished by the Greek prepositions with which they are formed, *ek* (ex) for "out" and *eis* for "into." Exegesis, broadly speaking, refers to the process by which a text is systematically explained. The goal of exegesis is understanding the message that the sender (author) transmits through a text to the receiver (reader). Eisegesis is a distortion of exegesis that reads a message into a text instead of receiving that text's message. All interpreters struggle with varying degrees of eisegesis.

**Form (7)**—a term derived from form criticism. It refers to the unit of saying or narrative that is categorized according to type.

**Form criticism (3) (7)**—a means of studying ancient documents that are believed to be based on oral tradition. It attempts to isolate, identify, and speculate on the forms of a document that represent the literary counterparts of what were originally oral traditions.

**Four source hypothesis (5)**—B. Streeter's proposal (*The Four Gospels* [London: Macmillan, 1924]) that Matthew and Luke each had four sources.

**Genre (1)**—a French word meaning "form." It is used to identify the specific types of written documents (gospels, letters, and so forth).

**Gnosticism (12)**—derived from the Greek word meaning "knowledge." It refers to a religious ideology prominent in the first three centuries. The ideology was dualistic and viewed the impartation of knowledge as the means of salvation.

**Gnostics (1)**—those who held to gnostic beliefs. *See* Gnosticism.

**Gospel (1)**—at first the proclamation of the early Christian community (Jesus' death, burial, and resurrection) and later a written document preserving the proclamation of the early Christian community.

***Gospel according to Thomas* (5)**—a collection of 114 Jesus sayings that is dated to the second century and earlier. A majority of scholars believes its material is late, but some sayings may be authentic.

**Hasmonean (15)**—the dynastic name given to the descendants of Mattathias (also known as the Maccabees) who ruled the Jews after their successful revolt against the Greeks (142–63 BCE).

**Healing miracles (7)**—miracles performed by Jesus on people, such as raising the dead.

**Hebrew Bible (1)**—the collection of 24 books recognized by Jews as inspired and holy. The title refers to the language used in these books. Protestant Christians divide these books into 39 books and use the title Old Testament. Roman Catholic and Orthodox Christians do the same but add additional Jewish texts, commonly known as the Apocrypha, to their Old Testaments.

**Heretics (1)**—those who deviated from the normative or common teaching of the Church. Their dissenting beliefs are known as heresies.

**Hermetism (12)**—a term derived from Hermes Trismegistus (meaning "Thoth thrice greatest"). It refers to a religious movement that began in the first century BCE. Hermes is the reputed author of a number of treatises that make use of myth and have as their themes God, the world, and humankind.

**Heterodox (1)**—unorthodox or nonnormative beliefs that deviated from the common teaching of the Church.

**Historical Jesus (3)**—Jesus as he lived in first-century Palestine according to historical research.

**Ideological (6)**—derived from the word "ideology." It denotes the ideas and beliefs that express a point of view.

**Imperial cult (1)**—the religious institution based on the divinity of Rome's Caesars.

**Interpolation (9)**—a passage that was added to a text.

**Intrinsic probability (4)**—what an author was most likely to have written. It is used in textual criticism when scholars are deciding on the more original reading of a variant text.

**Jesus Seminar (3)**—a project of the Westar Institute, a private, nonprofit research institute devoted to making scholarship in religion—especially what scholars can claim for the historical Jesus—available to the general public.

**Jewish Bible (1)**—another title for the collection of 24 books recognized by Jews as inspired and holy. *See* Hebrew Bible and Old Testament.

**Jewish-Christian (2)**—a term that distinguishes Christians who are Jewish in background from those who are non-Jewish or gentile in background. In truth, the earliest followers of Jesus were all Jewish. The term is also used to distinguish certain texts and communities whose Christian faith evidenced a devotion to Jewish traditions and interests.

**Kingdom of God (20)**—the rule of God that was a prominent expectation of Jews in Jesus' day. Many believed that God's rule was connected to the coming of a messiah who would succeed to the throne of David and bring about great victories over Israel's foes.

**Legend (7)**—a form criticism term. It identifies a type of narrative (in contrast to miracle stories) that is religiously edifying but not necessarily historical, although there may be an historical element in it.

**Literary criticism (3)**—a method of biblical analysis that developed in the nineteenth and early twentieth centuries.

**Liturgical (1)** (or liturgy)—a term that refers to religious rituals and rites.

**Maccabean revolt (15)**—Mattathias and his sons, known as the Maccabees, led a successful Jewish revolt against their Greek rulers from 167–142 BCE.

**Majuscules (4)**—upper-case letters. The term is used of New Testament documents written in capital (upper-case) letters.

**Mandeism (12)**—a gnostic religion whose members represent the sole surviving remnant of ancient Gnosticism. Scholars debate whether Mandeism has a pre-Christian, Palestinian (Jewish) origin and, if so, whether it can be related to New Testament texts like the Gospel according to John.

**Manuscripts (4)**—generally handwritten documents. The term is used specifically by biblical scholars to refer to the handwritten versions of the biblical books, whether they are the originals (none of which have survived) or the subsequent handmade copies that were eventually superceded by printed copies in the fifteenth century.

**Markan priority (5)**—a term used in source criticism to identify the idea that the Gospel according to Mark was written before Matthew and Luke, whose authors used them as a source for their own Gospels.

**Messiah (1)**—a transliteration of the Hebrew word meaning "anointing." It referred to a deliverer (sometimes thought to be a descendant of David) who was expected by some Jewish communities in Jesus' day.

**Midrash (23)**—a Hebrew term that means "exposition." It describes the rabbinic activity of interpreting the Jewish Scriptures. Rabbis of the second century CE and later had two types: *midrash halakha* (legal midrash) and *midrash aggadah* (nonlegal midrash).

**Minor agreements (5)**—a phrase used in source criticism to describe those places where Matthew and Luke agree in wording over against Mark.

**Minuscules (4)**—lower-case letters. The term is used with reference to New Testament documents written in lower-case letters.

**Mishnah (7)**—from the Hebrew word meaning "to learn." It designates the ancient code of Jewish law reputedly collected, edited, and revised by Rabbi Judah the Prince around 200 CE.

**Mithras (17)**—the name of a popular god of the Roman empire. Mithraism, the ancient Roman mystery cult of the god Mithras, began in the late first century of the common era and flourished from the second through the fourth centuries CE.

**Myth (2)**—in common usage, stories that are fictional and unhistorical.

**Nature miracles (7)**—miracles performed by Jesus on nature, such as the stilling of the storm.

**New Testament (1)**—the collection of 27 writings, generally dating to the first century CE that Christians identify as the divinely inspired supplement to those writings known as Old Testament (Hebrew Bible/Jewish Bible), that together make up their Bible.

**Oracles (1)**—divine messages that were granted to ancient priests and prophets.

**Oral Tradition (1)**—any body of material that has been handed down orally—by word of mouth.

**Palaeography (4)**—derived from the Greek words meaning "old" and "writing." It refers to the science of describing ancient writings.

**Papyri (4)**—the plural of the Latin name of an Egyptian plant whose stems were used to form sheets for writing (called papyri). In textual criticism, *papyri* refers to the earliest surviving witnesses (which were written on papyri) to the New Testament writings. They date from the second and third centuries.

**Parables (3)**—comparisons. They are identified as dominical sayings (authority sayings) by form criticism. As comparisons, parables can come in different forms, such as similes, metaphors, and allegories.

**Parchment (4)**—animal skin that was processed for writing. In textual criticism, parchment refers to the surviving witnesses to the New Testament that were written on parchment and date from the fourth to the fourteenth centuries.

**Passion (1)**—a transliteration of a Latin word used to translate "suffering" in Acts 1:3. It is used to identify the narrative of Jesus' suffering and death in the New Testament Gospels.

**Passion narrative (5)**—the gospel narratives that describe the suffering, death, and resurrection of Jesus. "Passion" is derived from the Greek word meaning "suffering."

**Passover (2)**—the most important annual festival of Jews in Jesus' day. It commemorates Israelites' exodus from Egypt, which followed the tenth plague of Moses—when the "Destroyer" slew the firstborn of Egypt but "passed over" those who followed Moses' instructions.

**Pericope (5)**—a transliteration of the Greek word meaning "a cutting." It is used in biblical studies to refer to any self-contained unit of biblical material.

**Pharisees (3)**—the name given to a Jewish sect that encouraged observance of the purity laws of the Torah.

**Piety (23)**—derived from a Latin word and refers to one's religious duties and practices.

**Platonism (12)**—a set of beliefs about humankind and the world that have their origin in the philosophical teachings of Plato, a fourth-century BCE Greek philosopher.

**Pleonastic (5)**—a literary term that refers to a redundancy.

**p–Luke (5)**—a term provided by source criticism. It refers to the special source (both written and/or oral) of Jesus traditions used by the author of the Gospel according to Luke. This material distinguishes his gospel from the other synoptics and John.

**p–Matthew (5)**—a term provided by source criticism. It refers to the special source (both written and/or oral) of Jesus traditions used by the author of Matthew. This material distinguishes his gospel from the other synoptics and John.

**Prefect (15)**—a Roman imperial governor appointed by Caesar. For much of Jesus' lifetime, Judea was governed by a series of prefects, the most famous of whom was Pontius Pilate, who governed from 26–36 CE.

**Primitive (5)**—with reference to a gospel, an early gospel that is no longer extant.

**Primitive Mark (5)**—an early version of Mark that Matthew and Luke may have used. *See* Ur-Mark.

**Proverbs (3)**—short, provocative sayings that embody an insight into life. Form criticism classifies them as dominical sayings (authority sayings).

**Pseudepigraphical (1)**—a text that has been ascribed to someone (usually a famous biblical figure) other than its real author.

**Q (3)**—derived from the first letter of the German word meaning "source." It is used by source criticism to designate a source of Jesus materials that is common to both Matthew and Luke.

**Qumran (7)**—a site in Israel where ancient Jewish scrolls, dating to the time of Jesus and earlier, were discovered in 1947. These scrolls are usually associated with a Jewish sect known as the Essenes.

**Rabbi (2)**—a transliteration of the Hebrew word meaning "master." It was used as a title of respect for Jewish teachers of the Law in Jesus' day.

**Rabbis (15)**—those Jewish teachers of the second through sixth centuries who are identified with what is called rabbinic Judaism and who were responsible for the creation of the Mishnah and Talmuds.

**Redaction (7)**—a transliteration of the German word meaning "editor" that is used by form criticism to identify the hands (additions) of the authors in the Gospels.

**Redaction criticism (3)**—a means of studying the Gospels that aims to identify the theological perspective of their authors by analyzing their editorial and compositional techniques.

**Sacrament (18)**—a Christian rite (such as baptism or the Eucharist) that is believed to have been ordained by Jesus and is held to be a means of receiving divine grace or to be a sign or symbol of a spiritual reality.

**Sadducees (3)**—a Jewish sect that was priestly and focused on the Jewish Temple.

**Samaritans (11)**—a name given to the descendants of the northern tribes of ancient Israel. They lived in Samaria, a region in central Israel, and had religious traditions and practices that were similar to yet distinct from the Jews, the descendants of the southern tribes who lived in and around Jerusalem.

**Sanhedrin (15)**—a transliteration of a Greek word meaning "council." It refers to a body of Jewish leaders who, in Jesus' day, enforced religious and civil law among Jews. It was made up of Pharisees and Sadducees and was presided over by the high priest.

**Scribe (4)**—one who was paid for the service of reading and writing. Scribes were often employed to copy written documents. In Jesus' day Jewish scribes were experts in Jewish law and were called on for instruction and guidance.

**Scripture (1)**—a term derived from the Greek word for writing. It was used by Jewish and Christian communities to refer to writings considered to be inspired and holy.

**Second temple era (14)**—a phrase used by historians to refer to the period of Israel's second temple in Jerusalem (late sixth century BCE to the first century CE).

**Sect (1)**—a religious subgroup that holds to beliefs and/or practices that distinguish it from the larger religious community. Jesus' early followers were viewed as a sect of the Jewish faith.

**Septuagint (6)**—the name given to the third-century BCE Greek translation of the Hebrew Bible.

*Sitz im Leben* **(7)**—a German phrase meaning "setting in life." It refers to the sociological and/or ecclesiastical setting of Jesus' deeds and sayings as identified in form criticism.

**Source criticism (3) (5)**—a means of studying the Gospels that seeks to solve the synoptic problem of why the synoptic Gospels are so similar and yet so different and thus to explain the relationship of the Gospels to one another. Source criticism has argued that the authors of the Gospels used sources and that these sources, sometimes used by more than one author, explain their similarities and differences.

**Synagogue (10)**—a transliteration of a Greek word meaning "gathering." In Jesus' day it referred to places (private homes, separate buildings) where Jews gathered on the Sabbath for the reading, study, and interpretation of the Jewish Bible.

**Syncretism (15)**—a term that refers to the mixing and/or combining of religious beliefs and practices.

**Synoptic (1)**—a "look alike." It refers to the Gospels of Matthew, Mark, and Luke because of their similarity in content and structure.

**Synoptic problem (5)**—a term used in source criticism to describe the dilemma of explaining the similarities and differences of the synoptic Gospels.

**Talmud (2)**—a term taken from the Hebrew word meaning "to study." It is used to identify the Mishnah and the commentaries upon the Mishnah. There are two versions of the Talmud. One is called the Palestinian Talmud (300 CE) and the other is called the Babylonian Talmud (500 CE).

**Textual criticism (4)**—the name given to the task of reconstructing the original wording of literary works, like the New Testament Gospels, from surviving copies. This task involves comparing existing copies to develop a critical text.

**Theology (3)**—a term that generally refers to religious beliefs. When used by biblical scholars in the analysis of biblical texts like the Gospels—for example, the theology of Mark—scholars have in mind the religious interests and messages of the writer.

**Torah (10)**—a transliteration of a Hebrew word meaning "guidance." In Jesus' day it was used by Jews to refer to either the law of God as revealed in the books credited to Moses (Genesis, Exodus, Leviticus, Numbers, and Deuteronomy), or to those books themselves.

**Tradition (7)**—a term used in form criticism to identify gospel materials relating to the Jesus traditions of the early Church that do not come from the hand of the gospel writer (redactor).

**Tradition criticism (8)**—a means of studying the Gospels. It seeks to identify the more original reading of materials that appear in more than one gospel. This task usually involves deciding whether Matthew or Luke preserves a more original reading of their common source called Q.

**Transcriptional probability (4)**—the kind of change or error that a scribe probably made when copying a text.

**Two source hypothesis (5)**—the source criticism proposal that postulates two sources, Mark and Q, for the Gospels according to Matthew and Luke.

**Uncials (4)** —upper-case letters. The term is used of New Testament documents written in capital (upper-case) letters.

**Unction (24)**—derived from a Latin word meaning "anoint." It refers to the pouring of oil on a priest or king when he is installed in his office or on a worshipper during a religious ceremony.

**Unorthodox (1)**—a term for persons or views that deviate from the normative or common teachings of the Church.

**Ur-Mark (5)**—a term used in source criticism to identify an early ("Ur" is German for early) version of the Gospel according to Mark. Many source critics believe that Matthew and Luke used an early version of the Gospel according to Mark when they wrote their Gospels.

**Variant (4)**—a reading that is different in two or more copies of the same text.

**Versions (4)**—translations of the original Greek New Testament writings.

**Yahweh (18)**—the transliterated English spelling of the sacred Hebrew name for God. English Bibles usually translate the Hebrew word as "LORD." In English Bibles "God" is usually the translation of *Elohim*, another Hebrew word for God that is derived from a common word for God in Semitic languages.

**Zealots (3)**—first-century CE Galilean Jews who used violence as a means of ending the Roman occupation of Israel.

# Bibliography of Primary Sources

Aland, K. et al., eds. *The Greek New Testament*. Fourth Edition. New York: American Bible Society, 1994.

Barrett, C. K. ed. *The New Testament Background: Writings from Ancient Greece and the Roman Empire that Illuminate Christian Origins*. Revised Edition. San Francisco: Harper and Row, 1995.

Cartlidge, D. and Dungan, D. eds. *Documents for the Study of the Gospels*. Revised and Enlarged Edition. Minneapolis: Fortress, 1994.

Charlesworth, J. ed. *The Old Testament Pseudepigrapha*. 2 volumes. Garden City, New York: Doubleday, 1983 and 1985.

Colson, F. H. and Whitaker, G. H. trans. *Philo*. 10 volumes. Cambridge: Harvard University Press, 1929–62.

Coogan, M. ed. *The New Oxford Annotated Bible: New Revised Standard Version with the Apocrypha*. Third Edition. New York: Oxford University Press, 2001.

Danby, H. trans. *The Mishnah*. Oxford: Clarendon, 1933.

Elliot, J. K. ed. *The Apocrypha New Testament*. Oxford: Clarendon, 1993.

Epstein, I. ed. *The Babylonian Talmud*. 35 volumes. London: Soncino Press, 1935–52 with reprints.

Foerster, W. ed. *Gnosis: A Selection of Gnostic Texts*. Volume 2 (Coptic and Mandean Sources). English translation edited by R. McL. Wilson. Oxford: Clarendon, 1974.

Lake, K., Oulton, J. E. L., and Lawlor, H. J. trans. *Eusebius: The Ecclesiastical History*. 2 volumes. Cambridge: Harvard University Press, 1926–32.

Roberts, A. and Donaldson, J. eds. *The Ante-Nicene Fathers*. 10 volumes. Grand Rapids: Eerdmans, 1989 (American reprint of the Edinburgh Edition).

Thackeray, H. St. J., Marcus, R., and Feldman, L. H. trans. *Josephus*. 10 volumes. Cambridge: Harvard University Press, 1926–65.

Vermes, G. trans. *The Complete Dead Sea Scrolls in English*. Allen Lane: The Penguin Press, 1997.

# Bibliography of Secondary Sources

Bloomberg, C. *Jesus and the Gospels: An Introduction and Survey*. Nashville: Broadman & Holman, 1997.

Bock, D. *Studying the Historical Jesus: A Guide to Sources and Methods*. Grand Rapids: Baker, 2002.

Bockmuehl, M. *The Cambridge Companion to Jesus*. Cambridge: Cambridge University Press, 2001.

Chilton, B. and Evans, C. eds. *Studying the Historical Jesus: Evaluations of the State of Current Research*. Leiden: E. J. Brill, 1994.

Cunningham, P. *Jesus and the Evangelists: The Ministry of Jesus and its Portrayal in the Synoptic Gospels*. New York: Paulist Press, 1988.

Dane, J. *Jesus and the Four Gospels: An Illustrated Documentary*. San Francisco: Harper and Row, 1979.

Evans, C. and Porter, S. eds. *The Historical Jesus*. Sheffield: Sheffield, 1995.

Evans, C. and Porter, S. eds. *The Synoptic Gospels*. Sheffield: Sheffield, 1995.

Funk, R. ed. *The Acts of Jesus: The Search for the Authentic Deeds of Jesus*. San Francisco: HarperSanFrancisco, 1998.

Funk, R. and Hoover, R. eds. *The Five Gospels: The Search for the Authentic Words of Jesus*. New York: Macmillan, 1993.

Goodacre, M. *The Synoptic Gospels: A Way Through the Maze*. Sheffield: Sheffield, 2001.

Green, J. and McKnight, S. eds. *Dictionary of Jesus and the Gospels*. Downers Grove: InterVarsity, 1992.

Hengel, M. *The Four Gospels and the One Gospel of Jesus Christ: An Investigation of the Collection and Origin of the Canonical Gospels*. Harrisburg: Trinity Press International, 2000.

Koester, H. *Ancient Christian Gospels: Their History and Development*. London: SCM, 1990.

McKnight, S. *The Synoptic Gospels: An Annotated Bibliography.* Grand Rapids: Baker, 2000.

Nickle, K. *The Synoptic Gospels: An Introduction.* London: SCM, 1982.

O'Grady, J. *The Four Gospels and the Jesus Tradition.* New York: Paulist Press, 1989.

Powell, M. *Fortress Introduction to the Gospels.* Minneapolis: Fortress, 1998.

Reddish, M. *An Introduction to the Gospels.* Nashville: Abingdon, 1997.

Sanders, E. and Davies, M. *Studying the Synoptic Gospels.* London: SCM, 1989.

Schnackenburg, R. *Jesus in the Gospels: A Biblical Christology.* Louisville: Westminster John Knox, 1995.

Stanton, G. *The Gospels and Jesus.* Second Edition. Oxford: Oxford University Press, 2002.

Stuhlmacher, P. *The Gospel and the Gospels.* Grand Rapids: Eerdmans, 1991.

Tatum, W. *In Quest of Jesus: A Guidebook.* Revised and Enlarged Edition. Nashville: Abingdon, 1999.

Thiessen, G. and Merz, A. *The Historical Jesus. A Comprehensive Guide.* Minneapolis: Fortress, 1998.

# Indexes

## Biblical Passages

(including the *Gospel according to Thomas*)

| | | | | | | |
|---|---|---|---|---|---|---|
| Gen. | Chp. 14 | 278 | | | 21:23 | 210 |
| | 17:2 | 6 | | | 24:1 | 262 |
| | 17:4 | 6 | | | 25:5–6 | 190 |
| | 17:7 | 6 | | | | |
| | | | | 1 Sam. | 16:3 | 271 |
| Exod. | 3:14 | 134 | | | | |
| | 19:5 | 6 | | 2 Sam. | 7:8 | 194 |
| | 19:6 | 167 | | | 4:10 | 2 |
| | 20:7 | 105 | | | 18:22 | 2 |
| | 20:17 | 262 | | | 18:25 | 2 |
| | Chp. 24 | 202 | | | | |
| | 24:8 | 6 | | 2 Kings | Chp. 17 | 174, 175 |
| | 24:17 | 279 | | | | |
| | | | | 1 Chron. | 29:11–13 | 40 |
| Lev. | 15:19 | 253 | | | | |
| | Chp. 16 | 183 | | Ps. | 2:7 | 274 |
| | 16:24 | 184 | | | 8:4 | 277 |
| | 19:17–18 | 264 | | | 22 | 107 |
| | 19:18 | 266 | | | 22:1 | 210 |
| | 25:36–37 | 176 | | | 22:18 | 210 |
| | | | | | 41:9 | 203 |
| Num. | 1:17–47 | 250 | | | 69 | 107 |
| | | | | | 69:20 | 210 |
| Deut. | 18:15 | 179, 182, 273 | | | 69:21 | 107, 210 |
| | 18:18 | 182, 273 | | | 82:1 | 278 |

**300**

## Modern Scholars

# Subjects

# Abbreviations

| | | | |
|---|---|---|---|
| *Ant.* | *The Antiquities of the Jews* | Jer. | Jeremiah |
| BCE | Before the Common era | Lev. | Leviticus |
| *BPes.* | *Pesahim* of the Babylonian | Mal. | Malachi |
| | *Talmud* | Matt. | Matthew |
| *CD* | *Damascus Covenant (or* | Num. | Numbers |
| | *Damascus Document)* | *Numa.* | *Numa Pompilius* |
| Chron. | 1 Chronicles | P | Papyri |
| CE | Common Era | p–Matt. | p–Matthew |
| Col. | Colossians | Pet. | Peter |
| Cor. | 1 Corinthians | Q | Quelle (source) |
| Dan. | Daniel | Phil. | Philippians |
| *Dem.* | *Demonstrations* | Ps. | Psalms |
| Deut. | Deuteronomy | *Rec.* | *Recognitions* |
| Eph. | Ephesians | Rev. | Revelation |
| Exod. | Exodus | Rom | Romans |
| Ezek. | Ezekiel | Sam. | Samuel |
| Gal. | Galatians | *Sanh.* | *Sanhedrin* |
| Gen. | Genesis | *Strom.* | *Stromata* |
| *GosThomas* | *Gospel according to Thomas* | Thess. | Thessalonians |
| Heb. | Hebrews | Tim. | Timothy |
| *Hom.* | *Homilies* | *War.* | *The Jewish War* |
| Hos. | Hosea | Zech. | Zechariah |
| Isa. | Isaiah | | |